Elk Hunting Guide

Elk Hunting Guide

Skills, Gear, and Insight

Tom Airhart

STACKPOLE
BOOKS

To all my family, including all the dogs,
on either side of that misty pass over the great divide.

Published by
STACKPOLE BOOKS
5067 Ritter Road
Mechanicsburg, PA 17055
www.stackpolebooks.com

Printed in U.S.A.

10 9 8 7 6 5 4 3 2 1

Second edition

Cover design by Tessa J. Sweigert

Cataloging-in-Publication Data is on file with the Library of Congress.

ISBN 978-0-8117-1092-3

CONTENTS

PREFACE

There's a widely quoted theory that the underlying motivation of most authors is a love of the subject. I subscribe to that theory. My other motivation is the absence, in the opinion of most serious elk hunters, of a single source of information that covers all aspects of elk hunting in enough depth to be practically useful in taking elk and finding good places and arrangements for hunting elk. What this book will do is give more depth than the many general interest publications available that touch on the general subject, even the same topics.

Elk hunting is different from other big game hunting. Part of the difference is the elk; part of the difference is the places that elk are hunted. Elk hunting is a lot more than actually bringing an elk back. If that were the case, I would have stopped going back to the mountains years ago. But this particular book does not try to do more than touch on all of those other aspects of elk hunting. This book is about bringing an elk back.

My basic premise is that the reader of this book is seriously interested in elk hunting. This serious interest can occur on two levels. A first-level reader wants to know specific and detailed information regarding what elk hunting is like and how to train and equip to get the most out of the experience. I've been there: It's a serious matter for the prospective elk hunter considering shelling out as much as a few thousand dollars total for that first hunt. The second-level reader has been elk hunting several times, has maybe even taken an elk, and truly enjoys the elk hunting experience—with one reservation. It seems that other hunters in camp always seem to have the luck, particularly the trophy-class-elk type of luck. I've been there too. A lot of elk hunters stay there.

Years ago, I made a deliberate decision to learn how to get "lucky" on a consistent basis. I began to take a more analytical perspective on my experience and that of others in a search for the keys to successful elk hunting. I had made a daily record of my own experience, hunting out of professionally run outfitter pack camps of the Northern Rockies at the time, and I'd listened to tales from friends and business acquaintances of hunting other regions with a wide range of hunting arrangements, from the economical to the very expensive. I set about expanding my own experience base, sticking to the more economical end of the hunting arrangements scale.

There are two ways to improve your chances of taking an elk, particularly a trophy elk; they are not mutually exclusive. Using the first approach (instructions included toward the back of the book), you can make arrangements to hunt where hunting pressure is controlled— perhaps by limiting the number of licenses issued for the area (requiring hunters to have the patience to wait out enough seasons to draw a permit) or by landowner rights and the associated prerogative to apply other deterrents (extreme expense, mostly). The elk in such an area will be less hard-pressed and therefore easier to hunt, and more of them will have a better chance of surviving to full maturity and developing a trophy set of antlers. The second approach, involving less expense but requiring more dedication, is to become a better hunter and go after the elk in the hard parts of public hunting areas.

My outfitter pack camp experience has given me the opportunity to observe master guides in action. They usually accompanied the "lucky" inexperienced hunters. Gene, one such an outfitter/master guide friend, sold out of the outfitter business but decided to go together with some partners to make up a little pack outfit of their own and invited me to join. I bought a couple of well-behaved little mules that I knew from the old outfit and a big old pack horse that could carry most of a camp in one load as long as he didn't stumble and turn upside down. With a series of riding horses that were good for some world-class buckoffs still talked about around campfires in the Northwest, I was in, and we had ourselves an outfit, the "Association."

I took a detached look at what I was doing, comparing my hunting style with the style of these experienced and consistently successful hunters, watching what actions came as second nature to them in particular situations, and learning what made the difference between an extended walk in the woods and a successful elk hunt. I started considering the hunting tales around the evening fire in a different light, looking past what had happened to why it happened. I suspect that it would never occur to most of the really good elk hunters I have known to consider elk hunting from this perspective. To them, it's just what you do.

What is the key to elk hunting? It's the mindset of the hunter. No, make that mindsets—a different one appropriate to each phase of the hunt. Definable techniques and skills that can be perfected with practice are associated with each mindset. The hunter moves along with all senses pulling in information from the surroundings to locate the elk; moves toward where the elk should be; looks where the elk should be; and assumes the mindset of the stalk. The trophy is assessed if that's of interest; the shot is planned mentally using the essence of the image. The hunter's focus expands momentarily to clear the shot, and then contracts to a 6-inch spot on the elk. The hunter has practiced precision shooting until it becomes second nature as an extension of this focus.

My fascination with elk hunting and these principles behind it compelled me to attempt to reduce them to writing. This book is what resulted. It's my cave drawing. Its intention is to help the reader make that hard-to-define next step in hunting.

I must make the reader aware that while in the process of practicing, defining, and writing these principles, I have discovered another essential truth: Sometimes, while in pursuit of difficult elk in difficult places, the elk hunter can indeed be lucky and just be in the right place at the right time and make a lucky shot. Any experienced elk hunter would agree that being lucky is not a bad strategy. But luck comes in two different flavors. The understated folks whose opinion matters to me would express it as the difference between making a lucky shot and being able to consistently be a Lucky Shot.

NOTE ON THE SECOND EDITION

To say that response to the first edition of Elk Hunting Guide has exceeded my expectations wouldn't be precisely correct. There were absolutely no expectations at all on my part as I set about writing it; I was putting the results of encounters with elk hunters of all types— potential and experienced, lucky and un-, old western types and city folks—into writing just for my own enjoyment. After the magazine article, then articles, that I never got around to sending finally got completely out of hand and organized into what looked, at least to me, like a book, I sent the entire mess off to Stackpole, the publisher of some of my favorite outdoor books. As my scribbles took form into the first edition, I now realize that I drifted toward addressing the folks that had been asking me questions for years—potential or inexperienced nonresident elk hunters. (In the world of elk hunting, there are two types of hunters, residents of states that have elk you can hunt, and everybody else.) So the book came to be a comprehensive reference for the nonresident beginner, and, as it turned out, seems to have helped a lot of elk hunters with quite a few elk hunts under their belts to make sense of some of their experience. (As I've noticed myself, experience is always inexperience while you're accumulating it, and at the time it often doesn't make any sense at all.)

So my first book came to answer those questions that are easy to ask, and easy to answer, with straightforward, explicit information that lends itself to being written down. The kind of information that's passed around by the ton using all the marvels of the information age that we live in. But there were questions left unanswered. All elk hunting "how to" books, including my own, are good, to varying degrees, at presenting explicit knowledge. But there's another body of knowledge that pertains to elk hunting. It's more vaguely expressed, to the point that the one asking the question needs a lot more background information simply in order to formulate the question that he or she would like to have answered.

This other knowledge, tacit knowledge, is an essential part of being an effective elk hunter. I'm sure you've heard it said that "speed kills." And for speed you need instinct—the ability to make straightforward decisions and take action without conscious thought—and intuition, the ability to make complex decisions without complicated reasoning.

You can get this tacit knowledge in different ways: You can be born into circumstances where it comes with the territory, or you can deliberately seek a lifestyle that gives you the experience to quickly accumulate tacit knowledge. For elk hunting, this means being born in or moving to elk country—not a possibility for most of us nonresidents. Fortunately for us, there is another way. We can study explicit information, which is internalized and nurtured by experience into tacit knowledge.

Throughout this book, I'll provide examples and application of these ideas, how they can be developed by anyone, and, more importantly, how they can be applied to attain greater success.

Enjoy the read! And good luck in all things.

INTRODUCTION

This book is intended to be a practical and comprehensive "how-to" book on the knowledge, strategies, equipment, and skills, basic through advanced, you need to hunt elk with a rifle or bow. It's addressed to hunters of all levels of skill and physical conditioning, hunting experience, and financial and time resources, from the gifted elite to the rest of us. It's written chiefly with nonresident hunters in mind—the folks who can really use a book about elk hunting—but then, I've had some favorable comments on the first edition from the locals as well. And while the first edition was primarily addressed to the beginning elk hunter, my intent in this edition is to give you a product that you won't outgrow. At least not in forty or so seasons.

OF ELK
In Chapter 1, we'll examine the nature of elk and how they came to be the way they are. An understanding of elk—what they eat, how they communicate, their senses, their instincts—is fundamental to being a successful elk hunter.

ELK AND THE EUROPEANS

I might begin with an aside to point out that the correct common name is advanced wapiti. With some variations, the locals on the North American continent referred to them as wapiti before the Europeans came over and started to confuse things.

Long before the Europeans observed elk for the first time as they "discovered" and explored the eastern seaboard of North America, the true discoverers of this continent in its original state came from the opposite direction onto the Northwest corner of the continent, following the same trails used by the great deer. Like these humans, the elk themselves were a recently evolved species, and both had expanded their ranges from their Asian homelands. The latest DNA data indicates that the ancestors of Asian and European Red Deer diverged from the sika-like deer ancestors around 1.3 million years ago, and the ancestors of East Asian/Northern American Wapiti diverged from the same ancestor shortly thereafter. The western branch of the family spread across Asia to the west and into Europe, progressively developing through stages of eco-adaption into distinct species until they reached their pinnacle, the European Red Deer, adapted to survival in temperate forests. Similarly, relic subspecies of the Wapiti family progression remain across eastern Asia, and we can trace their progression from mountain forest residents into a species that could survive in the most extreme conditions of winter in the harsh landscape of the land bridge between Asia and North America, then exploit the bounty of spring unique to this region and climate. And then the melting ice sheets parted to allow the wapiti into the continent of North America, where they are still in the process of adapting to the milder (and sometimes still too warm for them) climate, and their new neighbors—whitetails, mule deer, and the descendants of human immigrants from all directions.

Tradition has it that the very first English-speaking settlers to reach the eastern shores of North America, upon taking their first look at this most magnificent of the round-antlered deer, referred to them as elk, a mispronunciation of "ech" used in various German or Scandinavian dialects as the name for the European Moose, and the incorrect name stuck. Eventually, scientific-minded lettered gentlemen sorted it all out, and in their scientific journals, the common name of the great deer of North America became "wapiti." This translates to light or white, as in "the great deer with the whitish rump," in the language of the Shawnee of what is now the eastern United States, or the Cree of southern Canada west of the Great Lakes and Montana.

But you'll find that they're referred to as "elk" on the advanced wapiti tags that go with your hunting license from that state out west where you hunt for them. And in the title on the cover of this book too for that matter.

OF ELK COUNTRY

For the dedicated, and the successful elk hunter, the places where elk are found are more than the backdrop for the elk hunt. Elk look for habitat that meets their fundamental requirements, which are, in descending order of priority, immediate survival of the individual, general survival of the species, sustained subsistence, and comfort in extreme weather conditions.

The general characteristics of elk country at any particular area and time will affect the number of elk found there, and to some extent, their behavior. Be aware that there are always more of the "sweet spots" that are ideal for elk than there are elk herds to fill them. That's why it's important to take a look at the physical conditioning advice in Chapter 18 so you'll be able to move through all, or lots of, the places where the elk are *not* in the process of finding where they *are.*

Knowledge of and intuition into the interaction of elk with their environment are essential to success in elk hunting—but most serious elk hunters find that, over time, the intangible value of being in the camp and enjoying the beauty of elk country become as important as any other measure of success.

From the information on habitat and how to hunt it presented in Chapter 2, you'll be able to understand how elk behavior and habitat fit together, and have a general idea of how to apply that insight. Then the political breakdown of elk country in Chapter 3 goes through all of the annoying but necessary regulations that people come up with to allow hunting but still preserve it.

OF THE ELK HUNTER

Like elk, elk hunters also have factors that drive their general behavior and specific activities. They include why, when, where, and under what arrangements we hunt, and, most importantly, the equipment we use for hunting.

Every individual elk hunter has his or her own priorities, as well as a set of expectations. Both priorities and expectations are often unexpressed, and that's perfectly okay. But everybody needs to come to grips with the hard, cold truth that expectations of success need to be matched with capabilities. And capabilities don't just happen by themselves. They need to be paid for in time and effort just as surely as the trip and hunting arrangements need to be paid for in money. About the only factors over which we don't have control are the general level of physical capability that we can build on, and how much experience we bring to the hunt. Both can be offset, with physical conditioning and development of skills in the first case, and with explicit instruction and acquired insight in the second. I introduce your main choices and their implications in Chapter 4, with more on how to meet the challenges your choices bring throughout the rest of Part I and Part II. Then, in Part III, I'll present a review of elk hunting arrangements. Priorities and expectations are key again here, as is the same interchange of commodities: How much assistance do I need to hire? How much can I afford to pay for it?

One of these priorities and expectations is the desire to get a trophy bull. This goal can affect every part of your hunt; as I present different aspects of elk hunting throughout the book, I'll point out how trophy hunting can change the techniques, tactics, and strategies you use. You'll understand why trophy hunting doesn't mix well with the objective of taking any elk to fill the freezer.

OF ELK HUNTING

Immediately after introduction to the elk and elk country in Part I, I'll cover the guiding fundamental concepts of each phase of the elk hunt-location, stalking, and making the kill-along with the practical techniques required with each of the equipment options. The prospective elk hunter has three main options when it comes to equipment: high-powered rifle, muzzleloader, or bow and arrow. Your selection of equipment, one of those choices I've referred to, effectively determines the nature of your hunt-the tactics and techniques you'll use and the area and time of year you'll hunt-as well as the skill level required for success.

I would recommend that the first-time elk hunter use a modern high-powered repeater rifle (see Part II for specifics); this will allow you to enjoy the challenges of elk hunting in a wilderness setting without the extra limitations that come with a muzzleloader or bow and arrow. Elk are difficult enough to take without limitations from your equipment. For those who can afford it, I would also recommend that your first elk hunt be a guided pack camp hunt run by an established professional outfitter. With this kind of hunt you get the feel and flavor of elk hunting with the full package of intangibles under the safest and most convenient conditions. In addition to handling all the logistical details, even to the point of assisting you in getting your license and tag, the outfitter will have the general locating done for you when you arrive, provide guides who can give advice and allow you to concentrate on hunting rather than trying to keep your bearings, and get the meat and trophy out to the road for you (a formidable task unless you're set up for it). Save the backpack archery hunt on your own until you have some idea of what's involved.

If you're willing to put more effort into preparation, you can arrange a successful elk hunt without the expense associated with a professional outfitter hunt. Within these pages, you will find all the details on how to select and scout your hunting area from home by means of maps, how to outfit and provision your camp, how to secure the necessary licenses and permits, and everything in between, from how to hunt to how to cook in camp.

OF THE BOOK

From the couple of references to parts I've dropped, you've probably guessed that the information about to inundate you is organized into three parts. In case you weren't paying attention, or just skipped on to this heading, here's an overview of the book.

Part I presents my take on everything a person needs to know about to successfully hunt elk: the mind of the hunter; the elk; the interaction between elk and habitat; and the techniques and skills for all stages of elk hunting using any choice of equipment. Part II presents everything a person needs to acquire in the way of skills, conditioning, gear, and equipment to successfully apply the knowledge contained in Part I. Part III presents everything a person needs to know about planning a hunt and choosing among all the different arrangements available throughout elk country.

The Elk Hunting Tales that appear in this book need their own note of explanation. The Elk Hunting Tale, as traditionally told, is intended to teach a lesson as well as entertain. Tales are the case studies of the evening college of elk hunting, conducted around the campfires at the dawn of mankind and the wood stoves of countless hunting camps in present-day North America.

An Elk Hunting Tale is not simply the narration of the facts pertaining to an elk hunting experience. Narrations of various styles appear in many books and articles pertaining to the outdoors and hunting in general and elk hunting in particular. They're almost always from the perspective of the professional outdoor writer, who is usually either recounting first-person experiences or interpreting the experiences of a professional outfitter or guide. At their best, they convey the beautiful tapestry of the hunt, the sensations of the experience, to the reader, an observer of the work of art.

An Elk Hunting Tale, in contrast, is part of the fabric of that tapestry. And it's intended for the person who would also become part of that fabric. It's always told in the style of the traditional oral storyteller speaking from first-person experience. The narrator of the Tale doesn't necessarily have to be the star of the show, but, with just a few exceptions, was present when the proceedings of the Tale transpired. Its context is the elk hunt, and it teaches a lesson pertaining to elk hunting. Some of my hunting buddies and I, in company with some truly credentialed anthropologists and historians, have theorized that this type of tale, along with tales of territorial battles meant to simultaneously entertain and teach, is the predecessor of our literature, performing arts, and system of education, originating long before the cave paintings that left us our earliest tradition of visual art.

The Tales and other asides are identified by this different typeface. Like the case studies in a textbook, they can be skipped and the book doesn't lose continuity. If you're reading the textbook for the first time the night before the exam, or this book the night before the season opens, you'll skip the cases or the Tales; if you want to take more time and study the cases or the Tales, you'll get more insight as you go.

PART I

Of Elk,
Elk Country,
and Elk Hunting

In Part I, you'll learn the strategies, tactics, and techniques of successful elk hunting, and how they are based on knowledge of the elk. The first chapter gives you information on the nature of elk. Then we'll discuss the drivers that influence elk behavior—which include where they'll be found. The consistently successful elk hunter, with insight into the nature of elk, knows how to recognize those particular little spots that elk will be drawn to at certain times of the day or the year. This is location, the first of the three phases of elk hunting.

After you get a legal bull located comes the second phase of the hunt: the stalk. Like location, the stalk is fairly straightforward once you know the techniques appropriate for your equipment (bow or rifle). Straightforward but not always easy. The equipment you use will affect the nature of the stalk. Your stalk with a bow during the early archery season may involve closing to within 20 to 30 yards of a rutting bull; alternately, with a high-powered rifle slung over your shoulder, you may only need to approach as near as the opposite side of the canyon.

Making the kill is the third and final phase of the hunt. As opposed to location and stalking, which depend upon the behavior of the elk, making the kill is primarily a matter of the skill of the elk hunter with the equipment of choice. We'll discuss your mindset when making the kill as well as specifics of shot placement and clearing the shot.

CHAPTER 1

Understanding Elk

GENERAL DYNAMICS OF THE DEER FAMILY

The survival secret of the deer family is that they're supreme opportunists, quick to exploit new sources of subsistence and quick to adopt evasive tactics in reaction to emerging predators. The approach to survival of all the deer species is almost directly opposed to that of the grazing specialists. Bison and domestic cattle, adapted to process a steady diet of rough grass slowly through a complex digestive system to extract every last drop of nutrients, wake up on the plains every morning within a herd of thousands of their own kind and graze on a steady diet of the same grass every day, all year long. Elk, or deer of any species for that matter, have a diet that changes throughout the year according to what's available. They graze the newly emerging grass in the spring, but move upslope as the snow retreats and the succulent forbs emerge. Then, as that plays out, they'll graze the grass, the tender shoots of the bushes, and succulent growth in the vicinity of the emerging streams of the upper ridges. They'll come back down the slopes with the deepening snows of early winter and concentrate in larger herds to browse the tips of brush and, in desperate situations, even bark of trees.

Elk share the nutritional requirements of the other members of the deer family, they just need more and better quality food to produce their large calves and antlers. After all, an antler is a complete body part—hair, skin, blood vessels, and a massive, solid bone. Then this entire body part, grown at considerable nutritional expense, is cast off every year only to be grown again in the spring.

A point often lost is that growing this ornamental body part is an analogue of the nutritional requirements of giving birth to and raising an elk calf; even the timing of antler growth is in sync with final gesta-

The forbs of spring are the key to big antlers in the fall.

tion and critical early nursing period (the same time of the year when the mineral-packed forbs emerge in vast quantities, far in excess of the forage requirements of the elk). Cows prefer mates with the potential to develop big antlers. So the sire that carries the genes to efficiently convert this bounty of the spring forbs into impressive antlers passes on to his daughters the capacity to bear and nourish a well-developed calf—and also, sort of incidentally, to his male offspring the capacity to produce impressive ornamental analogues of those vigorous babies.

PHYSICAL AND BEHAVIORAL CHARACTERISTICS OF ELK TO AVOID PREDATION

Alpine mountain and cold plains deer, of which elk are typical, have an extensive repertoire of strategies and tactics to evade several types of predators.

Elk originated as a species by adaptation to life on the plains, or edges of the plains, of cold, windswept Beringia, and, by extension, to alpine biomes as summer range with migration to areas free of very deep snow for winter range. This adaptation was an overlay to the behavior for survival in woods and mountain niches of their immediate predecessors in the adjacent areas of northeast Asia. Many of their adaptations to conditions prevailing on the plains, such as incredibly sharp vision at great distances, speed, stamina, vitality, and a strong herding instinct, remain with them even though they now occur in greatest numbers in mountainous terrain, often in areas of heavy cover.

Their behavior under these conditions emphasizes traits derived from evading predators in heavy brush.

SENSES

The vision of elk is good, unbelievably good to experienced deer hunters. I once observed a hunter on stand turn his head; a few elk, about 1,000 yards out, went instantly on alert, staring in unison at the hunter, then slipped away. They will also become suspicious of a motionless human animal at about the same distance if they can recognize the distinctive shape, balanced on the hind legs, with a bare face and forward-pointing eyes. I believe that they can be fooled up to a point by the right kind of camouflage that breaks up the human form, or if the human can adopt a form of locomotion that mimics another animal. They seem to have more difficulty identifying a threat (or the nature of a threat) when they sense danger by sight rather than by smell. I use a rolling-gaited duckwalk of my own design—head lowered, face hidden—which allows me to hold a rifle or bow with a strung arrow. A more conventional high crawl on all fours seems to work, per the old paintings depicting Indian hunters covered with wolf skins. Since I'm probably something not much more than a quarter Indian according to family research, I don't go with the animal hide; anyway, some trigger-happy flatlander hunter might think he has a tag for what I might look like. I *do* go with the theory of avoiding washing hunting clothing in detergents with whiteners, or brighteners. I have proven the ultraviolet theory of animal recognition to my own satisfaction.

Elk have a sense of smell as keen as that of any grazing animal. This sense is often what they depend upon in the mountains, where variable breezes transmit odors unpredictably. I would rather avoid having a strong human odor while hunting and try to keep as clean as possible, but I don't roll in unspeakable stuff to cover it up, as have some of my short-term hunting companions.

The sense of hearing of elk is also keen; but, according to my experience, they seem to ignore random noises such as rolling rocks and breaking sticks. They do respond to rhythmic sounds such as two-legged types moving through low brush in noisy leg coverings, and, in areas where they have been hunted from horses, they may take off at any sound that's associated with horses, especially the clank of shod hooves on rocks. Human conversation will move them out, but a whistle doesn't upset them, for some reason. Their sense of the direction of threatening sounds is unbelievable to me, and I've seen plenty of demonstrations.

HERDING INSTINCT

In common with most prey animals of the plains, elk have a very strong herding instinct. They will attempt to regroup if scattered in a panic stampede, and then put a lot of distance between their group and the perceived source of danger. A member of the herd, if separated and left behind, is highly distressed at being left alone with a predator nearby— and for good reason, as an individual is less likely to survive. It doesn't have the extra eyes and ears of the rest of the herd or the experienced decision making of the old lead cows about the extent of danger and the best direction of flight to rely on.

The elk hunter should be aware of this characteristic of elk as it may afford some opportunities for stalking that may be particularly important in close terrain and heavy cover or when using short-range equipment. If you can get between the separated animal(s) and the rest of the herd, you can let the compulsion of the separated animal to rejoin the herd work to effectively drive it toward you. Your chances of success can be enhanced if you are skilled in the use of the cow call and answer the call of the separated elk with a reassuring call to join up. Another trait apparently derived from the strong herding instinct is that elk disturbed by heavy hunting pressure but not aware of immediate danger will move along single-file behind a lead cow, with each elk intent on keeping the elk immediately ahead in constant sight. The lead cow under these circumstances also tends to look ahead along the direction of movement, so that the entire herd is less perceptive to danger from the side. This instance is one of the few in which a hunter can stand and bring a rifle or bow into shooting position as elk pass, or even approach an alerted herd (from the side only), without arousing the attention of several keen-eyed elk cows.

A bull, even one going to a great deal of effort to keep a gathered herd of cows together, will still defer to the judgment of the lead cow, or another senior cow, as to the extent of danger from an intruder and the direction of flight if necessary. This probably is because a herd bull is usually five to seven years old, a youngster in terms of experience when compared to a twelve- to fifteen-year-old cow. Bulls usually fall to hunters or predators, or to the elements in the winter after the exertion of being a dominant breeder in the rut has reduced their energy reserves. The fall of such bulls represents a hard but extremely effective arrangement to minimize inbreeding while ensuring that the most superior sire available in any particular area during the breeding season passes its characteristics along to future generations.

THREAT PERCEPTION AND BEHAVIOR RESPONSE TO THREAT

The response of elk to threats is to evade or flee from them. The fearsome-looking antlers of mature bulls function primarily as weapons to fight other bulls during the rut. This is not to say that old bulls fully equipped with a rack of antlers and all of the aggressive juices of late summer and fall won't go after anything, including other bulls, trees, natural predators, or elk hunters not patterned as such. But the natural instinct of the species is to avoid or escape from danger.

My experience indicates that the threat response pattern of modern elk appears to be a combination of those of plains and woodlands prey animals. The classic prey animal of the plains, such as the caribou, routinely lives within sight of predators. Flight is triggered by behavior of the predator, the "perceived intent," rather than sensing their presence, and the objective of the flight of the prey animal is to put as much distance as possible between itself and the predator. During flight, the prey animal usually attempts to keep up with the location of the predator. The prey animal relies on its keen vision, for an early start, and on a running speed equal to that of the predator for survival.

For the classic woodland prey animal, such as the white-tailed deer, the presence of the predator is always perceived as a threat. The prey animal remains continually alert to sense the presence of predators, relying on its senses of scent and hearing as much as vision, which is usually less keen than that of the plains animal. The perception of a predator in the immediate vicinity triggers sudden, often panicked evasive flight for just enough distance to avoid the immediate attack. The prey animal immediately returns to its normal stealthy behavior as soon as it successfully manages to remove itself from the immediate area of danger. It may remain motionless for a while to watch its back trail, and then return to its normal deliberate movements while constantly on the alert to sense the next potential predator. Deer don't seem to have a strong urge to regroup immediately with the rest of the herd as elk do.

If elk sense a potential threat from a predator, they often initially wait motionless and let the threat pass as they watch the source of danger for clues of intention, in the habit of the classic plains prey animal. A bull elk will sometimes remain motionless if an approaching hunter hasn't been perceived as a threat and appears to be on a track not directed toward the elk. It follows that an appropriate response for the predator or hunter is to appear harmless. The hunter can avoid threatening behavior like direct eye contact and change gait to imitate something harmless to confuse the elk's threat pattern. If the threat appears to diminish, the elk will relax but remain wary. If the patterned threat continues at the same level, or appears to increase, the elk will move off as a herd behind the lead cow along an established route. The appearance of a sudden, immediate threat usually triggers a panic stampede. Pursuit, other than a quick move to intercept a single elk attempting to rejoin the herd, is usually useless or counterproductive. The elk in flight will attempt to keep the threat in sight and vary their direction to keep an obstruction between themselves and the threat as they create distance between themselves and the threat. They can easily outdistance the human pursuer and will watch their back trail. Most experienced hunters usually start the location process over again rather than pursue elk in full flight.

It's interesting to note that not all responses of elk to threats have come down through the ages. Some appear to be distinctly modern, indicating that elk can be fast learners when it comes to surviving with the lowest expenditure of energy. Wilderness areas and other areas of very low population are often designated as "free flight" areas for military aircraft, allowing supersonic flight operations for training. The resulting sonic booms tend to startle elk hunters when they occur, but the elk have become accustomed to the sound and don't perceive it as a threat. The sound may be a single loud boom or, more often, a double boom. It's not uncommon for elk to pay little attention to a first shot, or even a second if it follows closely, in such areas. But that third shot will always bring on a panic stampede.

I've noted a couple of adjustments in the threat responses of elk to predators over the span of my own elk hunting experience (a blink of the eye in the history of the elk). Not too many years ago, human predators carried elk tags good for either sex in the Bitterroots of Idaho. Both bull and cow elk were conditioned to humans as an immediate danger and responded accordingly: The perception of a human was certain to bring on a stampede of the entire herd. Then the humans stopped carrying cow tags. The younger cows that came along after that time weren't prey for humans and acted accordingly. But the old cows never forgot. And somewhere along the way, bull elk, having picked up the tactic of keeping something, anything, between themselves and the line of sight of the predator with the upright stance that kills from a distance, found that one handy moving bit of cover that's just the right size is a cow elk. This tactic came so quickly and so universally that it's probably derived from some aspect of the selfish herd behavior. In the selfish herd, individuals are acting in their own best interest; if there's no place to hide on the coverless plains, they hide behind the other herd members. The less capable get forced to the rear and outside of the herd. In the case of the cows being less threatened and the bull more threatened, the bull makes more effort to get behind the cows.

ELK COMMUNICATION—A DEFINING CHARACTERISTIC OF THE SPECIES

Elk use three common calls in communication: the bull elk bugle and grunt or growl; the various forms of the cow call, also used by bulls; and the alarm call.

The bugle of the bull elk during the rut of early fall is considered one of the defining characteristics of the elk as a species and one of the most spectacular and exciting aspects of elk hunting. It's also the most difficult and least understood, most frustrating, and most difficult luring technique to master of any outdoor sport. Particularly for the dedicated bowhunter, the results can be well worth the investment of effort once you reach the level of skill required to be successful.

The bull elk bugle has many variations, and its sound is often, but not always, an indication of a bull's size and maturity. A mature bull has a melodious sound throughout the full range of the typical bugle. An immature bull produces a high-pitched, reedy bugle and will often leave out the terminal grunts. A big old bull may just go with the growl or grunt part, if he's really mad, or just a part of the highest pitch of the whistle if he doesn't care much.

The bull's bugle is most commonly used during the rut as a challenge between bulls, but may be used by a herd bull to challenge other intruders. It can be translated, "I'm a big, mature bull and I'm collecting all of the cows in the area, and they're all mine, all through the rut, and if you interfere or intrude, I'm going to whip your tail and send you running." The bugle of the challenger is, politely stated, a rebuttal of the herd bull's position.

The second major form of elk communication is actually an entire repertoire of vocalizations collectively referred to as "cow calls." These are less familiar to most people than the bugle, but are actually used by all elk much more extensively during all seasons in their normal activities. Whereas the bugle is restricted almost exclusively to a challenge between bulls during the rut, the various cow calls express a wide range of elk signals. My friends who hunt late-season black powder hunts have observed bulls walking along together making continuous conversation with these vocalizations . . . maybe working out any little misunderstandings left over from fights over cows during the rut.

The last sound an elk hunter hears from a herd before every elk in the vicinity disappear is the alarm. Its pitch is similar to the yap of a frightened small dog but with a different pronunciation. The quality of tone reflects the size of the animal. It's usually accompanied by a stare in the direction of the cause for alarm. This call may be repeated until other members of the herd see the same thing as the originator and also sound the alarm, or the entire bunch may take off at the first call. I suspect that the herd's response may depend on the credibility of the first member to sound off. If it's a spike, they get verification; if it's the old lead cow, they're gone.

ELK TALK TRANSLATED TO ENGLISH ACCORDING TO OLD TOM

Most folks even remotely interested in elk are familiar with the bull elk bugle through recordings. Recordings usually don't do it justice, but they're better than the written word. I'll attempt to spell it out for you, though. It starts with an extended low precursor moan or growl quickly going up in frequency and volume to a high, then even higher, whistle that subsequently falls to a low grunt in the first breath; the terminal grunt is then typically repeated two or three times with progressively lower pitch, a separate breath being used for each repetition: *OOooEEEeeeeeeeeeeeeooooough, Eeeeough, EeeeooOUGH.*

A related bull elk sound is termed the "chuckle." It's often heard at the end of a normal three-breath bugle and sounds like *eeeEEyuck, eeeEEyuck, eeeEEyuck,* with a separate breath for each chuckle; it may be repeated up to eight times, with each subsequent repetition at a lower volume than the one preceding. It can be generally translated as a chuckle with the attitude of "I'm just so cool!" At the same time, the bull perfumes himself with a controlled urine spray or mist to the belly or, on occasion, into the face and thick neck mane, which is lowered into the spray between the front legs.

Herd bulls also make a low growl, which they use to urge the cows to leave an area if they sense danger.

A lot of elk hunters term the cow call a "mew" to express that it sounds a little like a cat's meow. It's normally rather short in duration, either side of a second, and not very loud, although it can carry for a considerable distance. It may strike the listener as a high-pitched chirp. Its various forms include something to the effect of *meeeak,* or *eeeeak,* meaning "Where are you, baby?" (from cow to calf) or, from any elk to another, meaning "I'm over here and things are okay." With a little more anxiety, it can become *eeEak,* meaning "I'm over here and something's making me nervous, but I think it may not be a danger; let's get together and check it out or leave together." A slightly more drawn-out, plaintive, *meeeaak,* which sounds like a mature elk mimicking the lost calf call at a lower pitch, means, "I'm over here lost from everybody else and I want to get with the rest of the herd."

One cow elk call that receives a great deal of attention from elk hunters, far out of proportion to how often it's used by elk, is the call made by a cow elk during the rut when she's ready to breed. While the bull is always ready to breed any and every cow in the area, the cow will refuse all advances of the bull until the time that conception will result from mating—and the bull will not force himself upon her until the cow signals that she will stand. The call that signals to the bull that the cow will accept breeding excites and attracts the herd bull to approach. It also attracts every other bull within hearing distance. You'll very seldom, if ever, hear this call under normal circumstances; elk just don't use it that often. You will hear attempts to reproduce it by every elk hunter in a practice calling session and anybody trying to sell cow elk calls. It usually sounds like a drawn-out, bleating, two-note (in a single breath) *eeeeeeeEEOOOeeeeeeeeeoch,* but I've heard a cow in heat (estrus) produce a short, urgent, low-pitched version too. Many elk hunters who hunt the rut believe this call to possess almost magical powers over trophy bulls to the point that they lose all caution and will charge toward the hunter that can create a reasonably close reproduction of it. It's been my experience that the urge to reproduce still comes second to the survival instinct in the scale of priorities of trophy bulls.

Cows in a fighting mood make a distinctive, high-pitched, drawn-out, aggressive scream of rage, *eeeeeeeeeeeeeeeeeeeeech.* The vanquished in a cow fight may let out a submissive *meeeuk.* I've heard from old guides that the loser of a fight between bulls may make the same cry.

The alarm call is always a loud, sharp, anxious, snorted *EAK,* and it has just one translation: "Danger!"

A final note in regard to elk calls (as actually used by a herd of elk, rather than by hunters attempting to call elk) is that the time between repetitions of any call, whether made by either bulls or cows, varies greatly. According to my experience, a bull will repeat a bugle every thirty minutes or so under normal circumstances. He has to be really excited to bugle, grunt, growl, chuckle, and bugle again without interruption. Talkative cows in a herd under undisturbed conditions may chirp two or three times over a fifteen-minute interval. Calling by both cows and bulls seems to be very frequent only during the excitement of the rut. Experienced callers take their cue for cadence from the elk. If the hunter caller isn't in sync with the elk, the elk will simply shut up. If they have the slightest sense of an intruder, they'll not make a sound until the dreaded danger call, and then they're gone. Often, they'll leave without a sound.

Elk communicate without vocalizations as well. Every elk in the herd keeps up with the other elk, particularly with the lead cows. If any one of them sees something out of the ordinary, a long stare shortly has every other elk looking in the same direction. The legs and ankles of walking elk make a very audible clicking sound with every step. If one or more come to a full stop and hold in place, the other elk quickly notice the absence of the sound and go on full alert.

ELK ON THE MOVE

Elk can be runners when faced with what they pattern as an immediate deadly threat. The elk that exist today are the descendants of elk that survived pursuit by predators on the plains and the brushy fringes of the plains for much of the existence of the species. They're not in the antelope class for flat-out speed, but, after they've had a little time to get started, they can run at about 30 miles an hour for extended distances through rough, uneven brushy terrain that would hold up the most swift plains runners. (The flat-out top speed in the sprint has always been a good topic for opinionated evening sessions, but we can address that with measured data shortly.)

The top-speed gait of an elk is a hard gallop, with the back feet coming through the grounded front feet and thrusting forward to produce a momentarily airborne leap. It's not unusual to see lighter elk like young cows and calves running at a graceful leaping gallop, with one front foot in contact with the ground and the other bent and coming forward to come down in front of the grounded foot, while both back legs are coming forward for their next touchdown ahead of the front feet. Lighter elk often use this leaping action to plunge through thick stuff when they're in a hurry. If sufficiently spooked, young bulls and some older, heavier cows will run with a shorter gallop that resembles a stiff-legged leap as they spring forward. It strikes the observer as inefficient locomotion on flat, clear ground, but it appears to be very efficient in thick brush on rough slopes. Heavy bulls in a hard gallop (very seldom observed) appear to bring their back feet forward close to, but not through, the grounded front feet, and their leap forward covers less distance than that of a lighter elk. But they can pick 'em up and put 'em down fast.

Sustaining such a gait in the case of an animal the size of a large bull elk consumes a very large amount of energy, apparently a prohibitive amount for everyday use for a large bull, according to my observations while hunting. It's been my experience that you'll very seldom see a mature bull elk running along with the easily recognized leaping action of the flat-out hard gallop. I've seen plenty of them in a big hurry to get away, in my misdirected elk hunting experience, and they were using the fast trot, an energy-conserving run. In the escape, the really big old bulls tend to plow ahead through both the thick stuff and the relatively clear areas, often appearing to simply move with a faster walk, which is actually a high-speed trot.

I have it on good authority that big bulls will routinely gallop for short sprints when chasing a wandering cow back to his gathered herd or when the winner is chasing the loser of a fight, if they still have the energy. (We might conclude that they'll expend more energy in breeding-related activity than in escaping mortal danger, but we won't follow down that philosophical trail since it's not important to our interests.) You'll normally see the fast trotting action used in the escape, unless you're chasing the elk with aircraft, which is the source of misleading photos, or when one decides to pass you on the road.

BIG BULL ELK PASSING ON THE RIGHT

One of the less widely known facts about elk behavior is that they share with their deer cousins a dreadful compulsion. When they see a vehicle moving along a road at high speed, they are possessed with the desire to cross the road. That, in itself, wouldn't bring on too much trouble, but they also feel compelled to cross *in front* of the vehicle.

On the occasion of this encounter, the four humans involved were driving in the dark just before first light, trying to find a jump-off for the day's hunt at a trailhead that we'd never seen before. This isn't unusual for hunts that are planned by map when you don't have a chance to look over the area before the morning that you plan to hunt. It's usually easier to do than it sounds, but not on that particular morning.

The eastern sky was already getting light and we were still driving along at gravel-road speed, all four of us starting to get a vague, pre-lost feeling as we looked ahead for the right combination of landmarks—the road turning to the south and crossing a small creek at the bottom of a grade with a mountain looming to the east—that would indicate that we were there. The twisting road had us traveling to the south without any of the rest of the terrain features that we were looking for in sight. The group had fallen silent and a little glum as we bounced along the road and started to top yet another grade.

Suddenly from the passenger side of the cab, in a rising volume and a peculiar tone, came a question to nobody in particular. "What's that shadow? . . . What's that coming around? . . . *Look out—it's an elk!!!*" The person sounding the warning jerked back and started to brace himself against the impact to come. The rest of us hadn't seen a thing and had absolutely no reaction as a big bull elk broke around us as if we were parked in the road.

Everything was in slow motion except the elk. It was almost in contact with the side of the truck as it shot across directly into the glare of the right headlight and shot ahead of us before I had time to react with either brake or wheel. It easily cleared the front of the truck and crossed the road as I slammed on the brakes. The elk scampered over the 8-foot bank on the uphill side of the road, outlined against the light of the eastern sky in fine detail, right down to each heavy tine of an oversized five-point rack. The four of us sat silent and absolutely motionless as the truck slid to a stop. The bull was long gone in a few seconds. No point trying to chase that one down. We were still lost and running late. I took my foot off the brake and the truck rolled forward.

There was no sound in the cab of the truck other than the background sounds of the engine and the tires on the rough gravel road surface. Finally someone spoke. "Probably too early for legal shooting." As if we could have shot anything in our immobilized state of shock.

Then the floodgates opened: "Illegal to shoot from the road anyway." "You could see how it extended its front legs with one a little higher than the other so that the front feet hit the ground with a good bit of front to back separation." "I wouldn't want to shoot one right next to the road anyway. Wouldn't be the same as getting one on top in the big timber." "You could clearly see the bottom of both back hooves as the back feet came forward during the leap." "Makes you feel a little dumb to climb 2,000 feet lookin' for 'em when they're right down here at the road." "Did those back feet come completely through the grounded front feet? Did anybody notice that?" "All I saw was the rack!" "That was a big rack!" "Big enough for me to shoot at." "That's the one I'm looking for." "How fast were we goin'?" "Thirty or a little more, I looked at the speedometer." "Thought you said the racks wouldn't be that big with the hunting pressure in this area." "What was its speed relative to the truck?" "Damn sight faster than my jog." "The oversized, high-pressure tires on this truck make it a little faster than the speedometer reads." "He came around faster than my run." "He came around faster than anybody's run." "He was doin' thirty-five?" "At least." "Faster." "Across the ditch on my side. Up onto the road and around and still gettin' ahead before you finally got on the brakes." "He was doin' forty." "Maybe more." "Not quite." "Kinda slow gettin' on those brakes, Tom." "And the speedometer read thirty?" "Yeah." "What's the insurance company with the outline of the elk for a logo?" "He looked just like that against the sky, didn't he?" "He wasn't comin', he was goin'." "You're tellin' me!" "So he was doin' at least thirty-five." "More." "Were the back feet comin' forward all the way through the front feet on the ground?" "Too fast for me." "Need an instant replay on that one." "I never thought they actually did on a bull that big." "Sure didn't have much up and down motion to it when it ran." "Kinda reminds you of a Blue Heeler in a hard run." "Or a great big lineman." "Lighter elk definitely hop more going through brush." "The ones you've seen hopping through the brush weren't trying to outrun a truck." "Why do they always try to cross in front of the vehicle?" "They're deer. It's a deer thing." "Damned big deer." "Fast too." "forty?" "Easy." "Less." "Definitely more than thirty-five." "Definitely." "Yeah." "If we were doin' thirty, it was doin' over forty when it came around this fender."

We went 10 miles past our jump-off that morning, but eventually concluded that a bull elk can maneuver past a pickup over different ground surfaces, top a high bank, and proceed up a mountain at well over forty miles an hour.

For the elk hunter, there are a couple of practical aspects of elk locomotion. The first is a quick way to tell if the elk is walking or running. It's surprisingly difficult at a distance, with brush or timber obscuring your view of the elk across a little canyon, to distinguish between the slow moving walk and the fast moving trot. Because of the difference in speed between the two, while a shot at a slow walking elk can be considered, a shot at the same range at a fast trotting elk should be avoided as unethical for most of us.

If we discount the easily recognized, and seldom used gallop that tops well over 40 mph, the bull elk has two gaits: walking and trotting. An elk's walk looks at any distance like an even plod at maybe 3 to 5 mph if they're about grazing along, with an action resembling an old carriage horse amble, but can be stepped up to 7 or more mph if the herd is disturbed and sneaking out of the area. An elk's trot looks like the trotting action of a harness racer and can be sustained at 20 mph through brush, uphill and down, and can be bumped up to 30 mph if there's an immediate threat. As opposed to the galloping run, the fast trotting run of the bull elk shows no wasted motion; the movement strikes you as that of a planed-out power boat. You don't need to see the entire elk to read the difference between the gaits. The key to reading the speed of gait is the carry angle and the movement of the antlers, which you can often see more clearly than the body and legs. The antlers of a slow walking elk appear to bob up and down, with a slight fore and aft rocking. The relaxed neck carries the head at a nose-down

Running elk (A, B) carry their heads more upright with stiffer necks and antlers tilted back; walking elk (C, D) carry their heads pointed more downward.

angle so that the antlers appear to have a slight forward tilt. The fast walk, when they're moving along with purpose, is characterized by an upright carry of the head; the antlers appear to float smoothly along. The stiffened neck carries the head in a slightly nose-up attitude, so that the antlers are tilted back, with the main length of the beams parallel with the elk's back. The faster the trot, the higher the nose. The angle of the antlers generally resembles their angle when the elk is bugling.

The antlers often strike trees with a distinct whacking sound as the elk moves along at high speed; tilting them back helps keep them from becoming entangled. In the process, the antlers of a large trophy rack rake the hair of the rump. The transition from a walk to a trot is a deceptively smooth acceleration. If the elk is moving fast and slows down, the antlers will make a few pronounced rocks as they move back to the slight forward tilt of the walk.

There's one other point to be made on the subject of moving elk that might be of interest on some future day when you find yourself trying to clear a killing shot at about the time that the elk patterns you as a threat and starts to take off. It usually comes as a surprise to new elk hunters to learn that for all of their superlatives as to size, vitality, vision, sense of smell, power, range, and speed, elk aren't very fast to get up to speed off the mark. This slow start off the mark comes from the elk's plains ancestors, who relied on a long-duration run to escape a coursing predator seen at a distance. You or I can just about sprint fast enough to keep up for a short distance on clear ground with a bull elk coming up to speed. (Try that with a whitetail!) This sprint maneuver is usually limited to attempts to cut off the elk's escape or get into position for a clear shot at the fleeing elk. It works best when used intuitively to cut off an elk attempting to rejoin the herd or head off in the direction of the preferred escape route. The other side of that statement is that the elk can move at the same speed straight up the side of a steep, rough, snow covered, brushy slope, picking up speed all the while, and keep it up for the rest of the day.

CHAPTER 2

Elk Habitat

THE NATURAL ASPECTS OF ELK COUNTRY

Learning how to hunt elk amounts to being able to recognize the places most likely to hold elk, then knowing how to hunt for those places, then how to hunt for the elk in those places. Sounds straightforward enough, but those places look different in different regions. You have to work from the fundamentals of elk requirements and capabilities, which are the same everywhere. Elk require habitat that provides their absolute necessities of subsistence and security. That's 24/7/365 and a quarter. Subsistence requirements include forage, water, and cover for undisturbed resting during rumination. The elk population that a given area will carry is the number that can be sustained under the most severe combination of circumstances (usually hard winters in the north and high country, severe drought in the south). Security amounts to an acceptable level of disturbance—a perceived immediate threat low enough to allow successful breeding, followed by gestation and birthing, and survival of the young.

THE SMALL SCALE—RECOGNIZING SWEET SPOTS THAT ATTRACT ELK

Places with quantity and quality of the essential elements of subsistence and security will always be gathering places for elk.

Natural Cultivation of Forage

Cultivation is any process that enhances the growth of desired vegetation. This is easy to understand in the familiar context of a farmer plowing a field to destroy weeds and break up compacted soil so that water can transport natural soil nutrients and fertilizer to desirable plants, but

Lush secondary growth several years after a "cool" burn.

A very hot burn is a scene of desolation for decades. This area is barren more than thirty years after the fire occurred.

natural processes are more subtle than a big green John Deere trailing a 41-foot-wide gang of cultivators and a fertilizer tank. Natural cultivation processes include fires that remove trees and brush shading desirable forbs; floods that deposit nutrient-rich soils; soil from runoff filling up mountain lakes; mountain slides that locally disrupt soils, rocks, and existing vegetation; and direct weathering of igneous rocks that releases nutrients locked up in the rock. But the most effective natural cultivation results from glaciations. Glaciers are the ultimate cultivator, grinding rock into flour, and they have only recently melted in high elevations in the northern region.

Fire is one of the dominant cultivators today. The aftermath of a fire can range from rejuvenation of forage for elk and other animals to a hellish landscape effectively uninhabitable by wildlife. The intensity of a fire is determined by many factors, including the amount of dead vegetation interspersed with living plants, the dryness of ground and vegetation (determined by preceding precipitation and atmospheric conditions), wind, relative humidity, temperature, and terrain features. The severity of damage to different elements of the forest varies based on the type of plants and details of the landscape features. In scrub oak–covered basins in the dry southern region, fires replenish soil and remove brush so that stands of grasses are rejuvenated. The thinning of heavy terminal stands of old timber in the north lets the sunlight in, bringing forth another succession of plants used by the grazers and browsers.

Reliable Sources of Water

Another part of subsistence is water, which is required in copious quantities for the efficient digestion processes of the ruminants. Elk also seek out water for cooling during hot weather (note that hot for elk starts around 70 degrees F). Particularly desirable are elk-sized standing muddy pools located preferably in the vicinity of cover in a cool location. These places are used as wallows to cool. With onset of the rut, wallows are often converted into mud baths that bulls improve upon using urine, where they soak to enhance their attractiveness to females. Big antlers and big odor make for a sharp-dressed bull elk.

Cover with a View for Resting

Elk require cover for a low activity period each day to chew their cud, an essential part of their ruminant digestive process. This cover takes many different forms according to the local vegetation and landform patterns, but the common denominator is that it has to provide physical comfort and relief from disturbance. Elk feel more secure (and stabilize at a lower level of disturbance) when surrounded by cover so that they're not in view of predators at a distance. They also prefer to have a view from cover so that they're forewarned of approaching predators. They'll attempt to create space between themselves and immediate threats. They also grade threats into levels of severity, preferring to winter in proximity to human populations because such areas are low in a greater threat, wolves.

Predicting Preferred Routes of Travel

Sites of forage, water, and resting in very close proximity are preferred, as there's always risk associated with movement. Edges where cover and feeding grounds border may hold elk, as is the case with other, more territorial deer, but when travel is necessary, elk will use a less direct route that furnishes some cover. Fringes of timber or brush or erosion-formed defile features are likely places to look for traveling elk.

Comfort in Extreme Temperatures

Elk seek cooling in all but the coldest weather. The result all year is that they can often be found in heavy timber: It's shady during warm weather so that it stays cooler than the surrounding area, but in extremely cold weather, it forms a thermal blanket that makes it warmer than the surrounding area.

The Big Picture of the Natural Characteristics across Elk Country

The backbone of the Rockies, formed from the eroded remnants of ancient batholiths, can be traced by the green timber on the higher elevations along the center of the satellite image, beginning north of the snow-dusted ranges at the top and center of the image. Coastal ranges formed by volcanic activity rim the Pacific. The ranges divide to the south as the continental divide separates to the east. There are a few breaks as the main divide of the Northern Rockies offsets to the east, then forms an unbroken line from the Yellowstone hotspot south into the massive Wasatch and associated ranges east of the Great Salt Lake. Another offset to the east and the high and wide ranges of the Central Rockies extend to the south, with the painted deserts to their west. The extensive basin and range area between the Central Rockies and the Pacific ranges is composed of folds in the surface, as the Pacific plate tends to drag the west coast along in its relentless slide to the east under the continental plate. Wide areas between the Southern Rockies and the Pacific ranges have been subjected to major uplifts, leaving large mesas at high elevations and spectacularly deep canyons cut by existing rivers as the land was uplifted.

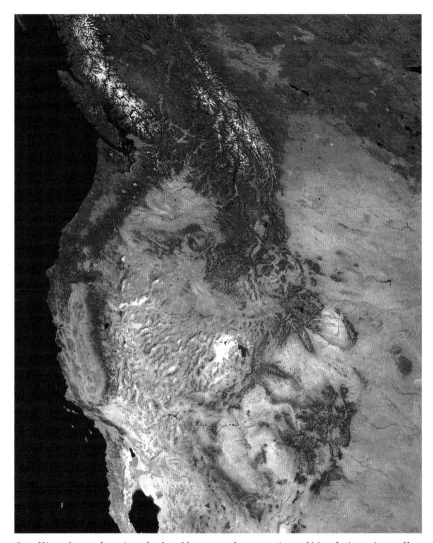

Satellite photo showing the landforms and vegetation of North American elk country. NASA. PHOTO AVAILABLE AT VISIBLE EARTH (HTTP://VISIBLEEARTH.NASA.GOV).

The atmospheric circulation that defines the climate across western North America is predominantly moisture-laden air in from the Pacific moving west to east or southeast; occasionally during winter it is interspersed with arctic surges of cold continental air. Moving west to east, the air from the Pacific crosses landforms that extract the moisture derived from the ocean. The first mountains encountered by the water-laden air extract the most moisture, and subsequent ranges wring out more or less, depending on their elevation and the nature of any atmospheric disturbance associated with the currents.

Landforms and climate combine to form vegetation patterns to complete the landscape. The combinations and patterns are more complex and we'll look at them on a smaller scale.

ROCKY MOUNTAIN ELK HABITAT

The Northern Rockies of Canada and the United States provide good to excellent elk hunting with a high-quality wilderness experience. It's a land of hard winters that cull the depleted breeders of the last fall. The most hardy of the young would-be breeders of last year's rut will be the herd bulls next fall, and there won't be many from that rut to inbreed with their daughters the following year. Complex landscapes are formed by weathering of exposed ancient batholithic intrusions, as typified by the Bitterroot Range. The level of moisture in this region is more than adequate for growth of spring and summer forage.

Big River Landform Habitat in the Northern Rockies

A typical landform encountered in this region is the sizable basin that drops off toward a large river. I'll illustrate how to recognize habitat sweet spots along with tactics and techniques of hunting this type of landform. The discussion will follow the way I'd explain it to you if we were there—climb up on a ridge and look around. We'll take a look at the landforms, and then I'll tell you how to hunt them.

First illustrated is a typical uneven ridge looking northwest toward Chateau Rock, a landmark pinnacle up from the Big Bend of the North Fork of the Clearwater. To the west is the small basin of Sprague Creek, as rich a forage area as occurs in the region, with meadows like the one in the foreground of the top photo on the next page interspersed with cover. The lower photo swings to the left to look across the mile-wide Sprague Creek basin. Note the timbered finger ridges coming down from the main ridge.

Routes of elk movement in this region are controlled by terrain. I've often hunted this area on the opening week of the season by taking a temporary stand around the rocks overlooking the basin. To the east of this ridge, the Squaw Creek basin drops off into the North Fork of the Clearwater. Steep sides and cover including timber falls impossible to negotiate make it a refuge for pressured elk pulling out of Sprague Creek, so these ambush stands along the ridge could be productive if somebody spooked elk out of the basin. Elk could also escape the basin by moving toward Chateau Rock to either drop off into Squaw Creek or go around Chateau Rock and over the top into upper Cave Creek and into an excellent feeding area with plenty of cover and water. The

Pinnacles along the rim of a large basin.

Turning 90 degrees to the west from the first photo (the little meadow behind the near pine is visible in both photos) shows how broad these basins are. This is as rich a forage area as you can find in this region, with meadows interspersed with cover.

ridges around the upper three sides seemed to mark the boundaries of the herd bull of the area, a small range since it didn't take a big area to support his average-size herd of cows.

On a season opening morning, Herm and I decided to take a stand overlooking the west part of the mile-wide basin to the west of the photos on the previous page.

HUNTING A BIG RIVER BASIN

Our printed diagram is a poor substitute for the scratches in the dirt next to the fire we made to plan this day. The spaced curved lines represent contours of 50 feet change in elevation, showing the shape of the slopes; our diagram is about 1,000 yards across. The arrowed lines show routes taken, with dark and light tracks representing man and beast, respectively. The small circular bursts represent rifle shots.

Herm and I walked through the early morning darkness down the draw behind our mountain camp. We silently moved down through the timbered drainage until it opened up on a series of brushy fingers falling off toward the river. Without a word or signal, we stopped and eased into a sitting position on the steep slope (A) as we sensed movement on the adjacent brushy finger, about 300 yards off to our left (B). A single cow fed through the brush, then another, then another. The herd continued moving out of the timber and across the face of the finger adjacent to the ridge from which we watched, straining in the weak light to see antlers or even a darker neck, which would indicate a bull. "Phere is zee?" ("Where is he?") I quietly hissed, to myself as much as to Herm, not even showing major movement of my face to the sharp eyes of the cows as they individually paused in their feeding to scan the slopes for movement. We remained motionless in our camo, and they did not notice us. The cows leisurely fed about the brushy finger for an hour, a motionless eternity for us. Still no bull. The cows eventually worked their way around the point of the finger (C). We slowly flexed stiffened limbs and shifted our weight from the numb contact points against the rocks where we had eased down a century earlier, it seemed.

We shortly noticed another movement on a brushy finger (D) almost 900 yards off in the same direction as the now unseen elk on the opposite face of the intervening point. One man, hardly more than a small figure in red at that distance, slowly labored up the point of the distant finger to rest on some low, flat rocks. Another presently joined him. They had apparently come up from a camp of local hunters below.

Suddenly, Herm and I were startled by shots in our direction from the far point. Then we relaxed as we realized that the shots were directed at the elk on the slope (E) facing the distant hunters. "Well, those twenty shots should about stink up this area for a while" was Herm's only audible indication of the frustration of an opening morning spent without results.

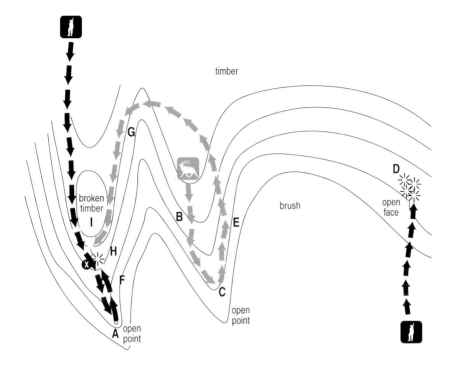

It hadn't been a complete loss, though. The scenery was pretty from the point, and watching the cows was entertaining if nothing else, and there still might be a chance for some action. The elk, pushed by the shooting, would leave the area under cover of the timber on the upper slopes and head for heavy cover. That cover might be the heavy brush on the slopes below, and, in that case, the herd might come down the point where we had taken their stand. It took only a forward lean and a flex of their legs to change from sitting to standing on the steep slope.

We made our way back up the slope we had descended much earlier and were shortly into the dark timber (F). Speaking in low tones, as is the habit of hunters, we wondered aloud if the hunters from the camp below somehow had cow tags or simply good enough vision or powerful telescopes or imaginations to see antlers at over 600 yards on that bunch of cows. We had thoroughly investigated the same bunch at a distance of less than 300 yards. A cow coming down the slope in the opposite direction interrupted the entertainment. We stood motionless as she walked on by a few yards off. We grinned at each other and whispered something about our fancy camo coats from Army surplus rendering us completely invisible. Maybe the cow's mind was somewhere else. We moved up the slope a short distance and the entire sequence was repeated with another cow. Then again with a pair. We were meeting the entire herd we had watched earlier, passing "like ships in the night"! The elk, spooked by the artillery barrage, had obviously moved well back up the slope toward the camp location, then, after a lateral movement of several hundred yards (G), were slipping off the mountain, heading into the brush of the lower slopes along the trail down the point we had been sitting on.

Without a word, I slipped off my daypack and handed it to Herm, who took it as if we were of one mind. Just in case interest picked up even more. We moved on up the slope, stopping as more cows passed, and finally, as if the now nonchalant attitude of the elk were infectious, even moving around a cow that had stopped to graze. The daypack changed hands a couple of times in the indecision as to what was going on. It was becoming obvious that we should have by now passed through the entire herd and, sure enough, there was no bull with it. I returned the pack to my back and the rifle to my shoulder. We began to ascend the final steep pitch (H) up to the rocky, pinnacle-like knoll that formed the top of the finger.

Then we instantly froze in place as a pair of cows, moving at a trot, broke over the brow of the knoll (I). Approaching around the edge of the knoll, the elk first appeared through the dense, interlocking but almost bare lower limbs of three small trees on the break of the knoll, about 50 yards from us. As the cows changed their direction of travel to cross in front of us from right to left, I saw the almost surreal sight of a disembodied full bull elk rack seemingly floating along behind them. Under that rack was an as yet unseen big bull moving at a fast trot.

The entire mass of the largest elk I had ever seen instantly materialized behind the three small trees. Unlike the headlong flight of the two cows ahead, the bull broke its pace at the break of the knoll to momentarily look to its left. With my right hand grasping the rifle by the small of the stock, I had already slipped the slung rifle from my shoulder and with the automatic reflex of countless repetitions begun the inverted spin to bring it to my shoulder. Within about a second, the rifle was up, the safety off without conscious effort. Only the head and neck of the bull were clear of the tangle of the limbs. No shot. The bull moved over the brow of the slope behind the tangle of the trees to follow the cows. Still no shot. I directed my attention along the path of the bull and almost instantly selected the first opening between two trees that would offer the possibility of a shot as the bull passed. The scope was to my eye as the bull appeared between the pines. Time and the bull seemed to pause as the crosshairs appeared over the bull's heart in the exact mental image I had seen thousands of times on the targets I always chose at the archery range. It wasn't a true memory but an ingrained pattern from practice. I was only aware of the barely perceptible recoil of the .338 in response to that image. With unconscious reflex I worked the bolt of the rifle to chamber another shell, aware from that image in the crosshairs that I had killed the bull. The huge animal continued down the slope unimpeded for a full 50 yards before his

Landforms along the North Fork of the Clearwater.

hindquarters wobbled. With that falter, he spun around in his tracks and fell in a heap (X). Movement ceased as we carefully approached.

A thought flashed through my mind. There was something wrong with the image. The head was too small. Then the true size of the antlers came into focus.

We took pictures, then we dressed the carcass and packed it into camp, ready for the trip to the river and on to the locker the next day. On the porch of the cook tent Herm proceeded with a long-delayed caping job for me. He paused in his meticulous work.

"Tom, it sure took a long time to show you a big one like I promised, and you needed a lucky shot to get him at that."

The photo above shows the view south along the ridge from the distant pinnacle in the bottom photo on page 23, and provides a good perspective on landforms along the river. Note how little pockets drop off from the long ridge. They usually have feed, water, and cover. Elk will move up or down the ridges according to conditions, all the way on top during summer heat, and down to the river when the snow gets deep.

The photo on the next page shows some high-elevation landforms above one of the big rivers of the Bitterroots. Meadows will be along the sunny slopes on the south sides of these landforms, and cool timber areas where the elk rest on warm fall afternoons will be on the north slopes; there will be (relatively) easy trails from one to the other, channeled between the rocky outcrops. The trails that elk use to get to feed

Left: Typical basin divide landforms. Right: An almost filled-in lake at high elevation is usually a draw for elk (as well as moose). Mountain lakes are very transient landform features, quickly filled in by rich soil.

are usually the trails they'll take moving away from pressure if they're not panicked. This high rough country where feed, water, and cover intermix becomes a refuge for elk as their disturbance level goes up. You can organize drives across upper sections of drainages to push elk upslope toward standers stationed along the trails. Alternately, single hunters or pairs of hunters can move silently along to intercept elk that are on the move, feeding early or late in the day, or bedded in the middle of the day.

High Divide Landform Habitat of the Northern and Central Rockies

Another landform type of the Northern Rockies with habitat sweet spots sprinkled throughout is widely encountered along the major divides. Long side ridges drop away from the main ridges. Small, often seasonal, tributaries arise from springs at the juncture of ridges in well watered pockets. Thin soils composed of recently weathered granite provide rich forage for elk, and, on steep slopes, treacherous footing for elk hunters. Ridges along the divides are often highly mineralized, and fires caused by lightning strikes are a common occurrence; the new

The photo above, taken at the top of Cave Creek just over the pass from Sprague Creek, shows some ideal holding area for elk, with feed, water, cover, and escape routes all in one place. In contrast to the wide open big-country landforms of preceding photos, these close little pockets are more suited for bowhunting during the rut and as the rut winds down.

Landscape near a divide with feeding areas adjacent; elk will find cover and water in the creases of the ridges.

growth after fires supports a good elk population. Security for the elk is good in these landforms—translates to difficult hunting. Thermal breezes carry the scent of intruders to the elk, and we make a lot of noise stumbling through downed timber. Escape routes are uncon-strained. I've come to prefer early hunts in these landforms, trying to get trophy bulls to come to calls.

A well-watered cool pocket surrounded by heavy timber cover. Elk have a short commute under cover for everything they need in this summer range. Always approach as if the big bull is in there, and chances are, someday— you'd better be ready to get lucky.

On early season hunts (usually archery) during the rut, you can count on bulls being around the herd of cows, and on there being no disturbance due to wolves or lots of hunters in the area; a good approach for these situations is to move up those ridges from the bottom, staying along the crest of the ridge. Those open areas are feeding locations and elk will be there at breaking light and then begin moving toward the cover and shade of the timbered pockets, which will hold springs and streams. Bugle every thirty minutes or so. If you get an answer, your locating is done and you can move on to stalking. Get sneaky and move in. If elk are disturbed due to wolves or human hunting activity, they may be reluctant to answer a bugle. Then it's best to work as a bugler/shooter team, with the bugler working along the bottom of one of the long drainages and the shooter moving along the top of the ridge. Bowhunting drives are slow and quiet so that elk drift along. The shooter may need to move fast and stealthily to keep position on the elk so that thermals won't drift human scent toward the elk. If the elk move away from the bugler upslope to go over the top, the shooter will be covering the passes into the adjacent drainage. If a bull answers the bugle, the shooter moves down toward the elk. If elk seem to be slightly disturbed, both caller and shooter may use cow calls. If the elk leave the area at the slightest sign of hunters, you'll have to hunt as if the general season's on.

The musings
smithereens by a
Acre come alive. I
mule. He was loo
tion from earlier ii
going silent, it hac
stood there like s
still. Must have be

Then a bull ⟨
below us. And frc
Without consciou⟨
as the .338 slid of
caller located exa
brush and low lir
working the low li

My internal
approaching bull.
instinctively cut m
a low sneak. Full r

The rifle was ⟨
of the elk sudden
alert and the body
tree obscured the
time was standing
of the upper rear l⟨
remained frozen ir

I worked the
bull running direc
than I'd like . . . ,"
few breaths to ge⟨
30 yards or 300—⟨
Bill, well ahead of
the slope. "You di⟨

Then to Bill, "
just made it befor⟨
more than 'a thou
down right here a
did. Then we took

Bill, ever the
"Gonna be a skull

During general season rifle hunts, two or three, or more, hunters may work as a team, with one moving up the bottom of the long drainage, one along the ridge (or ridges, if there are enough movers to cover adjacent ridges) and one or two located way up the mountain where the ridges come together. The hunter or hunters covering this last area will have to leave camp very early and go around to get on top without going through the area of the drive. If you don't have many people in your party and there are a lot of other hunters in the area, get out early, get on top, and let everybody else be the drivers for you! Also note that in the general season after the rut, the bulls will pull away from the herds of cows and retreat to higher elevations. They'll be found in spots of thick cover with escape routes around the little open areas you can see far up in the vicinity of the rock outcrops on the very tops of the mountains where the air is nice and thin.

During the rut, bull elk with small herds of cows will be in scattered pockets among the creases where secondary ridges drop away from the big ridges, and even more bull elk—usually, but not always, the younger, immature ones—will be hanging around without cows. The elk hunter's chances, during early rifle seasons that may overlap with the end of the rut, are greatly improved if the bulls can be enticed to answer a bugle. Cuts way down on the location effort.

The following Tale, of hunting an old bull along the big divide between Idaho and Montana, illustrates how speed (from instinctive action) coupled with making the right move at the right time (intuition and situational awareness) make for success in encounters with old bulls savvy to most elk hunter moves.

HUNTING HIGH DIVIDES:
THE OLD GNARLY HELL'S HALF ACRE BULL

It had turned out to be one of those opening mornings that start out full of excitement, but by noon, per B. B. King, some of "the thrill is gone." The bulls that answered our bugels were strategically located about a third of the way up on far slopes. They would answer bugles, then wait for the intruder to come across. That intruder, when it's an overwrought opening-day elk hunter, upon crossing the bottom of the drainage, gets winded by the elk on the fickle late-morning upslope thermal currents, and, after putting out all of that wasted energy and wasted opening morning time, ends up being left to wonder why all of the bugling elk have gone silent. Bill, my guide, had suggested that we pass on a couple of sucker offers to come across and play early on—and, looking across the big, steep drainages to our south, I heartily concurred—but as noon

came and went w
like it might have l
deal at all. Elk hur

By noon, we
along the long ric
the Montana borc
Church River of N
some bugling acti
look of the place t
twentieth century
of the Bitterroot c
area. Smoke hang
tionally dry summ
been like.

About one o
results would hav
been successful ir
gave out with a n
check out on the
morning working.
ing bull brought tl
forth again. Anoth

I had noticed
trees as we had
around as Bill bu
and there around
my excitement, I
ourselves into his
play into a hunter
direction of the w

Picking up on
And kept getting
note into an angr
said that." The bul

I realized tha
phony. The bull w
slope of the drair
directions, always
moving in. "Dam
bull's probably pla

"Really hadn't thought about it much yet." But I was beginning to think hard and fast as Bill started the field dressing and I looked the rack over and began to appreciate just how unique it was. Completely symmetrical, it was in the 300 or more class past the number three tine on either side, then faltered, and finished well under a 250 class from that point on out. Near the skull, the brow tines were twisted in odd ways and the beam had knots and bumps and stringers. The number threes swept out and up, approximating the girth and length of the number fours. It was an old bull. A very old bull.

Finally, as we came to the point that I had to decide, I said, "It's a weird thing and has a great tale to go with it. Think I'll leave my options open for a full mount—a sneak mount just like I first saw it." Maybe I was still getting over being excited.

"You got it." Bill was still the calm, experienced guide as he began a long cut between the front legs starting up the bottom of the neck.

"You sure 'bout that cut, Bill?" I respectfully inquired of the calm, experienced guide. He stopped and looked at me as I watched the wheels turn behind the squinty old guide eyes. What passed for a sheepish grin showed through the full gray beard of an old calm, experienced guide. He stopped what he was doing and just sat down to help me as I went back to working on getting over being excited for a little while as we both enjoyed the moment.

"Must have mistook this thing for a bear."

"No sweat. The undertakers for animals can fix just about anything except stretch spreads—or adding more or bigger tines." After a bit he moved around to more easily reach the thick hide along the back behind the shoulders where the cut really needs to start for an elk mount.

"How far back you think, Tom?"

"Doesn't need to be as far back as that bullet hole." We both grinned.

"It was good enough on this openin' day."

"It was the only shot I've seen so far on this openin' day—and not for very long at that."

"Yeah, just as it crossed my mind that that elk might try and pull a sneak on us, the whole world went 'Kaboom!' around me."

"Guess it was sort of loud in those thick trees. I didn't notice at the time." Time stands still. Colors go black and white. Sounds go unnoticed at the time, but they're recalled later.

The sun was sinking into the smoke of the fires to the west as we finished our field dressing duties. Riding back to camp, we cast long shadows in the red glow of the sky. The Halloween effect was impressed upon me.

A couple of days later, when I opened the camper for the taxidermist to take a look: "Whoa! That's a gnarly one."

Pulling the old bull up out of Hell's Half Acre through smoke from the fires.

Well-Watered Habitat in the Central and Southern Rockies

Precipitation predominantly crosses over western North America from northwest to southeast, with higher elevations catching the moisture along the way. The higher elevations of the Central Rockies catch enough moisture to support heavy timber growth. The elevations of upper and lower timberlines get progressively lower as you move north.

This is gentler habitat than that of the Northern Rockies. The aspen of intermediate elevations grades into scrub oak and brush in the basins. The rivers that carry snow runoff are typically of modest size. Winters are on average less severe the farther south you go, and the effects of predators are minimal. Elk herds are large where moisture is sufficient to grow forage.

HUNTING WELL-WATERED HABITAT IN THE CENTRAL AND SOUTHERN ROCKIES: A TALE OF BOWHUNTING IN THE LATE RUT

The first glimmer of light found the three of us scrambling up the slick bank of the gravel mountain road. We were a mismatched set of bowhunters. Robert, the youngest, was taking a few days off from school to make the last week of the Colorado archery season. Dan was the master bowhunter: With almost twenty years' experience bowhunting, he was expert at calling and

Cedar cover in breaks of the Upper Colorado River, northwest Colorado.

Aspens firing up along the Dolores River in southwest Colorado.

These open aspen stand pastures are used by both game and cattle.

A sweet spot where elk range comes up to the barn and into the hayrack when the snow is heavy. Private land along the roads blocks access to the public land in back, creating an area of low disturbance that can be accessed through the places where the public land comes out to the road, or by coming in from the back.

shooting, and in peak physical condition. I rounded out the threesome. The senior citizen of the group, I was also least experienced, and a retread rifle hunter to boot. But these fast movers had welcomed me to their hunt with a lot more patience than I deserved. That's the way of real elk hunters. They'll recognize any legitimate member of the fraternity, even a member of a distant chapter with a musty set of credentials. So we made up a hunting party, even if one of the party was scrambling a little harder to keep up than the other two.

This hunt was actually a continuation of the action of the previous evening. Robert and I had worked our way up along the bottom of the small stream, starting where it crossed the road about a quarter of a mile up the slope from our jump-off point. A bull started making a few interested bugles late in the afternoon in response to cow calls. Robert began working it with a combination of cow calls and bugles, and before long the bull was getting worked into a frenzy. We were set up with me acting as shooter in front of Robert. The bull moved toward us several times but would then back off as he reached bow-shot range in the fairly thick growth near the bottom of the little stream. As dark fell, he backed out around the crest of the ridge that dropped off toward the west to form the north side of the draw. As we described the action back in camp, Dan concluded that it was probably too late in the rut for bugling. Challenges were probably over for the big bulls that were now running with herds of cows already bred. Late-blooming or recycling cows in heat were the only action that would command their attention. If a bull—or, for that matter, all of the bulls in the area—perceived a rare opportunity to breed at this time when the vast majority of the cows were no longer available, no force on earth would deter them in their still-aroused condition. So here we were the next morning, early if not bright, in company with Dan to check the theory out.

We continued to climb up and around the nose of the ridge that dropped off toward the west. Dan would sing out with a convincing simulation of the call of a lonesome cow as we stopped to listen and replenish our oxygen in the thin mountain air. All of the bulls in the area remained silent as the sky grew light in the east. Finally, as we topped out onto a more level part of the top of the ridge, just above where our action of the previous evening had taken place, an interested bull sang out a reply to Dan's cow call.

The bull was due east of our position at about our own elevation along the crest of the ridge when he made his first reply to the cow call. We moved as fast and as quietly as possible toward the east, using the scattered stands of aspen interspersed among the open meadows along the ridge as cover. More aggressive and more frequent bugles rang out up ahead as the bull moved from the top of the ridge back down into the upper basin of the little creek. Three small streams arose from seeps and springs in the boggy upper reaches of the draw and converged to form a single stream, as is very typical in the high country of southwestern Colorado. These cool, wet, brushy hideouts are often the favorite home areas where big bull elk will hold their collected cows. We continued to move as fast as possible down the steep slope of the side of the draw, which was covered with low, noisy brush and treacherously slick wet grass. We moved as silently as possible, but Robert was wearing rain paints, and yours truly was wearing rip-stop camo rather than my usual wool due to the prevailing warm weather. It wasn't quite silent enough for the brushed-cotton-camo–clad Dan, from the hard looks over his shoulder and the few not exactly under-the-breath comments he made as we slid and swished along. I made a note that I'd better get my own brushed-cotton camo, which makes absolutely no sound against brush, on my next trip.

We moved fast into the little upper basin, and managed to do it undetected from all indications. The bull that was the object of our attention was still sounding off in response to our calls, but he was moving off. By the time we reached the bottom of the basin, he had moved up the far slope to the upper part of the south ridge. Now a second bull sang out a couple hundred yards down the south slope of the steep little draw. The bull that had drawn us in seemed to have moved into the second bull's comfort zone and was drawing a warning. We were trying to move in on the first bull but lost his location; he had gone silent as he moved around the top of the basin. So we turned our stalk toward the new bull downstream. A bugle sounded off behind us, from the very upper reaches of the basin. Then from farther downstream. It went through my mind that those two bulls were really moving around fast.

Then it seemed that any number of bugles went off from different locations at the same time. Robert and I looked at each other. Yup, there were at least five of 'em, maybe six. Probably two or three that we heard at the upper ridge at the back of the basin as we approached along the crest of the north slope had been drawn in by all of the excitement, along with another over the south rim to add to the ones that we were after. All probably less than a couple hundred yards out. For an instant my oxygen-depleted brain fantasized that I must have really done myself in coming down the treacherous slope we'd just descended and followed some of my ancestors to the happy hunting ground.

I snapped back to my place on the space-time diagram of this universe as we nocked arrows on our bows and set up facing a couple of the hottest-sounding bulls moving in on our position from down the draw. Robert and I took positions about 30 yards apart, facing a small tributary stream that crossed the route of approach of the two enraged bulls. Dan was centered between us, about 20 yards back. The bulls approached, unseen but definitely heard, through the thick brush and timber of the opposite slope, came to the far edge of the open ground along the stream—and then, still sounding off with enraged bugles every minute or two, dashed back up the slope. Then they came back down the slope, coming tantalizingly close to our position but not within bow range or close enough to be seen. Then back up the slope. Then around the slope. Then back toward us, but turning just out of bow range. They weren't moving together. On the contrary, they seemed to avoid close proximity to each other, and sang out with an agitated challenge to each other whenever their paths came together. The bugling was constant now, every fifteen to twenty seconds. Finally, both bulls moved back from the stream, one heading back up the slope, the other around the slope downstream. Dan started to throw some bugles in with the cow calls to see if he could work up enough excitement in one or the other of the bulls to lower his caution for a moment. No luck.

We unnocked our arrows and crossed the small stream so that we would have a chance at a shot if the bulls again approached to the same points that they had just occupied in their crazy routes. The two bulls closed in on each other, all the while bugling in a frenzy to Dan's calls, but still wouldn't move in close enough for a shot. The more powerful sounding bull would approach, then retreat to a point along the top of the ridge. He finally stopped and stayed high. The lesser bull, from the sound of his bugling, was then joined by another, then a third bull that moved around the top of the basin, above our position but below the larger bull.

We started around the slope single file along an elk trail, Dan in front, Robert in back, me in the middle, in an attempt to get into position on one of the new arrivals. Suddenly a smaller five-point bull lost all caution and came sneaking in fast but absolutely silently through the brush behind us. Robert caught sight of it over his shoulder and was having a fit trying to alert Dan and me without sound or noticeable motion, while our attention was fixed on the bulls making all of the racket ahead of us. I finally noticed and moved back to join Robert as the bull ducked back into the brush. Dan, unaware, moved off as Robert and I took position and tried to get a shot at the five-point that had been shadowing us. We finally decided that it had moved off as well, and, removing our arrows from the strings once again, moved on up the trail to rejoin Dan, who had slowed down, wondering what had happened to us.

We thought we heard another bull approaching silently, and set up, nocking our arrows once again. We waited. No action. It looked as though the big bulls with cows were making a lot of noise but were disinclined to approach either a serious threat or a lesser challenger, or even an interesting cow. Dan was doing a convincing job of sounding like all three, but the bulls moved away as the exchanges became heated. Finally, the bulls all backed off and went silent as the morning wore on and the temperature climbed. Our arrows went off of the strings and back into the quivers. Down the stream we went, toward the road.

Water is key in drier parts of elk country like Lone Cone, Colorado.

VOLCANIC PEAKS AND MESAS OF DRY SOUTHERN HABITAT

The arid southern and southwestern regions around the painted deserts visible in the satellite photo on page 21 are characterized by broad sedimentary deposits that have undergone uplifting and are often pierced by volcanic intrusions. The climate is arid due to the mountain ranges that remove moisture from air coming from the Pacific. So many of the sweet spots in these regions are based on availability of water. High elevations that intercept moisture are generally areas with good elk populations, and springs and streams become sites of concentration.

In these regions, elevation translates to marked climate change: More snow catches and holds on mountains at higher elevations. Green timber with active streams on top of a volcanic mountain provides meadows for feed, water for drinking and cooling, and cover. This favorite elk habitat grades to deciduous trees (aspen) and brush and finally to oak scrublands at lower elevations. The key to the spots where elk hold at lower elevations and on the sides of mesas is moisture.

Our next example is a Tale of tactics pure and simple. Two of the four hunters involved, Craig and Tom W., had never hunted elk before; another, Wes, had made two or three trips but had never taken an elk. The final participant was yours truly, Old Tom. The moral of this little aside is that preplanned tactics allow the novice elk hunter to engage in the hunt as fully as the experienced hunter on a personal hunt as well as a professionally arranged outfitter hunt.

The sketch on the next page, which covers an area of about 2 miles in either direction with 200-foot contour lines, illustrates how this saga unfolded.

HUNTING ARID SOUTHERN HABITAT: DRIVING A MESA

Our four hunters rolled out of the vehicle and into the early morning darkness, knowing generally what to expect even though they hadn't seen the place other than on a quick drive-by the day before. According to my assumptions from map scouting, elk trails would be found around the steep sides of the mesa. Elk forced to move would follow the elk trails in a more or less predictable pattern. Otherwise, the hunting pressure associated with Colorado's general season would keep them bedded down under cover during daylight hours. Grass covered the areas indicated to be without timber cover on the topo map, and they would be easy going unless the slope was steep. The steep places without timber cover were rock slides and rock fields, and they were treacherous to cross.

But it turned out that the drives I conjured up in the comfort of the easy chair back home were a little on the ambitious side in the rarefied air above 11,000 feet elevation, even for the fit and ambitious. Change of plan. Rather than drive around the entire mesa, we would circle half of it, staying above the rock fields. The standers would take a position along the small drainage to the west that headed into a similar drainage to the east, forming a pass that elk would be likely to use to move off toward the east. Another likely route of escape would be around the slope of the western drainage and into the heavy cover of the south half of the mesa.

Craig and I left the road in the same general area (A) and took off around the slope. Craig made an immediate swing downslope through the scattered timber below the broken open areas along the road to kick out any elk holding along the lower north slope out in front of my route around the contours of the north side of the mesa. Craig then made a swing to the south (at B) over the almost flat top of the mesa (C) to move any elk holding in the upper timber cover either toward me or toward the standers in the drainage below. He would also cut off any elk moving over the top from my direction to the west, around (D), or moved by Tom W. and Wes east and southeast as they moved west down the drainage after leaving the vehicle (at E). An unexpected development that the experienced elk hunter comes to expect when hunting under crowded conditions came along in the form of additional help for Craig. A couple of pilgrims in the wilderness on ATVs came from the direction of the road onto the top of the mesa—ensuring that all elk were moved from that vicinity. It's always good practice to be in or on the other side of cover when the motorized elk hunters using whitetail techniques show up late. They'll usually inspire hidden elk to move.

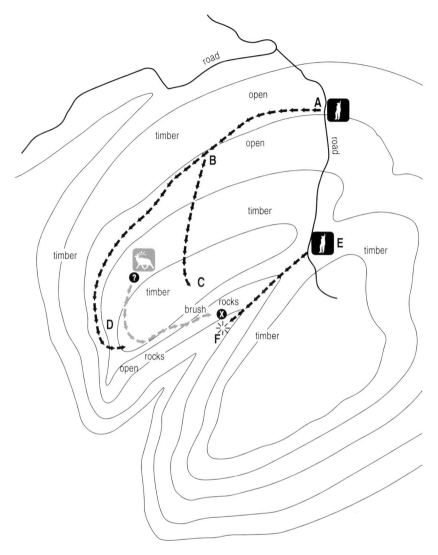

Driving a mesa.

The primary standers in the scheme were Wes and Tom W. They left the vehicle along the road in the pass formed by the drainages, then moved down the western drainage to a point where they could see any elk moving around the slope, headed either through the pass or across the upper section of the western drainage to the timber-covered south slope. They moved along at a much slower, and more stealthy, pace than the drivers. The entire party had come to realize over the first couple of days of the hunt that Tom W., on his first elk hunting trip, was a natural "moving stander" with a talent for moving without noise and blending into cover so that he could always see elk before they could pattern him. Wes, normally a tireless fast mover, moved along in the rear. This would be Tom W.'s show. He would take or pass on the first shot. If he passed, Wes would be ready.

Exactly according to plan, the two standers brought their rifles to battery at the clatter of fast-moving hooves on rocks coming in their direction around the slope (F). Cows followed by a bull. Big bull? Little bull? Tom W.'s rifle came down. He'd wait for a big one. Wes took his cue from Tom out of the corner of one eye. The other eye was on the bull. He'd made a few "dry-run hunts" and was ready to take some elk venison home. The bull turned his head to look back as he moved. Wes counted four tines big enough for Colorado, and that was big enough for him. Instinctive reactions took control as Wes went into the mindset of making the kill. Tom W. went into the mindset of getting the heck out of the way. Things were moving fast for him. For Wes, time stood still as he cleared the shot. The elk kept moving around the slope for a short distance, then turned downslope, faltered, and fell at X.

"The perfect hunt," Tom W. declared, speaking for all, since some of us were gasping for breath in the thin air as we each packed our load of elk parts toward the vehicle. The plan had worked. The entire party was part of the hunt. The pass on the shot for one. The shot for the other. "Exactly," went through the mind of the older hunter in the back of the line. "Maybe more than a perfect hunt."

The intermediate zone between oak scrub and green timber. Note how the aspen along the small stream form a fringe of cover across the open slope—this is the most likely route for elk to use between feed, water, and resting cover.

Dry scrub oak in thick stands covers the floors of basins.

Fires tear through the scrub basins quickly—but these areas recover quickly too.

Some aspects of where elk are found remain completely counterintuitive. In southwestern Colorado, volcanic cones rise above surrounding scrub brush basins to an elevation high enough to catch and hold moisture, supporting that heavy green timber interspersed with browse or grass-covered meadows and small streams on top. So I'm always drawn to the tops of these features, well above the sorry-looking scrub oak below. But the brush holds lots of elk as well. Relatively mild winters and early springs are the norm here, and predation is not a driving factor. Elk populations may expand for many years without the punctuations of severe winters that are catastrophic to the elk population in northern regions. That high population has to spread out somewhere, and feed and water are sufficient to support elk in the lowlands. So while I slip and slide through the rock fields around the tops of the mesas looking for elk in the company of lots of other hunters, more savvy types familiar with the area take stands and wait for elk pushed down by other hunters to come by through the brush below. "Just like big whitetail."

CHAPTER 3

Elk Hunting State by State

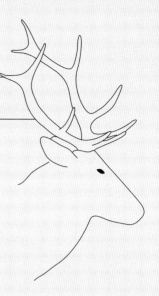

In order to hunt elk in the natural settings described in the previous chapter—without going to jail—we have to comply with certain rules and regulations of the various states we hunt in. In this chapter, I'll give you an overview of the nature of elk hunting in different regions. All of the interacting characteristics of topography, climate, land ownership, and human population tend to give elk hunting a different flavor across different areas. If you'll put up with a load of oversimplification, I'll try to give a general idea of the nature of elk hunting and hunting arrangements in each of the states and provinces. I combine the elk hunting states of the western United States and Canadian Provinces into five regional groupings, each with general regional characteristics. The groupings are loosely based on location, with associated prevalent landforms and climate, but also consider game management and policy. And so the beautiful natural patterns of the satellite photo in the preceding chapter give way to the arbitrary political boundaries created by the hands of humans.

The areas of the best elk hunting are indicated on the map, but I'll include for each state location references to cities, national forests, and major landform features that should be useful for orientation and ordering maps during planning and in interpretation of state hunting regulations that will refer to game management districts.

The information that follows, like everything else pertaining to elk hunting (except the mountains), is subject to change. It was all good, to the best of my knowledge, at one time or another, but it's a big area to keep up with. You should develop your own up-to-date information—tailored to your own areas of interest—through various techniques of "scouting from afar" (see Chapter 5 for more on this). You can find lots of information on the national forests, major landforms, tribal reservations, towns, and cities mentioned in the pages that follow by searching online for their names followed by the words "elk hunting." You can find more fine-grid search terms with the help of a road atlas that notes all landforms, from major features down to local spots (my favorite is put out by Michelin). Every outfitter, lodge, guide, and wannabe has a site. (Keep that wannabe in mind and keep your BS radar on.) You'll also turn up the old "'round the stove" crowd with their circle of pals with tips, opinions, and the normal BS about your favorite topics. The fundamental concept to grasp is that the best forum for hunting and fishing information exchange is no longer the outfitter woodstove or the pot-belly stove in the old country store glowing red hot with nostalgia. It's the cold glare of the screen of a computer hooked up to the 'net.

The states and provinces covered here all contain elk in numbers sufficient to allow at least some hunting by out-of-state hunters along with state residents. That seems to translate to an elk population greater than around 10,000. There are other states that have ongoing programs to transplant elk from populations in the West; these herds number from a few dozen up to thousands. Kentucky is a notable example, with a well-established herd that is reported to exceed 10,000. Hunting is available on a draw basis in several of these states, usually with long odds.

The states with the most mountains without many people in them also have the most elk: Colorado, Wyoming, Idaho, and Montana head the list. Over the last few years, I've come to add a couple of qualifiers to conditions for an extensive elk population: It's where the winter range is sufficient and the predators like the bears, cougars, and wolves haven't thinned them out extensively. The point is that the density of the elk isn't a static situation, and it depends on a lot of variables.

The elk population spills out with less density into the areas around the mountain retreats, sometimes literally in the form of winter migrations. Generally, elk exist as local permanent populations with lower densities as they mingle with ranching and farming land. These surrounding areas are within the blue line. The natural environment shapes some of the outline; for instance, elk are not permanent residents of hot, dry areas. Not shown are all of the holes within the outlined areas due to local environmental and human-related factors, such as population centers and land ownership and use.

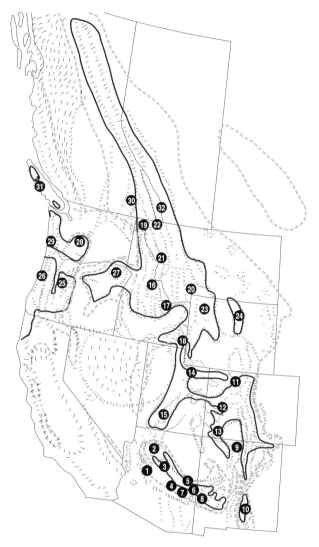

A rough sketch of the areas where elk are found in the western United States and Canada, superimposed over the major terrain features (stippled marks) and political boundaries (solid black lines). The solid red line encloses areas of highest concentrations of elk population; the dashed blue line catches the areas of lower density of elk. But remember how complex the satellite photo of terrain features is compared with this map. The reality of the actual elk population is also complex, and changes with the seasons. If we zeroed in on part of the red area for a high-resolution look at where the elk are actually located, we'd find them in smaller patches, with the shapes and sizes of the patches controlled by the season and the particular conditions and terrain features found in that area.

THE INTANGIBLES—SOME CONSIDERATIONS FOR YOUR HUNT PLANNING OTHER THAN HUNTING

There's a lot more to elk hunting than taking an elk. When considering the different areas where you might arrange an elk hunt, don't lose sight of the fact that, along with your elk hunting, that's also where you're going to spend your vacation time. The area where you hunt has a lot to do with the intangibles of the hunt, the memories of the hunt that you can count on bringing back with a lot more certainty than the trophy mount. I've concluded that I return time and again to the Bitterroots as much for clear mountains above rivers with morning mist rising, for the forests broken by meadows and steep little creeks just below the pinnacles and down through the cool places underneath, as for the elk. I'm also drawn to the high country far to the south, where a change in a few hundred feet of elevation can create a complete change of landscape. I want to hunt in a place where I have a good chance of getting shots at elk—but it's also important to me to be somewhere where I can just stand and look in wonder at where the aspen meet the pines, and the pines meet the sky.

Now we consider the political aspect of our geopolitical map to get at the burning questions of the elk hunter: "Where can I go hunt elk?" and "What do I need to do in order to legally hunt?" The authority to control hunting and fishing on both private and public land rests with the individual states. They tend to favor their own residents: Licenses and tags are available to them in greater numbers and cost less for them than for nonresidents. The number of permits issued in different areas usually corresponds to the density of the elk there, but also involves lots of other factors, some of which don't make much sense to those of us not involved in the process. Usually, but not always, the areas within the red lines are areas of general hunts with permits being issued to both resident and nonresident hunters. These areas holding the most elk are also usually public land (with lower human occupancy and therefore less disturbance to elk), and access is easier than in areas where private holdings predominate. Hunting in areas of lower elk densities (blue outline) will be more restricted, with licenses and tags often being issued by some form of drawing. Special hunts may be conducted in either type area for purposes of game management. Residents are usually favored in the number of licenses and tags issued in all areas for all kinds of hunts.

The exception to the preference given to residents over nonresidents is booked hunts on private land and/or with outfitters. Private landholders and outfitter concession areas get individual assessment and consideration on allocations of tags and permits (which translates to favored treatment in the opinion of many residents, resulting in laws passed to restrict such arrangements in some states). Well-financed private individuals and organizations acquire ownership of large tracts of prime elk habitat to set aside for private hunting or preservation or both. The juxtaposition of these various interests, not to mention the intricacies of natural factors of habitat maintenance and the impacts of weather variations and management policy regarding predator preservation or control, can get extremely complex, especially when federal statutes and regulations protecting endangered species (like wolves or other predators of elk, or plants that provide winter forage for elk) are involved. And thus the real world intrudes on our desire for the thrill of the hunt and the solitude of the wilderness. Sorry 'bout that.

In addition to the allocation of permits, the answer to our question of "Where can I go elk hunting?" needs to consider land ownership and control. A large part of the land area in the elk hunting states is held by the federal government and administered by various agencies. Much of this land, primarily the national forests and designated wilderness areas, is accessible to the public, so that with the proper state license and tag and whatever other permit the state requires, you're in. Some of the Forest Service land will have a road network for logging; other areas, wilderness areas and rough land not suitable for logging, will have only trails. Other federal land, notably the national parks, isn't open for hunting. Tribal lands usually have hunting, very good hunting in some cases, available at a price (a very high price in those same cases). Likewise, entry to private land for hunting comes at a price. Some private land has hunting with outstanding trophy elk available. The relative density of the elk population may be low so that the elk hunter has to enter a drawing to obtain a permit, but control of access by the landowner keeps hunting pressure practically nonexistent, which allows the elk to reach full maturity and grow the big racks. The terrain is often not too rough in the privately held areas, which makes for relatively easy hunting.

THE ART OF THE DRAW

In addition to the licenses and tags for the general hunt, the game management agency of each state and province of elk country annually issues permits to state or province residents and nonresidents for taking a limited number of elk in designated game management areas on the basis of a draw or lottery arrangement. The intent is often to manage the elk population to better match the carrying capacity of a particular area. Cow permits may be offered in an otherwise all-bull-tag area. The meat hunters take notice. Sometimes, in areas that carry few elk, the intent is to offer the opportunity to hunt mature trophy bulls. And the hell-bent trophy hunters go crazy!

The details of the rules and regulations, including the distribution of the opportunities between residents and nonresidents, are included in the annually issued Big Game Hunting Regulations for each state. The rules of the draw (even more so than the general regulations) are subject to multiple influences other than game management practices, and therefore are not the most straightforward and easy to understand passage that you'll ever read. Phone up the state game management agency and you'll eventually get somebody to translate it all into plain English for you. The applicant may sometimes, not always, be required to send payment for the permit with the application, to be returned if the application is unsuccessful. Some states have complicated alternatives that allow accumulation of points to improve chances in the draw in future years for areas of particular interest.

Art comes into play for the true nonresident enthusiasts, who may have applications, accumulated points, theories of optimum chances of success, wistful thinking, and other mental games going on in several different states all the time—and at the same time. To top it all off, many, maybe most, of these individuals are residents of states with elk hunting available. It naturally follows in these cases that they're concurrently working draws for several draw areas in their own state, which may favor residents. To this particular point, as the blood pressure of you nonresidents rises in indignation at the very idea of the injustice of such favoritism, note that the residents of some states want to throw the whole bunch out down at the state capital for allowing nonresidents to come in and take all of the permits away from the long suffering locals. But nonresident hunters bring in a lot of money to the state compared to the "sleep on the ground, don't need a guide or outfitter" locals.

THE SOUTHERN REGION

High mountain forests surrounded by very dry brushland at lower elevations characterize this area. Water distribution is often limited. Elk hunting is tightly controlled by game management and land control and ownership.

Arizona

The best elk hunting in Arizona is the forested high country of the Mogollon Rim, which runs generally east and west from around the cities of Flagstaff and Prescott to the New Mexico border. It includes the

Vegetation patterns are a function of elevation and landform in the southern and central regions.

Prescott (1), Kaibab (2), Coconino (3), Tonto (4), Sitgreaves (5), and Apache National Forests (6) and the White Mountain Apache and San Carlos Indian Reservations (7). It's adjoined on the east by New Mexico's Gila National Forest.

Hunting in Arizona is generally characterized by tightly controlled management on both public and private land. Public land hunting is moderately priced, although it is limited. Arizona controls nonresident hunting on public land by limiting licenses and tags to a drawing. Applications must be received by a specific date each year, usually around the middle of June. Nonresident general hunting license fees are around $150 and elk hunt permit-tag fees are around $600. Drawing success percentages for the general hunt range from 1 to 8 percent for a bull permit and 15 to 55 percent for an antlerless permit. Archery draw success is better, with the chance for a bull permit between 5 and 34 percent. After successfully drawing a permit, the chance of success on the general hunt is around 50 percent, with archery success ranging from 20 to 50 percent.

Elk management information is shared between tribal and state Game and Fish Departments. Forage management is coordinated with private interests. Elk numbers continually increase in the benign climate, and management consideration has to be concerned with such issues as damage to key riparian areas.

Tips and References: Begin with the Game and Fish Department to find out the deal and the best place to start to draw elk permits. The tribal lands of Arizona are well known for trophy bulls available on expensive hunts. (Word on the elk trail as of this writing has it that the old guy holding the premier six-figure tag for the last several years hasn't taken a shot as he looks for "the big one," but I haven't checked that tale out any further than the individuals I've talked to at shows. It's probably true. Same for the five hunters holding the economical mid-range five-figure tags.) Arizona is a good bet for elk hunters to research and work the involved draws for the once-in-a-while trophy opportunity as elk populations push limits in particular areas.

Contact
Arizona Game and Fish Department
2221 W. Greenway Road, DORR, Phoenix, AZ 85023
(602) 942-3000
www.azgfd.gov

New Mexico
The best elk hunting is found in three separated areas of the state. The first, along the border with Arizona, lies generally north of Silver City, from the Black Range west to the Mogollon Mountains, and includes the Gila and adjacent Cibola National Forests (8). A second area extends from the vicinity of Santa Fe north within the Sangre de Cristo and San Juan Mountain Ranges to the border with Colorado. It includes the Carson and Santa Fe National Forests and the Jicarilla Apache Indian Reservation (9). The third area, in the south-central part of the state near the city of Ruidoso, extends from the Jicarilla Range in the north through the Sierra Blanca to the Sacramento Mountains in the south and includes the Lincoln National Forest and the Mescalero Apache Indian Reservation (10).

There is some hunting on public land available, but hunting in New Mexico, particularly for nonresidents, seems to be mostly found on privately owned ranches and tribal reservations. They provide guided, high-dollar, tightly controlled, limited numbers of hunts with very high success rates on outstanding trophies. New Mexico has proportionally less public land than most of the rest of the elk hunting states and the hunting on the privately owned and reservation land with restricted access tends to come at a high price. These land holdings are extensive enough to afford fair chase hunting and a quality experience. These hunts are usually not physically demanding. The climate and management practices in the state provide conditions for excellent body growth and antler development of elk. The long growing season with less chance of very severe and extended winters than farther north combine to produce more consistent high-quality hunting than in areas farther north.

New Mexico allocates elk hunting licenses according to a draw quota system with residents receiving 78 percent of the available licenses, nonresidents using outfitters receiving 12 percent, and nonresidents not using outfitters receiving 10 percent. Elk licenses obtained through private land authorizations are not subject to the quota. Hunting on tribal lands (which cover a large part of New Mexico) does not require a license, but arrangements must be made with tribal authorities; contacts are available through the New Mexico Game and Fish Department. National forests, Bureau of Land Management lands, and designated state lands are open to the public for hunting. Hunters must be aware of any restrictions as to access. Nonresidents who plan to hunt using the services of an outfitter are cautioned against fraudulent operators.

The *New Mexico Big Game and Furbearer Rules and Information* give detailed instructions on making arrangements with landowners and obtaining licenses to hunt on private land. Access to private or tribal land is expensive. Elk license fees for nonresidents range from around $300 for anterless elk to around $770 for a quality mature bull.

Tips and References: Start by contacting the Department of Game and Fish for general information. From the information above, you can see that the good deals for elk hunting in New Mexico are special arrangements. So, if you haven't been working on your hunting deal all year because business was too good, use that extra money on a last-minute landowner deal. Information on outfitters and tribal lands can be found online, and the high-dollar arrangements are usually represented at the big regional outdoor shows. I'm also acquainted with experienced nonresident elk hunters who regularly hunt their favorite spots in areas open to hunting during the general season, and they out-maneuver both the residents and the elk to regularly take good bulls on public land.

Contact
New Mexico Department of Game and Fish
Villagra Building, P.O. Box 25112, Santa Fe, NM 87503
(505) 827-7885, (800) 862-9310
http://www.gmfsh.state.nm.us

THE CENTRAL REGION

This region is characterized by mountain ranges with green timber at the high elevations, with stands of aspen on the lower slopes. Lower elevations may be covered by more open stands of timber that change to brush or farmland in the valleys. Water distribution is limited in the southern part of the region but becomes more general in the north. There are large population centers within this region. Short general hunting seasons for the different types of equipment are managed to accommodate the considerable numbers of state residents as well as nonresident hunters who want to participate. High-quality elk hunting is available in areas of lower elk population with permits allocated by drawing.

Colorado

Colorado has the largest area of good elk hunting and the most elk of all of the elk hunting states. The area of high elk population extends from a north-south line just west of the line of cities along the Front Range (including Fort Collins, Denver, Colorado Springs, and Pueblo) westward to the border with Utah. It includes the Roosevelt, Routt, and Arapaho National Forests in the northwest (11); the White River, Grande Mesa, Gunnison, and Uncompahgre National Forests in the central west portion of the state (12); and the Rio Grande and San Juan National Forests in the southwest (13). Land in any given area may be owned and managed by the federal or state government or by private individuals. In some areas, the elk hunter may encounter all three, criss-crossed with complicated boundary lines that may be poorly marked. Be sure to get a good map (see Chapter 5 for more about maps for hunting).

Colorado elk hunting consists of a series of seasons for each of the three types of equipment. Hunters must choose one type of equipment, one season, and one area (hunting unit). The archery season begins around the end of August and runs through the end of September. Many hunting units allow unlimited permits for this season, while others are on a draw basis. The muzzleloader season overlaps with archery around the middle two weeks in September, and is currently all draw. There are four separate centerfire rifle seasons all about a week long and separated by a couple of days, beginning in mid-October and extending through mid-November. The first of these seasons is an elk-only season; the last three are combined elk and deer. Colorado limits the licenses to nonresidents to no more than 40 percent of the total licenses, unless there are licenses left after the draw. The nonresident license fee is $570 for bull elk and $350 for cow elk. As of this writing, selected Colorado game management areas are among the few places left where you can decide to go elk hunting in September or October, buy a license on your way to the mountains, and go hunting. You'll need an ID and proof that you've completed a hunter education course in any state that Colorado has reciprocity with. You're better off if you get a copy of the Colorado hunting regulations, available online, so you'll know the exact dates of the seasons for the game management area of interest, the deadlines for licenses, and so on. This situation may change with time since the demand for elk hunting is always increasing, and the public land is starting to get crowed in some places during the general hunts. The heavy hunting pressure on public land in some areas seems to result in a low percentage of quality trophies, although state Fish and Game data indicates a good success rate overall.

Ask some elk hunters about their Colorado trip and you'll get a quick answer that ends the discussion: lots of elk, lots of people. I can say from firsthand experience that this can often be the case. You can plan ahead to improve your situation, or you can learn to hunt with the crowd.

One solution is straightforward but a little expensive for some. A lot of the private land in Colorado is available for hunting. You make arrangements with an outfitter who owns the hunting rights to book a hunt on the land (the going price may range from $1,500 up to the $10,000-plus range). The price of the ticket for entry tends to keep hunting pressure low and the quality of the elk hunting high. The outfitter in this case is not necessarily the classic pack camp outfitter of the wilderness areas of the Northern Rockies. Hunting may be out of a lodge and may use some form of gas burner for transport. Other outfitters on both private and public land use hay burners (that would be horses and mules, for the readers not in on the joke).

For hunters who want to hunt public land without the crowds, several approaches are possible. A lot of hunters now use four-wheelers or riding and pack stock transported by trailer from home to get back into less crowded hunting areas. The management of public land often controls the use of motorized transport, and the road network, or lack of it, often dictates the type of motorized vehicle practical for any given area. Some areas are restricted to horse or foot transportation. Investing in horses and the skills for handling them or improving your physical conditioning will buy some separation from the crowd in these areas.

You can find yourself sharing the mountains of Colorado with the nonhunting public during early seasons despite your investment in physical conditioning. A hunting buddy and I once unthinkingly scheduled a backpacking bowhunt over a holiday weekend. Big mistake. Unknown to us, our chosen hunting area included some scenic attractions popular with folks with different interests from those of the typical elk hunter. We were sneaking through a good looking area looking for elk, full camo, painted faces, the whole deal, and encountered a group—about a hundred or so—of highly conditioned nature-loving hikers. They seemed very curious about our equipment and interested in our motivation for doing what we were obviously doing out there. We had a long visit with the whole bunch of them; we figured our chances of seeing an elk around there were pretty low after that bunch had come through. After that, we moved on to a more remote area, where we saw a lot of elk and encountered only fellow elk hunters.

Several of my friends have mentioned to me that booking with an outfitter, with the associated expense, doesn't necessarily mean that you won't run into a lot of hunters if the outfitter operates on public land, which is open to all. You need to ask the right questions before booking to understand just what you are getting for your money. I've been told of rather expensive deals to pack in by horseback that left the hunters, after a long horseback ride, camped along a logging road with four-wheelers roaring through early the next morning. Some special circumstances exist where private land blocks access to public land, which tends to make for less competition (and some resentment on the part of the public-land hunters). Some of these areas are hunted out of lodges located on private land.

A few of my affluent acquaintances have hunted free ranging elk on private land after successfully drawing permits for areas removed from the mountainous terrain normally associated with elk hunting in Colorado. They report that it's a good show if you can afford the price of the ticket. Another approach to quality elk hunting in Colorado is to be patient enough to draw one of the very limited permits to hunt public land in areas of low elk populations. This is reported to result in a very reasonably priced ticket for a very high-class hunt, but the line at this ticket window is slow. I understand from those participating that it's run by a lady whose name is Helen, Ms. Helen Wait. Yes, you're told to go to Helen Wait, and eventually you'll get your permit through a process of point accumulation. There's even a selection in the draw that gives you a preference point as your first choice rather than an outright shot at an elk hunt. The theory is that you get closer to Ms. Wait's window with this approach. Contact the Colorado Department of Natural Resources to get the full details on the process. Don't ask for Ms. Wait by name. They'll trace it back to me.

Tips and References: The Colorado Department of Natural Resources and the Colorado Outfitters Association are good places to start when thinking of entering a draw for special permit areas. As of this writing, you can still jump in the old truck and head out to Colorado and stop by the store (about any store) and buy a license and tag on the way up the hill. But, be advised that, unless you're hunting in the archery season, in a special permit area, or through a private property arrangement, you'll probably have some company out there with you. You can avoid the crowds by booking with an outfitter who operates in more remote locations in the high country in the north (check by map that it's really remote) or by hunting with private ranches (also referred to as outfitters) in the south. Closely check any arrangements in Colorado that promise a quality wilderness experience.

Contact
Colorado Department of Natural Resources
6060 Broadway, Denver, CO 80216
(303) 297-1192
http://wildlife.state.co.us/hunting

Colorado Outfitters Association
P.O. Box 1949, Rifle, CO 81650
(970) 876-0543
http://www.coloradooutfitters.org

Utah

The area of high elk population in Utah extends from the mountainous northeast corner of the state east of the cities of Ogden and Provo southwest almost to Cedar City in the southern part of the state. In the northeast, it includes the Uinta Mountains, the Wasatch Range, and the East and West Tavaputs Plateaus, including the Ashley and Uinta National Forests and the Uintah and Ouray Indian Reservations (14). Its extension to the southwest runs along the Wasatch Plateau and the Sevier, Aquarius, and Paunsaugunt Ranges and includes the Fishlake and Dixie National Forests (15).

Elk hunting permits are for one type of equipment—archery, muzzleloader, or centerfire rifle. The elk hunter is then restricted to that choice for that year's elk hunting. The type of elk that may be taken is determined by a combination of rules for the hunting unit and the type of equipment used. Some units are designated spike bull or antlerless elk only. Archery and muzzleloader hunters are allowed to take one elk of the hunter's choice in most units. The hunter using a centerfire rifle may purchase either a bull or a spike permit. Some units are designated as limited-entry hunts using a specified type of equipment, usually either archery tackle or muzzleloader rifle.

Nonresident elk hunting license and permit cost depends on the unit and the gender and maturity (i.e., spike or full antlered bull) of the elk desired. Some draw and special hunts may be applied for online. Statewide success rates are 14 percent for archery, 18 percent for muzzleloader, and 18 percent for centerfire rifle.

Tips and References: The pricing of licenses and permits has so many variables that the nonresident needs to specify exactly what and where he or she intends to hunt. The most interesting hunts require limited entry tags and a long-odds draw for nonresidents. Booking with an outfitter appears to simplify the process considerably. Outfitter prices I've seen quoted appear reasonable, and your chances of success are better with a guide if you don't know the territory.

Contact

Utah Division of Wildlife Resources
1596 West North Temple, P.O. Box 146301
Salt Lake City, UT 84114-6301
http://wildlife.utah.gov/dwt
(801) 538-4745

Nevada

Elk hunting units run north to south in the high country along the east side of the state; there is also one unit in the south to the west of Las Vegas. The prospective nonresident elk hunter needs both cash and luck for starters. A nonresident hunting license will cost about $150 and the tag runs about $1,200. Luck comes into play in the long-odds draw just for the opportunity. Private landowner tags are around $8,000 and are very limited.

Contact

Nevada Department of Wildlife
1100 Valley Road, Reno, NV 89512
(800) 576-1020
http://ndow.org/hunt

THE NORTHERN ROCKIES REGION

In general, this area has more elk and fewer people (both hunters and populations in the states) than the areas to the south. The sizes of the elk populations throughout this area permit sale of tags with fewer restrictions in terms of time and place than is the general case with the states to the south. Elk populations here are subject to pressure from especially hard winters, when prolonged deep snow can cover feed even in lower-elevation wintering areas, resulting in greater winterkill. Heavy snow also concentrates elk and makes them more vulnerable to predators, primarily wolves. The Bitterroot Region is the area most affected by pressure from predators and that pressure has increased significantly with the explosion of the wolf population over the last few years. Tags in heavily impacted outfitter areas along the wolfpack circuits have been reduced to a small fraction of what they were before the introduction of wolves. Areas with the best forage often provide the least security in terms of cover and escape routes with brush and obstacles to impede pursuing wolves. Many thousands of elk appear to have starved in recent years rather than return to areas of winter range that are thick with wolves. The recent issuing of a few wolf tags has helped bring some relief to the elk herds of the Northern Rockies.

High rainfall on the windward side of mountain ranges produces spectacular landforms in the northern and Pacific coast regions.

Low rainfall in the rain shadow of the high ranges results in low erosion, gentle terrain, and higher elevations between ranges.

The timbered high country along the backbone of the Rockies, with its sparse road network, is the domain of the outfitter pack camp. The opportunity to hunt for trophy elk in a wilderness setting makes this region a prime destination of large numbers of nonresident elk hunters season after season. There are usually road networks at lower elevations and a lot of elk hunting is done from camps along the road. Old logging roads may allow the use of four-wheelers to get into the woods in some places, but usually lots of downed logs or steep slopes require the use of horses or the physical conditioning to hunt and pack out game on foot.

These high ranges catch moisture-laden air coming in from the Pacific that mostly runs off, and erodes, the western slopes. About 20 miles to the east of the Montana-Idaho divide, the elevation of the gently flowing little streambeds has dropped less than 300 feet; 20 miles to the west of the divide, the streambeds of the rushing rivers have dropped 3,000 feet.

Idaho

A large portion of the state of Idaho contains high elk populations. The primary region is in the mountainous center of the state, north and east of Boise. This area extends northward along the east side of the northern panhandle of the state east of the cities of Lewiston and Coeur d'Alene. Included within this extensive area are the Salmon River Mountains, which cover the center of the state, and the massive Bitterroot Range. These areas contain the Sawtooth, Boise, Payette, Nez Perce, Bitterroot, Clearwater, and Coeur d'Alene National Forests (16). Smaller ranges include the Lost River and Lemhi Ranges between the Salmon River and the Bitterroots northwest of Idaho Falls. These ranges contain the Salmon, Challis, and part of the Targhee National Forests (17). Extensions of the Wasatch Range from Utah and the Caribou Mountains south and east of Idaho Falls contain the Caribou and parts of the Targhee National Forests along the border with Wyoming (18). North of Coeur d'Alene, the Cabinet Mountains extend into Idaho from Montana, and contain the Kaniksu National Forest (19). Idaho lies to the west of the high ranges of the Northern Rockies, which means that it catches a lot of rain and snow compared to other states in the region. The same high precipitation over the past millions of years has eroded the uplifted landforms of the Northern Rockies into seemingly unending arrays of complex, rough landforms. The vegetation cover is equally varied and the colors of fall provide an unmatched show, particular in the early part of the elk season, as the leaves change color. In the high country away from the roads, the hunter can expect hard hunting with spectacular views away from the crowds. This is pack camp outfitter country that offers a high quality wilderness experience along with excellent elk hunting.

Idaho tags and licenses for nonresidents may be obtained from out-fitters or purchased directly from the state on a first come, first served basis beginning in mid-December for the next fall's hunt. Either arrangement allows the hunter to make plans well ahead of time. Over the last few years, state game management has begun exercising additional control over the sale of tags in specific game management areas in order to keep down the number of elk taken by hunters in response to the pressures of hard winters and predators on elk populations. Tags are now restricted to the hunter's choice of one of twenty-nine game management zones, and one of two types of tags that allow the hunter to participate in different hunting seasons. Tags designated as "A" type include more hunting options for archery and muzzleloader; "B" tags include more options for the centerfire rifle. You can switch the type and zone of your tag, with some restrictions, until a designated time in late summer. Some zones with elk populations lower than can be carried by winter range have limited numbers of the "B" tags. Nonresident hunting licenses cost about $160 and the elk hunter will also need an elk tag, at around $420. The "B" tags usually sell out early in the year. Outfitters have a separate quota of tags, which means you can probably get one without problem if you book with an outfitter. Note that this doesn't necessarily mean that you can wait until the last minute to decide to commit to go elk hunting, since the outfitter might book all of the hunts available for any given year around the first of the year when tags go on sale. (Some of the best may stay booked a year or two in advance.) Also, in some cases, the number of tags allocated to outfitters is based on how many that outfitter has used during past years and other factors not necessarily associated with the number of elk in the outfitter's area. Idaho Fish and Game reports success rates of general and controlled hunts to be steady over the last several years at 18 to 20 percent, with about a quarter of the bulls taken being six points or better. That roughly squares with my own experience.

Contact
Idaho Department of Fish and Game
P.O. Box 25, Boise, ID 83707
(208) 334-3717
For brochures for seasons and rules call (800) 635-7820 or download from website; for licenses and tags call (800) 554-8685.
http://fishandgame.idaho.gov

Idaho Outfitters and Guides Association
P.O. Box 95, Boise, ID 83701
(208) 342-1438, (208) 342-1919
http://ioga.org

Idaho Outfitters and Guides Licensing Board (OGLB)
1365 N. Orchard, Room 172, Boise, ID 83705
(208) 327-7380
http://oglb.idaho.gov

Montana

The areas of greatest elk concentration in Montana are primarily in the high timbered mountains in the western and southwestern parts of the state. The southwestern area is to the south and west of the cities of Bozeman and Butte along the border with Wyoming and Idaho (20). The western area of Montana begins at this corner of the state and extends to the north along the Idaho border west of Missoula to the Canadian border (21). It includes the major landforms of the Absaroka, and Gallatin and Madison Ranges around Yellowstone and the south-west region of the state and the massive Bitterroot Range along the length of the border with Idaho north to the Cabinet, Purcell, and Salish Mountains and the Whitefish, Flathead, and Swan Ranges of the Rocky Mountains, which extend into Canada (22). The national forests located in these extensive mountainous regions include the Gallatin and Beaverhead in the southwest around Yellowstone; the Deerlodge, Bitter-root, Lolo, and Kootenai along the Idaho border; and the Flathead and Lewis and Clark, adjacent to the Flathead and Blackfoot Indian Reser-vations and Glacier National Park in the Northern Rockies.

Most of the high country of Montana lies just across the divide from Idaho, and the comments concerning the nature and quality of elk hunt-ing in Idaho apply equally to Montana. Some of the string of outfitters that operate out of the Bitterroot River valley have areas on the Mon-tana side, others operate on the Idaho side, and some have areas on both sides of the line. The precipitation is a little lower and the slopes are usually not so steep on the Montana side.

Pack camp arrangements predominate in the high country of west-ern Montana, while hunts from roads predominate at lower elevations. Outfitter late-season hunts are pushed to lower elevations and the road network as deep snow covers the higher elevations. Hunts often range far from the outfitter's base. The onset of deep snow also pushes elk downslope as it covers feed and makes escape from wolves more diffi-cult. They may be found on lower mountain slopes as the season progresses and will move out into agricultural areas as the hunting season closes. Recent years have seen elk moving into populated areas of the valleys of western Montana during winter due to pressure from wolves.

Nonresidents fees are $812 and tags are available through a draw. The arrangements for reserved tags for outfitters were recently abolished by voters.

High quality elk hunting is also available in the areas of lower elk density in central and eastern parts of the state. Accommodations for these hunts often involve hunting out of comfortable lodges on private land, riding on a vehicle or on horseback out to the hunting spots. A few permits are available by draw in some areas that offer a chance at high-scoring trophies.

Tips and References: Check with the state agencies and outfitters to keep current on arrangements. I recommend a book devoted to hunting elk in Montana: *Elk Hunting Montana: Finding Success on the Best Public Lands,* Jack Ballard, Lyons Press, 2007.

Contact
Montana Department of Fish, Wildlife and Parks
P.O. Box 200701, Helena, MT 59620
(406) 444-2950
http://fwp.mt.gov

Montana Outfitters and Guides Association
P.O. Box 1248, Helena, MT 59624
(406) 449-3578

Wyoming

The areas of high elk populations in Wyoming are the high forests in the mountainous west of the state, west of Cody and surrounding Jackson Hole and Yellowstone Park, then extending south toward Fort Bridger; a separate area to the east lies just west of Sheridan. The major landforms of the western part of the state include the Absaroka, Wind River, Wyoming, Salt River, Gros Ventre, and Teton Ranges, which contain the Bridger, Teton, Shoshone, and Targhee National Forests (23). The separate area to the east consists of the Bighorn Mountains, which contain the Bighorn National Forest (24). The areas of high elk density (indicated by the solid red line on the map on page 49) correspond to areas where licenses are offered by state authorities for the general hunt. Licenses are only issued for limited quota hunts in the areas with fewer elk (blue dashed line). The state requires that hunters in wilderness areas in the high country in the vicinity of Yellowstone hunt with licensed outfitters.

Wyoming issues elk licenses by drawings for both the general and limited quota hunts. Application dates are January 1 to 31. Three types of elk licenses are sold: special, priced around $1,100; full price, around $600; and reduced price, around $300. The full price allows the hunter to be drawn either for the general hunt or for a limited quota hunt in a selected area; the type of elk that can be taken with this license (i.e., antlered, antlerless, or any elk) depends on the regulations for the particular area selected. The special license allows the hunter to be drawn for the same hunts as the full price license, but in a separate drawing with a better chance of being drawn. The reduced price license allows the hunter to take a cow or calf. A hunter may apply for and receive both a full price and a reduced price license. While not many of the limited quota hunt licenses are sold, for the lucky hunters who draw this type of license, the success rate is high, from 30 to 70 percent, depending on the area. Success on general hunts runs around 20 to over 40 percent, again depending on the area.

Contact
Wyoming Department of Game and Fish
Attention: Information Section
5400 Bishop Boulevard, Cheyenne, WY 82002
(307) 777-4601
http://wgfd.wyo.gov

Wyoming Department of Commerce
Wyoming State Board of Outfitters and Professional Guides
1750 Westland Road, Cheyenne, WY 82002
(307) 777-5323, (800) 264-0981
http://outfitters.state.wy.us

THE PACIFIC COAST REGION

Three subspecies of elk occur in this region: Roosevelt elk in the thick tangles of the Pacific ranges; Tule elk in scattered areas of coastal California; and Rocky Mountain elk throughout the interior mountain ranges of the region adjacent to ranges of the high Rockies to the east. The northern states of this region are characterized by heavily forested mountains in the west that receive very heavy rainfall due to moisture-laden air carried by prevailing winds from the Pacific Ocean. These mountain ranges are not as high or as extensive as the Rockies, but hold a lot of elk (Roosevelt elk, to the surprise of many out-of-state hunters). The interior mountains extend into the Rockies to the east and south and hold Rocky Mountain elk. The small (as elk go) Tule elk are found in isolated areas north to south in western California. It has been demonstrated that these three ecologically adapted elk, once considered separate species, are actually all members of the same species, and will revert to the standard form over generations if transplanted to different habitat.

California

California has hunting available on a lottery basis for Roosevelt, Rocky Mountain, and Tule elk. Roosevelt elk occur in the northwest corner of the state in the Marble Mountain Wilderness; Rocky Mountain elk may be hunted in the northeast corner of the state, adjacent to Oregon and Nevada; and Tule elk occur in the coastal ranges. The exact areas of hunts are per the draw. The lottery, which requires purchase of a nonrefundable license costing $150 to enter, involves both preference points and random draw. For elk hunters successful in the draw, a permit is $1,200. Hunting on private property using landowner tags allows the hunter to avoid the lottery (at a price). Elk herds are managed to provide hunting opportunities for trophy elk of each subspecies.

Contact
California Department of Fish and Game
1416 9th Street, 12th Floor, Sacramento, CA 95814
http://www.dfg.ca.gov/wildlife/hunting

Oregon

Oregon contains extensive areas of high elk populations in the mountainous forests of the Cascade Range, which runs north to south across the western side of the state east of Portland, Salem, and Eugene and south to Medford. This area contains the Mount Hood, Willamette, Deschutes, Rogue River, and Fremont National Forests (25). The Coast Range contains a good population of Roosevelt elk and includes two fairly small national forests, the Siuslaw in the north and the Siskiyou in the south (26). A large mountainous area dominated by the Blue, Wallowa, and Ochoco Mountains covers the northeast quarter of the state; it includes the Whitman, Umatilla, Malheur, and Ochoco National Forests and holds a good elk population (27). Nonresident licenses cost around $150 and elk tags cost around $500. Roosevelt elk tags are available over the counter until opening day of the centerfire season. Rocky Mountain elk in the eastern part of the state may be bowhunted with a general tag, but rifle hunts in the east are controlled, for the most part, by draw for licenses and tags. Some areas generally have allocations equal to number of applications received; other areas can accommodate only a quarter of the applications received.

Contact
Oregon Department of Fish and Wildlife, Wildlife Division
3406 Cherry Avenue, Salem, OR 97303
(503) 947-6000 or (800) 720-6339
http://www.dfw.state.or.us

Washington

Washington's Roosevelt elk are found in tangles within the forested mountainous regions in the western part of the state. The largest area of elk population (28) is the Cascade Range, which runs north to south and is located east of the major population centers of Seattle and Everett; this range continues south into Oregon east of Portland. Another area lies to the west along the Pacific coast, south from the Olympic Peninsula along the Coast Range (29). The Cascade Range contains the Gifford Pinchot, Snoqualmie, and Wenatchee National Forests. The Olympic Peninsula is the location of the Olympic National Forest, which partially surrounds Olympic National Park.

Washington is the most even-handed of all the elk hunting states in apportioning elk tags out between the residents and nonresidents. The nonresident license and tag cost about $500, and are sold over the counter for Roosevelt elk in the west and for Rocky Mountain spikes; for antlered elk in the eastern part of the state there is a draw. Success rates tend to run between 5 and 8 percent for the general hunt. Special hunts with tags issued on a draw basis tend to run much higher, on the order of 50 percent in some instances. There is no limit to the number of licenses and tags you can purchase, but when you get them, you commit to hunting either the east or west side of the state.

Contact
Washington Department of Fish and Game
600 Capitol Way N, Olympia, WA 98501
http://www.wdfw.wa.gov

THE CANADIAN ROCKIES REGION

Most of the elk and elk hunting opportunities in Canada are to be found in British Columbia, which has populations of Roosevelt elk in the coastal west and Rocky Mountain elk around the backbone of the Rockies along the border with Alberta. A few elk have crossed into the Northwest Territories to the north. Free-ranging elk populations of another subspecies, Manitoba elk, occur in smaller numbers in the prairie providence of Manitoba but no permits are allowed for nonresidents. Saskatchewan has a growing elk population but hunting is limited to residents as of this writing.

British Columbia

The highest density of elk in British Columbia is found in the Rocky Mountains along the border with Alberta (30), extending to the northern extensions of the Rocky Mountains. Rocky Mountain elk also occur in lower densities in agricultural areas, where they help themselves to crops and to feed put out for livestock, particularly in winter. The province's populations of Roosevelt elk are primarily found on Vancouver Island, with small herds from transplants scattered along the mainland coast (31).

Hunting elk requires a license that costs around $200 and a permit that costs about $250; nonresidents are required to hire a guide. Some limited entry tags are reserved for outfitters, but they are a long-odds draw otherwise.

Contact
British Columbia Ministry of Forests
Lands and Natural Resource Operations
Fish and Wildlife Branch
P.O. Box 9391 Stn. Prov. Gov.
Victoria, BC V8W 9M8
http://www.env.gov.bc.ca/fw

Guide Outfitters Association of British Columbia
http://www.goabc.org

Alberta

Alberta elk occur in greatest density along the Rocky Mountain section of the border with British Columbia (32). They are expanding their range to the east and can be found at lower density far from the shadow of the Rockies in foothills, aspen parks, and prairies.

A nonresident license and tag costs a reasonable $255. Nonresidents are required to hire a guide, which kind of works out since your best shot of getting a tag is an outfitter tag, as opposed to the long-odds draw. See outfitter contact info below.

Contact
Alberta Fish and Wildlife
Alberta Sustainable Resource development
Main Floor, Great Life West Building
9920 108th St., Edmonton, AB T5K 2M4
(403) 427-2079
http://www.srd.alberta.ca/FishWildlife

Alberta Professional Outfitter Society
http://www.apos.ab.ca

CHAPTER 4

Hunting Strategy

The successful elk hunter assumes ownership of the elk hunt, with a strategy that includes tactics and techniques appropriate to his or her individual capabilities and preferences. Consider your choices of equipment, hunting arrangements, and objectives, along with an honest self-appraisal of your skills, conditioning, and knowledge. This practical evaluation serves as the basis to establish an appropriate and achievable hunting strategy to address the element of elk hunting that you don't have control over: the elk.

Your goals affect the way you go about your hunt. Consider the choice of hunting for a trophy bull. As we'll discuss when we look at locating elk, the trophy bull may not always be in company of the rest of the herd. So if you prefer to go after the trophy to the possible exclusion of a chance at a lesser bull or cow, now is the time to decide, before you start looking and making hunting arrangements. The consequences of your choice may be, of course, that you may not ever see the big bull. And if you commit to look for the big bull, you may not ever see anything else, either.

Likewise, the choice of equipment that you use has a direct impact on the timing of your open season and the techniques that you use to stalk elk. The archery season overlaps with the bugling bulls in rut, putting the trophy hunter at a possible advantage. This is one of the few times that the bulls set aside their own survival to ensure the future of the species. Going after a bugling bull with a bow will be difficult, but so is attempting to locate a silent "holed up" bull in the company of all the other rifle hunters later in the regular season. Here you have to make a choice and consider the trade-offs and your own abilities and goals.

In this chapter I'll be talking about different ways of hunting elk. You get to decide which kind of hunt you want yours to be. Decide on the basis of your realities before you're committed to something that you can't do, really don't want, or don't want to pay the price for. Early season hunts during the rut require a strategy of hunting with a bow and the bugle and cow calls far back in the wilderness away from other hunters. Another strategy—one that requires less skill but more money—is to arrange to hunt in an area of restricted entry (with bow and arrow or with the eaiser high-powered rifle) and use the services of an expert guide. Or, with adequate skill with the more effective high-powered rifle, and the physical conditioning to cover enough area to locate elk in more pressured areas, you can take elk, including trophy bulls, at the expense of less money and more time.

Different types of equipment to take the elk—high-powered modern repeater rifle, muzzleloader, or bow—require different types and levels of skills and conditioning for success. Your level of outdoor and hunting skills (as distinct from shooting skills) determine how you can approach wilderness hunting: alone, in the company of a hunting party, or with professional assistance as part of your hunting arrangements. The same goes for your level of physical and mental conditioning. Be assured that all of these requirements will be addressed in Parts II and III. They're under your control.

The elk are most assuredly not under your control. The way they behave changes according to the rut, level of disturbance, weather and season, and local characteristics of habitat, and this determines the skills and strategies used to hunt them. The following sections will provide insight into the techniques and tactics applicable under different conditions.

DISTURBANCE LEVEL OF THE ELK

Different tactics of locating and stalking will give better chances of success depending upon the extent to which elk have been disturbed. As a plains animal, elk are not panicked into immediate flight on perceiving a predator, like most woodland animals are. Their immediate response is instead an attempt to pattern the intentions of the predator. They will save their energy resources until it's absolutely essential to expend them in order to survive an immediate threat to life. But repeated close encounters do have an effect. The general disturbance level of elk in an area becomes progressively higher as these encounters accumulate. Sightings of humans, human voices, motor vehicles, the discharge of firearms, and, to some extent, the sounds of riding and pack stock all count as encounters. The effects of hunting pressure on elk behavior start at a low level each year at the beginning of the hunting season and rise as the season goes on. The higher the perceived threat level to the elk, the less time it takes for them to modify their behavior. The threat level stays low if hunting pressure is low, as in the case of truly remote wilderness or areas where hunter access remains low due to policies of land ownership/management. The elk hunter encounters and must accommodate the effects of disturbance on elk behavior during the stalk more than in other phases of the hunt.

NOTES ON LEVEL OF DISTURBANCE CENTERED STRATEGY

Elk hunters with insight into these effects arrange their hunts to take maximum advantage of the resources available to them. If those resources tend toward the economic, they pay the price to hunt areas with low hunter access. If those resources tend toward conditioning and the time and inclination to practice, they develop the skills needed to hunt the early seasons restricted to less capable equipment. Another, often overlooked, strategy is to attempt to arrange their hunts in particular areas and times to encounter elk from remote high elevations migrating through or to the area. An extreme example is the migration of elk from Yellowstone Park to lower elevations. However, for the optimum chance of success from this approach, timing is critical. It's difficult for most elk hunters to arrange a hunt to coincide with the exact time when heavy snow will force elk at a low level of disturbance down from remote high elevations into or through the selected hunting area.

THE RUT

The rut, that singular event that punctuates the annual cycle of the elk, is another factor that influences elk behavior, mostly affecting the stalk for hunters. In general, the rut provides the best chance for the elk hunter to get an opportunity to stalk an elk when survival as an individual is not the paramount driver of its behavior. This applies regardless of hunter objectives (trophy bull, any bull, any elk).

Here's an overview of the different stages of the rut and their approximate timing:

Pre-rut: From the second week of August through the first week of September

Early Rut: About the first two weeks of September

Late Rut: The last two weeks of September

Post-rut: From about the end of September until a couple of weeks into November, or until bulls and cows begin to gather into separate herds for the migration from their high summer ranges down to the lower winter ranges

Elk hunters, yours truly included, often refer to the effects of weather and other factors on the timing and intensity of the rut. According to scientists, that's only half right, but we are right about the only half that we can observe. Let me explain.

Bull elk are in the mood for breeding from around the middle of August on through the fall. Cows begin to come into heat, or estrus, beginning the first week or the second week of September, and they actually control the timing of the breeding. Most cows will have become receptive and many will have been bred by the third week of the month. In areas of high elk populations, competition for cows often seems to peak about this time, as the number of cows available for breeding decreases. Young cows breeding for the first time may be a little behind this schedule. Any cows not bred sometime during this first cycle will come into heat again three weeks later.

But what we can hear and see of the rut—bulls bugling and gathering their cows within an established territory—is primarily a function of the activity level of the bulls, and most hunters don't appreciate the one overriding factor that controls the activity levels of bull elk during this period: temperature. In late August and early September, bull elk are always suffering from the heat. They're creatures of the recent (in terms of climatic adaptation) ice ages. They only get comfortable at temperatures that humans find uncomfortably cold. As far as the hunters can observe, there is no rutting activity when it's warm, although the elk may be quietly taking care of any urgent and essential business during the cool of the night. So in the pre-rut weeks of August, and the breeding period during September, they storm around with bugled challenges and, on occasion, real fights only during times of cool precipitation and low overnight temperatures. But the insightful observer will note that after an unseasonably warm fall when elk activity levels seem low throughout the entire season of the rut, there'll still be a batch of calves dropped in the late spring right on time. Just like clockwork year after year.

The locals are usually at an advantage when hunting the rut due to greater flexibility in timing their hunts. But on average, by mid to late September, it's usually cooler and the cold fronts begin to make it through elk country, bringing in significant precipitation. This is also when the occasional cows not already bred come back into heat in an erratic pattern throughout the area, presenting breeding opportunities to the thoroughly randy bulls scattered about with herds of bred cows. The stage is set for a real commotion, referred to as "the peak of the rut" by the old-timers.

There's also an interaction between the intensity of rutting activity displayed by bull elk and the general level of disturbance created by hunting pressure. Relentless high hunting pressure increasingly elevates the level of disturbance as the hunting season progresses. Bugling will taper off slowly after the peak of the rut if the level of disturbance remains low. In areas of low hunting pressure, it will continue well into October after the general high-powered rifle season opens. High hunting pressure will stop daylight bugling immediately.

NOTES ON STRATEGIES OF HUNTING AREAS
OF LOWER HUNTING PRESSURE

Booking an outfitter hunt in a remote wilderness area, where casual hunters without the use of horses or mules cannot go, is an effective strategy for success, whether your measurement of success is in terms of venison, a trophy, or the wilderness experience.

Another approach is to apply for a draw hunt and play the sometimes long odds of pulling a quality hunt in an area of restricted hunting tags. Alternately, if you have the extra cash, you can book an expensive hunt in an area with controlled access, like tribal lands, for the big trophy bulls in herds managed for quality.

Finally, if you have or can develop superior physical capabilities to get into hard places where pressured elk hide out, you won't have too much competition. These places often have paved highway access part of the way there—all you have to do is take a rubber raft across the river, rock climb with your camp in a backpack, take the elk from an inaccessible pocket, and then carry it in several loads down the rock face.

Learning to Read Territorial Boundaries

About the time that the hormonal juices start to kick in for the bulls, and the other bulls they've been buds with since last year's headgear fell off start to get repulsive, even annoying, and it seems like a good idea to wander downslope to drop in on the cow herd and see how they're getting along, the local landforms start to take on a new character as far as the elk, particularly the bulls, are concerned.

The cows actually choose the bull's area for the fall rut, since the bull goes to join the cow herd and they've been on location since early summer, but the bull takes the initiative in deciding which features are boundaries and then defending them. I don't think any human has the formula for what constitutes a boundary to an elk, but some patterns emerge. Major terrain features that serve as a wall or barrier to keep intruders out of line of sight are likely boundaries; the same arrangement prevents an intruder from making any audible challenge directly at the bull claiming the territory. Bulls also like terrain features that would put the challenger at a disadvantage in a belligerent meeting, like a steep uphill scope that the challenger would meet when the boundary is crossed. Rims around basins and creeks with steep banks might be boundaries of this kind.

The size of the territory is determined by a subtle interaction between the number of potential herd bulls in the area and the natural boundaries made by the landforms. In rough country along rivers with lots of elk, the territories may be less than a half mile across and extend a couple of miles up from the creek to the ridge. The herd may consist of a bull and six or eight cows. In Colorado one year, after snow drove elk down while the general season was still open, resulting in an extensive bull kill, I ran into a herd of six cows with a five-point, and a half mile farther along the old logging road, an overgrown raghorn three-pointer with three cows. In a special permit area of open rolling country away from the mountains of Idaho, I've tried to get the drop on a six-point herd bull accompanied by a five-point sidekick, a raghorn, a couple of spikes, and about thirty cows. His territory must have been several miles in all directions.

Aside from territorial boundaries, a different sort of barrier may be encountered when trying to call a bull into shooting range. Very minor landscape and even vegetation features can drive bugling elk hunters to the point of distraction. A vaguely linear feature such as a stream, ditch, or faint logging road can sometimes stop the bull coming nicely to a call dead in its tracks. It's a good idea to place the shooter of a caller-shooter team on the far side of the tiny hop-over creek with the bull, with the well-concealed caller back away from the creek, so that the bull can walk back and forth along the creek and maybe pass close to the shooter. The stream sometimes actually turns the bull from coming around to wind the caller. Thermal air drift always causes problems, but the bull is usually inclined to come around above to have the advantage of elevation on what it takes to be the bugling bull in case of an encounter.

CHAPTER 5

Scouting: Location in the Most General Sense

Scouting could be considered the first step of the process of finding an elk in that it narrows down the area of the search. But it includes familiarization with the area to be hunted as much as general location of the elk to be hunted. It establishes not only whether or not elk can be found in a general area and in what numbers, but the requirements that need to be met in order for you to be in that area to find and legally take an elk. Scouting takes many forms.

Scouting begins with general planning of the hunt. Defining the area you're going to hunt is very important in cases where land open to hunting borders land where hunting isn't allowed, or where access is limited. A map of land ownership and control is essential to scouting in this situation. Scouting will also make the hunter aware of the areas of lower hunting pressure (in the controlled access area). General familiarity with what the landforms and vegetation cover look like help your map-based tactical planning. General location probabilities are determined by how many licenses and tags are allocated in any given Game Department administrative region or area.

Who does the scouting and when it's done depend on the hunting arrangements that you choose. If you book a guided hunt with an outfitter, the guide(s) should have a good idea of the location of elk in the area. Outfitters will scout the area with the objective of locating elk before the first hunters of the season arrive. They know where elk have been taken under different conditions of weather and hunting pressure in past seasons, and can use that knowledge as a starting point for your particular hunt. When an outfitter acquires a new area, its guides will ride over the entire place, studying with the eye of a professional the best spots to place camps and exercise various tactics during hunts.

Good outfitters will send or take new guides over the area and instruct them as required in preparation for the arrival of the client hunters.

The folks who live year-round in elk country have the advantage of being able to scout prior to the opening of the season at their convenience. Many locals hunt the same area year after year, generation after generation, and don't need to put out a lot of conscious effort to have a good idea of where elk can be found. It's usually in Grandpa's favorite hunting spot. Those of us whose ancestors chose to settle somewhere other than elk country need to develop our own approach. An extreme approach is to become transplanted locals, folks native to the flatlands who, for business or pleasure or a combination of both, now live in elk hunting states. These "new locals" soon learn that it's best to intermingle with the native locals and soak up scouting the easy way. But those of us who are now and evermore will be flatlanders can take heart! With a little research, we can wake up on the opening morning of elk season in the wrong time zone but with the confidence that comes from having a good idea of where to start looking for our elk. And in contrast to the locals, we're not limited to a particular region. Our scouting from afar may indicate that our chances may be better in another area, or even a different state. We have all of elk country at our disposal!

SCOUTING FROM AFAR

Strategic scouting is the *general location* of elk that can be hunted legally and practically on a regional and statewide scale. This scouting takes on different forms according to the scale of effort. The traditional version, the one you'll generally find referenced in outdoor books and articles, means driving out to the woods a few weeks before elk season opens and checking out where the elk are holding. It's not too practical for us nonresidents to take off early enough in the afternoon from our regular jobs to run out that couple thousand miles to the western wilderness of our choice, check out the elk, and get back to make bedtime story time with the little kids. And the older kids need to be picked up from soccer. Or you might have a lifestyle that requires lots of eighteen-hour days to get the wheat harvested during the time when you "need" to be out there scouting the elk.

For most of us in the real world, strategic scouting is done late in the evening on the kitchen table or at the computer on the Internet. And, done right, it's a fairly sophisticated undertaking, which comes as a surprise to a fair percentage of folks when I run it by them. It involves method, maybe some logic, innate bias, silly unfounded wishes, and the deeply embedded intangible influences of some old book or movie.

When you do this kind of scouting, you are definitely thinking about chances at an elk of some kind, but it also has to do with the nature of the experience.

Before we get into the more methodical techniques of scouting from afar, we should remind ourselves not to ignore the people connections. Most elk hunters who have been at it for a while have an extended network of elk hunting friends and acquaintances. This group thinks and talks about elk hunting entirely too much, but, as a result, they can usually come up with a contact, or know somebody who can come up with a contact, to check out the deal on elk hunting almost anywhere. Another approach is to ease into a new area by making a trip with a group that regularly hunts in an area of interest, if your people connections turn up the opportunity. A ready-made group of connections can be found in the state Fish and Game Department listings you'll need to get when you're think about planning a trip. Contact the regional offices and go from there. Talk to the game wardens if you can; get your maps out and ask specific questions. "How's the hunting over in the [landmark] area?" These folks are friends of the law-abiding, and closer to the game than anybody, with the possible exception of the sheep herders. State Fish and Game Departments also maintain websites that often have a news page or put out a regular publication laying out the current situation, covering conditions, diseases, extensive fires, and other issues that might impact your planning for a hunt.

Scouting from afar is key even if you aren't organizing the hunt on your own. If you decide to use the services of an outfitter, which means you don't *have* to do your own scouting, an understanding of the topography of the area allows you to independently follow the outfitter's script of the hunt. If you don't engage an outfitter to handle all details, it's up to you to do the scouting by any and all means available. Incidentally, scouting from your armchair, computer, or kitchen table is the only technique in this book guaranteed not to spook the elk.

Topography is the key concept of the analytical methods of scouting from afar. The USGS topographical maps show enough detail of landforms and vegetation to allow an elk hunter with a fundamental knowledge of tactics (discussed in Chapter 8) to sketch out plans for a day of elk hunting in an area without ever setting foot there. The observant and intelligent beginning hunter can, after a little practice, develop hunt plans almost as effective as if several seasons of experience were behind the planning. Just pay attention during the location phase of the hunt, and fit your observations of location and movement of elk in the area into the overall context of the time of the season and the weather

during the hunt. The hunter scouting from a map can expect some surprises upon actually seeing the area for the first time—some pleasant,
some not. It's a good idea to have, in addition to your Plan A, a Plan B
in case conditions on the ground don't fit your expectations.

Regardless of how you do your scouting, unless you can be sure
that all of your hunting will be within the boundaries of a national forest or designated wilderness, and well away from any national park or
privately held land, a key map to have is the Bureau of Land Management 1 to 100,000 scale map, which indicates land ownership and
management. A road network usually means a confusing mix of irregular boundaries. Federally or state owned public land open for hunting
may be interspersed with privately owned or leased land closed to public hunting. The private holdings may be strategically located to legally
block off easy access to the public land. You probably don't need to be
advised that any trespass disputes that may arise will be settled by local
authorities.

SCOUTING FOR TROPHIES

Trophy hunting may be the most tangible of the important intangibles
of your elk hunt. It falls somewhere near the top of the list of choices
that define your strategy and the general approach to your elk hunt.

The availability of elk with trophy antlers is controlled by several
factors, both natural and human related. To develop a trophy-sized set
of antlers, an elk has to have the genetics to develop large antlers, con-
sume enough food containing the right nutritional elements at the right
time of the year (which, incidentally, can vary from year to year), and,
perhaps most importantly, survive the several years required to reach
maturity sufficient to produce that massive trophy rack of the hunter's
dreams. All of these factors are related to the area that you hunt. In
wilderness hunting, the acid test of a good trophy hunting area is to
find a large rack on a winter-kill skull.

Trophy hunting is often done from outfitter pack camps. When a
guide is involved, the guide needs to be aware of the hunter's objective,
and the hunter needs to be consistent. Hunting for a trophy bull
involves subtle differences in technique from hunting for any legal bull,
and the hunter usually forgoes the best chances to take any bull if the
choice is to hunt for a trophy. During the early season, the herd bull is
in the herd with all the cows, and calling and stalking are complicated
by the presence of all the cows. Satellite bulls on the fringe of the herd
don't have all of those extra eyes keeping watch. Post-rut, lesser bulls
form herds together, while the depleted herd bulls go to hideouts and

stay there undercover while they recuperate; again, the trophy hunter will be passing up the herds of lesser bulls to pursue the trophy.

The would-be trophy hunter should also realize that luck plays a big part in the opportunity for a shot at a trophy, and another member of the party may take a trophy while the self-defined trophy hunter goes home with an unfilled tag. True insight into all of the implications of trophy hunting, like insight into many other aspects of what we perceive as the important things in life, comes only with experience and reflection upon experience.

Where to Find Trophy Bulls

Big trophy antlers require superior genetics, timely nutrition, and years of maturity sufficient for the bull to grow antlers to its full potential. You need to find an area that not only contains mature bull elk with the genetics to grow large antlers, but also provides the elk sufficient nourishment to grow them. The nourishment an area provides is a function of soil and climate in general, and in particular, a spring that comes early enough to remove snow in time for early-growing forbs to provide quality and quantity nutrition during the critical time for antler growth.

The place to start your quest for a trophy is with the various state Fish and Game Departments, which can usually furnish information on the best locations to hunt in order to get a shot at a trophy. This normally ends up being a location with some form of restricted access. The restricted access can result from land ownership, where the owner controls the number of hunters allowed and charges them for access, or game management control, with state agencies limiting the number of elk taken.

Alternately, the restriction on the number of hunters in a particular area can be due to the sheer difficulty of access to the area. This situation usually occurs in rugged mountainous areas, where the distance from roads requires that hunters pack into the area using pack stock or packboards to take in the camp and bring out the elk. Occasionally, the difficulty of access can be very localized, in the case of a small, difficult-to-reach pocket that becomes the refuge of old bull elk when they feel hunting pressure. The ticket into such an area is being able to recognize the characteristics of a bull hideout and having the skill and conditioning to get in on the bull unnoticed, then bring out the kill on your back. Don't kid yourself when you sign up for the packboard clause of the deal. That clause covers more than the equivalent of carrying 100 pounds of well-balanced load around the block of your flatland suburb. More like 100 pounds of poorly balanced elk quarter or boned venison over several miles of steep trail at around 10,000 feet elevation. Maybe with a foot of snow or lots of slick mud thrown in. It's hard to acquire the balance and footwork finesse to avoid a tumble on unsure footing with an unfamiliar heavy load.

As far as more specific location goes, in spring and early summer, old bulls will hold to high pastures with the best nutrition, at the risk of more exposure to predators. After they join the cow herds and stake out their claim to a harem, the oldest and most careful will often move with the herd, but off to one side, when escaping danger. After they're depleted and exhausted by the rigors of the rut, they'll hole up alone and hide out to avoid being the least capable, and therefore the most vulnerable, member of the herd.

SCOUTING ON THE GROUND

Many hunters, if they can manage it, scout on the ground in the area of the planned hunt. For state residents who live a short commute from the area of the planned hunt, it's a big advantage easily come by; nonresidents have to be creative to fit scouting into their routines, if it happens at all. Some of my hunting buddies usually manage to make a trip out to their prospective hunting locations a couple of months before the season. These scouting trip types usually have their own businesses, or travel on business, and can either take or make a few days in the vicinity of the hunting location. They usually try to stop by the regional Fish and Game office if at all possible. One of those facts that make perfect sense if you think about it for a minute is that if you plan to make a hunt without an outfitter, the area probably has some kind of a road network. With a suitable vehicle, some road scouting with the right set of maps can make you reasonably familiar with the parts of the area that will hold elk and help you figure out how you could go about hunting them.

In preseason scouting, you cover a lot of area with low expectations of encountering elk. If you can use a four-wheel-drive vehicle or an all-terrain vehicle, you can cover a lot of ground in a short time. You'll also get a good idea of the condition of the roads or trails through the area. Keep in mind that weather conditions will likely change with the approach of the hunting season, so evaluate what the roads will be like after rain or snow. You don't need to worry about stealth. These trips usually end up being well before the start of the hunting season. That translates to warm weather, and that translates to most of the elk in the area being found at high elevations or at least in the vicinity of shade and water. Unless the weather turns drastically colder, that's also where the elk will be located at the start of the early hunts. If you plan a late hunt, make sure that you check the most likely routes of elk movement down from the high country at the onset of heavy snow, as well as holding areas with cover and feed at lower elevations. The general techniques used to locate elk while scouting well before the hunting season are less thorough versions of the techniques for locating a specific elk to stalk while hunting. Any disturbance of the elk produced, short of permanently driving them from the area, is usually unimportant.

INTERACTION OF TOPOGRAPHY AND ELK BEHAVIOR

The key to a successful scouting trip visit is a thorough understanding of the topography of the area. Study the terrain by map and/or aerial photography before you arrive in the area. The photos will indicate areas covered with timber and heavy brush, which elk will use for rest and cover, open meadows and areas covered with low browse where elk will feed, and streams or other watering locations. The map contours and vegetation cover patterns will give you a general idea of elk movement between areas. Undisturbed elk will usually move around steep slopes rather than straight up and down for any distance in order to minimize expenditure of energy. They prefer to change elevations along the less steep slope, even if it means a considerably greater travel distance, and they prefer crossing long ridges at locations where erosion has produced local areas lower than the ridge on either side. Such locations, particularly if traversed by game trails, are termed "passes" by elk hunters, and "saddles" by everybody else. Passes are prime locations to check for sign when trying to locate elk (more on this in Chapter 6). In areas of less well defined terrain, elk will prefer moving along routes with better vegetation cover—for example, fingers of green timber stands through more open stands of aspen. Slopes and cover seem to combine in the central and southern regions to cause elk to prefer to move around the sides of mesas and cone-shaped volcanic mountains.

If your arrangements work out such that the first time that you ever see the place is at the beginning of your hunt, you can still get off to a good start. If at all possible, try to arrive at your selected hunting location at least a couple of days before the season opens. In addition to giving you time to set up camp and acclimate to the local elevation, arriving early will allow you to check and update your information from scouting. You may locate passes that fall within the contour interval of maps, or small details of vegetation cover that control elk movement might not be shown on maps.

Pay attention to the current situation as well. Weather and ground conditions can have an impact on your hunting plans, but often more important are the number and location of other parties. It's seldom that the most dreadful of developments that can be imagined—like a group of campers showing up where you planned to take a stand on opening morning—actually come to pass, but there might be others in the vicinity. If you're aware of the unanticipated company, you might want to exercise your Plan B, or modify your Plan A to take into account the extra pressure that might be applied by your unexpected hunting companions. It's been my experience that it's better to drop in on their camp for a visit rather than going about your plans as if the unexpected company didn't exist. A little conversation will usually give an indication of the personalities involved and what they intend to do in the way of hunting. Then you can decide whether to cooperate with them to some extent, to carry out your own plans and make them generally aware of what you intend to do for safety's sake, or just leave them the heck alone and give them as wide a berth as possible.

Once you arrive in the area, get an overview of the ground from an elevated vantage point. Note areas of feeding grounds, locations of water, resting areas, and how landforms might constrain travel between these areas. Familiarity with the information in Chapter 2 should help you recognize the elements of habitat in the region of your hunt. Check out vantage points where terrain contours force trails to converge— places where you'll be able to take a stand for a break or to sit for a while and glass for a shot using binoculars. Also remember that you'll need an access route to avoid detection as you take your position on that lookout before light on opening morning. Note any elk trails in the area and their general directional pattern. The direction that elk take when disturbed will become key to the success of tactics that your party may want to employ.

Finally, in case preseason scouting just doesn't work out as planned, as expected, or at all, I would still have a plan for the morning of the first day of the elk hunting season. You're welcome to my default plan with my elk hunter's blessing. Use a well-defined trail or old logging road to avoid confusion in the dark, and head for the high country before it gets light. Let daylight find you somewhere on the edge of the dark timber, looking out over some open areas. Wait there for an hour or so after shooting light. If there's no action in the vicinity by then, start moving and try to find an elk using the techniques of location presented in the next chapter. And don't stop on that opening day until dark. Other hunters will probably be out, and some of them could be acting as drivers for you and not know it.

CHAPTER 6

Location

The problem to be solved now can be phrased as a question: Where should the hunter begin the search for elk (or for sign of elk)? Incredibly, every season, there are literally thousands of would-be elk hunters who never ask this question, and therefore never receive an answer. They make the investment in time and money to go on an elk hunt, and then just go out and sit down someplace, and wait for a trophy elk to walk by! I know; I've talked to a lot of them. You walk by them, usually on your way back to camp. Any luck? Naw. Any sign around here? Blank look.

"Location" refers to finding a legal and desirable elk to stalk. In a sense, it picks up from the activity of scouting, taking us from the general idea of where elk are located to finding a particular elk that we want to stalk. Unlike stalking, location is done out there where the elk are. While it may seem like a preparatory step, location *is* elk hunting. Out there, moving fast along the slopes as you eliminate all of the places where the elk are not on your way to finding where they *are,* you're elk hunting. I've been using the term "location" in a general sense up to now. From this point forward, it refers to this process of locating a specific elk so that you can make a stalk and get into position to take a shot.

There will always be more places where elk might be found than there are elk to be in those places. The method of the location phase of the hunt is basically to cover the places where they aren't until you find one where they are. The elk may be in 5 to 10 percent of the areas where they could be, and some of those areas where they are moving around are large. A trophy may be in no more than 1 percent of the possible places, and the elk are not moving around for most of the time that it's legal to hunt them; and during the rut when they *are* moving around, they may have twenty sets of eyes looking out for them.

The location phase of the hunt requires a deliberate absence of focus. All your senses must be equally tuned to pull in information, to search for clues, or the absence of clues. If you find this sort of abstract concept of mindset hard to swallow, just go with it for now. If the techniques of location make sense, the mindset will eventually take care of itself.

A thorough understanding of location is essential for the elk hunter planning to hunt without the services of a professional guide or outfitter. It's also a cheap insurance policy in the unlikely event that your professional arrangements fall flat. Even if you do book with an outfitter and everything works out, knowing how to locate elk is still important. Yes, you'll have a guide available to assist you in finding elk; he or she will have a good idea of the general locations where elk can usually be found under different conditions, and may have done some preseason scouting. But you can't expect to have the specific location of elk as part of the outfitter package. Some locating is required at the opening of each new season, even in a familiar area. Elk are often found at different locations and elevations in different years depending on weather, timing of the rut, and other factors and interactions controlling their movement that may seem completely random to us. Even if early scouting or archery hunting had them located at one time, they may have moved in the meantime and will have to be located again.

FIRST-ORDER STEPS OF LOCATION

So we're back to that original question: Where should the hunter begin the search for sign of elk? Glad you asked: A good place to start would be where factors influencing elk location intersect. Find a cool place, which translates to a high elevation early in the season before the snow flies, with timber cover, feed, and water suitable for drinking and cooling, where rough terrain constricts easy movement and pushes elk trails together.

These places with feed, cover, water, and constricted terrain can always be found in areas with a significant elk population. Sometimes they are all found together; other times they will be in separate locations, in which case the places occupied by elk will vary based on the time of day (as well as the weather on that day and where the day falls in the hunting season). These places will be connected by well-worn trails, whose locations, in turn, are determined by terrain and cover.

Begin by checking the connecting routes for sign of elk. If sign indicate elk are present, their location can be deduced according to the time

A good place to look for elk sign—-water and cover at high elevation.

of day, level of disturbance, and whether there is rutting behavior or not. Undisturbed elk will feed early and late, and seek water and cover during the middle of the day. Cover will be in deep shade with a breeze in warm weather, or in timber out of the wind when it's very cold. Sources of disturbance will overlay this basic pattern of behavior. Onset of disturbance, hunters arriving at season opening as an example, will influence elk to move away from the strange activity. Preferred cover will be thick and have multiple avenues of escape into very difficult terrain. If the rut has concluded, bulls will separate from the herd and hole up in a restricted spot with feed and water close by and move only after dark. If the rut is under way, disturbance will curtail bugling.

ELK PATTERNS OF LIFE THROUGHOUT THE YEAR

Location is the phase of elk hunting that doesn't translate well from experience hunting other deer—that is, territorial New World deer, which is all of the New World deer except the migratory caribou/reindeer (their New World/Old World names). Individual white-tailed, mule, and black-tailed deer will usually be found holding to their home territories so that individuals are distributed throughout the range. Mule and black-tailed deer will tend to hold to preferred locations within their range: mule deer on open rocky slopes with an overview where they blend in with obstructions, and blacktails along edges of feed and cover in spots of cover with a view. Moose will be around or in the water. It's not so simple for elk. If undisturbed, all of the elk in an area will be in one herd in one place, and the place changes with the time of day and the season. If disturbed or threatened, that place will be in the most inaccessible location in the area—or, they may, all of them, simply leave the area altogether. And the areas just referred to can stretch for miles in all directions.

Imagine a checkerboard pattern drawn over a square-shaped hunting area under average conditions. Make it large squares, 1 mile to the side, so that you only have four squares to the side of the board—sixteen squares on the board, 16 square miles in the area. In the case of the whitetail, each square might contain five or more deer on average. If you got out and started hunting for them, you could probably carefully cover a square and eventually locate a couple of deer. You might sit down on a trail at the right time of day, and have a good chance of deer moving past you. Depending on the stage of the rut, you might find two does running together, a doe and a buck, or a single buck. If you spooked them, they would probably run around within their square and take cover. They'd still be in the square that afternoon or the next morning. They're territorial.

Elk will be different. A hunting area of the same size might have an elk or two per square. In the entire area, there might be a big bull, maybe two, or maybe a couple of five-point wannabes instead of the second big bull; two to five spikes or raghorns; and one to two dozen cows. Try to find them. How they are dispersed will be highly dependent upon when you look for them. During the rut, all of the cows will likely be in one herd with the bulls of different ranks close by: a single herd in a single part of the 16-square-mile area. In rough terrain divided by distinct drainages, two bulls might divide the entire area according to drainage patterns if it doesn't crowd their space. In wide-valley big country, a single herd bull might be attempting to hold three dozen or more cows together.

The level of the commotion of the rut usually depends on the (weather-driven) activity level, and may help with location. The herd bull will be attempting to keep all of the cows he's managed to collect together under his control in an around-the-clock vigil. The challengers—the other big bull if there is one, the five-point and raghorns if there isn't, and maybe a couple of spikes trying to get lucky while the herd bull is preoccupied—will be hanging around the fringes of the herd. There will be bugling, and a brief tussle might break out as the big bull moves the lightweights off. Occasionally, a serious fight may occur between the herd bull and an equally matched challenger.

BUGLING AS A LOCATION TECHNIQUE

It's appropriate to mention calling at this point in the context of location. During all stages of the rut, the time of most bow seasons, experienced bowhunters conduct a form of scouting designed to lead directly into the stalk. They cover as much area as possible by the most efficient means available and listen to bulls calling to other bulls; the hunters may bugle to get a response from elk in order to get a measure of the level of excitement of the bulls in a particular area. In order to cover as much territory as possible, they may move along the main trail during predawn or dusk, or, if they're hunting along major creeks or rivers with an adjacent road, they may drive very late at night or early in the morning before daylight and listen from the road. They gauge the relative intensity of the bugling activity in different areas to pick the most productive places to concentrate their efforts. Sometimes particular bulls may be selected for the next morning's hunt if they seem particularly "hot." A small, low-activity camp within hearing distance of elk not only is good entertainment, but also can serve to measure the general mood of the elk in the area. Location early in the rut may involve moving quickly to cover lots of area, stopping to bugle at landform features that might mark the edges of a bull's territory.

Bugling as a location technique, or even as a stalking technique, may not be productive if elk are at an elevated disturbance level due to the presence of human or natural predators. But intermittent, quiet cow calls might bring a response.

Normally, by the time the regular rifle season starts, things have settled down a lot from the frenzy of the rut. Elk will return to normal patterns of feeding early and late, moving to and from rest areas in between. The herd or herds of cows will usually still be together, maybe

Stopping to bugle on an early ride out along a high ridge that forms the edge between an old burn on one side and cool timber on the other. An answering bugle from below determines the plan for the morning hunt.

with a spike bull among them. The herd bull may still be in the vicinity, but you can't count on it. He might be in the general area of the herd with a couple of late bloomer cows that are still interested. The bachelor bulls are often found together in little herds of two or three. Now you have elk in three or four squares within our sixteen-square grid, and they're not making any sound to tip you off as to where to start looking. Feeding may bring them out into the open early and late, but they will otherwise be resting under cover during the day. The elk's movement and preferred locations are controlled by so many complex factors and interactions of factors that they can appear random to humans. Their inclination to change elevations in mountainous terrain in response to weather and seasonal changes often results in their complete absence from locations where they had been spotted by scouting a few days earlier. And if they're thoroughly spooked, they're gone, possibly from the entire sixteen-square area (or even from an area of thirty-two or sixty-four squares)!

A week or two into the regular rifle season, even with light hunting pressure, it becomes more difficult to see an elk, particularly a bull elk, as most of the elk movement turns nocturnal. If hunting pressure is heavy, the herd bull has gone to his hideout and he's not moving at all; the bachelors are also lying low. As the season wears on, changes in the weather and lighter hunting pressure cause movement to pick up. Late in the season, as snow cover deepens, you may find all of the cows collected from a very large area, often at a lower elevation than earlier in the season, or at the edge of a drop-off into a lower elevation. Small groups of bachelor bulls will be moving about, leaving tracks and yellow dribbles in the new snow. Surviving herd bulls may be with the bachelors, but are more often still back in the high country, where they will stay even with light pressure from human hunters or wolves until driven down by the deepening snow, or trapped.

So, given these circumstances as rules of the game, how do you go about locating an elk? Well, it depends. It depends on what kind of elk you are looking for, what time you are looking, what part of the hunting season it is relative to the rut, and what the weather conditions are.

VARIABLE FACTORS INFLUENCING ELK LOCATION

In addition to the more or less constant effects of terrain and elk behavior discussed above, some variable factors influence the location of elk at any given time: Chief among them are water and weather.

Elk always need a lot of water regularly for drinking. They'll get it as part of their daily routine. In hot weather, they also use it for cooling. In normal weather—fairly cool for most elk habitat—elk will feed and rest within walking distance of water. The distance of the walk is influenced by the availability of feed. If feed is in the vicinity of water, they'll be around somewhere in the vicinity of the two most of the time. As feed and water become scarce, they'll be pushed into a longer trip for their daily routine, and rest under cover and cooling shade and breezes somewhere in between the feed and water, probably closer to the water. Hot, dry areas with little water just won't have a permanent resident elk population. They may temporarily occupy such an area for a while to escape hunting pressure or similar disturbance, but they'll return to the preferred area when conditions improve there.

If water is generally available in the area, which is the usual situation in good elk habitat, the weather becomes the most significant influence on elk behavior. With two exceptions, the influence of weather on elk behavior is subtle, and it interacts with other factors so that it is often obscured as an independent effect (or at least, obscured to just about all humans). The main, hard-and-fast exception is the onset of heavy snow late in the year. That can be counted on to force all elk except maybe a few old bulls down from the summer range to lower elevations. Those few holdouts may stay in hidden pockets until they're snowed in. The other weather effect that can be counted on is a sudden onset of cool weather or rain at about the time of the start of the rut. The change in the weather seems to throw the activity level of the rut into high gear. Unseasonably cold, wet weather can jump-start the onset of the madness stage of the rut, sometimes moving it forward by weeks. A lazy, warm, late summer going into fall without a sharp weather change can result in a gradual onset of observable behavior of the rut and string out the activities of the proceedings at a low level. Note that breeding still takes place; the calves are dropped right on time the following spring after a hot, dry early fall. The elk just take care of essential business in the cool of the night without fanfare.

Now that we've covered the more or less predictable weather effects, we can get into the weather effects that are more vague and make for better, or more lively, opinionated, discussions. The onset of heavy, prolonged rain or snow seems to influence elk to lie up under cover for a while. After a day or so, they'll probably be back out feeding again on their regular schedule, rain or shine, unless it's an intense storm. Sometimes they'll be active just before the onset of heavy weather, but you can't count on it. I have observed them to be very active and nervously moving about with the approach of a summer evening thunderstorm. One behavior that I would put in the common but not absolutely predictable category is for elk to suddenly appear on the slopes feeding at any time of the day just as an extended storm of two or three days clears. I've often heard that elk don't actively feed as much on dark, cloudy nights, and are therefore more likely to be out feeding later into the morning after a cloudy night than after a clear night. This is consistent with the common phase of the moon theory that elk feed at night during a full moon and therefore tend to lie up quicker after a bright night. I think there's an extension of that theory that says that they're then more likely to come out for a short time in the middle of the day after a bright night with a full moon. It's my opinion that, with the two exceptions noted in the preceding paragraphs, all of the effects of weather and phase of the moon on elk behavior become secondary to an increased disturbance level, or increased hunting pressure, at the start of the general high-powered rifle season.

I've observed another pattern of behavior (which may not be universal) that doesn't seem to have any reason behind it but which is nonetheless useful: If undisturbed, most of the elk in a given area will tend to stay at the same general elevation. It has been my experience that this tendency is strongest at the start of the season. If you find elk (or their sign) at a certain elevation in one part of an area early in the season, then when you start looking in other parts of the area, you should begin with likely spots at the same elevation. An altimeter has long been a handy tool for this type of location. A GPS will serve the same function as long as you keep up with the contours.

AVOIDING DETECTION WHILE MOVING TO LOCATE ELK

You want to locate the elk before the elk locate you. Walk quietly while moving. Breaking a stick or rolling a rock now and then is okay, but if you're with someone, keep the conversation to a minimum and keep it quiet. Wear camouflage clothing suited to the local vegetation. If you're required by state regulations to wear a blaze orange cap and vest, I recommend that you still go with camo for the rest of the ensemble to scramble your human shape.

Since locating requires a lot of hiking on the part of the elk hunter, it isn't practical to go full stealth, which can make locating less efficient by restricting movement and causing you to overheat. You're not likely to catch this flatlander wearing a full ghillie suit over a scent-suppressing coverall set, but I'll have washed, used odor-suppressing deodorant, and avoided washing my clothes in brighteners that give an ultraviolet signature. The commonsense approach is the bigger the area you need to cover, and the more open the cover, the more important cool headgear and freedom of movement are.

I find lots of new elk hunters are reluctant to cover the extensive areas required to locate elk because the elk might see them. Attention to technique can minimize that risk. Fast movement up the slopes while the early-morning thermals are flowing downhill keeps the hunter downwind of the elk above. Additionally, you can avoid presenting a skylighted profile of a distinctive, upright human shape and walking gait by staying aware of where the elk you're interested in will be, and of the line of sight from that general direction. In the photo on the facing page, the nose of the ridge we're standing on is about the same height as the ridge in the background, and we're coming up the face. We're going straight upslope to the top of the ridge where it flattens (in the Idaho sense), so that the line of sight from elk above is obstructed by brush and trees. They'll usually lie up on the flat over the crest of the ridge from us. Elk will seek out a flat spot with enough area to let the herd bed down together in sight of each other so that they can communicate without sound, using body language (cow elk stare with elevated neck in the direction of a predator).

Dress code of the day for hard location, beginning with a fast 3,000-foot elevation gain.

The elk hunter has some flexibility in deciding which parts to camo or not to camo. You might not realize that you have that kind of freedom if you don't look past the ads of suppliers of camouflage clothing. The pictures in the advertisements always depict matching jackets and pants. However, wearing different patterns on top and bottom is more effective for breaking up the human form. The outfit pictured above is optimum for hard location—stretchy jeans, a light jacket for chilly early mornings or light showers, light boots, athletic (non)headgear, and photosensitive glasses for alternating shade and glare. Camo is less important when working wind direction and cover to remain undetected.

Obviously, if you're interested in locating elk across a canyon, you can't move up an exposed face directly in their line of sight. That perfect spot to wait for the cross-canyon shot toward the facing brushy slope might have the disadvantage of an exposed entry that will allow elk to pick you up taking your stand. You'll be sitting in your well-chosen vantage point wondering why they aren't coming out on that slope you have so well covered. If you move onto a lookout spot before daylight, it goes without saying that you turn the flashlight off before you cross any areas exposed to the facing slope. Even without the light, it's best to keep a screen of vegetation between yourself and possible locations of elk that are probably out in the predawn darkness. The low-light vision of elk is probably better than our vision in full daylight.

It's unavoidable that elk hunters who have hunted a given area for several years gravitate toward a favorite spot to take that stand at breaking light on opening day of the season. Whether they call it the "sweet spot," the "honey hole," or the "murder spot," or don't even name it (or mention it around their campmates), that's where they'll be. My place above the Big Bend of the North Fork is the place our group came to know as the "Low Shooting Rocks" on the east side of the breaks above the "Kitchen" (and no, names of favorite spots don't necessarily need to make any sense). In any event, that's where I am on the morning of this little tale.

SKYLIGHTED

The situation was better than usual, since Herm would eventually work into the brush below with the chance of getting a bull moving even if it might not be so inclined. It's usually not a good idea to move into this particular spot before first light because there's a lot of excellent opening-morning hunting area to move through before you get to this good sit-for-a-while place. It's usually a bad idea to "burn" or "stink up" a good area by traveling through it before it's light enough to see elk that might be moving about as you pass; they can see you with their UV-sensitive, "see-in-the-dark" vision, and they'll move out and you'll never know that they were there.

So it was already a little bit light as I picked my way down to a good position on the low rocks using scattered brush as cover to limit my visibility from sharp elk eyes below. Access to these particular rocks isn't from the absolute cover of heavy timber, as is often the case with the pinnacles in the area. As I made my approach across an unavoidable gap in the brush, a bull bugled from the heavy brush below. Just a couple of tootles up and down the scale. I peered intently into the brush below without ever getting a look at him. I presently heard the swish, swish of brush on his legs and flanks as he made his way past my overlooking position. I never saw even so much as a hair, much less an antler tine.

Back in camp that evening, I relayed my experience to Herm and how my favorite opening-morning spot had let me down. My sad tale was very entertaining to Herm, who then filled me in on my story from his angle. He had guided his hunter in below as planned and, sure enough, got a quick, tail-end look at a bull escaping past my lookout, also just as I had planned. But, not according to my plan, the bull kept to a little depressed fold in the slope so that it was hidden from my view for the entire, more or less leisurely escape to the thick timber and high brush on the lower slopes. "Just like he knew you were there, Tom." The translation of that bugle I heard was "Gotcha!"

Always be aware of the wind direction—often easier said than done in rough mountain country where thermal and terrain effects interact with the prevailing wind. Many experienced hunters always carry a small butane lighter, a piece of chalk to scratch dust off of, or a squeeze bottle to poof, or tie a feather to the brim of a hat to continually check the wind.

Being aware of the senses of elk that can detect hunters so effectively in several ways, the beginning elk hunter, and sometimes the hunter who has made a few hunts, can become reluctant to risk the movement required to locate elk. Intuition to know when, where, and how to move eventually comes with experience, but until that time comes, here's a general approach that can be applied to specific situations you'll encounter when hunting.

A SUGGESTED STANDARD APPROACH TO LOCATION AND ONE LAST CAUTION

The technique instinctively used by many experienced elk hunters to locate elk while avoiding detection by elk is to work along the upper slopes of ridges and rims, staying below the ridge crest to avoid being skylighted. Elk (usually) tend to look downslope and into the wind for approaching danger. If the prevailing winds are coming up the slope, they carry the hunter's scent back over the ridge away from the elk. Less obvious is the effect of a steady wind coming over the crest from the other direction. The air often rolls over the crest and creates an upslope flow over most of the upper slopes of the downwind side, to the advantage of hunters moving along those upper slopes. In the absence of a prevailing wind, the rule of thumb is that thermal effects usually form an upslope flow during the morning hours as the sun shines on the lower slopes and the warmed air rises. Then the thermal air movement turns downslope into the evening, and often through the night and into the very early morning (when smart hunters get started), as cooler, heavier air slides down the slope under the warm air. Check those rules of thumb every so often with a wind indicator: a lighter (note that this will create a distinctive odor), dust spray, goose down feather tied with light thread to the hat brim, or the ever-handy if unsanitary mouth-moistened finger (the cool side is the direction the wind is coming from). In areas of mixed cover of meadows and heavy timber, morning heating warms the open areas first, causing air to rise locally to be replaced by heavy, cool air from the shady timber areas.

A hunter moving (and stopping to look) along upper slopes is in a good position to see elk on the slopes below and take a shot with the rifle, or begin a downslope stalk into the wind with the bow. Use your glass to carefully cover particular features of terrain and vegetation that are attractive to elk. Look for them moving along terraces around steep slopes or holding in pockets below rims. They are also likely to be moving along fringes of cover through more open areas, feeding along the edges of meadows close to cover, or resting just inside the edge of cover on flat spots. Cover the secondary ridges by working along one side, around the point, then along the other side. Note particularly the little pockets formed where secondary ridges intersect the main ridge. The south and west sides will often be open or brushy; the north and east sides will be timber covered, cool, and better watered. It's sometimes productive to stop and rest a spell overlooking passes along the ridges you're working. You can check any trails crossing the pass for sign. Lots of sign makes the experienced hunter move slower; absence of any sign creates a need for speed to cover more area until you find some sign. But while it is good technique to get over the less promising areas in a hurry so that you can concentrate on the places most likely to be holding elk, don't move too fast, and don't forget to keep on looking. This is a common pitfall for inexperienced hunters. Just about the time you've decided that there are absolutely zero elk in the entire area and you've stopped looking and are moving along like a fast freight train through the night—*EAK! EOUGH!* Thunder of hooves. (Human expletive deleted.) And it'll come back to you: "Old Tom told me so." Old Tom has been there many times before you, my friend, and, no doubt, will be there many times in the future too.

SURPRISE ENCOUNTERS WITH UNDISTURBED ELK

After the first hour or so of your first elk hunt, you'll have the impression that there aren't any elk anywhere in the area. Another fifteen minutes and you'll be sure that there were *never* any elk there. It's all a myth. A fraud to take your time and money.

And the sight of that first elk in front of you at any distance will be . . . nothing. And, unless you catch a glimpse as it jumps into the brush, or your annoyed guide pokes your ribs and says in a coarse whisper, "Dammit! That wuz a good 'un!" it's likely that all you'll ever see will be . . . nothing.

Clear your mind of those beautiful color photos of unobstructed, filter-enhanced elk standing in open meadows. You know, like the cover of this and every other elk hunting book, or the special elk editions of the outdoor magazines that show up on the racks in late summer. Your actual encounters with hunted elk in the real world hardly ever look like that.

Hate to disappoint, but when you're trying to locate elk during elk season in an area that allows elk hunting, you hardly ever see elk at all. In certain locations and at times when they're not hard hunted, elk may be seen in photo ops out on meadows or the sides of slopes, but then you can't hunt them. When and where you can hunt, you'll almost always locate them at a distance as patches of russet summer coat very early in the season or creamy light brown winter coat later, blinking on and off as they move along behind cover. *Do not think about shooting at these patches!* You have no shot in this situation. And you're not going to be fast moving across rough elk country with those expensive binocs up to your eyes finely adjusted to whatever distance the elk happen to show up. You're going to be stuck with having to use those unaided natural eyeballs you come equipped with, all bloodshot from getting up at 3:30 excited to get out there for the hunt.

I brought the next few photos home from a recent hunt. Gorgeous looked 'em over and gave her assessment in that usual flat tone reserved for her assessments of my photos: "Your pictures of nothin' came out just as nice as your pictures of dirt this season." (A flattering reference to my photo studies of tracks.) But if you enlarge the picture of nothin', you can make out several elk, including a five-point, moving around and looking about in a casual way. In contrast to the glossy close-ups in outdoor magazines, these photos illustrate what you're actually going to see when you're out there looking for elk—and they'll help you learn how to look for what you want to see.

The first photo was taken a while after I was surprised—you're always surprised—while I was moving fast down the old logging road during bow season to get to the next good ambush point.

I made out a couple of elk shapes before they patterned me as something of danger to them. (I wasn't—I was about 270 yards short of where I needed to be for a shot.) We had an unobstructed view of each other across the intervening distance of maybe 300 yards along the road. I immediately crouched low and melted in behind vegetation to one side of the road—partially hidden, and somewhat obstructed, so they wouldn't pick me up until I moved. Which I'd need to do if I were going to get one of those graphite arrows from my bow quiver. I very slowly wiggled around to fish the little returnable camera from my daypack I lay back against. Might as well document the dumb situation I'd deftly maneuvered myself into.

Elk! Where?! Where?! Right in front of you, (colorful western descriptive adjective) flatlander!

In these photos, you can see the antlers lit up in the sun, turning one way, then back the other way. The shape of the antlers indicates that it's a five-point. There are cows in these photos, too—but it's a lot harder to pick them out!

More elk appeared—five cows and a five-point right out there in the open in the old loggin' road. I took a snapshot or two. As the sun came up and the bull moved around, I conducted my own personal clinic just for me on the topic of why I was seen by elk before I saw them. In the weak light at the first break of dawn, the cows in shadow were almost impossible to see without enough light to create the russet hues I always look for. Red bird cocks, I recalled, look black in poor light. Russet just goes invisible, like black over dark brown brindle cattle (or dogs), even with the washed-out strawberry-blond rump. But the bull was a different story. Even at a great distance—as you can see from the pictures—the antlers light up. There're intended to be seen to impress both cows and rival bulls!

Note that it's difficult to make out individual tines in a long-range photo; it's also difficult without binocs out there on the slopes. And it's a bad idea to waste time with the attention-attracting motion involved in getting them in place. Judge by the shape for a first-order assessment of rack size (for more details, see Chapter 9). The bull in the photo is a five-point.

ELK SIGN

Elk sign is the unmistakable evidence that elk have been in a specific location. Elk sign verifies our guess that elk could be found in a particular area. Location of elk sign is essential for a successful hunt.

Tracks

Tracks are the most widespread form of elk sign, and therefore the easiest find. They're also the most predictable. When you're scouting for elk in an area, and you can't immediately find a convergence of the factors influencing the location of elk, a good technique for initially locating elk is to begin looking for tracks in places where movement would be constrained or funneled between areas of feeding, resting, and watering. I would begin by checking out all passes, beginning with the major landform patterns, then moving toward the smaller features. If the season is dry, check in the vicinity of running water first, if it can be found, then around pools of standing water. Keep looking until you have covered the entire hunting area. All of the elk in a rather large area may be concentrated in just one part of the area. Focus your search according to the behavior patterns that should be prevalent at the current time of year. Stay with it, and you'll locate the elk if they're anywhere in the area. If you find a likely place where elk should be feeding, watering, resting, or moving between all of the above, and there aren't any elk tracks or other sign around, make a big move. Put your efforts into a more promising area.

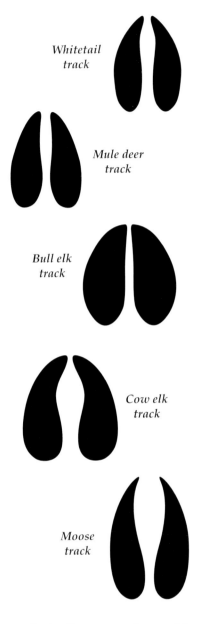

Whitetail track

Mule deer track

Bull elk track

Cow elk track

Moose track

Elk leave distinct cloven tracks with a very round pattern compared to most other animals that can be encountered in elk hunting areas. Cloven tracks are divided into two ground contacts so that the track pattern appears to be split in half. Each half of the hoof is a separate toe. They're just slightly longer than they are wide. Elk tracks in a soft surface such as snow or soft ground will show more of the back part of the hoof, which is normally above ground contact level. Such tracks will appear to be more elongated than those made in firm dirt.

The sketch illustrates elk tracks along with some other possibilities of cloven tracks that you might encounter while elk hunting. I have shown single tracks rather than patterns of several tracks because under typical ground conditions, you usually see tracks here and there, one at a time. The size and shape of elk tracks are very similar to those of mule tracks, except for the fact that the elk tracks are cloven. The rounded tracks of horses also have only one toe. Elk tracks are easily distinguished from deer tracks by their size. Elk tracks are always very symmetric. The only other tracks in elk country that could confuse the beginning elk hunter might be moose or domestic cattle tracks where cattle grazing overlaps with elk range. Moose tracks are extremely elongated compared to elk tracks and are significantly larger. Cattle tracks are closer to the size of elk tracks and only slightly more elongated than elk tracks; the more rounded shape of the elk track and the somewhat irregular appearance of cattle tracks compared to those of elk can differentiate elk from cattle.

If you're still confused about whether you're looking at tracks of elk or cattle or both, the question can usually be resolved by other sign, to be discussed shortly.

Tracks of a large bull may in very rare cases approach 5 inches across, but most of the bull tracks that you'll ever see, other than in your wildest dreams, will be around 4 inches, less for younger bulls. I always relate them to the width of my boot tracks or a .300 or .338 Winchester Magnum cartridge, which is slightly less than $3^1/_2$ inches long. Tracks of cow elk are somewhat smaller in diameter but the tracks of an old cow can be almost as large as those of a small bull. Tracks of old cows may be slightly more elongated than those of young cows or bulls. It's easy to distinguish bull tracks from cow tracks, since the greater weight of the bull tends to result in deeper tracks. Bull tracks appear to be almost solid; cow tracks, in contrast, appear more distinctly divided with more indentation into the ground around the outside of the pattern.

Most tracks you'll see are left by walking elk, with the imprint of the back foot over the front foot. Walking elk place the back foot almost exactly in the track of the front foot. Running elk leave tracks that appear to be of separate impacts, and the hooves will appear spread apart at the center of the front of the hoof; the force of the impacting hooves landing and then pushing off for the next bound forces the ends of the toes apart. Running elk tear the ground up in random ways, and dirt will usually be thrown to the side.

When studying elk tracks, the relative sizes of the individual tracks give an indication of the animal that left them, but the best way to make a quick scan for bull tracks is to look for deeper tracks. In snow, look for

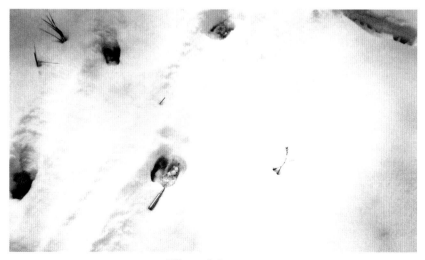

Elk track in snow.

Typical-size dried track of walking elk in mud (pictured with a .338 cartridge for scale).

signs of a wet dribble down the center of the bull's track pattern. The tracks of a very old cow elk are the only tracks that may lack symmetry.

How fresh the elk tracks are is the main point of interest for the elk hunter. Recent precipitation tends to make judging the age of tracks difficult.

The appearance of elk tracks in snow, where you can easily follow the pattern, should be interpreted according to the amount of time elapsed since the most recent snow. If there has been no snow since the tracks were made, they will retain their sharp appearance for a matter of several hours in the absence of thawing, which makes the tracks indistinct and larger. If tracks in snow are frozen hard overnight, frost will distort their shapes to a minor extent. An example of an elk track in snow is shown in the photo on the previous page. Note that the appearance of the tracks is altered by the way the hoof went into the snow, the drag over the surface, and loosened snow falling back into the track.

Tracks in mud are a little more difficult to follow and interpret because of the variation of the ground surface and its effect on the tracks. If the tracks are left in shaded areas, they will retain a fresh appearance for a matter of days, whereas in an exposed location they will dry and deteriorate in a few hours. An example of a track made by a walking elk in mud after it has dried for a few days is shown above. The pattern of drying of the mud will change the appearance of the track from the way it looked when it was made. Look for little details as an indication of the age of the track. If there are leaves in the track, determining whether they were pressed down there by the hoof or

A bull elk track of impressive size, shown with a size 14D Herman Survivor boot (5 inches across).

The same track in the afternoon of the same day.

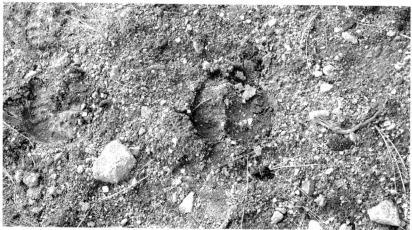

simply blew into the track later may indicate how long the track has been in place. Close examination can yield additional information. By looking closely at this track, you can see indicators that it's a bull track. The pattern is large and round, uniform, and pressed deeply into the surface. The picture isn't sharp enough to show the very thin division down the center of the hoof, but the division is visible under close inspection of the actual track.

The photos above show an elk track that's way bigger than normal. That's a size 14D Herman Survivor adjacent to a fresh bull track in wet, weathered granite mud. Most references say bull elk tracks top out at

A fresh track of a running elk in soft dirt.

just over 4 inches wide. The sole of that boot measures exactly 5 inches wide.

The same track late in the afternoon of same day appears to be very old compared to the first photo of the track, taken in the early morning when it was still fresh. Tracks appear to deteriorate faster in weathered granite mud than in weathered shale mud (clay).

The photo above illustrates the track of a running bull elk. The increased force on the impacting hoof tends to force the two toes apart, leaving a wedge-shaped space in between. The track will usually be impressed deeply into the ground, as can be seen in the picture. The cartridge is across the width of the track, and the separation shows as a pie wedge shape beginning under the cartridge and opening toward the top of the page. In moist ground, the track will show the initial pattern of the landing with the toes together, then a deeper pattern with the toes spread as the full weight of the running elk comes down on the track, and a deep indent formed by the ends of the toes, the front of the hoof pattern, formed by the push-off for the next bound. The tracks of running elk are usually made by the one that got away, often unseen. They're useful in correcting the hunter's tactics to cover an unforeseen escape route.

Tracks in standing water of puddles, wallows, or watering locations might give a little more information, depending upon the appearance of the water. Muddy bottoms might leave a murky suspension in the water for a matter of an hour or so if the water has little or no flow.

You may note that I categorize tracks and tracking with location rather than with stalking, the common approach in classic outdoor books on the general topic of big game hunting, which usually had a predominantly deer hunting flavor. The old-time writers seem to always refer to tracking within the context of stalking for all big game. It's been my experience that the technique works a lot better on deer than on elk. Deer are reluctant to leave their familiar area. Elk don't have that problem. Once they've determined that you're after them, they're gone. Often miles-away gone.

The reason that I make the distinction and emphasize it is to counter the usual tendency of all hunters on encountering easily followed elk tracks such as in fresh snow. Full of enthusiasm and stamina, we tend to take off up the trail, following the tracks like a pack of hounds. The elk, meanwhile, are performing their age-old "J" maneuver, doubling back and watching their back trails for tracking predators, and then putting plenty of distance between themselves and anything suspicious on their trail—such as an excited hunter.

These two Tales, although they took place years apart in time and miles apart in distance, are almost identical in seasonal setting and circumstances. They take place late in the season as the snow begins to fall in heavier amounts and remain in place, while the old herd bulls, exhausted from the rut, instinctively retreat to their hideouts to recover from the exertions of the rut in preparation for the ordeal of survival through the winter. Meanwhile, the lesser bulls and cows congregate in separate herds prior to moving downslope to their common wintering grounds. The bulls will usually be found in groups of two to four, while the cows may form large herds of forty or more. A fresh snowfall of a few inches overnight transforms flatland dude hunters into expert trackers, at least in their own minds. Pack camp guides are duty-bound to go out with these greenhorns while they slide and tumble around in the snow in a fool's quest to run down the little groups of bulls. This tactic is usually unsuccessful; elk have managed to survive natural predators for the last several million years, and have developed the habit of hooking around, stopping to take a break and look over their back trails from concealed locations. The stop may be just a pause, or they may bed down in a good location for the day.

The first fishhook maneuver Tale takes place early in my elk hunting career, my second season to be exact, when I hunted with a lot more misguided exuberance than skill, or good judgment, for that matter. I had booked a late-season hunt with the idea of tracking down a trophy bull through the snow.

FOLLOWING THREE LITTLE BULLS THROUGH THE SNOW ABOVE STANLEY HOT SPRINGS

Herm thought maybe we could improve our luck by beating our frozen butts through the snow of a more distantly removed steep, slippery slope rather than the ones we had been over in the vicinity of our pack camp. We saddled up and rode over to the face of Old Greensides, a hairy old mountain reached by fording ice-cold Boulder Creek and taking the trail past the Stanley Hot Springs. The springs were a popular destination of day packers, but, as I expected, no "skinny dippers" graced its warm, steaming pools as we rode past and on up the mountain on this heavily overcast, cold, foggy, snowy early morning. It was one of those days that a person would have to be young, or crazy, or an elk hunter—or all three—to be out in.

We cut three trails of bull elk–sized tracks—fairly fresh but with a dusting of snow from the intermittent flakes still coming down. We eventually came on three vacant bull elk–sized beds in the snow, with the unmistakable yellow spot centered in the depression. We followed the tracks leading away from the beds. Three times we found beds and three times we followed, doing our best to peer through the thick timber, fog, and snow as the elk led us on another wild goose chase until we came again to their latest lookout where they had stood to watch their back trail, then left another stain in the snow and more tracks leading off.

Finally, Herm pulled one of his Master Guide Tricks out of his pack. He would follow the three bulls without pressing them too hard. I would loop around to intercept them when they moved off. He would ensure that they headed in my direction by his direction of approach to their most likely next lookout. Foolproof. I was sidehilling along through the deep snow, trying to keep from slipping and breaking my neck as I made a loop down the slope, toward their most likely path of escape, when, well ahead of me, I just made out three large shadows carefully sneaking down the slope through the dark, snowy timber. I was excited to finally see my first elk of the trip, but I was more annoyed than excited to see that they were giving me the slip again.

Whatever the reason, I was highly energized as I backtracked along my trail for a short distance, then dived off down the side of the mountain in an attempt to get ahead and cut off the elk's path of escape. I crossed the government trail a short distance down the slope, and took off to try to cut off the elk as they crossed the trail ahead. I picked up speed along the trail, since I was much less likely to slip with each step than when I was moving cross-country.

I was at a dead run, poncho flapping in the wind, rifle at the ready as the trail flattened out a little. In my wild headlong rush, I didn't notice that I had moved down the slope to the point that I was at the level of the hot springs.

But as I rounded a corner of the trail I did notice, although my brain didn't react immediately, that I was running through a group of about twenty or so nature-loving college-age hikers that had come up the trail behind us. Some were resting, strung out along the trail and taking in the winter mountain scenery; others were in the pools of the hot springs, contributing to the quality of the scenery. I was moving too fast to notice the scenery (Herm told me about it later after he had come through at a more leisurely pace on the horse). I mostly noticed that there were people along the trail because of the bloodcurdling shrieks of a few of the co-eds as they dived off either side of the trail into the underbrush. And they were the ones with clothes on. I managed a soft "Good morning" that, with my generally agitated state of mind and out-of-breath physical condition, probably sounded like a hoarse foghorn to the hikers enjoying the stillness of the wilderness morning.

I didn't stop to visit. I continued running down the trail for a few hundred yards, figuring that, at the very least, the three bulls would veer off of their escape route, heading directly down the slope. I eventually slowed and stopped to wait to get a look at the elk if they crossed the trail. They didn't. After a while, Herm came riding down the trail, leading my horse. At the sound of the commotion along the trail, the elk had made a 180 turn and headed back up over the mountain, moving fast. Herm had tried to turn them around, even firing his revolver into the air, which only terrified the hikers even more. We headed back to camp, worn out by the morning's entertainment.

This next Tale takes place during a late-season hunt about twenty years after the preceding fishhook maneuver tale. You would think that I had been hunting long enough by this time to know what was going on—and, as it chanced to happen, I was accompanied by the same guide, Old Herm, so you'd think that both of us would have saved the effort. But, in this instance, the terrain made it practically impossible to cut across the trail of the elk in front of us due to the impossibly steep slopes on either side. We were hoodwinked even before we jumped off into the steep-sided canyon.

THREE LITTLE BULLS IN SNOW AROUND THE TOP OF SQUAW CREEK

We had intercepted the bulls on flat ground along the rim of a big, rough (even for the Bitterroots) canyon carved out by a drainage called Squaw Creek. We apparently "jumped," or surprised, three bachelor bulls traveling in their own little herd. The bulls dived off into the head of a very steep part of the canyon. The trail, or what passed for a trail, actually more like a crease in the snow-covered exposed rock, immediately dropped around just under the steep pinnacles of the hogback ridge dividing Squaw Creek from the next drainage. Against any hint of good judgment, we followed.

We followed them down and around and back up again and then back down again and around once more and then back around once more. We eventually realized that the tracks that we were following might not even be following a real trail. This realization came at about the time that we were again along a real trail across a steep slope almost straight up on one side and straight down on the other. No chance to circle ahead to intercept the elk. Slipping and sliding in the fresh snow, we followed the steep trail down into the creek, then back up again, all the way up to the end of the canyon just under the rocks of the pinnacles, then up under the rock fields and overhanging boulders and up to the crest of the canyon. There, at the perfect lookout, we found where the three bulls had stood shoulder to shoulder for a considerable time, watching us labor up the slope—three sets of tracks with little yellow drippy stains around yellow holes in the snow centered in each set of tracks. Tracks that then took off over the divide into the next drainage.

For all but the most athletic and skilled elk hunters, the most feasible way to use fresh elk tracks to get elk in sight is to figure out where they're going from their direction and the terrain ahead. Then you head them off to make an intercept. Then you have to use stalking techniques. Your enthusiasm and stamina will be very useful when it comes to practicing this approach in rough country, since the elk are going to use the easiest route to their intended destination, and you'll have to cut across the rough parts to intercept them.

The elite among us, who have both the physical conditioning to keep up with alert, moving elk and the intuition to predict the most likely next move of the elk, can have success using the tactic of "doggin' elk"—and yes, it does pertain to running them down in a literal sense. Be advised that it's a tall order, lots tougher than doing the same with whitetails. Successful tactics normally fall into two variations: bugling while following a bull with cows during the rut; or following elk through late-season snow with the intent of jumping ahead of them and cutting their trail at an ambush point. The intent of both approaches is to transition from locating to stalking on the move. A fast move at some point, as it usually works out.

The first approach requires enough stamina to keep up with the herd of cows, which the herd bull is attempting to keep moving along. And all the while, the caller is attempting to annoy the bull. It's much more effective to work as a caller-shooter team traveling along separate paths. The shooter continually maneuvers to keep downwind of the elk and move in for a shot when the elk turns on the caller. The caller mimics an enraged but lesser bull, sometimes throwing in a few amorous hot cow sounds to push him over the edge.

The second approach is like a drive on afterburner when practiced by a single hunter. A really good hunter. A team approach is usually more effective for us normal humans. One hunter works to keep the elk moving without too much disturbance while others attempt to get ahead for the ambush, usually at a pass over the divide into the adjacent drainage, sometimes toward cover or a likely point where elk will likely lie up and watch their back trail. Sort of turning the J-hook move around.

Droppings

Every publication on any kind of big game hunting has to have a section on what was once politely called "other sign"—in somewhat more descriptive terms, droppings. There's no denying that even the stealthiest old bull can't avoid this tip-off. However, to sort of paraphrase and clean up for publication the observations of any number of old guides: Excitement over excrement is often misplaced exuberance. First you need to separate the elk poop from all of the rest of the poop in the woods. Domestic cattle leave big splats, usually in one place; horses leave distinctive sort of rounded clumps either in one place or strung out along the trail—tight, hard clumps if they're eating dry hay, soft, messy clumps if they're eating grass; elk, deer, sheep, and goats leave small, round pellets of different sizes. Elk droppings are about the size and appearance of a black olive, more or less.

Bull droppings.

Cow droppings.

Without extending this discussion any more than necessary, here's what's important. The reason the experienced hunters don't get too excited by the mere appearance of droppings is that with a little rain on them, those pellets can look pretty fresh and yet be weeks old, which doesn't say much about elk in the area now. The old hands do get worked up if the pellets are still steaming. And, yes, some do pick them up to feel for warmth. Of the most interest is the sight of fairly recent bull droppings. They can be distinguished from other elk by the amount in one pile. Cows usually leave a pile of individual pellets or string pellets along while the bull is more inclined to stop and dump the entire load on the same spot with a lot of the pellets fused into solid clumps.

During all of the excitement of the rut, the bull doesn't graze much, so this sign isn't very important. But, about two weeks into the regular rifle season, which equates to well after the rut, you may, if you're really lucky, blunder into an area where big piles of large pellets are all around. The area will usually be removed from the most heavily used elk trails. Get ready. You have located a "bull's nest," his hideout to recover from the rut. He will also hang out in this hideaway through the first part of the general elk hunting season if the hunting pressure is high. Closely cropped grass and the piles of droppings will be the only indications of the bull's presence. And he usually has to be forced out of the place at the point of a gun. Don't make a move until you've assumed the mindset to instinctively make the kill.

Rubs

Another indication of a bull elk's holding ground is the rub. While a rub is an absolute indicator that a big bull has been there, close examination usually reveals that he has not been at the location for some time. Bulls, particularly big ones, will stay in a restricted area while the velvet sheds from their antlers. As opposed to the hideout nest, these areas are often in the vicinity of main elk trails, and on hillsides to catch the breeze. The elk usually pick one or two small trees to rub off the tattered velvet as it dries. As their hormone level rises, the rubbing turns more vigorous until the bull is fighting the tree as he would a potential rival. The rubbed tree illustrated is about average; sometimes you'll find small trees with all of the bark and small limbs removed from ground level to as high as 10 feet. The tree may even be broken off. It's pretty spectacular, and makes for an interesting report when you get back to camp. During the general season after the rut, though, usually nobody gets too excited over such reports because the rub activity takes place long before the season starts. This may not always be the case for archery or

Rub.

early rifle seasons. A perk to make the archery season more interesting is that it is scheduled close to or overlapping the time of the rut.

Odor

You'll usually have seen tracks and know that elk are in the general vicinity before you can smell them. However, there are times when the mountain breeze may bring the odor of a raunchy old bull to you as your first clue of his presence. If the breeze is light and the accumulated odor is noticeable, he will likely be bedded down in the immediate vicinity. Go into a stalk immediately, moving carefully into the wind without making a sound. Search the area in front of you thoroughly as you move. Remember, you are probably looking for a bedded animal whose resting body will be obscured by low brush and ground cover. Your visual clues won't come from a standing profile until he jumps to run. You might see an ear twitch, but you are more likely to catch the gleam off an antler of a perfectly motionless animal. You might get a stationary bedded shot, but more likely you had better be quick with your offhand shot when he jumps.

Sounds and Vocalization

Most people who have hunted deer are surprised to learn just how much noise elk make moving along. They rub brush, break sticks, and roll rocks, seemingly oblivious to the sound they create. On numerous occasions, I've frozen in place thinking that a herd was near at hand from the sound they made, only to find that they were hundreds of yards up the ridge. On a very few occasions, I've heard the faint clicks of their lower legs, which they share with other herding deer, notably the caribou.

Hearing elk bugle is one of the greatest thrills of the hunt for me. Hearing the bugle of a big bull down in a canyon on my first hunt is what I like to hold responsible for this elk hunting problem of mine. As far as location of elk is concerned, a bull sounding off is as about as absolute as anything you ever get in this elk hunting business. There he is; begin your stalk. Note that here I refer to a bull sounding off without being prompted by an initial bugle by the hunter. The technique of bugling as you move along in the process of locating elk, then waiting for a possible answer from a bull is also a proven location technique. The bugling is usually done at fairly long intervals, just to see what happens, or as the hunter crests a division between drainages, a feature that often forms the territorial boundaries of bulls. This technique is best practiced during the rut under cool, wet conditions. Note that if a bull isn't "talking," you just serve to locate yourself by this practice. The elk, of course, know when it's time to talk and when it's time to shut up. Most of us humans usually don't.

A very few highly skilled hunters—the particular individuals I'm aware of happen to be Native Americans who've lived from infancy in the woods—can vocalize the entire repertoire of every creature they've ever heard. And a big bull not in the mood to start a rhubarb by answering a bugled challenge might tweet or grunt back at a raven or jay or owl or eagle or even a pack mule. So these experts will sometimes make one of these alternative calls, just to see what happens—and, sometimes, unexpectedly, a bull sings out. And if he doesn't, he isn't on alert to be looking or listening for another elk, or maybe one of those things that walks on its back legs all the time and sometimes makes a sound like a bugling elk, which it is not.

CHAPTER 7

Stalking Techniques

Once you have located a desired elk and go into the stalk, your next choices depend on your equipment. Whereas the way you go about locating elk is almost solely dependent upon elk behavior, the techniques you use in stalking must consider the equipment to be used in making the kill—and your level of skill with that equipment—as well as the senses of elk and their response to perceived threats.

This stage of elk hunting is practically the same whether the hunter is on a guided hunt with an outfitter or hunting alone with a personal outfit. There's an advantage to the beginner if you have an experienced guide literally at your elbow for coaching as you make the shot. But this is not always the case even with a guided hunt, and, in any event, you still have to make the shot.

In this chapter, I'll first discuss general considerations and techniques for different equipment, then address in more detail specific techniques that can be used for elk at various disturbance levels.

THE MINDSET OF THE STALK

There's a transition in the mindset of the hunter where the activities of locating and stalking meet. The successful elk hunter learns to make this transition without conscious thought or effort. The change in mindset between these two distinct activities may be practically instantaneous and may be necessary at almost any time, usually when least expected. That's why it's important to always be not only alert, but also mentally prepared to make the transition into the state of absolute focus required to make the final stalk and kill. It's been my experience that many opportunities are lost because the hunter is not mentally prepared to actually encounter the elk, particularly the trophy elk.

The mindset of the hunter during the stalk is split between focus on gathering visual and auditory information about the elk and avoiding detection by the elk. The hunter must also have a mental image of what he or she will do if an elk is located—an ongoing planning of the next move based on what's going on at any given instant and the most likely development. Furthermore, that response must realistically accommodate the limitations of the equipment the hunter is using. You may not have time to figure it all out in a deliberative process after action begins. When time is limited, this practice of planning ahead for every situation is invaluable. It allows you to develop those instinctive reactions that have to come into play when there's no time to think.

As you're stalking with your bow, you should be thinking, *If I come upon a bedded elk on this slope and see it before it sees me, and if it's 25 yards away, I'll shoot it; if it's 200 yards away from my path through this timber on the far brushy slope with broken timber cover, I'll consider the way the wind is blowing, then approach it along a route that appears to cover my approach and keep me downwind from the elk as I get within bow range.* (And that's based on a realistic appraisal of my own physical capabilities to move quietly and quickly across that intervening terrain and make that shot from that angle through the obstructions.) Or if you're carrying a high-powered repeater, you might be thinking, *If I see an elk 200 yards away, I have time to take a good shot, preferably from a solid rest or the sitting position that I've practiced on the shooting range.* The quick decision whether to take the shot in either case must take into account ethics and your capability with the equipment. And you must have practiced to the point of absolute confidence that a shot can be accurately made at the range limitations of your equipment under all circumstances. Again, it's a matter of ethics.

Your plan has to include the kind of elk you're looking for. The trophy hunter will be seeking to locate a bull elk with a set of antlers meeting a preconceived standard. If you locate elk but it's not clear that they include a bull with a rack meeting that standard, the locating phase must continue—but you need to use stalking techniques due to the presence of other elk. The trophy hunter will take a careful look to assess the antlers with binoculars or variable scope on high power before deciding to shoot if a shot is presented.

And if for some personal reason you have chosen to hunt with an old family rifle, or a modern preference of a large-caliber but short-range lever-action rifle, you can't change your equipment or its range limitation once you see the trophy of a lifetime across a wide canyon. Your mental response in this situation must be appropriate, again with ethics considered.

STALKING TECHNIQUES WITH THE BUGLE AND BOW

The rut usually coincides with the archery season in many western states, giving the bowhunters, who must stalk to within about 30 to 40 yards of the elk, a fair chance at a trophy. During the rut, undisturbed bull elk are often preoccupied with mating activities to the point that they show little threat response to humans. There are several different sets of techniques and tactics used to bowhunt for elk: calling; waiting on stands; stillhunting (which includes locating and stalking); and specialized driving. The last technique may include close following and annoying with calls or "dogging" a rutting bull without pushing him into flight until his rage overcomes his caution. The most effective of these options, when practiced by competent and experienced elk hunters, is calling using bugles and/or cow calls during the rut.

Successful bowhunters must have adequate shooting skills as well as the physical conditioning to quickly move on elk in the most difficult terrain; bowhunting also requires superb calling skills with both bugle and cow calls and the hunting experience to make the transition from calling to making the kill. Most of the elk killed with bows are taken by these same expert bowhunters season after season. Intuition and instincts make the difference. Those of us who don't have their level of calling skills would like to think that these masters of the calling art possess some mysterious natural talent, but the best of them will tell beginners that the secret is mostly some good instruction, followed by practice, practice, practice.

OF ELK CALLS, ELK CALLING, AND THE CRUEL TRICK NATURE HAS PLAYED ON OLD GUYS WHO WOULD BE ELK CALLERS

Becoming an accomplished elk bugler, if you're a male under the age of thirteen, or a female of any age with a reasonably high-pitched voice, is no problem. Get your hands on a grunt tube or any other piece of 1- to 2-inch-diameter hose about 2 to 3 feet long. If your dad is an expert caller and he starts you early enough (say, before you can speak human), or if most of your ancestors showed up with the early group out of northeastern Asia, you don't even need a tube. My friend Dan's son learned to speak perfect elk before he mastered human English. Imagine little kid talk punctuated by unbelievably precise elk bugles and cow calls. Otherwise, you can get a tape or CD at an outdoor sports store or order one from an outdoor sports mail-order outfit like Cabela's so that you know what you're supposed to sound like. Then all you need to do is to make the appropriate sounds by singing the notes or grunts into the tube (which is just an amplifier), and you'll produce an excellent elk bugle naturally. You are now set up to invite yourself along on the elk hunt with the old man around the place, while you laugh at him because he can't make the correct pitch for an elk bugle, no matter how hard he tries.

If you're one of the old guys, welcome to the club. The rest of us need to buy all of the calls, tubes, diaphragms, and instructional tapes that we can get our hands on, and choke ourselves trying to learn how to make the sounds that those other groups can make without trying. This cruel prank of nature is funny only to those lucky ones—and to old guys who can manage to get a family member with these qualifications to go hunting with him. They just squeal through the thing and a perfect bugle tone comes out. Then the boys grow up and their voices change and the girls become women and go out and buy their own bows and the old man is just along for field dressing unless he gets one of these devilish devices and practices (a lot) with it.

Calling generally mimics the vocalizations made by both bulls and cow elk during the rut, but expert callers often use variations and unusual combinations of the natural calls of elk to get the elk excited and lure a bull into bow range or distract him while the hunter or the shooter of a caller/shooter team moves into shooting range. The specific techniques of calling used should be appropriate to the stage of the rut and the mood of the elk at any particular time. Some experienced callers will mix bugles with cow calls of different types to create the impression of a herd with breeding going on.

CUTTING BETWEEN CALLERS AND ELK THEY'RE WORKING

Elk hunters new to the bugling bowhunting game need to be aware of an occasional type of interaction between callers and other hunters that doesn't make the outdoor sportsmanship awards list. The muzzleloader seasons of some states, notably (at the time of this writing) Colorado, are set sometime during the archery season. Licenses are usually issued by a draw. Muzzleloader hunters don't usually work on calling skills as an essential technique. They do often take advantage of a bugling bull locating himself. There are lots of reported incidents of muzzleloader hunters mistakenly stalking bugling bowhunters, although dangerous situations as a result appear to be rare. It's almost always passed off as a case of mistaken identity with congratulations to the expert caller, but sometimes it's obviously a deliberate tactic that goes over the line. To be fair to the muzzleloaders, my only firsthand experience with this sort of thing involved catching a bowhunter from another party sneaking in between me and a bugling bull I had going. My raghorn bugle isn't that good, as everybody who's heard it will verify, so I suspect that my fellow bowhunter knew I was another hunter. I've reached that point in life where I recognize the downside of pointing out the error of his ways to a demonstrated slow learner with a bad attitude and a bunch of sharp-edged broadheads. Anyway, if he thought that I was an elk, he probably thought that elk made one helluva loud danger call to run off every elk on the side of that mountain for the afternoon as I eased back off the hill.

During the pre-rut stage, from mid-August until the first of September, bulls will gather a herd of cows, which actually amounts to joining an existing herd, and defend a claimed territory. A common calling technique is bugling a challenge to excite a herd bull into approaching the hunter. Cows are usually not in heat at this time, and bulls may be suspicious of cow calls until close enough to the time of breeding that the caller can sound like an unclaimed but lonely cow.

Bowhunters may use a decoy to entice bugling bulls to move in a little closer. Elk decoys are usually easily portable two-dimensional rollup representations of an elk body. They may be placed as part of a caller/shooter setup.

During the early rut stage, herd bulls will be defending their gathered herd and breeding cows as they come into heat. This stage builds up to the peak of breeding activity. Dominant bulls will be excited with the heavy breeding activity, but occupied with the cows under their control, which normally tends to make them less inclined to come toward a challenger. But despite this focus on breeding their gathered cows, they're sometimes spoiling for a fight due to their agitated state, and may be lured into bow range by the hunter mimicking a challenge. In simulating a challenger, the experienced caller avoids the extremely deep and powerful bugle of the very large bull. The bull with the cows might be intimidated to the point that he simply leaves the area with the cows he has so far rather than risking their loss to the new boss bull. As the cows in the herd are bred, so that the herd bull begins to run short of breeding opportunities, a caller with a good simulation of an individual cow or a small group of cows in an agitated condition may bring the old bull over to investigate. Less dominant bulls without cows are more likely to respond to this tactic.

The bowhunter caller/shooter(s) team is much more effective than a single hunter bugling. Any bull elk responding to a human-produced call will usually attempt to check out the source of the racket before charging in, and you can be sure that he has an accurate fix on the location of the caller. The responding bull will usually attempt to circle around downwind to check out the scent of whatever is making the noise. A hidden shooter can get position on a likely route of approach toward the bugler. A two-hunter team can have one member do the calling while the shooter tries to get position on the answering bull, or the caller may attempt to move the elk over the hidden shooter. And the bull's options are wide open—anything from moving away to charging the challenger, with or without his herd of cows. This is another situation where decoys have come into use, to give the elk a visual distraction during the dynamics of the hide-and-seek that sometimes develops as both hunter and prey call, then move in an attempt to get the other in sight. A caller working alone attempts to enrage the bull to the point that he turns back on the tormentor. Expert callers who are also superbly conditioned will sometimes follow and challenge a herd bull that attempts to break off the encounter and move the cows away from the intruder.

But caution notwithstanding, during this stage of the rut, the bull elk will bugle, day or night, with or without encouragement by human attempts at bugling—when conditions are right. And only bull elk and a few master elk hunters know when that is. This is the time when serious fights develop between big bulls. If you are lucky enough to find yourself in a situation where elk are bugling to each other, you have the advantage of knowing their location without having to reveal your own. This is the trophy hunter's dream.

A real fight between bugling bulls is a real show in itself. The bowhunter can take advantage of the preoccupation of the fighting bulls to move in on the altercation for a shot. Your scent is about the only thing that will spook the bulls involved. In this case, you should focus on stalking one of the bulls, trying to get in for a close shot—and the best choice of the two bulls is usually the one that gives you the best angle on the wind, the bowhunter's nemesis. In lining up a shot, make sure screening vegetation will not deflect the arrow.

You may need to move through cows when going for a bull. I have been able to walk past them like a human on occasion, but have had better luck with a bear impersonation. Move along on all fours or in a duckwalk on a course that is obviously not directed at the cows that are usually looking at you. Don't make eye contact or look at them in a full-faced stare. You can attempt to add to their confusion by using a cow call as you move.

By the time of the late rut, the first round of breeding has been completed. Most cows have been bred, and those that failed to breed on the first cycle are coming into heat again. Bulls are highly competitive for the few breeding opportunities available. A single cow coming into heat in an area is cause for great excitement, not only for the bull controlling that area, but for bulls in surrounding areas as well. Even the cows become agitated, calling and sometimes fighting among themselves. The cow in heat may make a distinctive call, urgent in some cases, indicating her condition. This usually throws all of the bulls within hearing distance, which may be a considerable number, into a frenzy. They sound off with bugles unique to each individual bull, each differing in tone and in the number and sequence of notes. Bugles may initially be spaced a few minutes apart but rise in cadence until they form a continuous chorus. Under these circumstances, dominant bulls are thrown into a quandary. They won't be inclined to respect territories of others but at they same time they are usually reluctant to risk losing a gathered herd of cows in the confusion created by moving in on a cow in another bull's herd. Satellite bulls with no gathered cows to lose will often sneak in quietly in an attempt to get lucky while the dominant bulls are preoccupied with challenges to each other. In this stage of the rut, cow calls mimicking a cow in heat or multiple excited cows are effective. As would be expected, the satellite bulls are more susceptible to these techniques than herd bulls, but, if the caller can do a credible imitation of unattended, excited cows, an old herd bull will occasionally allow himself to get worked up to the point that he throws caution to the wind and comes in to the call.

During the post-rut stage, bugling activity is very dependent on the level of disturbance. In areas of limited access due to either remote location or controlled entry, bulls may bugle on occasion throughout the general rifle season. Elk will sometimes bugle for no apparent reason, or at least for no reason that's apparent to humans. A herd bull will keep company with his gathered herd for some time after breeding should have been completed. Under conditions of low disturbance, it's not uncommon for a bull with cows to walk out on a point, so that he can be heard for the maximum distance, and give a bugle in the middle of the morning or in the middle of the afternoon. He may repeat the performance every day if not disturbed.

A bull's bugle, whether in response to the bugle of a hunter or for some reason known only to himself, may serve to reveal his specific location so that a successful stalk may be initiated. The rifle hunter, with greater range capability available, won't need to call the bull in close, as the bowhunter does. A cow call may also draw a response, particularly in situations where a herd has been scattered and individual elk are attempting to join the rest of the herd.

Most beginning elk hunters will be hunting with a high-powered rifle during the general season after the rut; elk bugling at this time is unusual and the elk is probably upset about something. Bugling to call the elk in isn't as straightforward or effective under most conditions as published articles and demonstrator videos might lead you to believe— and it is almost never effective during the general rifle season. It generally works only when the elk are in the peak of the rut and undisturbed by hunting pressure. However, I can state from firsthand experience hard gained from almost forty seasons of plodding along the elk hunting trail after this elusive beast that bull elk might do anything. I've heard a bull bugle well after the rut, and, before I was able to put together a plan for a stalk and dive off into the hole where the bull was located, lost him to a hunter from another party already in position across the canyon, who answered the bugle. I was moving up the trail toward a better approach when I was surprised to hear the bull bugle again. I was not surprised to hear a single shot a little while later. Our packer saw the six-by-seven rack packed out to the river by the other party. This little tale stands out in my memory because it makes the point of the exception so well.

Usually, in my experience, bulls are most likely to stay cautious and avoid any life-threatening stunts. Except during the heat of the rut, the more experience a particular bull has had in past years with hunters that have bugled and missed, the more cautious he will be. An immature bull without cows will probably be more likely to answer a bugle, and then move toward its location, than a bull with cows. A bull that has managed to gather some cows is usually reluctant to leave them. He has the cows and he likes the tactical situation as it is. The bugle of a herd bull should usually be translated as a warning for the intruder to stay away. The herd bull is usually more inclined to move off, herding the cows away to separate them from the intruder.

A couple of particular points are of interest to the trophy hunter: A bull with cows is not always a trophy; and the old, experienced herd bull that is a trophy will probably not be inclined to leave the company of the cows that he's rounded up and go out to meet a challenger. If the bugling hunter is too convincing in producing the sound of another big bull, the trophy bull may leave the area and take the herd of cows with him to avoid a showdown. Fighting won't be that bull's objective; breeding the cows will be. This is one of those situations where a cow call may be more effective in bringing a bull in than a bugle. The aggressive tone, or not, of the terminal grunts of a herd bull's bugle is usually the tip-off of his next move.

The trophy hunter, whether using bow or rifle, will usually need to move in on the herd and go after the bull. It's not as preposterous as it sounds if the cows of the herd haven't reached a high level of disturbance. Effective camouflage and good work with a cow call will work to settle lookouts if they sense your approach. If you can sell the idea that you're another elk to the old cows, you might get away with a little noise, but if they pick up the human scent, they're usually gone. On occasion, the hunter gets a second chance. A herd that's disturbed, but not to the point of panic, may have scattered animals, including bulls, likely to be attracted to the reassuring version of the cow call. Other times, the best of efforts don't pan out—that's elk hunting, my friend. If you can't get in a good, ethical shot as they go, drop another coin in the slot and start a new game.

A bull will sometimes bugle if he or the herd is disturbed by a perceived threat. The bugle may have a pattern different from the one used during the rut, and won't coincide with the timing of the rut.

A hunting buddy and I once heard a bull bugling repeatedly over a period of more than an hour during the middle of the day. This particular occasion was much later than the peak of the rut, but hunting pressure was light in the area. That bugling was just the start of one of the more weird episodes of attempted stalking of my experience. It illustrates how sometimes an elk hunter will be in the right place, or close to the right place, at the right time, and have an unexpected distraction show up at the same time to throw the hunter's mindset over the bluff.

WES AND THE BULL AND THE BEAR

It was a good morning for elk hunting, and Wes and I were moving through a nice area that hadn't been hunted so far that season. Still, despite elk tracks and other signs that they regularly worked the area, we hadn't seen a thing as we sidehilled around high pockets of the mountain where little springs gave rise to the creeks below. The morning wore on to lunchtime (which tends to come a little early when all you need to do to arrange lunch is to stop and reach into your daypack). We sat down on a flat rock overlooking the next pocket.

Our focus immediately turned from lunch back to bull elk at the distant sound of something generally resembling an elk bugle up ahead at about our elevation. We relaxed as it repeated the same general notes. Apparently, some elk hunter up ahead had decided to take a break and kill some time during the middle of the day practicing on his elk bugle. From the sound, he could use the practice—but he was also going to clear all of the elk out of the area. He might have come through the area that we had just covered, which would explain the absence of elk. We decided to finish our lunch. Wes would stay on the rock where he would be able to spot any elk that the inept hunter might chase our way. I pulled back to catch a view in the other direction.

The bugling, or rather variations on the bugle-like sounds, continued intermittently for thirty minutes or so. I finished my snack and eased back up onto the rock to join Wes to plan our next move. I had just whispered something to the effect that I wondered if that guy was ever going to get any better when he threw into his efforts a series of high-pitched *eeeeeucks* that instantly yodeled down the scale of elk notes into a series of extra-low notes. And I mean really kettle-drum low. Unbelievably low. Inhumanly low.

I instantly sat straight up and gasped some utterance that was more profane than profound, which drew a funny look from Wes. "A human can't make a sound like that!" Wes joined me at full attention.

We quickly got our stuff together and moved out in the direction of the bugling. In a short time, we had covered the distance between ourselves and the general vicinity of the elk. I say "general vicinity," because the bull was moving around a little brush- and timber-covered point in a very irregular pattern. Up close, we could hear it making various sub-bugling bull elk sounds in between the full-up bugling variations. The vegetation was so thick that we couldn't get the bull in sight. I indicated to Wes that this was as good as it gets in heavy cover, with the bull moving about while keeping himself located by sound. There was still no sign of a herd with him, but I suspected that there would be some cows in the vicinity that would sound the alarm if they picked us up.

We quickly formed a plan for Wes to move in alone for the final stalk and to make the kill. A lone hunter usually has a much better chance of avoiding detection by sound or scent at close quarters than a pair of hunters. I would move back to keep my scent away from the elk and try to position myself to cut off the bull if I could tell from the sounds that he was attempting to circle back to check the scent of the intruder or to escape.

Wes moved in on the sound of the bull, keeping the breeze in his favor. As we'd expected, there were some cows in the vicinity, and they were upset— upset to the point that their preoccupation allowed him to move past two of them in an upright stance without setting off their alarms. He hadn't been able to get a look at the bull through the thick brush yet, but from the bawling and agitated bugling sounds Wes could tell that he was close. Another confused cow elk showed up at the same time without any reaction to Wes's presence.

It would be an understatement, but more polite than Wes's own graphic recollection, to say that he was startled when suddenly an *Ooooof . . . oof . . .*

ooof at his back announced the presence of the source of all of the commotion. A large black bear bounced down the hill in a menacing stiff-legged semi-charge in Wes's general direction. It was apparently attempting to move in on the elk herd using the same downhill approach into the wind that Wes was taking, and it didn't want any competition.

We regrettably have to digress for a moment and leave poor ole Wes there on the side of the mountain with the hair on the back of his neck standing up in order to understand the state of mind that influenced his next actions. Just before he left for the trip, a trusted advisor—his mother-in-law, to be precise—had given him a specific caution: "Don't turn your back on a black bear." The advice was prompted by a news story to the effect that, a few days earlier, a couple of missing elk hunters had been located in the Northern Rockies. From clues at the scene, it appeared that they had been field dressing an elk and had been surprised from behind by a black bear. It had somehow managed to dispatch the both of them, and then proceeded to devour the soft parts of both hunters and the partially field-dressed elk. Enough of the details had been included in the newscast to keep the ratings up, and anyone with a slight bit of knowledge concerning predators in general and black bears in particular could fill in the blanks. Wes, with a master's degree in wildlife science, understood more than most. He also knew that his advisor's admonishment didn't come from the naive perspective of a person who knew nothing about bears in the wild. She had spent some time in the same mountain range looking for black bears with a .300 Winchester Magnum slung on her shoulder and a bear tag in her pocket.

Trouble with a grizzly usually derives from their territorial instinct. If they perceive that they've taken care of you in that regard, a grizzly is through with you—hence the official advice to play dead. By contrast, a black bear, if it's so inclined and perceives that it can take you unaware, doesn't want to go to the trouble of dispatching you and then let you go to waste to be eaten by the ravens or the coyotes. There's no point in playing dead for a critter with disembowelment as the next item on its agenda. If a black bear perceives that you're aware of its presence, it either backs off, or sits down and looks to one side to signify that it's not looking for trouble, or backs off to circle around for another approach in hopes that you won't notice the next time. Wes was aware of all this. And it was all going through his mind as time stood still and this particular black bear in front of him just kept glaring at him with its beady little bear eyes and making disconcerting bear sounds: *oof . . . oof . . . oof.*

So Wes was having a little trouble maintaining his focus and, without turning his back on the bear, making the appropriate next move on the bull elk, which was still moving around making agitated sounds, attempting to keep track of the perceived threat on his flank, to get the cows organized and moving away, or to figure out what the old lead cows had decided to do. Finally, after about a millennium passed, according to Wes, with the bear still holding its ground and threatening to charge again, Wes turned his back on the bull elk to deal with the bear. Maybe the rifle's safety came off about that time, as Wes now recalls. Suddenly, the entire saga faded to black. The bear finally patterned Wes as a threat, rather than competition, and raced off back up the hill. The bull, with the rest of the elk herd, moved off down the side of the mountain in the other direction. Wes was left standing alone in the sudden stillness of the wilderness. When the hillside went silent, I had the feeling that a big party had happened and I must have missed it. I kept wondering when I was ever going to hear Wes make that shot.

Here's a final word of caution on bugling, based on my experience. If you sing out on the bugle call and mess up, which you'll likely do unless you've taken the time to practice a lot, you'll be a lot worse off than if you had remained silent. You'll just contribute to the education of the elk and locate yourself for every elk on the mountain. Squeeze-activated cow calls are a blessing for those of us without a lot of natural ability in the calling department.

PRODUCTS FOR STALKING
Bugles and Cow Calls

You'll usually find a limited selection of elk bugles and cow calls in larger outdoor stores. A better selection and training tapes are available from the major mail-order companies, through either their catalogs or outlets. I definitely recommend getting these training aids so that you know what you should sound like.

Most commercially available bugles and calls use some type of vibration source to create the original tone, which, in the case of bugles, is then amplified and changed in quality by passage through a tube. The vibration source may be a vibrating reed or elastic diaphragm. All operate on the same general principles as musical instruments. And just like with band instruments, some types are easier for a particular individual to master than others. No matter how good it sounds on the demonstrator video, you're going to ruin the effect if you always have a terminal gag and coughing fit at the end of each call. I would suggest that you try some of the different types before you settle on one that you'll invest a lot of time in learning to operate. Learning to operate one of these calls amounts to creating just the right pitch to put through the tube. Some of the best calls currently available, according to my expert bowhunting friends, are the Primos Hyper LIP single- and double-reed bugles and cow calls and the Carlton Squeeze Me Estrus Cow Call. Other good bugle selections include the Terminator and Bull Call, both by Primos. All these and more are available from Cabela's and other outdoor stores.

One type of elk bugle that may not show up in the stores or catalogs operates on a different principle. They're usually fabricated by the bugler, often with the assistance of another old elk hunter whose voice changed a long time ago. These bugles are made from the connection tubes for the gas space heaters you can get at the hardware stores of little country towns out where the houses don't all have central heating. You wrap the tube a couple of turns around a 2-inch or so diameter pipe and you're in business. You'll still need a recording of an elk bugle unless you've heard one and remember the correct pitch. You fiddle with the wrap and the pressure of the air that you blow until you have just the right pitch. All bugles of this type produce a sound that simulates the reedy, high-pitched (non-threatening) call of an immature bull. This often results in a more excited response from a herd bull than a bugle that mimics a mature bull.

Decoys

Several decoy designs have been developed for elk hunting. The most widely used ones are easily portable and quickly deployed, handy for fast-moving bowhunters who need to move to keep the wind on elk coming in to a bugle. Which brings to mind something else you should consider when selecting a decoy. It needs some provision to keep it from becoming airborne in the mountain breeze. If your clever decoy goes flying away, it tends to lose its desired effect on the elk.

Camo Face Paint and Covers

Generally included in bowhunting gear is some means to obscure the distinctive human face for close stalking. Whether you camouflage your face or not, you should still try to avoid the two-eyed predator stare.

THE END OF THE RUT

Toward the end of September and into the first two weeks of October, all of the breeding cows in the collected herds have been bred, and rutting activity gradually tapers off as the general rifle season approaches. Bulls will stay in the vicinity of the herds for a time, then drift off into hideouts to rest and feed to replenish their fat reserves in preparation for the fast-approaching winter. The techniques you need to use to stalk them are now determined by the level of disturbance of the elk.

STALKING ELK AT A LOW LEVEL OF DISTURBANCE

The techniques presented in this section apply when elk behavior is not influenced by heavy hunting pressure or the excitement of the rut. This is the usual situation during the latter part of the archery season and at the start of the rifle season. It can extend on through the rifle season if hunting pressure is light.

The usual technique of the bowhunter after the rut is to wait in a stand, either a tree stand or a well-hidden ground-level stand, along trails elk are using to move between feeding and resting areas. This usually allows the bowhunter to get a closer shot than any other strategy after bugling goes out of style with the end of the rut. The rifle hunter, with the advantage of greater range, will usually take a position that allows him or her to cover a larger area. Good locations are lookouts from timbered sides of canyons where the opposite broken timbered or brushy face can be watched using binoculars. To be successful, both bow and rifle hunters must be absolutely motionless while taking a stand (hunter-speak for waiting on a stand). In addition to the image of an entire elk, look for shades of russet early in the season or creamy tan late in the season, or the glint of sunlight reflecting off of antlers. Closely scan one small area, then another, then the original area again. Your mind will instinctively pick up a change in the image. It might be the bull! Long-range, unhurried rifle shots using a rest are the norm in this situation. This technique favors the beginner in that assuming the mindset to make the kill is straightforward since you have plenty of time. It's also good for hunters who physically can't run the ridges and brushy holes. On the other hand, it's a handy way for some outfitters and guides to keep hunters entertained without much effort on the outfitter's part even if the hunters involved can get around well enough for more effective techniques under prevailing conditions. When elk aren't inclined to move, it's time to consider some of the tactics that will be presented in the next chapter.

Conditions of low disturbance after the rut are also good for still-hunting quietly through possible resting areas of elk during the middle of the day. Note that the "still" part of the term refers to absence of noise rather than the absence of motion. Move along slowly into the wind as you look for bedded or standing elk. Visual clues might be a patch of russet in or through the green foliage, the glint of sunlight on an antler, the poorly defined bulk of a large animal through a screen of vegetation, or a set of symmetric, upward-pointing sticks above a brushy or grassy area. You might consider using yellow shooting glasses to improve your ability to pick up color variations, particularly if you wear prescription glasses. (You should take precautions to prevent fogging up your glasses with your warm breath if you get excited in this type of situation.) Listen for sounds of sticks breaking, rocks rolling, or muffled hoofbeats. Pay attention to your nose as well. The pungent odor of a bull during or just after the rut, once sensed, is never to be forgotten; if you smell it, immediately turn your attention into the wind.

Always be alert and ready to transition to making the kill. Even if you fail to see the elk before they jump up to move off, they might give you an opportunity for a shot just as they stand. Often, even after elk have moved off a short distance, they may pause to look back, depending upon whether or not their threat response is triggered. Camo clothing seems to help in this situation. Some experienced hunters and guides will also use a cow call in this situation. I have hunted with some old-timers who would let out a sharp, loud whistle to get elk to pause before they took off. It sometimes works to get a bull to stop and look, particularly if he hasn't made up his mind as to what you are.

A good technique at the beginning of the rifle season is to move along a ways, then pause for a time to watch routes elk might be using to evade or escape other hunters. Masters of this technique can move with absolute stealth from one location to blend in with another. They're true "moving standers" and can utilize the advantages of both stillhunting and waiting on stands. It's best to watch from a vantage point off of the trail the elk might use, but you never can tell. I took my elk of a lifetime (at least up to now) after moving through the herd on a collision course until I intercepted the bull at the end of the herd of over a dozen cows. (These techniques start to merge with the tactics discussed in detail in the next chapter.)

Stillhunting can be productive for bowhunters as well as for rifle hunters, particularly when elk are not disturbed. During the middle of the day, they tend to hold to resting areas, and are susceptible to approach to within bowhunting ranges. You might as well give it a try; they're not going to be moving by your stand anyway, and you could use a change of scenery. If you are stealthy, keep the wind in your favor, and, of course, manage to stay lucky throughout a stalk, you can get within shooting distance of bedded elk. If you are noticed by elk but haven't startled them into a panic, you may be able to move in on them by casually dropping to all fours or using a duckwalk and moving confidently and steadily forward. This move should be instinctive and automatic—and it will be after you've forced yourself to initiate such a bold move the first time or two. Don't give the old cows time to think about it too long. They'll always decide that it's a good idea to take off if they think about it long enough. Take care not to give them the full binocular predator stare or make any kind of eye contact. Make your draw from some kind of crouching position to avoid presenting a recognizable human stance.

You may encounter moving elk at any time while stillhunting with a bow. Always think ahead and have a mental plan of an appropriate response ready. As we'll cover in the chapter on making the kill, concentrate on the shot location, not on the antlers and not on the trees you may need to shoot between. I'll drill these concepts home later, but they're worth mentioning here because it's particularly difficult to get in focus for the kill when you've just been startled.

STALKING WHEN ELK ARE SOMEWHAT DISTURBED AND WARY

The techniques and methods of the successful elk hunter undergo changes, some obvious, some subtle, as the level of disturbance of the elk being hunted increases. Clues about the level of disturbance are taken from the behavior of the herd. You can note a great deal of difference in the behavior of herds at different levels of disturbance. Resting elk herds at a low level of disturbance may be easily observed and will appear to be relaxed. The herd may be found in an area of shady overhead cover, with some animals lying on the ground resting with their heads up looking casually about, while others are standing or walking about in the general vicinity grazing. The bull will be walking about the area and may even bugle for no apparent reason from time to time as if to warn off possible intruders.

Initial indications of disturbance—other than the fact that the elk are much less likely to be observed at all—are that elk will be inclined to stay under cover, but will move away along established routes if disturbed by a perceived threat. You may find fresh tracks indicating that they've moved out ahead of you. This is the prevalent situation at the start, or just after the start, of the general rifle season—after the first few days if hunting pressure is light, and after the first few minutes if it is heavy. Elk that have been hard hunted in seasons past reach this state of disturbance before the season even opens as the hunting parties begin arriving in the area. The normal feeding, moving, and resting cycle of the elk has been disrupted to some extent by continued disturbances of hunters to the point that they have gone to a primarily nocturnal movement and feeding schedule. They will hold in resting areas under cover during the daylight hours. If an intruder is sensed, escape usually takes the form of deliberate movement, as a herd, away from the intruder along established trails.

A progressively higher level of disturbance will result in the cows of the herd as a group hiding absolutely motionless under low vegetation, with the bull also bedded down, either in closer cover in the general vicinity or in the middle of the herd of cows. If disturbed, the entire herd may be spooked into a panicked headlong stampede, with individuals scattering in all directions.

When elk have been disturbed, the techniques of elk hunting diverge from those used in whitetail hunting. As discussed earlier, the techniques used to hunt undisturbed elk are combinations of stillhunting and waiting on stands for moving elk, very similar to the techniques of whitetail hunting. If elk have been disturbed, stillhunting by an individual hunter is usually not a productive tactic. When stillhunting for deer, the usual uniform distribution of the deer makes the odds of an encounter good. The hunter hopes for a shot before the deer bolts from cover after it senses a human presence by scent or with its relatively short-range vision. The whitetail, when forced from its hiding place, will usually move off for a short distance from the immediate threat and seek cover again. The hunter usually gets another chance, or will come across another deer for another try. In contrast, if elk are alarmed to the point that they flee the threat, they're often gone too far for practical pursuit; moreover, all of the elk in the herd—meaning all of the elk in that vicinity—are gone. Classic stillhunting techniques essentially move game from cover by the presence of the hunter. In the case of elk, they are a one-shot throw of the dice, and a low-percentage throw at that, considering the acute long-range vision of elk. Better luck (and better technique) next time! Experienced elk hunters will sometimes refer to would-be elk hunters who hunt disturbed elk using whitetail tactics as "whitetail hunters."

When hunting in crowded situations—like opening day of the season in an easily accessed area—an experienced elk hunter hunting alone will often use a tactic in which the "uninformed masses" are utilized as drivers. Elk will move from areas of high hunting pressure toward less disturbed sanctuaries, even if the area of lower hunting pressure looks like a sorry place as elk habitat. Hunting pressure translates to an immediate threat to elk, and security becomes the main driver of elk behavior rather than long-term subsistence. The appearance of prime elk habitat is transformed. Cover and removal from the presence of the threat become the most important characteristics of habitat. The smart hunter sets up along a likely route (that's the route with the most cover) and waits for the elk to move past. If the crowds start showing up around the hunter's stand, it's time to move into the area where the elk are hiding and slowly, quietly move along looking for elk, which may be found sneaking away from pressure or lying in cover. A very occasional quiet cow call may get a response from a separated elk—or an inexperienced elk hunter, the type that has been known to take a shot at suspicious, or interesting, sounds. Use caution above all else in crowded situations.

STALKING WHEN ELK ARE HIGHLY DISTURBED

Highly disturbed elk are very wary, only freely moving at night for normal activities. They will be hiding, resting under cover during the day, and must be closely pushed to move; and when approached, they'll panic into full flight in any direction. This situation develops when elk feel that they are directly threatened over an extended period of time. Their response is to leave the area or hole up, ready to take full flight, possibly completely out of the area. It seems that different elk have different thresholds for this condition. The entire herd will reach this point if they are continually hard-pressed by lots of hunters. This can occur in areas of easy road access and liberal issue of tags, which invite large numbers of casual hunters. It can also develop in an outfitter's area that is heavily booked over a period of time. Elk response may be to leave the area and migrate to a more remote location with less pressure. And it's surprising where they might go. They can leave heavily timbered areas for cut-over areas with small, isolated areas of brush, for privately held agricultural or ranching areas where permits or tags are not issued, or hard, dry areas with little feed. The heavy pressure is often associated with short hunting seasons, so the elk just wait it out for the short run in the poor habitat, then return to their normal range.

The entire herd seldom reaches this point if cow permits are not issued for the area. The cows soon learn that they're not the objects of attention. On the other hand, the bulls catch on that they are. However, it seems that the bulls are not inclined to leave the area if the rest of the herd stays. Their response is to separate from the immediate area of the rest of the herd and to hide out in a small area of thick cover with poor access. They prefer unrestricted escape routes in all directions with plenty of brush—which means noisy access by clumsy intruders. That would be us.

This entire situation is referred to in summary as "hard hunting" and about the only way to address it is to use the locating and stalking techniques discussed in this book. If the entire herd has moved, you have to cover the fringes of the area you are in, or go into adjacent areas, assuming hunting is permitted there. It's often hard for experienced deer hunters to believe, but if the herd feels threatened enough to move, it's gone. Unlike with deer, you won't always find the elk hiding around your immediate area, regardless of how hard you may look. As far as elk are concerned, if they're gone, they're gone.

The successful hunters under these circumstances are the persistent hunters. And a good package of instincts (example: the "speed kills" two-second sling-to-battery transition, covered in Chapter 12) and intuition (knowing what good habitat looks like to elk under different conditions) is very valuable. That package can be either your own, or one that comes with an old, slow-moving hunter, if you can get one to come along. A team of two or three die-hard hunters working together seems to be the most productive general plan. They'll try to cover a lot of area in an effort to locate elk, then use coordinated tactics on a small scale when elk can be located in areas of cover. If fresh sign is found but no elk, look for hiding places close by. If old sign is found but no elk, look farther away, maybe on the other side of what appears to be a natural boundary, like in another drainage. If no sign is found, make a big move. Note that if it's still early in the season and you can get a herd moving but can't see a bull with the cows, the bull will likely be somewhere in the general vicinity, probably with a cow or two that are still of interest to him.

WORKING IN CLOSE ON A HERD BULL WITH COWS

Both rifle hunters and bowhunters should be aware that, within the defensive structure of the herd, the cows are always on the lookout, using their senses of sight, smell, and hearing to scan for any threat. While feeding, they instinctively take turns to pause and look around both their immediate vicinity and all distant slopes in their line of sight. Anything that arouses suspicion brings on the sharp bark of the danger alarm as the cow continues to stare at whatever drew her attention. All of the other cows follow the stare, and if they don't like what they see, they each let out a yap and start walking around, heads up in alarm. If they all agree that it's a threat, or take the cue from an old lead cow who thinks it's a threat, they're gone in a trot, usually before you get a look at the bull, if he's around.

If you're seen at a distance, your best technique to avoid detection by the entire herd is to remain motionless and to trust in your camo. When you've been seen at close range—a common problem for the bowhunter when attempting to move in for a kill—you should try not to spook them, which is tricky, but it can be done.

Working in close with the bow is characterized by deliberate speed and subterfuge. Assume a form they can't perceive as a human. Move using a crawl on all fours or duckwalk, penguin masquerade, or alligator crawl (low crawl to the military types). Some hunters use a cow call in this situation. Never make predator-prey eye contact before you're ready to strike. All prey animals panic on seeing a predator stare from a set of forward-pointing eyes. This pertains to elk from 10 to 400 yards; remember, they're not deer from the woodlands, they're plains animals that instinctively look for danger at long ranges.

When moving in on a bull through an area where cows are scattered about, your best chance is to get close for the shot before your scent collects in the surrounding area. If one elk picks up your scent, they probably all will, and there isn't much you can do about it. If you can't quickly pick out the herd bull for a shot before they're gone, they're gone, and so is the bull. You can sometimes buy yourself a little time—if you're close to the herd and if they haven't completely spooked and if you're lucky—by going into the wolf, bear, or penguin masquerade. If the elk see you moving and you don't look like a human, you might get their minds on what they're seeing rather than what they're smelling. Maybe. The main point I would make to the bowhunter in this situation is not to let yourself be rushed into a shot that you will regret later.

If elk hear you without scenting or seeing you, they may simply ignore a single stick breaking or rock rolling. Some experts use cow calls that they keep in their mouths while stalking for just such an occasion. They use them to give a reassuring chirp that it's just another elk out there stumbling around. Those of us who aren't experts with cow calls are usually better off leaving the elk to their own imagination as to what's out there.

Be aware that bull elk will instinctively use cows as cover. The cows of the herd are usually the first to sense danger and can sound the alarm to end a stalk before it can get started. If you manage to work your way through the sentry system and close in for the kill, particularly at close range, the herd bull may use cows as direct screens in making his escape.

The next Tale illustrates the slickest use of cows for cover that I have ever encountered during my quest for the Big One. It occurred in an area where elk routinely encounter humans during all seasons of the year, and where cow permits hadn't been issued for years. The elk in the area didn't automatically take off in a panic at the sight of a human, and the cows were particularly nonchalant in regard to humans. All the bulls to some extent, and especially the old herd bulls, were a different story. This bull elk tactic is probably a variation on the principles of the "selfish herd," the term used to describe the groups of grazers that attempt to escape rather than fight predators. It's up to each individual in the herd to escape, and on the open plains, the only place to hide is behind another member of the herd—so the least capable members are forced to the edges of the herd.

TALE OF THE BLURRY EIGHT-LEGGED SIX-POINT

This Tale took place in an area with very little terrain relief. It's usual in this type of terrain for the dominant bull to gather all of the cows from a large area into a single herd. Lesser mature bulls will follow the cows to challenge the dominant bull, and spikes will hang around the fringe areas outside of the herd in hopes of an opportunity to move in on a receptive cow while the big bull is preoccupied with a more serious challenger.

At the time of this story, the rut was well along and should have been over, but the composition of the herd was still what it had been during the peak of the rut. The herd bull was focusing on the few young cows yet to be bred rather than trying to keep the entire herd of cows together under close control.

Before daylight, I moved out from the camper in the general direction of bugling I had heard during the night. My general plan was to head toward a clear-cut area in that direction where the elk might be feeding at night. As I approached the general area of the clear-cut through a screen of fairly thick timber, I began to encounter scattered elk cows milling about without any particular direction. As I picked up the movement of an elk, I would stand motionless against a tree or area of thick brush until the elk moved past, then move on toward the clear-cut, hoping to see a bull. It seemed that the cows I encountered were paying little attention to me, but I nevertheless took care to avoid any quick or threatening movements in case one of them saw me first. As I moved on, the elk continued to move past me in the opposite direction, now with little groups of three or four mixed in with the individuals and pairs. My interest was turning to excitement as I realized that I was moving through the entire herd, and that the herd bull might show at any time. My sense of urgency was also rising with each passing second. My experience told me that the longer this episode lasted, the more likely it was that it would end in a major stampede instead of a killing shot. The little morning breeze that favored me could change at any instant and it would be game over for this stalk! I had no way of knowing where the bull was in relation to me. Had I slipped past all of the cows and worked myself in between the cows and the bull? Had the bull slipped past me out of sight on the other side of the cows, or even behind me? Both of these possibilities had happened before.

My problems compounded as I came to the edge of an old logging road that ran transverse to my line of travel. If I caught the attention of a cow while trying to sneak across the road, there wouldn't be anything to freeze against to obscure my great big upright human form, and dropping to all fours to assume the identity of a bear while under observation might not be too convincing. I paused at the edge of the cover just short of the road. Maybe the bull was trailing the herd of cows and would step out into the road and give me a chance of a clear shot.

Then the problem of deciding what to do next, along with what little control I had over events, was taken out of my hands. The bull didn't step out into the road; a cow did, and looked straight at me. I looked back, which wasn't a good idea. Our stares locked, and the elk instantly patterned the two-eyed stare of a predator. A second cow emerged from the trees onto the road as the first broke across the road to head toward the rest of the herd. Then, on the edge of my peripheral vision, I caught a glimpse of what I had been looking for: a big, herd-bull-sized, six-point set of antlers. The cow in the road just ahead of the bull moved to cross the road. The bull started to follow as my rifle swung up. I picked up the full outline of the antlered bull in the crosshairs of the scope as he moved out into the road.

But something was wrong with the picture. Double vision? Stress-induced brain failure? I struggled to unscramble the image and finally realized that I was looking at two superimposed elk bodies with one big set of antlers carried by eight fast-trotting elk feet. The bull had pulled alongside the second cow and was moving exactly in tandem with her!

An aside. There are two possible endings to this tale. The first ending—the correct ending and, I think, the ending that would happen if I found myself in the same circumstances today—would be short and simple: No shot. No shot opportunity; no shot taken. End of Tale. But this Tale took place many seasons ago, and I wanted to try for a lucky shot. I'm telling what did happen on that morning many seasons ago in the hope that you won't try it. In this no-shot situation, I attempted to make a shot, and, in fact, I was fortunate enough to make a very lucky shot under the circumstances. It was a clean miss.

As my brain focused on the now unscrambled image of the eight-legged apparition picking up speed as it crossed the road, it was apparent that there was a lot of bull elk exposed around the cow being used as cover. I had reached such a focused mindset that everything was moving in slow motion and I had time to look for a shot location. In general-interest hunting publications like the ones I read too much of at the time, you'll see diagrams put together by outdoor writers and illustrators with good imaginations illustrating various (questionable) shots, one example being the spinal cord shot. And this shot—a shot at the bull elk's spinal cord over the back of the cow—was the one that my desperate mind conjured up in that instant just before the rifle went off. Both elk cleared the road before I recovered from the recoil of the .338. I followed as they trotted through the trees behind the rest of the herd.

And followed. And followed. No elk dropped; no blood showed along their trail. My reactions came in waves. I was disappointed at first, when the bull didn't drop. My spirits lifted as I came to full realization of the downside of the stunt I had attempted, and I was thankful that the wrong elk didn't drop. As I followed the elk, my rationality returned in stages, and I took a second look at the still-fresh image in my mind of the sight picture when the shot went off. I had held the crosshairs well above the back of the cow and maybe slightly above the spinal column of the bull—but there's a good bit of bull above the spinal column, and he hadn't flinched. A hit would have produced considerable shock and some sign of damage. It dawned on me that at the range of the shot, a little over 50 yards, my rifle was sighted to shoot at least a couple of inches high. I had held a little high, and the shot had actually gone a little higher than I held.

My last glimpse of the bull was through a little opening far ahead as he left the area without any sign of damage.

Another incident illustrating the tactic of bull elk using cows for cover occurred once when I was hunting in the company of a master guide who is good with a bugle. It's a pretty good example of the animals' sharp sense of hearing and their practice of keeping cows and other cover between them and the hunter.

A BIG SIX-POINT ANSWERS THE BUGLE—
BULL COMING IN AT A GALLOP

Gene and I were moving along a well-used elk trail around the side of a timbered slope when he decided to sound off with one of his patented elk bugle tunes produced by his professional-grade coiled gas stove tubing bugle. Gene speaks several dialects of elk using various types of bugles, including cupped hands. I don't know the exact elk-to-human translation of the particular notes he blew on that particular occasion, but it must have been something to the effect that "I'm a skinny little raghorn spoilin' for a fight—and your mama's in your herd—and your urine spray just ain't cuttin' it this mornin', cream cake!" Or somethin' like that. Whatever it was, an infuriated bull over a mile away instantly screamed and bawled back an answer; I didn't know the translation of that one either, but I could tell that he was big and he was mad. We started moving in the direction of the bull at a near trot through the timber, our objective being to get position on his route of approach. In just a few minutes, as we were crossing a steeply sloping brushy opening in the timber where a huge old tree had fallen, my fearless guide and I both about jumped out of our boots. An unearthly-sounding bull elk scream shook the leaves, and us too—and it was right there.

We froze in our tracks, pulses pounding, as a dozen head of elk crashed at full speed through the shoulder-high brush and swirled around us in a panic as they sensed our presence. The brush was just tall enough to almost completely screen the milling elk, allowing us an occasional glimpse of russet. Trying to regain control and look around for antlers over the brush at the same time, I caught a glimpse of movement up the slope. I turned toward a surreal image of Gene's head framed by a huge set of elk antlers. As he stood slightly upslope and 4 or 5 feet to my right, still looking in the direction of the bull's last bellow, Gene was unaware of the bull standing upslope about 30 yards, its head back so that only its eyes and antlers appeared over the top of the brush, checking us out. In the short time that it took for me to recover from the shock and surprise of that image, roughly throw my companion out of the way (at least a 10-foot free flight according to him), and get the old .300 into battery, the elk disappeared. No shot.

I instantly took off at a sprint up the slope, fighting my way through the brush. I should make the point in lame defense of my sanity that a human running at top speed can keep up with an elk for a short sprint when both begin from a standing start. Elk aren't particularly fast out of the chute. That is, of course, on flat ground with no brush. Under the prevailing conditions of this particular race, I was a good distance behind when I broke out of the brush in time to get a look at the bull as he went up the slope, screened by a thick tree. I ran to the point where I cleared that tree, and caught a glimpse of the rear end of the bull just as it was screened by another tree farther up the slope. Gene cleared the brush behind me to watch the rest of the show. As I moved to clear a shot past the intervening tree, the bull, with me in sight, would move in the opposite direction to keep the tree between us. I would move one way; the bull would move the other, all the time moving farther up the slope. The bull cleared the crest of the slope just out of my sight, stopped, and let go with the most obscene-sounding elk bugle I've ever heard. Moving over the ridge, he crossed paths with another of my hunting companions, evaded him as well, and went on over the ridge into the next drainage, still bugling.

As a herd moves along a regularly used trail under normal circumstances, the herd bull will often move along with the cows, but off to one side if the trail crosses an open area. In some situations, the bull may deliberately shove the cows along ahead to indicate any danger in his way. If they show alarm, he'll veer off the trail to investigate from a safe vantage point. If you should accidentally intercept a herd that scatters at the disturbance, you may have a couple of seconds before the old cows get their collective thoughts together and head out along the best escape route. Use those seconds wisely. Don't waste time or attention on all of those cows—look everywhere else, particularly toward the rear and off to one or the other side of the bunch. Where are those antlers?

WORKING IN CLOSE ON A SOLITARY BIG BULL AFTER THE RUT

Toward the middle of the general season, the herd bull will finish up with the young late-bloomer cows and pull away from the herd to retreat to a more detached hideout. All you need to do is find that one "hidey hole," the "bull nest." I reached this point in the discussions of locating techniques, and left it there with the promise that we would get back to the particulars of how to stalk a bull in this situation. Here goes.

The rifle hunter encounters close hunting less frequently than the bowhunter, usually only in surprise encounters. One common case is a chance meeting while both elk and hunter are moving; another is walking up on a bedded elk. The bed may be a normal bed-down place, or the bull hideout introduced previously.

By the time you've figured out you've found a "bull's nest," the bull is likely looking at you, so keep cool and try not to spook it. Your intuition should scream, "No quick moves!" Immediately go into stalk mode. One school of thought says: With deliberate movements, bring the rifle to battery. Using deliberate, slow rotations of your entire body so that you are ready to shoot in the direction that you are looking, carefully scan the entire area. I'm with the school of thought that says: No threatening moves without positive, absolute identification of the desired elk—then make the kill faster than the elk can react so that he doesn't have time to pattern you as a threat.

Try not to stare at a specific place too long. Be aware of any quick movement out of the corner of your eye. As noted above, be ready to switch to the kill mindset when the bull jumps, rather than jumping out of your own skin. If nothing happens, just stand there a minute and get used to the idea—that's the polite way of telling you to take a little time to get over the shakes. Now, after getting a grip on yourself, get a grip on the situation. Assess the area to locate the likely escape routes and make a plan for your response. Then just stand there and check the entire area once more for any visual clue, like a limb with a different texture or shape. Antlers are usually easier to see than a mostly hidden bulk of an elk's resting body.

If there's still no action or clue, again, there are two schools of thought as to the next action. One group says that if you could improve your situation regarding wind direction and visibility from another angle, back out and come in from the better direction. If two hunters are together, one stays in place while the other backs out to come in from another approach. The idea is that the bull will be very reluctant to attempt to slip out from his safe location. I'm with the other group that says that you usually don't improve your situation that much and the bull is likely to slip out while you stumble around in the brush. The best approach is to move on into the hideout a few feet at a time, carefully looking around from the new location each time you stop. If two hunters are together, they attempt to spread out and approach along parallel paths.

CONCLUDING THOUGHTS ON STALKING BULLS LATE INTO THE SEASON

The big old herd bulls may stay in their bull nest in a state of exhaustion and withdrawal from the hormonal excitement until the onset of heavy snow. In rough high country they may become trapped and die in their hideouts. I've chanced across the big racks early in the next fall—or the one after that. Gnawed by rodents but still attached to the skulls, they have a tale to tell if you examine them. Absorb the feelings of that place, ghosts and all. That feeling will come again while the live bull yet to die in the winter to come is still there. If that feeling isn't in that place, then I move on to another place to find the one likely to die in the coming snow if I don't get him first.

Lesser bulls, and sometimes the big ones, start to herd together as the snow flies and they prepare to move to the winter range below. Small-scale tactics by two or three hunters laboring through the snow have a good chance of success with these gathered bulls. Your chances improve if your timing is good and you brave the snows during very late seasons and catch migrations of great numbers of elk moving to lower elevations. Stamina never trumps luck in the late season, but it's more reliable. And the disturbance level of the elk progressively drops as fewer encounters with hunters occur. Tends to improve the luck aspect for the die-hard few hunters remaining out there. It's cold and hard work, but, as some of us say time and again, it's still better than being in camp—or back at your day job in the flatlands!

CHAPTER 8

Introduction to Tactics

Several cooperative techniques involving two or more hunters are commonly used when hunting elk at an elevated level of disturbance. These organized strategies are often referred to collectively as elk hunting tactics. Tactics can be applied over a wide range of elk behavior in response to disturbance, but most of them are aimed at elk that prefer to remain under cover during daylight hours unless deliberately pushed by hunters. This behavior is usually a response to a threat such as hunting pressure, or, more rarely, an approaching storm. Under unusual circumstances, elk may lie up in response to a physical discomfort such as hot weather.

First, some definitions: For the purposes of this book, techniques are individual hunting skills; tactics are deliberate, organized practices of two or more hunters designed to improve chances of success by working together.

Tactics can be easier understood if first presented in their most general form rather than with specifics of terrain and hunter movement. I'll start with the "purest" concepts of tactics, then translate them into practical situations and examples.

THE CONCEPTS OF ELK HUNTING TACTICS

With elk hunting tactics, two or more hunters can make their locating and stalking efforts more effective than if each worked separately. Both locating and stalking require movement to find and approach the elk. When working together hunters may be able to position themselves, or at least some of their party, to their advantage for a shot during locating and stalking. This is more important in elk hunting than in other big game hunting, since when you spook the herd it's gone; you don't get a second chance like with deer.

THE THEORY OF ELK HUNTING TACTICS

Elk hunting tactics involve relative movement of two or more hunters to create shooting opportunities when disturbed elk aren't moving from cover of their own volition during legal shooting hours. The most basic, and most common, strategy uses a moving hunter (or more than one) to push elk toward one or more concealed stationary hunter or hunters. The objective is to create shooting opportunities for the stationary hunter, but the elk movement created can often lead to opportunities for the moving hunters as well, when elk set in motion by one mover cross in front of another mover. Organization and control of multiple moving hunters will increase the chances of shots for the movers. This control can be achieved by cooperation, with moving hunters keeping track of each other, normally by sight, or by coordination, with moving elements moving according to a prearranged plan. More movers or more complicated plans may be involved, but the additional elements are always simply multiples of the basic arrangement. There should always be a recovery or default plan in case movement becomes confused. Cautions should be issued to prevent any dangerous developments.

Tactics based on cooperation involve two hunters moving together, usually side by side, in a cooperative effort. The hunters control their formation by keeping each other in sight, staying far enough apart that they are just in sight of each other, either continuously or intermittently. In rough terrain with lots of cover, they won't be too far apart; in less rough and more open areas, they can spread farther apart to cover more area. Each hunter adjusts his or her pace as they proceed so that one doesn't get too far ahead of the other. This tactic is effective when stationary elk under cover are going to remain under cover unless forced to move; they may be located as they move away from one moving hunter and cross the path of the other. This situation is common when elk may be expected to attempt to escape by moving either up- or downslope to cross the ridge into the adjacent drainage or to get into thick cover at the bottom of the drainage. The moving hunters will be dispersed up and down along the slope, moving at constant elevations across the face of the slope—the ridge line on one side, the creek at the bottom of the hill on the other. In order for the moving hunters to get shooting opportunities, they need enough visibility so that elk made to move don't pass unseen between adjacent movers. With more than two hunters, you can increase your effectiveness by placing hunters with less experience or familiarity with the terrain next to more experienced

Checking for fresh tracks at a mineral lick, or around a wallow. Elk trails will converge in the vicinity of either. Elk trails often pass by the wallows, and when pushed by drivers, the elk will still go by the wallows unless panicked.

hunters, who can act as point guides for them. The point guides set the pace for forward movement based on their experience.

Variations on this tactic with several hunters moving in a line together may appear to involve more than just the basic model, but each hunter can cooperate only with the two hunters on either side, and then only as long as they stay together. Practically speaking, attempts to maintain cooperation in a long line of hunters using only visual control usually fail. The line tends to quickly break apart into pairs, if it stays together at all. Wide lines of separated elements can effectively move together, but it's nearly always by means of coordination rather than cooperation.

Tactics based on coordination involve two or more hunters moving according to a predetermined plan. The plan may be to arrive at a specific place or cross a particular terrain feature at a given time, to move along predetermined routes to meet at a given time and/or location, or to converge on a location to be determined by events during the hunt. The intent of the movement may be to locate and move elk that would otherwise remain stationary and under cover so that one of the hunters can get into position, or to move the elk into position in order to create a chance to make a kill. Sometimes the plan includes a response to a particular event: for instance, to converge on any bugling bull, or to take a stand along a likely escape route for a time after hearing shots from a given direction (then come and help the shooter with the field dressing if no escaping bull comes by).

This set of tactics is effective when elk are not moving or specifically located but are likely to be concealed in a particular area and will likely move along a known route or past a known point if disturbed. Either the hunters may move separately by different routes to converge on the same area, or one hunter may move to a predetermined location by a route selected to avoid disturbance and then take a stand, in the expectation that elk disturbed by the other moving hunter(s) will be forced to move past the stand.

Again, it may be noted that this kind of tactic in the most basic form involves only two hunters. In practice, it may appear to be more complex. For instance, when the terrain of the area forms two or more likely escape routes, they may be covered by different stationary hunters; in other plans, some of the stationary hunters may fall in with the moving ones to drive toward other stationary hunters farther along the route. Uninitiated newcomers to the group may mistakenly assume that the old-timers in the bunch are communicating in mysterious ways, but all of these movements are simply different exercises of the same basic tactic set being repeated in a series of separate plans. The same scheme may have been exercised by the same group for years so that they're very proficient at it. And the hunters' intuition from the shared experience helps them predict how elk along the route will react under different conditions and circumstances.

The specific terrain features of a given location will determine whether multiple stands should be occupied at the same time to intercept elk forced to move by a single moving hunter, or the stationary hunter should move to occupy different locations in a sequence. This can take the form of covering a series of passes across a long ridge running parallel to a long drainage that the moving hunter or hunters drive along from one end to the other. This approach is often used to great advantage when a single stationary hunter element can't effectively cover all likely escape routes. In other situations, it is impossible for a single individual to cover a likely escape route that is wide and brush- or timber-covered, and multiple hunters can be stationed there.

The moving hunters may operate in either a cooperative or coordinated approach. In the first case, control is by sight; in the second, control may be according to a plan to pass selected terrain features as checkpoints at a predetermined time. If a moving hunter arrives at a checkpoint too early, he or she waits until the planned time before moving on.

THE PRACTICE OF ELK HUNTING TACTICS
Now we'll translate the general concepts of tactics into elk camp jargon and practical situations. The common term used to collectively refer to

elk hunting tactics is the "drive," sometimes used with an adjective that tells what kind of drive it is. On its own, the term "drive" refers to movement by one group of hunters through an area with the purpose of getting the stationary and hidden elk up and moving toward another, often stationary, group of hunters. When an adjective is added to the name of the drive, it usually gives a broad suggestion of the strategy of the drive.

If the elk are likely to exit the area through a constricted location that can be covered by a single hunter, the drive is called "dotting the i." If the way out of the area being driven involves a broad exit or a group of likely exits, it's called "crossing the t." (Both are actually the same concept, but have a different appearance due to terrain features.)

"Converging drives" involve two groups of moving hunters who generally approach each other through an area that will channel the movement of elk ahead of the converging hunters into the other party. This kind of drive is used when an area is narrow in the middle but opens up on either end.

The "surround" is a drive variation where hunters approach the area where elk are thought to be located from many directions in order to block the elk's escape. If it's unlikely that elk will attempt to escape in a particular direction, that direction doesn't need to be covered. In the unlikely (but sometimes encountered) case where elk won't leave a route on either side, a surround can be accomplished by only two hunters.

"Driving and crossing" is a very common technique where hunters move through an area side by side with the intent that any elk they get moving will likely move across their general line of travel and cross the path of another member of the party to the side. It's typical for the line of hunters to move "sidehill," each member moving along at a constant elevation, with the line (more or less) straight up and down the slope. Standers will be located on vantage points on the crest of the ridge or around the rim of the mesa above, looking for a long-range unobstructed shot.

Directions of travel are planned, based on the wind and the possible escape routes of the elk, to improve chances of a shot. Obviously, hunters must take care with any of these drives to avoid shots in the direction of other members of the hunting party. Especially great care must be taken if a hunter in a moving line attempts a shot at an elk passing between the moving hunters.

The drive tactic amounts to one hunter or group of hunters (called the "drivers," "beaters," "bird dogs," "young bunch," or "ridge runners") getting elk moving so that they move past another hunter or hunters (the "standers," "sitters," or perhaps "old fat guys") so that they can take a shot. These roles correspond to those of the peasants and aristocrats in the hunting methods used in ancient and medieval times, but outfitters usually don't mention this association because it discourages volunteers for the driver group.

Driving is one of those simple ideas more difficult in implementation than in concept, at least in outfitter pack camps. You can expect to see any number of takeoffs on the basic drive model when hunting with outfitters. Outfitters are in the entertainment business and this is one activity where all of the booked hunters can participate, regardless of physical capability. The results of a drive are usually pretty entertaining, if nothing else. These operations often do not go according to plan, but it's better than sitting under a tree when nothing's moving otherwise.

The outfitter drive usually has several of the physically fit types, accompanied by guides, move through a constricted area in an attempt to get all of the elk they encounter moving. They are, of course, actually engaged in fast-moving stillhunting, and it's not unusual for the "bird dogs" to get all of the shooting on one of these operations. Drives as practiced in outfitter camps usually deteriorate as the drivers move along because they fail to grasp the concept of cooperation and lose sight of each other. Then they're just moving along through the woods as individuals, or, in some cases, individuals accompanied by guides. Due to the terrain and lack of sense of direction on the part of the drivers, the driver line is seldom straight or uniformly spaced. Elk tend to slip through the line, and some smart old bulls simply stay put and let the line pass them by. I have been on some of these operations where drivers were sharp enough to notice bulls standing in cover and shoot them where they stood. The result of all this is that the standers usually fail to get any shooting due to the lack of coordination of the driving. Sometimes, however, the standers actually do get the shot and take elk from brushy slopes as they move ahead of drivers who were unaware that elk were moving ahead of them.

This situation brings to mind an important safety point: You *must* be careful with these drives to prevent accidents. Usually the good, experienced outfitter arranges the operation so that the drivers remain out of the line of sight of the standers. The standers may be in actual stands along trails but more often are on outlooks so that they can cover a large area. Everyone involved usually has an empty cartridge case to use as a signal whistle. A little toot on the whistle avoids startling anyone you might walk up on, and prevents any rifles from being pointed in your direction. Usually, some old hunter makes a point of telling the

A driver checking for fresh tracks at a creek crossing. The driver should stand absolutely still when stopped, turning his or her entire body around to check other directions. Check for any sign of elk movement all the way around— drivers have a tendency to look only in the direction of the drive, or along the trail they might be following.

The driver continues the drive, striding off (at a fast stillhunt pace) along the general direction of the drive. The technique is to move at a fast pace through cover, then pause to check for moving elk before leaving the vegetation to cross an open area.

young drivers that if you hear a clickitty, clickitty sound followed by a boom in the distance, don't worry. It was a high-velocity bullet going over, and it's already past. A serious note of advice: When playing the role of a driver in one of these little skits involving standers I don't know, I am inclined to wear some hunter orange even if it's not required by the state Game Department. And all players need to wear a thick smear of situational awareness at all times.

Now, as promised, the deeper insight into the practice of drives for hunters going after elk without the assistance of professional outfitters or guides. The key to success in tactics is being able to predict the most likely routes that the elk will take to move away from the perceived threat of the drivers. This determination is usually a judgment call, and should consider all the factors controlling elk movement discussed to this point (factors you should have noted when scouting the area, preferably in person). The test of any assessment of likely routes is the presence of elk trails along the routes. Look for elk sign as the drive is made to learn whether elk were there recently and how they left in case the drive is less than successful.

The drive has to be executed so that the elk are made to move without becoming panicked. If elk pattern that they are in mortal danger from a source in the immediate vicinity, they may stampede in any or all directions rather than taking the route you predicted. Drivers should avoid the tendency to move fast in a straight line using long, quick, purposeful strides. Instead, intermittently move slower, with irregular stops to look around in all directions from screened locations, then move fast again across open places. All drivers need to use the same techniques to move at the same rate of progress.

A successful drive depends on attention to a lot of details orchestrated into one seamless team effort. Standers need to locate spots where normal elk routes pass through or converge, where clear shooting lanes can cover the routes, and where their odds of their being detected are minimized. The most important aspect of avoiding detection is making sure the scent of the waiting hunters is not carried toward the approaching elk by the wind. The direction of the wind should control the conduct of the entire drive. If the drive can't effectively be turned around to accommodate the wind on a particular day, put off driving the area until the wind does turn. The second most important detail for the standers is getting into position undetected, then remaining still and quiet until the elk or the drivers show up. No wiggles, no giggles, and absolutely no answering the call of nature while the drive is under way! It's really not as rough as it may seem. As

When taking a temporary stand, if faced with the choice between field of view and concealment, pick field of view (and then be very still).

opposed to the interminable hours spent waiting on deer stands in hopes that a whitetail will walk by, elk hunting tactics should be planned to minimize the time that the standers are required to remain in one place. The longer they stand, the greater the chance that they'll give away their position by a slight movement that a sharp-eyed elk can pick up from a distance, or that their scent will be carried to elk by the mountain thermals.

For the drivers, the task boils down to everything it takes to cover the entire area as they move through as a team. A ragged line invites elk to slip through the gaps, undetected. Individually, the drivers need to move along at a deliberate, steady (preferably erratically steady) pace, faster than stillhunting, but striding along at less than a headlong rush. They need to move slowly enough to look over every hiding place where an elk might be standing as the line moves past. Drivers may pause to check tracks at stream crossings or other locations that constrict movement, look in all directions while stopped, then move out again, head up, looking well ahead to detect elk that might be moving away or across the line in front of the drivers, offering a shot. Remember, elk, plains prey animals, are not compelled to flee at the *sight* of a predator, but at any *sign of threat* from a predator. The drivers should

A very obvious shooting lane.

A more subtle shooting lane.

understand that their purpose is not to throw the elk into a state of uncontrolled panic, just to create enough pressure to force them to move ahead along their normal route.

The photos above and opposite illustrate shooting points and lanes through timber from the perspective of the stander when drive tactics are in progress. You need to pick a spot to cover where the elk will most

An extended shooting lane across a burn and a sparsely timbered area.

likely come through and you see them before they see you, or actually recognize you as a threat, and you need to do it quickly without a lot of movement.

TACTICS FOR CROWDED CONDITIONS

Crowded hunting conditions are an absolute downer, a situation that makes many elk hunters want to head back home and never go elk hunting again. If your hunt turns out to be that way, make the most of the situation. The appropriate techniques can bring success even in— and even *because of*—crowded conditions. You can consider the comic relief provided by some of the intruding flatlanders as a substitution for the wilderness experience.

Drive tactics should be adapted to the level of hunting pressure and the number and location of other hunting parties in the area. As the number of hunters in the area goes up, the drivers should slow their pace and be on the lookout for elk moving away from other hunters in addition to their usual practice of trying to locate motionless elk resting under cover. This aspect of tactics has little effect on outfitter hunts in remote backcountry areas. However, it needs a lot of consideration by hunters conducting their own hunts during the general season, in easy-to-access areas, particularly on opening day and for a couple of days into the season.

TACTICS AND LANDFORMS

When thinking drives, think in terms of the equipment in hand. Tactics for large-scale landforms like those pictured on the next page require several drivers and standers using high-powered repeater rifles. You're moving along, covering lots of ground to get the elk out of the particular hole where they're lying. Great! Here we go . . . But give a thought to what you intend to do with them after you get them going. In the top photo, look at how the sunlit ridges on the other side are broad across the top, with thick trees. Rifle shooters will need to cover both sides. Will the party be spread too thin? Thick timber might best be worked very slowly by bowhunters.

The lower photo shows a more interesting landscape that you might run first. It looks to have small features superimposed over the big patterns; note the little pass that cuts the adjacent ridge near right center. A rock slide spills down through the center on this side and elk will go on one side or the other. You'll be able to determine how the elk trails run with a closer look. The thick vegetation will push the situation to close shooting, just what the bowhunters ordered. The subtle undulations of the long gentle nose down to the right from center should form spots for multiple stands to pick up elk drifting along in front of easy, slow drivers. This might be your best shot absent hot bugling . . . and sometimes it can be very absent. Rifle shooters will like the looks of open shots along the ridges with sparse vegetation to the left of center. Disturbed elk will move toward the heavy timber along the north slopes, crossing the open areas along the way.

Many novice elk hunters will try to hunt elk with the same tactics they use for whitetail—and as a result will scare all the elk out of the area. But these elk can be intercepted by careful drivers exercising proper techniques for elk hunting, and, in fact, these circumstances will often result in a chance for the drivers to "get in some shootin'" along with the standers. When you take a stand in this type of situation, be aware of hunters from other parties who are also taking stands in the area of the planned drive. Bearing in mind that the other bunch has every right to be there, you can move to take a position to "shortstop" the other party. This trick is usually easily turned, since inexperienced hunters typically don't take stands to effectively cover elk routes anyway.

If the stander or standers just can't get in a good location, a workable Plan B can be implemented on the spot. The stander becomes a driver, and the drive-toward-standers tactic becomes an all-driver sweep, with the converted standers driving toward the original drivers.

High ridges with side ridges and uniform timber cover.

Ridges with complex patterns of cover.

Safety first! Keep in mind that the other drivers aren't in on the new plan, and won't be expecting to see a stander show up as a driver. The converted stander should don some hunter orange even where it's not required by the state (other than the state of common sense).

The consistently successful elk hunter is an eternal, if sometimes misguided, optimist, and sees opportunity in what might be viewed as discouraging circumstances. Remember, for the diehard elk hunter, the absolute worst day elk hunting is still better than the best day in the office.

Now we'll consider some real-life examples of tactics and hunting techniques using tactical concepts.

The next Tale is an example of a quickly conceived drive to move elk from cover in an area of low hunting pressure. It also illustrates the other side of the driving coin, the side that usually turns up—no shot.

A PINCER SURROUND MOVE ON A BUGLING BULL

The setting of this Tale is the fringes of the timber just above a series of finger points dropping into the Big Bend of the North Fork, in the Idaho Bitterroots. These finger ridges have steep, brushy slopes on either side of the rocky points. Wes and I had the area around the camp to ourselves, but we hadn't managed to see a bull.

We knew from fresh sign that elk were in the vicinity of the spot we referred to as "the Shooting Rocks." A few mornings into the hunt, I gave the area another visit, and located a bull by his bugling. For some unknown reason, this bull was compelled to sound off at regular intervals even though it was well past the rut and into the start of the general season.

All of the action of this Tale took place within a space about a quarter of a mile square. The contour lines on the map are 100 feet. Wes and I were located at a slightly elevated point of the ridge (A). The bull was located in high brush below a series of pinnacle rocks, moving around the upper slopes and over the top of a small brushy knoll (B). I stayed concealed and attempted to get a look at the bull, but he remained hidden as he moved around. The show went on from midmorning until past noon. The bull quit moving and went silent as the day grew warmer. Since he seemed inclined to stay put, I developed a plan for a two-person pincer surround tactic to make him move. I headed back to camp to pick up Wes after he returned from his morning hunt.

Wes and I were back by early afternoon, full of confidence in ourselves and the "can't miss" plan. We refined the plan while looking over the brushy knoll from the vicinity of the shooting rocks. I would go around the knoll on the east

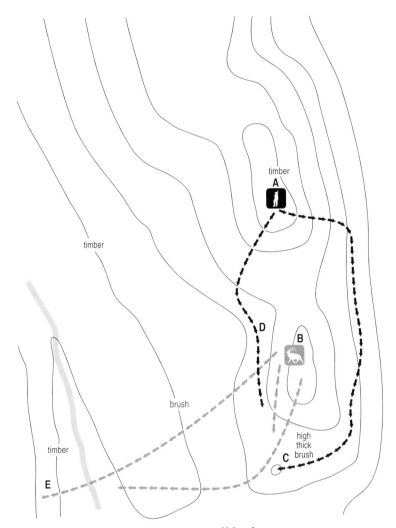

Driving a small knob.

side as quickly and as quietly as I could while staying out of the line of sight of any elk on top of the knoll. I would have a better chance of moving without noise on the "non-brushy" side while on my way to the opposite side of the knoll (C) from our planning position. There, I should be able to locate and position myself along the main trail assumed to go down the point, which should be the main avenue of escape for panicked elk.

Wes was to wait and watch from a position overlooking the brushy (west) side and try to spot any elk moving through the brush that might detect me by sound or scent as I made my move. After enough time had passed for me to have reached my cut-off position along the trail down the point, Wes would move through the brush (D) toward my general location. Any elk that he got moving should head for my position, then double back toward Wes if they detected my presence blocking their route of escape.

This was one of the few times in my elk hunting experience that a tactical plan was executed to perfection, even down to the timing of movement.

The elk were holding their position where they had bedded down in late morning. They weren't disturbed by my movement around the knoll to point C. When Wes made his move, they stampeded toward my cut-off position. I could hear them coming through the tall brush in singles and small groups. I noted that the elk created a continuous swishing sound as they moved through the tall brush, indicating that it was rubbing along the length of their sides rather than against the sides of their legs. The brush in my immediate area was taller than I had estimated based on my view from the rocks above. Moving at a fast trot through the brush, the elk apparently detected my presence and veered off to one side before I could get a look at them over or through the high, thick brush. But rather than turn back around the slope toward Wes, or head down the main trail off of the point, the elk took off down over the steep, brushy side of the finger and right out of the area (E). Wes and I had exactly the same results—neither of us ever saw a hair of an elk.

Another typical terrain form encountered in all parts of elk hunting country is what is referred to as a "hole," a steep-sided pocket with an open end. Small streams typically originate in these spots, and groundwater can usually be found standing in little pools—perfect elk wallows for cooling. The bottom of the hole is often timber-covered, while the steep sides may be thickly covered with small trees or brush. This combination will usually hold elk in the vicinity. A single element of one or more hunters moving into the hole from any direction usually results in the elk simply moving out of the area in the opposite direction along a well-established network of trails. A coordinated simultaneous movement of several hunters from different directions to cut off escape routes is usually much more productive. The sketch for this story covers about 1 1/2 miles in either direction, with 200-foot contour lines.

ANOTHER TALE OF TACTICS—DRIVING A HOLE

Everybody jumped off the vehicle (G) with a set time to drop over the edge of the hole. Wes, elected as the most physically fit rock climber, took the high road straight up the side to a jump-off position for the drive on the edge of the top (A). Tom W., Craig, and I started through the timber toward the western edge, staying together as long as possible for the best possible coordination of timing and position for the move into the hole. Just before we reached

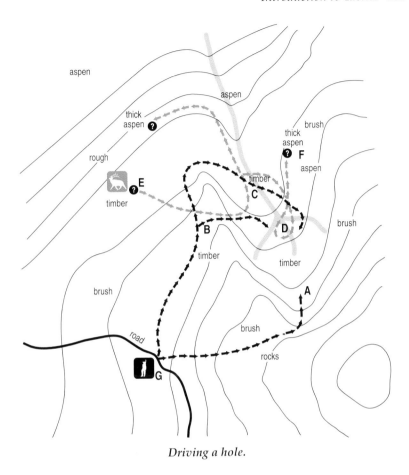

Driving a hole.

the location where we planned to split up, a very large herd of elk crossed our path just ahead of us. We immediately lowered our profiles and went motionless in hopes that the elk, with all eyes looking toward the lead cow, wouldn't notice. Luck was with us this time, and we had a good chance to look the entire bunch over as they paused, milled a little, then moved up the slope. No horns to be seen. A few of the herd hung back in the dark timber, however, keeping us from getting a good look at them.

Tom W. broke away from the rest of us at a point where several elk trails converged at a break in the west rim of the hole (B). There were fresh elk tracks through the area, but we had no absolute assurance that this was the route taken by the large herd we'd seen. Craig and I continued to move along the west rim of the hole with the intention of rounding the portal of the entrance of the hole at the level of the hole bottom. We missed the exact location of the break and had to slip and slide down a short distance of the west wall to the point where the floor of the hole leveled out to our jump-off for the drive (C).

At the planned time, all of us started moving along our planned routes. I crossed the small creek running through the center of the hole and proceeded up the east side, roughly parallel with the creek, but far enough removed to cover all escape routes between the creek and the sharp rise of the east wall of the hole. My route was to follow the main network of elk trails around the upper end of the hole until elk were seen or I encountered other members of the party coming around the other side.

Craig was to move slowly up the west side of the creek to block any elk escaping down the west side and drive any elk forced to move in the general direction of Tom W. or me across the creek.

Meanwhile, Wes moved straight down the upper end of the hole to a point where he could look over the network of elk trails around the upper end of the hole along the sudden change in elevation between the flat bottom and the steep end.

As it turned out, Wes was some distance above the point along the elk trail network where the two Toms met (D). Nobody had seen an elk. A check of the ground at different locations along the length of the hole indicated that the most likely route(s) of the elk were as indicated in the sketch (E). The herd must have been set in motion by hunters from another party, probably to the west. Tracks of elk in a hurry could be found along the steep west side of the hole (below C). We found tracks of a running bull elk circling around the spot where the small tributaries of the upper end of the hole came together to form the main creek. We couldn't determine whether the bull came into the hole with the herd, or was already in the hole with some cows when the large herd entered the hole from the west side. Also still an unknown was whether the bull left toward the thick cover of the lower east side of the hole (F) or went with the rest of the herd out the lower west end and into the rough cover below. The big one got away this time.

The examples to this point have illustrated applications of tactics by individuals and small hunting parties to hunt areas constrained by individual landforms. I'll now consider how tactics are applied in outfitter camps to cover larger areas while providing high-quality elk hunting experiences to clients with a broad range of hunting skill, physical conditioning, and enthusiasm. The following example is actually an amalgamation of several drives I was involved in over a period of time hunting in this particular outfitter area. These tactics work in terrain covered with open vegetation or with enough openings to allow drivers to see ahead and across advancing lines—not only so they can see elk, but also so they can be sure the other hunters aren't in the line of their shots. The standers will often be along ridges or across canyons to look down into brush and trees, which offers a more open perspective. The area covered should be large enough that it's likely it holds a herd of elk.

OUTFITTER TACTICS DRIVING A LARGE AREA WITH A LOT OF HUNTERS AND GUIDES

Tactics are used on a large scale by outfitters to provide interesting and pro-ductive hunts for entire outfitter camps, which may consist of up to ten or twelve hunters and three or four guides and a packer.

As indicated by the sketch below, the landforms covered by tactics of this scale are large enough to allow hunting by several hunters and well defined enough to allow the coordination of inexperienced hunters who are likely to become separated from guides and each other. The particular landforms shown allow two independent drives that may be done separately or at the same time by two separate camps. The advantage of driving two or more adja-cent landforms at the same time comes from the tendency of disturbed elk to move from one area to another. They'll usually use predictable route(s) of escape, which may provide several good locations for standers of limited mobility. This amounts to hunting in a crowd that's cooperating in an effort to get a shot at an elk for some, and sometimes all, of its members.

The scale of this type of drive is typically large. The area covered by the sketch extends for almost 3 miles in both directions, and the 150-foot contours indicate a change in elevation of about 1,500 feet from the trail jump-offs along the creeks to the trail along the top of the major ridge. The general scheme of the operation is for the drivers, usually guides along with some physically fit hunters, to be dropped off to start from the bottom (either A or B, sometimes both when multiple camps are involved). The standers will already be in position when the drivers start. They get an early start and ride horses from camp to drop-off locations along the ridge trail. They then make the easy walk out to stand locations with good fields of view, shown on the sketch by circles along slopes D, E, F, and G, while the packer moves on along the trail, dropping off the rest of the standers and leading a longer and longer string of driver and stander mounts. It's best to keep the horses together. If they're sep-arated from the herd, they'll stomp and paw and make unhappy horse sounds that can alert elk.

The drivers wait at their jump-off points until a predetermined time, when the standers should already be in position, then they fan out across as broad a front as the terrain and visibility permit and move along the routes with arrow points as shown in the sketch. (There's always a tendency for drivers to string out in line under constraints of the terrain.) They try to coordinate their move-ment forward by sight so that if elk moved from cover don't move straight

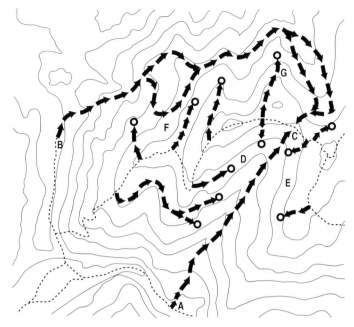

A typical outfitter drive.

ahead toward the standers, they will cross closely in front or to the side of another driver, for a possible shot.

The standers look for elk moving between trees and other cover in front of the drivers while keeping a close lookout for the drivers. Drivers in this type of operation should wear blaze orange for safety. Long-range shooting is the norm for the standers. A by-product of this type of drive is a lot of entertainment from the combination of inexperienced standers, unobstructed fields of view, clear mountain air, and telescopic sights set at high power. The normal flatland hunter tends to get a little excited at the sight of a bull elk and forget about details such as range estimation techniques, or anything else for that matter, and just blaze away at ranges up to 1,000 yards. Herm and Gene say it best: "You can only stretch rifle barrels so far!" There's often more than one set of red ears later as the tale is told, since this problem is highly contagious once the echoes of that first shot roll down the canyons. I've heard stories of major shootouts erupting all along the ridge and all drivers seeking cover behind large rocks and trees until after dark.

All too often, however, not a shot will be fired. The drive will just end with hot, tired drivers breaking out over the top along the trail at the predetermined location (C) or—just as likely—anywhere along the ridge line, trying to link up with the packer for the long ride back to camp, picking up frozen standers along the way.

CHAPTER 9

Making the Kill

Making the shot is the final, critical phase of the elk hunt.

AN ASIDE TO CONSIDER THE GRAVITY OF MAKING THE SHOT

Before we get into the details of how to make the shot, let's pause for a minute to get into the right mindset.

For the reader not familiar with the language of the western hunter, we'll first get some definitions straight. A "good shot" is one that makes a clean kill of the intended animal. A "clean miss" doesn't count. A bad shot is one that violates codes of safety or ethics. Once a shot is made, it can never be taken back.

The risk of a bad shot exists with each of the three types of equipment used to hunt elk. The lethal power at extended ranges of the high-powered repeater rifle and, to a secondary degree, the muzzleloader makes safety the primary consideration when using these weapons. A bad shot can easily kill or wound a person or animal that has not been seen or properly identified. The primary consideration when using a bow is ethics. Bowhunting requires the utmost in ethics and self-discipline, because in this case, you can often easily see elk that you can't kill due to the limited range and killing power of the bow, or due to obstacles. Precautions specific to each of the three types of equipment will be discussed later in this chapter, along with other aspects of making the kill. However, the same principles of being sure of your shot before you get into the mindset to make the kill apply in all three situations.

The key to making a shot, as with any activity that depends upon motor skills, is absolute concentration. Concentration involves shutting out all sensory input for the moment so that your brain has just one task. In this case, that task is to make the shot. You can tell that you have reached that point of concentration when it seems like time stands still during the activity. Everything seems to happen in slow motion except your own reflexes, which happen without conscious thought. The time to think about the consequences of a shot and to prevent the bad shot from occurring is *before* your mindset becomes that of absolute concentration and automatic reflexes. Before you reach the mindset to make the shot, make sure of the shot. Do not begin your attack with incomplete visual clues. I use the term "visual clues" deliberately. Sometimes your locating may be done by sound. But you must make sure that you have *seen* what you heard before you get too excited or begin to move toward the mindset of making a kill.

The hunter has to absolutely internalize this point: Never, *never* even *think* about shooting on the basis of a sound. Trouble arises when you hunt in an area that has a lot of tall brush cover. You get into the habit of listening for elk in thick areas as much as you look for them, and if the mules have gotten loose in the night . . . well, four or five mules with about the same weight, hoof size, and leg length as elk sound pretty interesting if you startle them some distance from camp while you are heading out in the dim light of early morning. One morning I was completely taken in, ready for that little herd of elk to break out of the thick stuff; then I got a look at those ears on otherwise slick heads (no antlers). I was in the company of an experienced guide, and he was fooled too.

Whether you're hunting with a bow or a gun, the first line of safety is good hunting ethics. No hunter should ever take a shot at a part of an animal that will not result in a quick, humane kill. An old friend of mine lost his leg and almost his life to a deliberate bad shot by a hunter who thought he saw an elk's legs. A deliberate bad shot is criminal in a legal sense as well as the ethical sense. Never consider taking a shot unless you have the complete image of a legal elk in sight. Never make a commitment to a shot without a complete image and absolute identification. Some strange things can happen as you attempt to make the transition from the stalk to making the kill. Straining to make out the image of an elk for some length of time is a very unsafe practice; your imagination tends to help you finish the image whether it's physically there or not. Hunting experience in general doesn't seem to help this tendency; trophy hunting, however, can help. Holding back your commitment to a shot until the antlers are sized up tends to assure that the half-hidden mass in the undergrowth is a big bull elk, not your companion, a hunter from another party, your or somebody else's horse or mule, a cow elk, or anything else that you don't have a legal tag for. None of these possibilities has antlers; a bull elk does. The rack may not be as big as you thought—I have my four-point hat rack as evidence—but it will be a bull. In those areas where a legal bull is restricted to one with antlers or brow tines of a certain size, you have some more sizing up to do even after you have seen antlers.

So what if you locate something that looks like it might be an elk but you can't quite tell? Don't stand and stare hoping that the confused image will become an elk with antlers; move and look at the same spot from a different angle. Yes, move to get a look from a different angle even if this spooks the elk and you miss a chance at a shot. If the object of your attention spooks, it was an elk. Too bad; better luck next time. However, the object usually doesn't spook—because it usually isn't an elk. A change of perspective on my part once transformed the large antlers of a bedded elk on a dark timbered slope below me into an overturned tree with exposed roots projecting up from reddish soil.

IDENTIFYING A LEGAL OR TROPHY ELK

A legal elk usually means a bull elk. This particular problem usually doesn't pertain to bowhunting, since you're closer and during the rut the bulls will be screaming anyway. But for the rifle hunters trying to distinguish the bull elk from cows, there are a few tricks to assist in the sorting process. In thick brush where it may be hard at first to see antlers, it's sometimes handy to know that the bull elk has a noticeably different color than the cow. The bull's body is usually lighter than the cow's, but the long shaggy hair covering the neck of the bull appears to be very much darker than the color of the necks and heads of the rest of the herd. This almost black color is sometimes easier to spot and follow than the light and dark variations of russet that seem to come and go as the herd moves through openings in the brush. The bull may have a russet tone early in the fall, but turns a creamy tan with the winter coat that sharply contrasts with the dark mane.

If a trophy bull is your objective, you have still another task before you assume the mindset to make the kill. Along with the size of the antlers in relation to the rest of the elk, the shape of a bull's antlers will give an indication of their size.

You'll commonly hear rules of thumb for estimating antler length and size in relation to the body size of the elk. One is that, from a side view, large antlers will appear to be about the same length front to back as the bulk of the body of the elk from shoulder to rump. Another is

The shape of elk antlers can be an indicator of the maturity of the elk and, secondarily, the size of the antlers. Look at the plane of the beams from tine 2 to tine 4; the more steeply tines 5 and 6 angle up away from that plane, the more mature the bull.

that while big bulls tend to be big in body as well as rack, head size is about the same for all of them: If the antlers appear to be too big for the head, it's a good one.

Shape can also be used to estimate antler size—even if the body is obscured by brush. It's common knowledge that the overall size of the antlers, along with tine count, generally increases with each year that a bull manages to survive. Less well known is that in any given year, this size is controlled by the availability of a sufficient quality and quantity of feed during the critical period of initial antler development. Good feed tends to give extra growth to the lower parts of the racks of less mature bulls. This effect is less pronounced in the case of more mature bulls. Focus on the length and mass of the part of the rack past the fourth (or "royal") tine. An immature bull in a year with an early thaw may develop a six-point rack, but the fifth and sixth tines will be small relative to the brow tines. The antlers of a mature bull will have terminal tines proportional to the brow tines even in hard years.

But there is a more consistent—and even less well-known—indicator of the maturity of a bull. As the years go by, a bull elk's rack assumes a progressively more curved shape as the angle between adjoining tines, particularly from the royal tines back to the terminal tines, increases. The antlers of large, mature bulls look like they're curving back along the main beams, regardless of the tilt of the head. Antlers of immature bulls will usually seem to stick straight up or curve slightly forward. In the case of the oldest bulls, as the fourth tine begins to emerge as a true royal, the rest of the rack, which develops along the axis of the fifth point, appears to curve back from the initial plane of the beam.

ART APPRECIATION FOR THE ELK HUNTER

Note that the art style used in these illustrations is old school—at least 35,000 years old school, in fact. The hunter-artists of prehistoric times just concentrated on the essentials, and we can see their mindset reflected in their art. Hunters of today need to do the same thing when comparing the size and shape of the antlers to the rest of the elk. You need to reduce the complex and confused image of the elk, as viewed through brush, bad light, fog (both mental and real), excitement, and confusion, to its simplest elements. Practicing reducing photographs and mounts of elk to this cave-art style in your head will improve your intuition with regard to judging antler size.

This will be the extent of the art appreciation in this book.

The symmetric rack with thinner fourth and terminal tines on the upper left in the photo on the next page are from a young bull taken in a year with

Immature and trophy-sized antlers.

good feed and an early spring. The rack shown in the lower center has lighter, less symmetric antlers with a greater angle of divergence between the fourth and fifth tines, which are heavy relative to the brow tines. This rack was that of a herd bull in a year with a late thaw and poor feed during the critical time of antler growth in the spring. In a year like this, you might pass on an apparently small rack, but not find a better one that year no matter how hard you look. A trophy rack from a mature herd bull taken in the same area during a year with an early spring thaw and plenty of feed is shown on the right. The plane of the rack breaks behind the royal tine, and even the sixth tine is long and heavy. The bottom drawing in the last sketch is intended to represent this bull.

RECOGNIZING THE SHOT

This section gives you information about skills that will ultimately need to be developed into instinct. Study the sketches here and internalize them in the "good shot, bad shot" file deep in your mind. Check it just before you pull the trigger or release the arrow.

Coming from any angle, the area on an elk where a shot will hit essential organs for a clean kill is about 6 inches in diameter. You'll often hear that area referred to as the "6-inch pie plate" (or, with more lenient guides, the "8-inch pie plate").

Regardless of the equipment you choose to hunt with, the shot should be directed toward the organs in the center of the chest cavity of

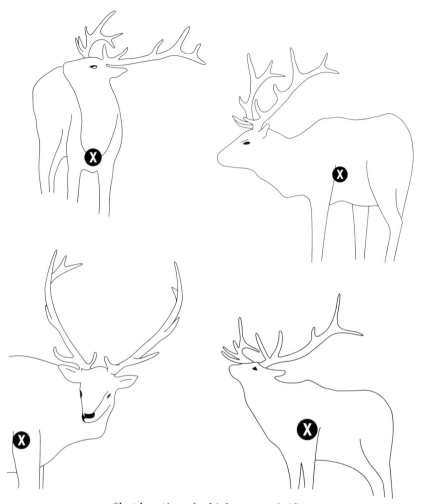

Shot locations for high-powered rifle.

the elk. The choice of equipment has some implications as regards the appropriate target on the outside of the elk. The high-powered rifle with premium bullets can be counted on to reach the center of the chest cavity from the side, front, or quartering angles.

Note the location of the shot in the lower left-hand image. When the body behind the front leg is covered by a tree trunk or other obstacle, the high-powered rifle shot can pass through the leg and lower shoulder and will reach both lungs and/or the heart, which extend forward between the front legs. Shoot forward enough to clear the tree, but don't be distracted by the tree. If you concentrate on the tree, are too aware of the tree, worry about the tree, and so on, you'll probably hit the tree.

Shot location for bow and muzzleloader.

The upper left image on the previous page illustrates the head-on heart shot, where the idea is to put a high-performance bullet between the legs and through the chest. However, if the range is too great for the shooter to ethically attempt the shot, if the hunter is using a less-than-premium bullet, or if the bull lowers its head, covering the target location with its thick neck or the long hair below the neck, this situation becomes a no-shot.

Shots with the muzzleloader or bow should be restricted to the side shot, which should be placed low in the front of the chest, just behind the shoulder blade, as illustrated above, placed so that the arrow passes through both lungs and/or the heart.

The shot location is about one-third of the way between the bottom of the bulk of the body and the top of the shoulders; the vitals of an elk are located rather low in the body. The shot is centered just behind the leg muscle, which appears on the elk's body as an extension of the leg. The major bones of the leg angle forward at this location to a joint close to the front edge of the shoulder, so that a well-directed shot shouldn't strike the major bones of the leg or the shoulder blade, which is higher.

No shots—best to pass.

A chisel-point broadhead will likely deflect around the rounded bones of the leg, but the flat shoulder blade will catch and stop it. Experienced muzzleloader hunters can take this shot at more of a quartering angle than the bowhunters. The key word here is "experienced." The new hunter should take it more carefully until he or she has a feel for the power of the rifle.

Some shots are best not taken, even with the high-powered rifle. Check out the set of sketches above: The name of the game is "What's wrong with this shot?"

The upper right image is large because it's at close range (when this situation is especially tempting). This is the neck shot, with a tree covering the part of the elk where you really need to place the shot. If you take this shot, you seldom break the neck and drop the elk in his tracks like you plan. You usually go through flesh just inside the long hair covering this area, and do little damage; or you may clip the esophagus, the windpipe, or a large vessel. None of this damage will slow the elk down as he runs off, but they all may result in death much later and far away from the location where the shot was taken. This is not an ethical shot.

The bottom center image depicts the classic rear-end shot. I have seen older publications that actually present this view as an ethical shot. As if that .270 or 30-06 soft-point is going to enter that little 1-inch-diameter soft spot from a range of 200 yards and penetrate straight through to the heart-lung area from the rear. Sure. If you're luckier than you deserve taking this shot, you *might* strike the spine just right and knock the animal down. You're much more likely to break a back leg or to produce the classic gut shot.

The center left head shot seldom results in that little hole square between the eyes you imagine. The more likely result is major damage to eyes or jaw, and an unrecovered slow kill.

The lower left presentation is that head-on heart shot again, only this time the bull is standing with front feet slightly lower than the back feet so that the hunter can't place the shot at an angle that will penetrate into the heart area. An angled-down shot like this is the worst case and will only result in head, neck, or front leg damage.

The lower right image is known as the "bowhunter's dilemma." It's really no better for the high-powered rifle. The same goes for the upper left image. How about those "brush buster" cartridges to take that bull on the other side of those low limbs? Do you really think that when a bullet weighing around 200 grains hits a tree part weighing around 200 pounds the tree part is going to fly off at a crazy angle while the bullet speeds unerringly toward the target?

SURPRISE SHORT-RANGE ENCOUNTERS WITH ELK

The fast encounter with an elk at close range has several surreal characteristics. If you're trained, time stands still, and all action other than your own is in very slow motion. You have no sense of controlling your actions. If you attempt to intervene and take conscious control, you lose control and your skill level plummets. If, in contrast, you're untrained and unpracticed (or out of practice), all actions move faster than you can think.

A peculiar aspect of the experience for me, and other hunters who can vividly recall the moment, is that the image of the elk will have no

A typical encounter with an alerted elk: Everything is blurry and in black and white as your brain scrambles to get your rifle from sling to shoulder for an offhand shot, clear the shot, evaluate whether it's a legal bull, and assess the trophy—all within the two seconds it takes the elk to recognize the threat, turn, and go. WALLIS AIRHART

color. Apparently, color is useful in leisurely situations when we have plenty of time on our hands. It's speculated that color takes time for the brain to process—and the hunter in a fast encounter doesn't have time. All that the predator side of our nature needs is shape and shade.

The practical consequences of these effects are that you need to develop your instincts. If they are fully developed, they allow you to move quickly without thinking while everything else is standing still. And don't think about what you're doing—let your motor reflexes in the primitive part of your brain handle the fast action. The key to success in this is to practice your motor reflexes until they are second nature, then exercise them in practice hunts (see Chapter 12 for more on this).

MAKING THE KILL

Making the kill requires a mindset of absolute visual focus on the selected prey while your motor reflexes, made automatic through practice, make the kill. This mindset is to be assumed only after you have closed to within killing range for the equipment you are using. Whereas the only effect of your equipment on the stalk is how close you have to get to the elk, techniques of making the kill are totally dictated by equipment used. Accordingly, I will go into three separate discussions of making the kill, one for each type of equipment. The information up to this point about clearing the shot before assuming the mindset of making the kill holds for each type of equipment. Situational awareness is critical.

The sections that follow present the techniques of making a clean killing shot. We'll discuss selecting equipment and developing the skills to use that equipment in Part II; to avoid any suspense or confusion, I'll state here that my eventual recommendation will be that the beginner use a modern high-powered repeater rifle with a high-quality telescopic sight. The high-powered repeater rifle is the most effective equipment for making the kill, which is why I recommend it for the beginning elk hunter. You need to put in a lot of practice to develop the skills required to make a clean kill with any weapon, but it is my opinion that the high-powered repeater rifle is more straightforward for the beginner to master than the muzzleloader or bow and arrow. Even more important to the beginner, stalking the elk is less demanding with the modern high-powered rifle since the hunter isn't limited by the equipment to a very close-range shot. The greater range and killing power of the high-powered rifle require a high level of discipline to ensure that the shot has been cleared before the transition from the stalk to making the kill.

MAKING THE KILL WITH A HIGH-POWERED RIFLE
The Deliberate Long-Range Shot from a Rest
In the opinion of most experienced elk hunters, a deliberate long-range shot is actually less demanding than a quick shot at close range. The reason for this apparent contradiction is that in the case of the longer-range shot, the hunter nearly always has more time and can afford to take the time to steady the rifle with a rest or a steady shooting position. The hunter also has more time to get into the mindset of concentration required to make the shot.

Once you have satisfied yourself that the elk has legal (or trophy) antlers, don't get fixated on them. Guides delight in telling tales featuring novice elk hunters who took carefully aimed shots from a rest at bull elk with magnificent antlers, with the only damage to the elk being a piece of antler flying off. Some of the sources of this entertainment might not be above a little embellishment at the expense of a client hunter, but I've heard enough such stories to be convinced that it does happen.

There are some things that you can do to improve your chances of success. First, get the range. It's best not to have to rely on your estimate, instinct, or luck—this is one case where actual measurements generally trump instinct. Many riflescopes currently have some type of rangefinder based on the size of a given object in the scope. I know how big an elk at different ranges looks relative to the crosshairs in my scope. I'll cover the details of range estimation using duplex scopes in Chapter 12. My relative sizes stop at about 300 to 400 yards. Don't even think about shooting if the elk is more than 400 yards away. Study some ballistics tables. Note that because of the trajectory of the bullet from any rifle, small errors in range estimation result in a big error in where the bullet hits at the 300- to 400-yard range. It takes time when you often don't have any, but a laser rangefinder can accurately measure these ranges. If you're on a stand, it's a good idea to measure distances to obvious locations where an elk might appear before any action starts.

Now, you're not concerned about extreme accuracy in range determination; that's the main reason you chose to use a high-powered rifle like I recommended, remember? Range here is not as critical as with the bow, or even the muzzleloader. But in clear mountain air, an elk 700 yards away can still look pretty close through a clear telescopic rifle sight. I don't recommend that you use a scope of greater than 4 to 6 magnification power for anything other than trophy assessment. In addition to the disadvantage of a narrower field of view with the very high powers, they tend to make you lose your perspective of the actual range. You can always see a lot farther than you can shoot, especially farther than you can shoot *and make a clean kill.*

If you're looking at an elk out at some distance on the side of a mountain, and you're a beginner, and you don't have coaching from an experienced guide at your elbow, don't think about shooting unless you have a stationary broadside shot at the front half of the body. Estimating the correct lead to hit the target shot location on a moving elk at long range is a pretty risky business. Even with the standing shot, ask yourself if you absolutely have to shoot, or will the elk get closer, or can you get closer? If you decide to take a shot because the elk looks to be within range, but you're not sure exactly how far away it is, don't hold over the elk with the first shot to compensate for bullet drop. Make the first shot 6 inches below the top of the back, and then hold over with the second shot if you're sure that the shot was short. If you hold over 3 or 4 feet and don't connect, wait a minute and collect yourself; the elk is out of range (ethical range, for sure) or your shot is off line. It might be off line as a result of a crosswind, or more likely, you're pulling it off because of your grip or your rest. Change your position to make sure you fix both problems before you take another shot. Make sure that you are not holding the rifle at a slant so that the scope crosshairs are not aligned over the barrel. The scope should be mounted with the vertical crosshair precisely vertical, which should help in holding the rifle without a cant.

BOULDER CREEK FIVE-POINT

I was hunting with a typical outfitter pack camp of six hunters and a couple of young—just graduated from John Rose's Guide School—guides in an area called Horse Camp, up Boulder Creek from the Lochsa. The weather was okay, the hunters could get around about as well the average bunch, and while the guides were inexperienced, Gene was the packer for the camp as well as part owner and could keep them going in the right general direction. But still, we just weren't having any luck. After several days, it was decided that we would expand our range up the Boulder Creek drainage and cover some new territory. The plan was straightforward. We would ride up the government trail to a good point to climb to the high ridge to the north across from the point where the basin containing Long Lake pushes up against the ridge, and return to camp using the straightforward tactic of driving abreast along the ridge while one of the guides brought the horses back to camp.

It was a hard climb up the steep slope to the hogback ridgeline. I got impatient and left the rest of the slow-climbing group behind, as several of them needed to get reinvigorated with a smoke break.

I took a breather on top of the ridge to rest from the climb, looking over into the small basin on the other side of the ridge.

Then I heard rocks clanking as if disturbed by hooves—it's a very peculiar sound. I noticed several head of cows in the edge of the timber. Looking closer, I picked up some cow elk and a bull elk as he walked out of the trees below about 400 yards out, more down than out from my location looking down into the little bowl basin below. He had a full rack of antlers. At that range, I couldn't tell immediately exactly how big, but it looked good considering the fact that we hadn't seen a bull for the entire hunt so far. I had plenty of time to wiggle into a fully supported shooting position draped over a large rock on the edge of the drop-off. The range was long, about 425 yards, as later paced by one of the guides during all of the comings and goings that go on after a kill. I held dead-on, using the standard instructions for distance shots taken in steep downhill direction, without any holdover. I centered the crosshairs exactly on the top of the back above the heart and lungs, and touched off a shot—my first shot in earnest from my new knock-'em-down .338 Win Mag. Absolutely no effect.

Puzzled but unfrazzled, I carefully touched off another. Identical non-effect. Twice down into the chest of the moving bull quartering toward my direction. Now slightly frazzled and figuring I was shooting too high, I lowered the crosshairs, which amounted to putting them right on the end of the nose of the bull. The shot caused the elk to flinch. It creased his nose, we later found out.

It was time for me to reload as the elk turned around and headed back toward the timber he came from. By this time the guide and the rest of the group topped out on the ridge, encouraged up the last part of the slope by the sound of my shooting. The young guide fresh out of guide school was getting a little excited at the sight of the bull moving toward the cover of the timber and started yelling, "Shoot, shoot, he's getting away!" Some of the other hunters finally saw the bull and one took a shot, then another, then another. One, Big Bob as I recall, moved in alongside me and fired a ported Magnum that took the bull down. My ears rang for a couple of hours after that. At least ten, maybe twenty, more shots rang out as the bull went down.

One of the guides and I went down the very steep slope to recover the elk. He expired as we approached.

"Is he a big one?" I called to the excited guide, who was well ahead of me on the trip down the steep bluff.

"No, not real big." It's strange how that rack never impressed me after that remark. But that not-real-big mount was the only mount I had for a few seasons during my early years, as I got snookered by the big ones, passed on the raghorns, or took a sundown spike for the collective skillets of the Association during my formative elk hunting years. And it was symmetric and made a pretty shoulder mount. A quick check showed that I had put the two shots into the top of the chest and then clipped the end of the nose when I held low, thanks to the distance-shortening effect of the steep downhill. The angle of the hits showed that my two shots had entered from the front as the elk moved in my direction. Out of the fusillade fired by the rest of the group as the bull moved away, only one more shot—Big Bob's, I'm sure—hit as the elk moved away.

There are several points that the new elk hunter can take from this Tale. First, it demonstrates that first-order conditioning and shooting skills put you at an advantage. Second, the energy of high-powered cartridges has its limits, as shown by this typical long shot; the new hunter needs to be aware that many long shots will have no immediate effect. Sure enough, no holdover is required when shooting steep downhill shots, just like the experts say. Also note that in the real world out there on the slopes, a bunch of outfitter hunters, coupled with inexperienced guides, can result in a less-than-textbook experience in making a kill. Happily, all went well in this case, but sometimes more than one hunter will claim a kill, which can lead to trouble.

Making the Kill with a Quick Offhand Shot

Now we consider the quick, offhand rifle shot. In this case, you usually don't have the luxury of the time to get "ready and steady," as they used to say on the army shooting ranges. Be sure of your target, and then get it done.

A close shot, by my definition, is about 50 yards or less. You should be able to hold a quick, offhand shot to within a 6-inch pie plate at that distance. To get a feel for this range, you can look through your scope, with the rifle unloaded and the bolt open, at something about the size of an elk at that distance. That would be something with a body length of 5 feet, more or less. A small mule or a Jersey cow would be about right, but ask permission of the owner first. The width of a standard pickup bed is also about that size, if you don't want to bother the livestock. You just need to have a feel for what an elk looks like at the outer fringe of the close shot so that you can immediately go into battery for the offhand shot.

There are some things you can do to improve your chances for success in this situation. I'll review tactical aspects in this section, and practicing with your equipment will be covered in Part II. First, unless you're very lucky, the elk will probably be moving. Don't try to follow a moving elk through trees and brush with a swinging lead. Your probability of hitting a tree is obvious when you notice what percentage of the area out to 50 yards is covered by trees. Look ahead to an opening that will allow you to see most of the body so that you can place a shot. The risk of shooting a tree or making a bad shot because branches blocked a good one is greater than the risk of the elk not going through your chosen opening. You have to pick the most likely opening. Good luck! There are elements of both instinct and intuition at work here. Keep both eyes open to check the animal's progress. That makes the likelihood of your selecting the right opening a lot better. It also helps you make sure that the first elk you see through the opening selected is the trophy bull you want and not a fast-moving cow that passed him. You should be in the under-50-yard range for this sort of activity, so don't worry about a lead or any other confusion. When the elk appears, shoot. You should have practiced this shot until you can hit a pie plate within a second or so every time. With close shots, speed kills, and speed has no time for deliberate logical meditations. And thus we begin our entry into the realm of instinct. Instinct comes from practice. Practice, practice, practice, actually. Practice to the point that your muscles "remember."

AN ELK CAMP TALE OF A SHORT-RANGE SHOT

The sketch illustrating this Tale is less than a half of a mile across with 20 feet of elevation change between the contour lines. The paths that begin with question marks represent the unknown route of the elk up to the point when the Tale starts.

It was a couple of weeks into the rifle season, and the elk were holding in cover during daylight hours, so Wes and I made a plan to try to kick them out. We separated in a low pass (A). Wes would veer to the left and take the lower, more direct route back to camp through an area of thick growth that might hold an elk hiding out at this point of the season (B); I would hold to the main trail and take the longer, easier route over the rise to the north (C), hoping that it would be easier on my ankle, sore from a slip crossing a little bad place earlier in the week. Our separate routes were about a quarter of a mile apart at maximum separation. If any elk were moved from cover in the drainage that we had to cross, they would probably move along the contour of the far slope, and one or the other of us might have a slight chance of seeing a bull. Chances had been hard to come by on this trip.

The main trail led up a steep, familiar pitch and over a small pinnacle. I stopped after the climb and looked over the view through my scope, checking the clarity of the scope as much as anything. The crosshairs weren't as sharp as they should be—probably a matter of my eyes getting a couple of years older since the scope was last adjusted. I proceeded down the other side of the pinnacle, and stepped over the little creek at the bottom of the slope (D). On the other side of the stream the trail went up another steep little grade. Suddenly I had the impression of faint hoofbeats. Unsure, I slipped the rifle from my shoulder and carried it at the "port," as they called it back during my Texas A&M and army days, while I continued to pull up the grade.

As I topped out over the abrupt change of slope, I was momentarily shocked into complete inaction by the sight before me on the trail. I was looking at two cows at quartering angles on either side of a completely stationary bull that presented a full head-on, no-shot image immediately adjacent to a full-tail, no-shot image. Two bulls rubbing shoulders head to tail between two cows? My reaction slowed as my brain attempted to unscramble the image before assuming the mindset of making the kill; I brought the rifle to my shoul-

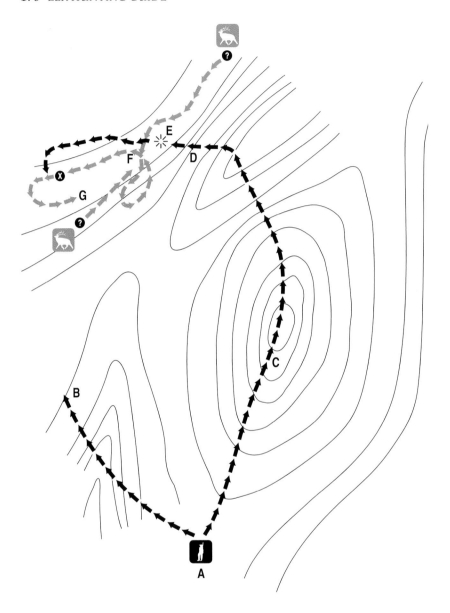

der just as the bull disappeared from the scope over another abrupt slope to the left of the trail ahead. My mental processes were restored. The bull had been facing in the opposite direction with its head turned completely around to look to the rear following the alarmed stare of the cows.

I assumed the stalking mindset, moving slowly forward along the trail in order to see over the break in contour of the ground (E). One, then another cow could now be seen milling through the trees in the shallow, 100-yard-wide secondary drainage off the trail to the left. I continued to move forward. The two cow elk were now to my left and slightly behind me. Three or four more heads were now evident and moving without apparent direction through the trees to my left and forward. They may have been confused by a scent on the breeze—Wes, downstream along the drainage.

One of the elk, a little farther out and larger and darker in the front than the others, drew my attention. It had stopped broadside between two trees. Nothing showed of its head or hindquarters. Maybe a belly patch in the middle. The bull? Maybe. But I couldn't see the rack or even where it should be. No shot.

My thoughts were interrupted as the herd spooked in unison and swirled about the little drainage as if caught in a vortex. Then the bull appeared on the near side of the depression, moving across my left front. Indecision resolved, he headed up the drainage in company with two cows in full flight.

My rifle came up again as I picked a space about 50 yards out between the trees ahead of the bull (F). I perceived the sight image of the crosshairs behind the near foreleg over where the heart should be and the sense of recoil as from a detached perspective, without any sense of time. The bull ran ahead up the drainage.

I automatically worked the bolt as I recovered from the recoil of the .338, and then moved ahead along the trail, which ran parallel with the general course of the little secondary drainage. Not absolutely sure of the shot, I strained to catch any movement in the brushy undergrowth along the direction of the bull's possible escape. Finally, a hundred yards along the trail, I picked up movement on the far side of the draw at about my own elevation (G). It was the two cows that had run with the bull, sneaking back toward the main part of the herd. No bull with them. "Good news? Bad news?" I wondered. I went another 50 yards along the trail, and then turned off toward the bottom of the draw to look for the bull.

I descended to a point where the side of the draw leveled slightly. This is where the elk would have run. Finding no fresh tracks of running elk in the immediate vicinity, I started back toward the area where I had last seen the bull. Then I saw him, his lifeless body turned full around to face back in the direction he had come (X). The crimson streak down the shoulder originated at the intended shot location, $1/2$ inch above my point of aim. I marked the way back to the trail and took off toward the nearby camp—I hadn't bothered to bring along all of the gear to field dress and quarter an elk on this casual morning stroll through the woods. I'd hear about that from my younger hunting partner.

THE TALE OF THE BIG FOOT BULL

Sometimes you make your best moves and take your best shot and all you take home is a Tale to tell. And some lessons learned, after you've had some time to figure out just exactly what they are. And they don't always have much to do with instinctive action or intuition or situational awareness. Sometimes it's simply "Check for the #@%$*& limbs!"

The setting was the top of the switchbacks behind Magruder Station along Magruder Corridor between the Frank Church and Selway-Bitterroot Wilderness Areas, Idaho. The characters: JoAnne, Bill, and me. JoAnne had a bear tag, I had an elk tag.

We climbed up steep switchbacks toward Pasture Ridge, hearing intermittent bugles, when we, mostly me, stopped to get our breath. As the trail broke out onto a (relatively) level section, we saw tracks of a herd of cow elk accompanied by a bull with very large tracks. We continued along the crest, heading toward Bill's favorite lunch place. Our lunch entertainment was listening to a pack of wolves hunting under the direction of what sounded like the senior female, which used unique deep yelp signals. After lunch, we retraced our steps of the morning back along the trail. As we approached the top of the switchbacks, we noticed a spike bull slowly moving in generally the opposite direction off to our left. We remained motionless to avoid spooking it. The spike had a "whipped" look as he plodded along, as if reluctant to leave the area. Bill and I were talking in very low tones, trying to come up with the right move to get the herd and the big bull.

Out of nowhere, JoAnne whispered, "Did you hear that elk?"

"What elk?" Neither of us had heard anything.

"Maybe I'll try a bugle," Bill said, I suspect possibly trying to humor her.

"OOOugheeeeEEEEEYUCH . . . EOUCH . . . EOUCH . . . eouch," from Bill.

"Eouch," came the reply, half-heartedly—but not from Bill and not that far away.

"OOOugheeeeEEEEEEEEEEEYUCH . . . EEEOUCH . . . EEEOUCH . . . eouch," from Bill.

"EOUCH," with anger and not from Bill.

"OOOugheeeeEEEEEEEEEEEYUCH . . . EEEOUCH . . . EEEOUCH . . . eouch," from Bill.

"OOOugheeeeEEEEEEEEEEEEEEEEEEEEYUCH . . . E EEOCH . . . EEEOCH . . . EEEeouch," not from Bill and coming in our direction.

"OOOugheeeeEEEEEEEEEEEEEEEEEEEEYUCH . . . EEEOCH . . . EEEOCH . . . EEEeouch," not from Bill and a lot closer.

And the game was afoot! Big Foot, to be precise.

The "big foot" bull stopped a short distance behind the three trees left of center. It was a very typical elk encounter—the elk could be clearly seen though the trees, but I couldn't clear a shot. Another common dilemma is where moving to either side might give you a better rest for the shot, but will completely obscure the elk behind an intervening limb. And movement is easy to pick up for the elk as well as the hunter.

View looking back toward my location shows the stuff in the way of a clear shot.

Big Foot was fast closing on our position and it was apparent that there shortly wouldn't be much cover between the two antagonists. My experience (up to the point of this episode) indicated that a smart herd bull would approach up to that magic boundary, then veer off on a route that took him downwind of our position and silently sneak through our scent plume. Then he could reconsider his options of how to make a close approach, or not, with more information. I began to move off downwind to try to find a vantage point so that I could see over the crest to our right and get 'im before we were patterned by Mr. Big Foot. JoAnne hung back in Bill's vicinity.

Bill quietly alerted me that he saw the bull coming straight in.

Incredulous that he'd come straight in, I nevertheless moved back up toward Bill, close to where JoAnne was still standing. She had the bull in sight and he was coming straight in along an open trail. She indicated a direction through the trees ahead of us, and, sure enough, there he was! For safety and to get some pictures from the perspective of the shooter, she moved in close behind me.

The bull was approaching straight on, head back with his antlers carried flat along the main beam. His antlers were very wide and appeared to be completely polished white. He approached along a path to our right and stopped behind a group of three trees. The late-afternoon sunlight came in at an angle so that it was dark under the shade of the trees, but the bull stood out in better light in the more open area behind the trees. The agitated bull was staring in our direction, looking for the source of the bugling while moving closer to the trees.

The bull stopped behind the trees to present a head-on shot between two of the trees, about 60 yards out. I was assessing whether to shoot now, or wait until he moved from behind the trees. The view past the trees to my left was obscured by the low-hanging limbs of closer trees, and the ground dropped off there so that the bull would be in defilade if he moved a short distance. If he moved far enough, he'd be behind a pile of large boulders and in our scent plume—and be gone. If he sighted us, which was likely since our profiles weren't broken by any cover in our immediate area, he'd likely turn tail and run back along his approach—and be gone. The only good move (for me) that he could make was to move to my right, possibly presenting a broadside shot. And that wasn't likely.

The time to shoot was now. The bull was likely to pick me up immediately if I moved, and would sooner or later even if I didn't. In either event, he'd be gone. The frontal shot made a small target but appeared clear between the trees. It was close enough for a good offhand shot, which eliminated the need to move to a tree trunk for a vertical rest. The front sight was waving slightly, but I was pretty sure I was holding it over the heart on shot location. I shot.

The bull jumped straight back. "Just like my first eight-point whitetail" went through my mind. "A clean heart shot. Now a stagger and fall."

I realized that it wasn't happening to script as I chambered another cartridge belatedly due to my unwarranted overconfidence. I mentally replayed the sight picture from the instant of the shot, which showed something flying in the direction of the elk. Something not a .338 Nosler. Which I couldn't see anyway. With JoAnne's "Dang, I didn't even get a picture!" I knew it was a miss.

To my amazement, the bull didn't run back up the trail, but continued his determined march to intercept our scent plume. I could follow his movement with intermittent glimpses through openings in the cover, but any shot was hopeless. I kept an eye on the trail to our left and rear and knew that he hadn't gotten behind us. He'd either veered off downhill behind cover or was hung up behind the piles of boulders that blocked our view. I began a close cover stalk, rifle at the ready, with JoAnne right behind me. I rounded the pile of boulders, unaware that Bill was catching up to us on our right. I picked up the elk to our far right out of the corner of my eye.

My rifle was swinging around and coming to my shoulder in an unconscious reflex. The scope came to my eye with the elk centered in the crosshairs. My voice of situational awareness—sounding just like JoAnne—came out with an urgent warning: "Don't shoot Bill!" just as I was becoming aware that the same Bill the Guide referred to was in one side of my view through the scope between me and the elk, which was 25 or so yards out.

"Bill, drop!" And Bill disappeared from the sight picture as my eye came away from the scope so that I could check to see what else was going on that I was unaware of. The elk had seen and heard enough and was getting into a big-bull getaway trot. I instinctively swung the rifle along his length, from tail to chest in a point-blank shot. At the same instant, the elk finished a sharp cut that was already under way to swing straight away as the barrel of the rifle continued its swing to the right. My sight picture at the instant of the recoil registered a clean miss, as was verified by the elk's big buff butt being carried off at a good clip by those four big feet. He ran straight away, then swung around to the left, heading out on the same trail that had brought him into this scrape as I chambered the last cartridge in the magazine.

That last Federal Premium Safari would make the trip back to Texas unfired, Nosler Partition bullet still in its nickel-plated case.

Assessing the distance, angle, questionable lead, intervening brush, and my level of performance up to this point . . . I wasn't going to contribute to even a remote chance that such a magnificent young breeder would go out as an unrecovered gut-shot heap off in a hole some place due to this old elk hunter having an off day. I wished him continued good luck.

The winter following the incident of this Tale was very easy; even the depleted herd bulls made it through just fine. And the winter migration amounted to a short walk downhill to the river below for a while, then straight back uphill as the green shoots appeared on the south slopes. Did my plans include a check-out of Pasture Ridge in September? Does a bear . . . ? Actually, it was a wolf—a pack of 'em—that left plenty of fuzzy calling cards where they'd set up shop on the point of the ridge in late summer. Was that the end of Big Foot and his harem? We extended our sweep of the general area. There were no responses to an occasional locator bugle. It was still early opening morning as we cut across a likely cool spot on the timbered north face above the main trail through the area, and . . .

TALE OF THE BIG FOOT BULL: EPILOGUE

Jackpot! Mashed-down beds just vacated, the wonderfully nauseating stink of bull elk, drops of urine standing fresh on the leaves of the huckleberries. We carefully moved through the bedroom. I was, of course, looking for a distinct, oversized track, but the debris covering the floor of the heavy timber precluded that possibility. The air freshened as we moved away from the gathering area. Suddenly the bull scent was back with a vengeance. I looked up from the ground in the direction of the light breeze. I was looking along a slight defile over the ridge. That's always the route of the elk. I nodded in that direction as a signal to Bill.

"That way," I said very softly as Bill came up.

"See 'em?"

"No, their scent plume is comin' up over the ridge; they're probably side-hillin' around the ridge to the right."

"Think I should bugle?" Bill asked.

"I think he swore off answerin' bugles after last year." Bill agreed with a grin and a nod. We took off, moving fast and silently to the crest of the ridge. The scent faded, then returned in strength. We'd cut it again. We angled down-hill, hoping any second to get a glimpse of russet.

No joy. Those elk, including Lucky Big Foot, had had enough of us, and were outta there.

We made one last pass after we'd let the area cool off for a couple-three days. A mini-drive had Bill moving down through the bedroom with me set up to stand directly on the other side from his approach in a little draw that should be the most likely avenue of escape. No luck. We back-calculated that Bill had likely missed the main gathering area.

To the best of my knowledge, Old Big Foot's still out there as of this writing. I hope to drop by his place again someday.

MAKING THE KILL WITH THE MUZZLELOADER

As will be discussed in the upcoming chapters on equipment, I strongly recommend that the beginning elk hunter who decides to use a muzzleloader choose a modern muzzleloader design. Save the flintlock and original cap-and-ball versions until you have some experience hunting elk. The ignition systems of these old designs are exposed and very susceptible to the elements, and ignition problems are something you can do without while you're trying to learn how to get in on elk at the same time. I also recommend that you mount a 4-power or lower-magnification scope on your muzzleloader, not so you can make long-range shots, but for precise shot placement when making close-in shots under poor lighting conditions with lots of shadows.

The low velocity of the muzzleloader ball or bullet doesn't create enough energy to produce hydraulic shock like the modern high-powered cartridges, so the muzzleloader kills with a penetrating, hemorrhage-producing wound. The muzzleloader projectile also loses velocity fast, resulting in trajectories with rainbow shapes and loss of penetration at even moderate ranges. On the basis of ethics, the beginner needs to have the discipline to pass on the longer-range shots in order to avoid the regret of a shot that only wounds without an immediate kill. (Remember, discipline weighs ounces, but regret weighs tons.) That puts you in the close-in shot business when compared with the high-powered rifle. That's okay when you consider that you often get an advantage in regard to seasons when you use the front stuffer. Beginners should limit themselves to shots of less than 100 yards on standing elk. The penetration of the muzzleloader bullet is limited compared to that of the high-powered cartridge, so the shot should be square broadside rather than even slightly quartering either to the front or to the back.

When you close in for a short-range shot using a muzzleloader, exercise caution and judgment when taking shots at moving elk. The high-powered rifle technique for taking fast-moving elk (looking ahead of the elk for a clear shot between trees) will not work as far out with the muzzleloader. The lower projectile velocity combined with the slower ignition of a muzzleloader can result in a shot striking behind the heart-lung area. The beginner should hold ranges to 30 yards or closer when using this technique.

MAKING THE KILL WITH THE BOW

Before getting into the details of techniques to make the kill with the bow and arrow, I feel obligated to make the reader aware of one major point: This is *much* more difficult than making the kill with a rifle. The skill, conditioning, and discipline needed to get close enough for a clear, ethical shot with the most effective archery equipment available, combined with the required savvy to predict what the elk will do under different circumstances, probably account for the fact that the vast majority of elk taken with the bow are taken year after year by the same handful of expert bowhunters. Then there's the skill you need to have with bugles and cow calls.

For all potential archery elk hunters, I repeat an important observation that applies here if it applies anywhere: Elk are big, tough animals. The applicable corollary here is that it's awfully hard to make a clean kill on one with a bow. I would encourage the beginning elk hunter who doesn't have any experience hunting deer with a bow to do some very serious consideration before taking on the challenges of learning to hunt elk *and* learning to hunt with a bow at the same time. The experienced archery whitetail hunter only needs to be prepared to handle an animal with five to ten times the size and vitality of their normal prey.

In Part II, I'll discuss in some detail the different types of bows and accessories used in elk hunting. You'll be well advised to read all of the specialized books and publications you can get your hands on along with all other sources of information; experienced hunters might be your best resource in that you can ask questions. I recommend that the new bowhunter choose the compound bow. Most of the discussions in this book have the compound in mind. The dedication to develop the level of proficiency to hunt any big game with the recurve bow or longbow, both usually aimed without sights, becomes a passion in itself. Enthusiasts tend to specialize in either the recurve bow, which has an arrow rest and is aimed deliberately along the length of the arrow, or the longbow, which has no arrow rest and is aimed instinctively. Some aspects of technique, such as taking care to hold the bow in a vertical plane so that the arrow will not fly to the side, apply to both compound and recurve bows with arrow rests and/or sights above the arrow. However, tilting the bow has much less of an effect on a properly adjusted recurve sighted along the arrow, and the longbow aimed instinctively is *normally* tilted, sometimes almost horizontal.

All the effort required to develop advanced skills of instinctive shooting results in tactical advantages for these most dedicated of bowhunters. Their foremost advantage is probably speed of operation. The truly skilled instinctive longbow shooter sees the spot on the elk, draws, and shoots an arrow into it. Another arrow is nocked and immediately on its way if required. Another advantage is adaptability to the space available; if the shooter is standing in a brush pile or sitting among the limbs of a tree, he or she can tilt the bow to make a shot in a tight space. True mastery of instinctive shooting skills and the associated upper body strength allow the hunter to make adjustments in draw length and anchor point to make any shot imaginable. Note that I say "mastery" here—I mean it. With anything less than the highest skill level, you may look at the spot on the elk but be aware of the adjacent tree, and nail the tree every time.

In addition to sighting, there are differences in the draw and release of the various types of bows. Compound bows are usually brought to full draw, followed by a pause before the arrow is released as the shooter makes a last-instant alignment of the sights. A common technique of the compound bow hunter is to draw while the quarry momentarily turns away or passes behind an obstruction—the idea is not to let the animal see the hunter move until the arrow is released, so that there's less chance that it sees and avoids the arrow. This technique is practical in the case of the compound bow, since at full draw the force required to hold the bow drawn is drastically reduced (this effect is called "let-off"). This can be extremely important when the elk is close and can easily pick up your movement when you draw the bow. In contrast, the recurve and longbow require progressively more force as the draw is made, so that the archer must apply maximum force at the peak of the draw, which is very difficult to sustain. Holding a stickbow at full draw while waiting for an elk to clear cover gets pretty shaky, in a literal sense, for most of us. (Take it from an old guy with a draw length of over $31\frac{1}{2}$ inches: The creaking is not the bow—it's the shoulder joints.) So the recurve and longbow shooters tend, for the most part, to draw, pause, and release in a single much-practiced smooth motion that includes sighting. There's no wasted motion, and it's fast—but it does involve more movement in clear view of the quarry. Trophy assessment and shot clearance are done before the draw starts. For success, you need to practice enough to make the operation of the equipment absolutely instinctive; conscious mental activity is reserved for the other parts of the hunt.

The techniques of making the kill with the bow and arrow vary somewhat depending on whether the elk approaches the hunter (say, a stationary hunter on a stand) or the other way around. In either situation, the hunter must accomplish three tasks: Operate the equipment while sighting with the correct range; clear a shot path between the bow and the elk; and locate the point of impact on the elk so that the arrow penetrates into the vitals. It should be noted that these are tasks that need to be accomplished as second nature before the archer assumes the mindset of absolute focus to make the shot; otherwise any one of the three can result in a distraction that will break the hunter's focus and ruin the shot. It's also worth noting that each of the three is more difficult than the equivalent task in the case of the rifle. Finally, due to the nature of the close-in stalking of bowhunting, the hunter must always be mentally prepared for a situation that seldom occurs when hunting with the rifle: the truly point-blank shot.

The hunter needs to be familiar, to the point of second nature, with the space needed to correctly operate the bow. This familiarity can be developed on the archery practice range by shooting from unusual positions such as kneeling or sitting and in other settings such as areas with lots of brush and tree limbs. Dedicated instinctive shooters can actually accommodate extremely awkward shooting positions. I suggest that the beginner—in particular one using a compound bow— select an arrow rest that provides some retention in order to keep the arrow in place while the bow is being moved around before the shot. Remember that the bow has to be vertical when the shot is made with a compound. A rest that holds the arrow in place just serves to eliminate one more possible distraction. Happily, compound bows are also short, much shorter than a longbow, so that much less space is required to operate the compound.

For the beginner, the range needs to be 20 yards or less. All sorts of devices and techniques for range determination are available and will work if you have time to use them. Many bowhunters use laser rangefinders to measure the distances to objects in preparation for an encounter with an elk. If you use an elevation-adjustable sight with a single aiming point or crosshairs, or a fiber-optic point, the surrounding sight support-protector can be used for instant maximum range determination, and it's always in front of your face and therefore available. You can detemine the range based on how much of the image of the elk you can see within the sight support-protector at a range of 20 or 30 yards. Usually the 60 inches between the feet and the top of the back of a bull just fits. Extreme precision is not required; the presence of mind to get the range while keeping up with the actions of the elk takes precedence. The sight should be set to strike the point of aim low on the chest at the selected range. If you're closer, the shot will be a little high but still through the lungs. Too far and you'll make a clean miss low. You want a good hit or a clean miss.

If you do use a multiple-fiber-optic-point sight, I would suggest using only three points until you've accumulated a lot of practice and hunting experience. Set the center point to be dead on at 30 yards and the arrow won't rise out of the lethal strike zone at closer ranges, then don't push the distance too far with the bottom point sight setting. And don't hold the bottom pin over the back of the elk. That's crowding the ethics of the too-long shot.

A change in elevation of the sight for ranging just adds to the problem of the arrow going off to one side if the bow is tilted. Just keep in mind the fact that if you're not positioned to operate the sighted bow in a vertical plane, you're not ready to attempt the shot.

Your narrow focus on the intended target should be relaxed and expanded for a moment to clear the path of your shot just before you concentrate fully on the sight in preparation for the kill. It's that situational awareness thing again. Concentrating on the target tends to make the intervening twigs, limbs, and brush invisible to you, but they're still there to deflect the shot and leave you wondering what went wrong. This point applies to iron sights and scopes on rifles as well as bowsights. Remember that the arrow rises up from the rest as it's launched. This initial lift, followed by the trajectory of the arrow, takes it slightly above your line of sight. Those twigs and limbs might be just above your line of sight to the target, but that doesn't mean you're going to be able to shoot under them.

Instinctive shooting eliminates all these mechanics of sighting—but it comes at the cost of a lot more practice for the beginner, and the trajectory curve still pertains.

A final word on aiming and range estimation with a bow: Laser rangefinders and multiple-pin sights can hit the 6-inch shot area on an elk at more than 50 yards—but that doesn't mean you should. The shot can be a little off; the elk can (and likely will) move; or the arrow won't retain enough energy to make a clean kill. The result? The elk may not be recovered and may either die a slow death or live a cripple. Draw your line at the 35- to 40-yard mark. There are a lot of things worse than an unfilled elk tag.

Another installment of Tom's Fall Frolics with the Bow: This little Tale illustrates from firsthand experience the results of not paying enough attention to clearing the shot.

ON CLEARING THE BOWSHOT, OR, HOW BOWSHOT PASS GOT ITS NAME

Herm and I were both learning about bowhunting for elk and checking out a new area during the archery hunt of my twentieth elk hunting season. We had worked tree stands at a couple of good places and tried ground stands at a few more. The elk didn't seem to be moving to our stands on their own, so we decided to try stillhunting and move ourselves to them.

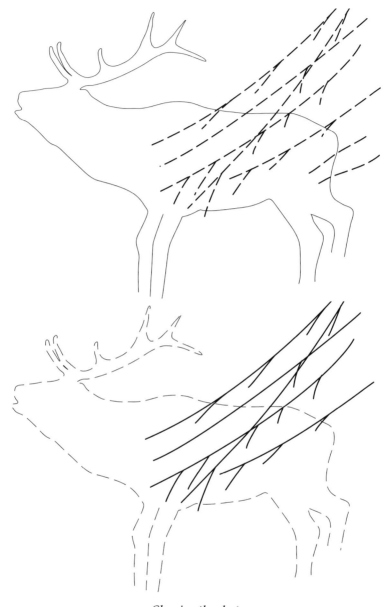

Clearing the shot.

We found an area with a lot of elk tracks and followed the contour of the ridge to a likely-looking saddle with the thought of finding a good place to watch for elk moving through. As we worked our way along the elk trail from the Chateau Creek side, we cleared a stand of brush just as we crested the midpoint of the pass, and found ourselves face-to-face at a range of about 50 yards with a small herd of elk moving up from the Squaw Creek side. Hunters and elk froze in place as we all saw each other at the same time. After just a second of reaction time, Herm and I got low, Herm on all fours, me in a squat, in an automatic attempt to assume the form of anything but two surprised human elk hunters. The startled and confused elk nervously milled around, and began to move back down the slope they had been coming up. A single set of large elk antlers stuck up over the russet mass of the swirling herd.

Still acting with instinctive reflexes, we moved forward in a awkward rush to close the distance between ourselves and the elk to a reasonable bow range, while the elk tried to put some distance between themselves and the strange beasts who were acting like predators and moving in their direction. Herm, moving on all fours in a reasonable imitation of an ambling bear, was making faster progress than I was, since I was trying to clear the low brush with my large compound bow as I moved along in imitation of a drunken penguin or overgrown duck. Herm got to the near side of the intervening stand of trees well ahead of me, and cut loose with his cow call with the most soothing, reassuring sounds that he could come up with in his agitated state. I pulled up behind the screen of brush, looking for an opening and trying to clear a shot at the bull—again, an instinctive reaction.

I picked the bull out through the screen of brush. I could see his head and the upper part of his back from my crouching position. He was moving toward my left across the slope in front of me. I stood up in a shooting position and moved to my left, looking for an opening through the brush and low tree limbs. When I found my opening, I focused on the bull, which was a little over 20 yards away.

From my standing position, I could see the full mass of the bull's body, and the heart-lung aiming point was in my line of sight, just above the intervening grass-covered ground. It looked like the arc of the arrow trajectory would just clear the ground. I brought the bow to full draw and released the arrow, holding on the elk with a good sight picture. I heard a muffled "thump" at the bull's location. The bull made a peculiar, flat-footed crow-hop straight off the ground, and then bolted around the slope and out of sight. The rest of the herd took off in various directions down or around the slope.

Soon after, we heard the bull bugle about 100 yards off to our left and slightly above us. We moved off a short distance in that direction, trying to pick up a blood trail. Failing to spot any sign of blood, we settled down to wait for the shot to tell. It had looked good and sounded good. I was euphoric at having gotten a good shot at a big six-point with a ground stalk. The only challenge to my confidence came from the bull, who continued his defiant bellows for a long time as he moved off. Usually not a good sign, but not always a sure indicator of a clean miss.

We sat down to wait a reasonable amount of time for the bull to lie down and stiffen up. An hour, maybe an hour and a half, was about all the waiting that we could manage before we moved out to try to pick up the bull's tracks, or maybe a blood trail. Moving in the direction of the last bugles, we picked up a well-used elk trail. Several sets of fresh tracks along the trail indicated that the part of the herd that had rejoined the bull had used the trail to leave the area. There was no sign of a blood trail (a better indication that the shot had failed to connect in the case of a bowshot than with a rifle shot). It became obvious that the entire herd, including the bull, was leaving the area. We decided to go back and check the area where the bull was when I took the shot before taking off on a long-range pursuit of a possible clean miss.

Back at the point of the shot, we realized why we hadn't found any sort of blood trail to follow, and weren't going to. The clean arrow lay in the trail at exactly the spot where the bull had been standing when I released the shot. It was not only undamaged, but also completely clean. It appeared to have been dropped straight down where it lay. There was no sign of the broadhead penetrating the dirt in the trail, or encountering any other obstacle, for that matter. It looked like we had the makings of one of those unsolved mysteries that float around evening elk camp campfires for years.

But this tale would have an ending. We climbed up the steep, grass-covered slope that the arrow had traversed, in an effort to find what sort of obstacle could absorb all of the energy of that heavy arrow without leaving a mark. As we neared the screen of brush and low tree limbs that I had been behind when I took the shot, there lay the answer to our little mystery.

On the ground, looking completely out of place, lay a very fresh green pine twig, neatly sliced through its $1/4$-inch-diameter butt end as if by a razor. Looking up, we saw the freshly sliced other side of the cut. I moved around the little stand of trees and underbrush to stand in my tracks where I stood to make the shot. There was the opening, through which I could clearly see Herm, standing where we had recovered the arrow. And there was the cleanly sliced twig jutting down from a limb just above my line of sight. I focused my sight on the twig 10 feet out and it was clear—much more clear, in fact, than anything else visible through the little opening. I focused my sight on Herm, 30 or so yards down the slope, and the twig wasn't so clear. The moral for the aspiring bowhunter is to focus far *and* near before releasing that arrow. Control the mindset to clear the shot before the mindset to make the shot takes over.

So this Tale had an ending, one that I've heard about ever since. Ever since then, that little pass where I took the shot has been known as "Bowshot Pass" among my hunting friends. And there is a song of several verses about it that starts, "Come all you young hunters and hear my sad sooong . . . 'Bout bow shots gone crazy and bow shots gone wronnggg . . . " It's one of the few things that Old Herm seems capable of remembering through the years.

A ground stand with small limbs placed in front of and behind the bowhunter.
DAN UHRICH

Stands

The tree stand is normally used by the bowhunter to wait unseen along a path where an elk is expected to pass within range for a shot. The stand is placed in the tree in a good position to make the shot, and while you're waiting you have plenty of time to clear small limbs and other obstructions from the expected line of sight and to make accurate estimates, or actual measurements using a rangefinder, of the range to the expected location of the elk. This way, when the elk appears in the expected location, the hunter needs only to focus on making the shot. Complications to this well-arranged situation can develop when the elk fail to cooperate and the trophy of a lifetime shows up in some place other than the expected location. Then the hunter on the stand has to maintain the presence of mind to operate the bow in a possibly confined position, check the path of the arrow, and verify that the elk is standing so that the arrow placement will be good.

The ground stand can involve the hunter waiting in a concealed position, as is the case with a tree stand; it can also involve a temporary position offering some concealment along the path of an elk that is being stalked, possibly in cooperation with another hunter who may be driving the elk or bugling to it. The concerns about having enough space to operate the bow, clearing the path of the arrow, and ranging the shot are the same in either case, the difference being that there will be more time to prepare for the shot in the case of the deliberately prepared stand. A problem common to both ground stands is that the hunter is much more likely to be seen when on the same level as the elk. Good camouflage helps in this situation, but the hunter may need to wait until the elk looks away in order to draw the bow without spooking it. Sometimes the terrain makes it possible to take a position on elevated ground that seems to help the hunter remain unnoticed. You should take care in selecting your position to avoid limiting yourself to difficult shot angles.

A Notch Past the Basics

A very remote possibility, but one you should contemplate before it's presented, is when the bull is right in your lap, the point-blank shot at less than 15 feet. There are more good stories than successful shots in this situation for a variety of reasons. The underlying theme of most one-that-got-away stories is that the hunter never considered this case as a possibility, and therefore couldn't get into the appropriate mindset to make the kill. I suggest that you do think about it, and practice for it just in case. It happens in bowhunting more than with other equipment. You can practice for this shot with a large area target that completely fills your sight picture. If you don't have a full-size 3-D target, you could stretch a large sheet of brown paper across the front of a conventional target to provide an area target.

Some hunters prefer to aim instinctively in this situation even if they normally use a sight. If you're normally a sight user, as I am, I would draw the bow to the point of aim as usual, and then look through and past the sight, without concentrating on the points or crosshairs, so that you see a lot of the elk. A common reason that this shot is blown seems to be that the hunter's vision is focused by looking through the sight. Rather than seeing an image of an elk with an aiming point, all they see is hair. For some reason the hunter doesn't shoot because it isn't obvious where the spot to aim at is, or maybe it just doesn't look right.

A stalk in close proximity to an elk in order to make a bowshot is probably the most challenging technique in elk hunting. The key to successfully making the kill in this situation is to take it one step at a time in a smoothly flowing continuum. You can attempt to make the entire approach unseen (which, if you are successful, will give you more time to make the shot, but carries the risk of spooking the elk if and when you are discovered), or you can make the entire approach attempting to pass yourself off as some woodland creature or at least something that the elk doesn't pattern as a predator. Different approaches may be better or worse in different situations.

A good opportunity for successfully making a bow kill—one that hunters often fail to take advantage of—occurs when moving elk and the moving hunter in the process of attempting to locate elk unexpectedly intercept each other. The key to success here is to instantly make the transition from the mindset of location either to that of stalking or directly to making the kill, depending on the distance and whether you have a good broadside shot at 20 yards or less. You must immediately determine whether the elk are aware of a human presence, in order to decide on the first step of the appropriate reaction. If the elk are unaware of you and the wind is such that they won't shortly get your scent, you're probably better off to freeze in place. If you have a suitable shot, draw and take it; if not, let the elk approach or move to present a shot, then draw and take it. If the elk are aware of your presence but you have a good shot, then draw and take the shot without making eye contact until the last minute. In the more likely event that you don't have a shot and the elk have become aware of you, immediately attempt to pass yourself off as something other than a human elk hunter while you move to a position where you *will* have a shot. I suggest that you get low and try to pass yourself off as a bear. As you move, don't stare at the elk, but stay aware of what they're doing; the elk may assist you by moving around and getting in position for you to have a shot. It's best if you can make an approach other than directly at the elk. If you're on a trail crossing a slope, move off the trail upslope; the elk are likely to move along the trail past you, and present a shot in the process. Check the breeze first.

Bow Options and Shot Timing

Bowhunters often encounter situations where they are close enough for a shot but the acceptable shot locations are covered. And all too often, the hunter is within the wide field of the elk's vision. You're stuck with waiting in hope against hope that the elk will step clear of cover. A variation is that neither the elk nor the hunter is covered, and the hunter attempts to stay motionless in hopes that the bull will turn to look in another direction, allowing the hunter to make an undetected draw. Or the hunter is in a situation in which he or she is forced to step clear of cover to make the shot in full view of the elk. There are variations without limit on this basic theme, but you get the idea.

Your options depend on the equipment in hand. The compound bow can be brought to full draw and held under much less weight than maximum draw. The hunter can make the draw and hold it for a considerable time, releasing the arrow using a trigger release when the opportunity for the shot presents itself. Releases that let the string go under precise control of the shooter work best in this situation. Stickbows increase in draw weight with length of draw and are difficult to hold at full draw for long periods of time. On the other hand, the stickbow draw, sight, and finger release tends to be faster than shooting with a compound with sights to align and string releases. Stickbow operators get off a shot quicker, giving the elk less time to react. Compounds with multiple sight points are more accurate for shots at long ranges. The downside of long-range bowshots is that the elk has more time to pick up the arrow and jump. Not as quickly as a whitetail, but you'd be surprised how agile the big boys can be.

CHAPTER 10

Recovery of the Kill

... WHEN EVERYTHING IS PERFECT

So, you've done everything right, taken all of the precautions, made the shot, and saw the elk drop in its tracks, or, at worst, trot off a few yards, stagger, drop, and expire in a few seconds. Congratulations! Take the pictures; attach the tag, and whatever else the state where you're hunting requires; recover from your excitement.

... IN THE REAL WORLD

This section addresses what we have taken all measures to avoid. That other case, when the real world intrudes into the Saturday morning Outdoor Hunting Show script and you need to recover the kill.

There are many techniques that can be used in different circumstances to recover an elk that doesn't drop immediately after the shot. The nature of the problem, and therefore the best technique, is often associated with the type of equipment used to make the kill.

The problems with the recovery of elk taken with a high-powered centerfire rifle are often associated with the range capability of this type of equipment. (It might be more precise to say the range of the equipment combined with the lack of experience of the hunter making the shot.) Beginning with the least odious circumstance, hunters often have difficulty in locating a clean kill when shooting across canyons from one side to the opposite slope. The shot is usually made at extended range, but still within the lethal range of the rifle. The elk is in clear view when the shot is made, since the hunter can easily see into the brush and broken timber of the opposite slope. The hunter sees the elk go down, and immediately takes off down the near slope, through the heavier brush and timber along the creek at the bottom of the canyon, and up the opposite slope toward the elk. Complications develop when the rough, thick stuff in the bottom of the creek results in a little disorientation starting up the far slope. It gets worse when the visibility through the brush and trees on the far side is much more restricted than it appeared from the original vantage point. You're on the same plane as the brush, and you can't see down through it as you can when you are looking across from the facing slope. Before long, the excited hunter has lost not only the original line of travel, but also the starting point from which the shot was made. A very exhausting search of both slopes often results before the elk is finally located, and sometimes it may not be located at all. If the shot didn't result in a clean kill, the hunter has a very small chance of locating the point to start to trail the wounded elk.

This problem can be eliminated by remembering to take a little time before you start toward the elk to pick out a couple of landmarks near the spot where you took the shot. Then use your compass to get a bearing on the location of the downed elk, along with some landmarks that rise above the brush in the vicinity of the elk. If two hunters are together when the shot is made, it's usually best for the shooter to stay where the shot was made to give directions by hand signals while the other one searches the far side for the elk. Just get your signals straight. Or a landmark from where the shot was taken might be used as a bearing.

GPS units and laser rangefinders are now available to assist the technology-savvy elk hunter, but even the best of these units won't have a "find elk" function. You'll need to be on speaking terms with topographical maps to keep from becoming confused in the brush and complicated slope patterns in rough country. One approach to finding the elk is to mark the spot where it dropped on the topo map in the GPS unit before you cross the canyon to find it. A rangefinder might come in handy to pinpoint the location, or you might locate a prominent landmark or terrain feature near the elk on the GPS map. You can then stow the unit in your pocket for the rough climb over to the opposite face and take it out again on the other side and go to the marked location. Alternatively, if you can't get a good location along the line of sight toward the elk, you can mark a bearing line on the GPS map that you can get back on once you're on the opposite slope, then work along that line looking for the elk.

Once you are standing at the location where the elk was when the shot was taken—whether you get there with the help of hand signals from your partner or by GPS—take a look around for the elk. At the distance of a long-range rifle shot in rough country, the elk that you couldn't see go down from where you took the shot might be lying in plain sight from the vantage point of the location where it was hit. If the ground is covered with brush tall enough to obscure the body of the elk, remember that you are looking for a single beam of the rack over the vegetation. If you don't see anything, look around the immediate vicinity for blood or disturbed ground that indicates startled movement. Particularly in the case of a rifle shot, the disturbance may not resemble tracks, but it might be your only indication of a hit, and might give an indication of the animal's direction of flight. A rifle shot might not produce a blood trail for up to 20 yards as the elk moves away. At this point, you might be well advised to hold your place for a half hour to an hour to give time for the elk to expire or stiffen up. If left undisturbed, it may not have moved too far, but if immediately threatened, the excitement might enable it to travel a great distance before it gives out, and you might never recover it. Waiting should be your usual procedure unless it is raining or snowing (which will ruin your chance of following a blood trail) or darkness is closing in.

Muzzleloader elk hunters shouldn't be in the business of cross-canyon shooting due to the inherent range limitations of their equipment. The moderate velocity of the muzzleloader projectile doesn't provide as much damage to internal organs from shock as the high-powered centerfire rifle does. Recovery of the kill is more on the order of what the bowhunter faces. It's not uncommon to have to do more trailing to locate downed elk hit by a muzzleloader.

For a bowshot, the best procedure is to hold your place after what appears to be a successful shot. The elk could be standing in the same area where it was hit, but out of sight. Without the noise of a firearm, a mortal wound through the chest cavity with an arrow may not disturb it at all. If it stands, you may have the opportunity for another shot if it is not aware of your presence. The decision whether to take another shot might depend upon your own mental condition as much as on the condition of the elk in these circumstances. You might just spook the elk and make it harder to recover if it is already mortally wounded. If not panicked by the approach of a perceived threat, the elk will likely hemorrhage and expire in the immediate vicinity. Another shot or an immediate approach might panic the elk and give it the adrenaline to flee for an incredibly long distance even if mortally wounded. Waiting for a sufficient time for the animal to hemorrhage and stiffen will usually greatly decrease the area you have to search. Recommendations on how long to wait vary from one to four hours (although excited elk hunters seldom wait over two hours, according to my observations). Falling rain or snow creates more of a dilemma for the bowhunter than for the rifle hunter, since the bowhunters need to wait longer.

After waiting for as long as you can stand, move to where the elk was when you made the shot, even if you are sure that the elk has moved off in a certain direction. You need to verify that nothing strange happened to your shot, such as an arrow deflection, and determine from the ground that tracks of the elk you hit do lead off in the direction you may have heard the elk going. Look for disturbed ground in the vicinity of the elk as it reacted to the shot. The bowhunter is more likely to find a good blood trail than the rifle hunter, and it will likely start closer to the point of the shot. On the other hand, the bowhunter is also less likely to be able to see a fallen elk from the point of the shot—but you should look around anyway.

At this point, the techniques of the rifle hunter and the bowhunter merge. The best situation is to have a continuous and unmistakable blood trail with easily followed tracks that quickly lead to the expired elk. That's not always the case. In the more likely event that either the blood or the track trail is intermittent or absent, remain calm and confident, and pause to look around to assess the most likely avenue of flight of the stricken animal. The factors that influence the direction of flight, in generally descending order of importance, are as follows: the escape route of the rest of the herd, if other elk were present; the apparent state of panic of the animal at the time of the shot; the direction of perceived threat; the type of wound (which might impede mobility); and the terrain, both in the immediate vicinity and surrounding the immediate area.

Look in the most likely direction first to see if you can pick up the trail. If you're not successful and other elk were present, it might be worthwhile to follow their more numerous tracks to see if the elk you are after rejoined them. You can assume that the herding instinct of the elk will dominate behavior when an immediate threat is patterned. If you run out of good directions to look for a blood trail or tracks and still haven't found anything, don't give up; switch to a patterned search, beginning at the point of the shot, then widening out in the most likely directions first, and finally in all directions. Don't quit searching until you have covered all possibilities, even the ones that seem completely illogical. If you're lucky, you'll locate the elk and you'll be able to explain why the route that seemed crazy was the obvious one that you should have gone with first.

Once the wounded animal is located, the final step of the kill is to make sure that the animal has expired before you closely approach or touch it. You may have the task of administering the killing shot. There are stories of animals stunned by a non-lethal shot only to completely revive and run off, with the rifle hanging from their antlers, in the middle of the picture-taking session. There are many more—but less often told—stories of wounded animals spooked by the hunter's approach that find enough reserve energy to get away to die a lingering death from a lethal wound that did not immediately incapacitate them. Indications that the animal has expired, in addition to the obvious cessation of breathing, are glazed, dilated eyes (open, not shut) and drooped ears.

FIELD DRESSING

Field dressing is the final stage of taking the elk. This is not the favorite aspect of most elk hunters, but it's an area in which you need to have at least adequate skills. It's the ethical responsibility of the hunter who has taken the life of the animal to preserve the meat—regardless of whether you have someone there to help you with it. You need to have some basic knowledge of the essentials so that you're able to field dress an elk (no style points to worry about here). You also need to have the few simple pieces of gear well maintained and on hand when you make the kill—not back in camp because you were just going out for the afternoon on the last day of your hunt. Not only is taking care of the meat ethical, but preparing and eating the elk venison are considered a major part of the enjoyment by many hunters.

Care of the meat and hide and trophy begins as soon as the kill is made. Well, in just a second. You might want to consider securing that rifle you're still running around with all excited and with the safety off. Hunter's prayers. Then congratulations are in order, along with attaching the tags and any other administrative actions required by the state you're in (that is, other than the state of excitement), and taking a couple of snapshots while the elk carcass is still in one big piece to embellish the tale in future telling. Then it's time to get to work.

There's no time to waste in getting the hide off and the carcass quartered and off of the ground so the meat can begin to cool. You can get away with a less thorough immediate job while you go back for heavier tools to split the backbone if the weather is cold, but you should always completely gut out the carcass, get most of the hide off, and separate it from the ground. At a minimum, it should be up on small log sections if you're not moving it around often, and you should hang it if you're going to walk away from it for more than an hour or so. If you're hunting far from camp or if the weather isn't very cold, you'd better have the full set of equipment at hand to do a complete job to get the meat hanging before you leave the carcass. If you're in coyote country, you'll want to leave it hanging at least 6 feet high; 8 to 10 feet for bear country. You'll also want to keep up with where you leave your rifle, preferably close at hand, and look around from time to time during the field dressing job.

It's been my experience that most people interested in elk hunting have some experience with deer hunting. So, if this is your frame of reference, the first time you see the carcass of a bull elk on the ground in front of you, prepare yourself for something of a shock. They're big. But more relevant to the job at hand—they're heavy. The live weight of a bull elk will range from around 500 pounds up to over 900 pounds. That would be a load anywhere, but the next shock you're in for is that place where it dropped. It's usually on a slope with several obstacles around and under the body to add to the handling problem. You will probably not be able to do much with the whole carcass other than to turn it over on its back and slide it around on the ground by struggling with one limp, massive element at a time, enough to rotate it so that you have the head pointed uphill.

Quartering an Elk Carcass

If you've taken a bull elk, the party starts in earnest with removal of the belly patch. You will find it to be even more awful than anything you have ever read or been told. And everything you have heard about its detrimental effect on the taste of any meat it comes in contact with is also not an exaggeration. I recommend that you go to any lengths possible to prevent that from happening. Bring along elbow-length rubber gloves that you *only* use once, and only on this task. Likewise, bring a small knife especially for this job, which you can clean up later at your convenience, but don't use that knife for anything else or even touch it with a bare hand once it's been used on the skin around the belly patch. Have a dedicated ziplock bag opened and ready. Once you've removed the hide around the belly patch, getting enough extra that you're outside the scented area, throw the hide far enough out into the brush that the pack animals can't even smell it; then remove the gloves by turning the sleeve part wrong side out while you hold the knife, and put the entire stinking mess into the plastic bag. Zip it up without touching any surface that has contacted the belly patch hide, or that has contacted anything that has contacted the belly patch hide.

Depending on the state where you're hunting, in the case of a bull carcass, the next task will likely be to make sure that a testicle remains attached to each hindquarter. This is done by first carefully slitting the hide covering the scrotum to start the skinning. This initial slit makes it easier to locally remove the hide from between the back legs before you get into any cutting. This will allow you to see the very small, soft secondary material that connects each testicle to the quarter immediately adjacent to it. Then you can safely split the hide forward to the skinned belly patch area and back to the anus, divide the soft tissue between the legs with a testicle still attached to each quarter to get at the bone and cartilage with a heavy knife, and use a small saw to split the lower part of the pelvic bone front to back so that the colon can be cleared back to the rectum. Whew! Carefully cut around the rectum to separate the intestinal tract from the hide. This allows clean removal of the lower part of the colon, along with the rest of the intestines and everything else forward to the windpipe, which is what we're getting set up for. The next step is to split open the abdominal tissue and muscle from the part already made between the back legs forward to the diaphragm. Cut the diaphragm away from the muscles around the ribs so that everything is separated all the way to the windpipe. Everything will be neat because you did make a clean chest-cavity shot, didn't you?

Working in the chest cavity, avoid broken rib bones—or you'll find out the hard way that those bones are hard and sharp enough to cut like a knife. Reach inside the chest cavity all the way forward and cut the windpipe and esophagus so that you can pull out the lungs, stomach, and everything else to the rear in one motion, all the way back to clear the hindquarters. Double whew! Cut around the anus and everything will be separated from the meat. Now you know why you went to the trouble to get the head of the carcass pointed upslope. You sure don't want to have to work against gravity to remove all of that stuff out the back.

Separate the heart and liver from the rest of the bear bait and put them in bags to take back to camp for special treats for the rest of the hunt. It's best to use an extra deer bag to carry the heart and liver; it will allow quicker cooling and keep flies off. It's a good idea to cool them in a cool stream if available. If you only have plastic bags, don't leave them bagged too long while they're warm. They spoil very easily.

Now all you have to do is remove the hide and cut the carcass into quarters. Easy. Right.

Split the hide down the inside of each hindquarter so that you can peel the hide back from the ham of the leg along with the flank of the back part of the body. If the hide is to be used in one piece, you'll have to tip up the hindquarters together to get the hide off before you halve the carcass. You can leave the hide on and cut it with the carcass at about the third rib with everything still on the ground, using a heavy knife and a saw to cut the backbone, but you're more likely to get hair in the meat with this less strenuous approach. Split the two hindquarters along the length of the backbone, using a medium-sized Wyoming-type handsaw with a bone blade or an axe. Remove the lower part of each leg by going through the ankle or knee joint using a heavy knife and a saw or axe. Put a deer bag around each quarter and hang it up. Now you're ready for the front-end assembly.

SHARPENING A KNIFE

Your skinning knife (knives) will probably become dulled sometime during this job. You'll need to have with you some means to sharpen them. You'll also need to have practiced the sharpening process beforehand—without the time constraints of your first elk field dressing job out on the side of a slope with dark or a storm approaching, or in a swarm of flies and hot weather threatening to spoil the meat before you get the hide off. Some hunters and guides use ceramic or carbide-bladed sharpeners set at fixed angles to restore edges during field dressing. These devices are quick and require little in the way of technique, but they remove a lot of the blade with each stroke in the case of moderate-hardness knives, and leave the edge rough. Many hunters restrict the carbide sharpeners to the axes and saws, and prefer to use a whetstone or hone for all types of knife blades.

To use a whetstone or hone, draw the knife across the surface of the stone for the full length of the cutting edge, with each stroke at a constant angle to the stone or hone, which takes a little practice. Knife experts with a lot of experience sharpening the modern high-hardness stainless blades recommend that the angle between the blade and stone be 22.5 degrees. It's not really that exact, but this angle is easy for knife sharpeners not into trigonometry to visualize. If the blade is positioned exactly perpendicular, or 90 degrees to the stone surface, then tilted to an angle that splits the difference between perpendicular and the surface of the stone, that's 45 degrees; split the difference again and that's 22.5 degrees. This differs a little from the technique that I was originally taught. The traditional way of sharpening traditional pocket and hunting knives, as practiced and taught by generations of granddads using conventional stones, was with a circular stroking motion at an angle of 10 to 15 degrees. Knife makers suggest stroking the blade into the stone as if shaving off thin slices of the stone at an angle of 11 degrees (using our angle-estimating technique, divide that 22 degrees in half one more time). The old granddad technique also requires application of a drop of spit every twelve strokes or so if you're not using an oiled stone. As a modern granddad, I don't have any suggestions on this aspect of their technique as applied to hard stainless steel or even harder ceramic blades against a diamond whetstone. Have your grandkids go online and check out the current preferred practice.

If you want to remove the hide whole to be used in making a rug or article of clothing rather than a trophy head-and-shoulder mount, continue the split along the belly all the way up the neck. Split along the inside of the front legs, then peel it off in one piece up to the head. Cut around the neck just behind the head. Sometime before you get rid of the skull, don't forget to remove the ivories, the small tusks just in front of the upper grinding teeth. Cut away the surrounding tissue and work the tusk loose to make extraction easy.

SKINNING FOR A TROPHY MOUNT

To skin for a trophy mount, you cut the hide behind the shoulders, leaving plenty of hide to go with the mount. Split the hide from the belly patch area forward along the center of the bottom of the chest cavity to a point just behind the front legs. Split the hide around the ankle or knee joint at the lower leg and down the inside of each front leg to the chest, then across to intersect with the chest centerline split behind the front legs. (You're not cutting the hide at the front of the chest because that annoys the taxidermist.) Then peel the hide forward to clear the front quarters and start up the neck. Cut the head off with the hide still attached.

Once you have the elk skinned, divide the front quarters along the backbone using a saw or axe, remove the lower leg at the joint, and put a deer bag around each quarter and hang it up.

So now you have five loads of around 100 pounds (four quarters of meat and the trophy) ready to be packed out to the road and then on to the processor or freezer. A reminder and caution—do not leave meat on the ground any longer than the minimum time required to get the hide off and the carcass quartered. And when you hang it, hang it high if predators are in the area. The work is over if you have a packer ready to bring in a string of mules to take it out, it's just begun if you're on your on.

Bringing an Elk In to Camp and Packing It Out to the Road
On that rare occasion when somebody in a pack camp gets lucky and actually gets an elk, the packer has another job along with the drop camps coming and going. If it's a trophy bull, it's a good job that means some good references and pictures for the outfit's advertising. The quarters of meat are brought in to the hunting camp from the kill location. The usual procedure is for the packer to bring the elk quarters in to camp with the front quarters packed on one load, and the rear quarters

on another, so that each load is balanced. When the trail is good and the rack is manageable, the trophy may be "top-packed" on the front quarters.

When the rack is large, and more of the neck is left attached to the head, the neck and head and cape may make up another load, packed on the most settled pack animal in the string, and brought in on a separate lead to hold down complications with the string coming up out of the typical hole where the bull goes down. Complications tend to occur when antlers catch on limbs and poke the horse or mule in the flank. It's easy to imagine how this can happen when you consider what an awkward load the head and cape of a large trophy make.

If the weather is cool, the elk quarters will hang on the meat pole until it's convenient to pack them down to the base camp to be taken to the wild game processor. If it's warm enough that the hanging meat might spoil, the trip out takes place right away.

If you're in for a long, uphill packboard pack out, you'll be tempted to bone out the quarters to make smaller loads. This practice has pros and cons. If not allowed to age on the bone for at least a day or so, the meat tends to shrink and take on a rubbery texture. Most dedicated wild game cooks don't bone out newly killed quarters unless it's absolutely necessary. And there *are* times out on the mountain where it is absolutely necessary.

THE "WHITTLE-AWAY" APPROACH TO FIELD DRESSING

Sometimes hunters in a hurry will use an alternative method for handling a downed elk instead of the standard steps of field dressing (gutting), quartering for packing, and saving the hide or cape intact for mounting. This short-cut approach is used when an elk has to be packed out on a packboard and time is short. It's recommended when there's a real need for speed due to hot temperatures that will spoil the meat in a short time, or, at the other extreme, an approaching winter storm. This method can be accomplished using only the essential daypack tools: a couple of knives and a small handsaw.

The carcass is laid flat on one side and the hunter strips the meat from the top side; then the hunter turns the carcass over to repeat the process on the other side. For each side, the entire hind leg is removed with the hide still on by cutting around the hip socket so that the leg can be removed whole like a ham (a ham with the hide still on). The front leg is removed by cutting underneath the shoulder. The lower part of the leg may be removed at the joint. Slit and peel back the hide along the backbone and slice away the backstrap for the length of the backbone, then continue forward to remove the side of the neck, and down to strip all of the meat from outside of the ribs. Saw through the ribs along the backbone to get at the tenderloin underneath the backbone. The meat cools better if the hide is removed and the meat is cut into smaller chunks. Place the chunks in deer bags in manageable loads for the packboard, remembering to keep the loads within your realistic limitations. Load up and head out for as many trips as it takes. Hope you have help.

One more caution before leaving this section: After you have finished the field dressing, if you leave the meat and hide cooling while you go back for help in packing it out, make sure that you can find it again. Even if it's a short distance to a main trail back to camp, hang markers in low tree limbs on the way to the trail, close enough together that you can always see the next flag from the one before it. Note some landmarks and check your direction on your way out as well. Some hunters carry surveyor tape for this purpose. Toilet paper makes good environmentally friendly flags, and can serve several other purposes as well. Its only drawback as a trail marker relative to surveyor tape is that you need to protect your markers from pouring rain, which is very unusual. As opposed to toilet paper, the surveyor tape serves no dual purpose.

The first cut in removing the hide and head for a trophy shoulder mount.

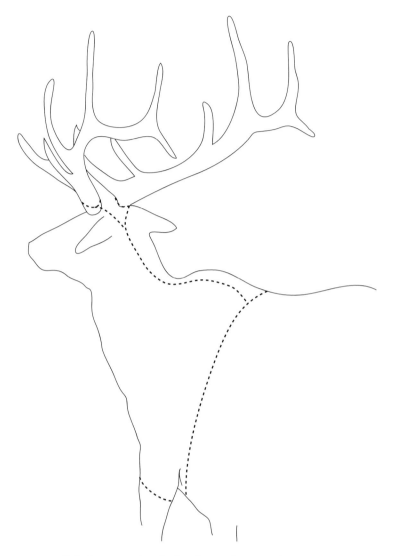

Cuts for removing the head cape for a trophy mount.

REMOVING THE HEAD SKIN FOR A TROPHY MOUNT

The meticulous process of skinning the head for a trophy mount is time-consuming and requires good lighting. The usual procedure in outfitter camps is to pack the trophy head back to camp, where the hunter has the option to do the job him- or herself with skilled help available for advice, or to have one of the experienced camp hands do the entire job, with an extra tip as partial compensation. Unless the hunter is an expert skinner, a better option is for the best skinner among the guides or the packer or sometimes the outfitter to do the honors while everybody else critiques the skinner's technique as part of the celebration.

The hide is removed from the head and neck by making a cut along the back or top of the neck through the thick hide and heavy mane-like hair to a point just behind the ears and antlers. Refer to the sketch on page 206 to see how to make the cuts.

The hide is peeled away from the neck and head as you go.

From this point behind the ears and antlers, make a cut to each antler.

Removing the hide from the back and top of the head and around the antlers is tough, and may require prying with a very heavy knife blade or some other prying tool such as a very heavy screwdriver.

Use a small finger-sized skinning knife to very carefully remove the hide from around the base of the ears, where you remove the hide from the more massive cartilage at the base of the ear, then remove the full thickness of the ear from about an inch or so above the base of the ear on out. From the ears toward the nose, you need to exercise care to keep from cutting through the thin hide that covers the front part of the head.

When removing the hide in the area of the eyes, take care to keep the eyelids with the hide.

The "ivories" are extracted during the skinning of the head and become a small trophy.

Remove the lips with the hide, keeping the trim close to the jaw so that the taxidermist has plenty to work with in preparation of the mount.

Now for the salt to prevent the hair from slipping. Any taxidermist will tell you that you can't use too much salt, and I'd be the very last person in the world to cross a taxidermist on any point. If you ever get to know a taxidermist, you'll understand. Hair slippage, which salt prevents, is about the only damage taxidermists can't finesse with their magic. Use 1 pound of salt for every 2 pounds of hide, which is a lot of salt, but that's what I've been told is needed. Use fine salt; non-iodized is preferred. The main thing is to cover every square inch of hide, including around the eyes, ears, lips, and any other folds.

Shoulder mount.

So just get all the salt you can get your hands on, and rub it in. And rub, and rub, and rub. You've used your tag, so what else are you going to do? Chop wood? Just keep rubbing. If you ever finish, roll the hide up, hair side out. As time passes, moisture seeps out of the hide, a process termed "sweating" by the informed. When the hide is dry, it's ready for transport. If you don't have a burlap bag to carry it in, plastic is okay for a short time, but take it out periodically, or moisture might collect. Keep the hide in a cool, dry place until you can get it to the taxidermist. Through a series of magical processes unknown to mere elk hunters, the taxidermist transforms the mess you leave into a beautiful shoulder mount. You just specify what you want it to look like. They can do anything except restore slipped hair—or make a big rack out of a little one.

The conventional, or shoulder mount, trophy requires that the rack with the top of the skull be separated from the head. You can do this

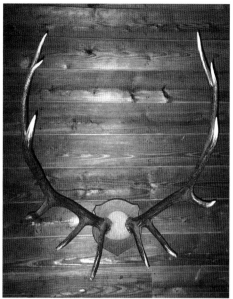

Antler mount.

Skull mount.

yourself or just take the entire skull and attached set of antlers to the taxidermist whole. Or you can keep the antlers attached to a section of the top of the skull and display it attached to a wall plaque. Kits are available for the handy and include a covering for the section of skull. An alternate way to display the trophy is with the European mount; this kind of mount leaves the rack attached to the entire skull, which is itself attached to a carved wooden base that hangs on the wall. The taxidermist removes all soft parts from the skull and bleaches the bone of the skull white. This makes a really nice trophy for racks that are not exactly perfectly formed or that didn't develop to their full size potential due to a hard winter. The commonly used name refers to the fact that this is the type of mount usually used in Europe for red deer, which are a cousin of North American and Asian elk, and have smaller racks that seem to usually have less symmetry.

Bugling mount of a big one.

The most popular trophy mount in terms of numbers, especially among elk country resident hunters, is the old-school country mount. Preparation is simple: a swipe with axe or saw across the top of the skull, and pack it out on top of the quarters. The preferred location for this type of mount is on the front of the barn—not in the house, since the hide is usually left in place, and gets a little ripe for a while. My uncle Dutch Kuykendall has a nice variation. He just hangs the rack over the cross braces under the barn rafters. His collection from over fifty years of hunting was always impressive to this visiting flatlander. Some are huge.

Protocol calls for the shooter to never mention anything about the horns, as they're termed, until a visitor mentions them—and to never score them to see "where they would go in the book."

PART II

Skills and Gear

This part of the book is about the stuff. Always a favorite. You'll find that hunters, and those in the business of selling them stuff, generally categorize all that hunting stuff into two classes: equipment (the implements used to "make the kill") and gear (boots, clothing, GPS units, packs, knives, and everything else). Some refer to archery equipment as tackle.

And then there's the other big category of stuff you need, separated from the rest by an easy divide to recognize—your hide. This internal stuff is the knowledge, skills, instinctive reflexes, and so on you need to use that external stuff effectively. The fundamental difference between the ways that the *internal stuff* and the *external stuff* should be addressed is this: You can never get enough of the internal stuff, but you'll always have way too much of the external stuff. The internal stuff is expensive in terms of time, but cheap in cost and easy to carry; the external stuff is just the opposite. In the hunting-supply industry, you're pretty much on your own regarding acquisition of the internal stuff; you'll find lots and lots and lots of help in acquisition of the external stuff, the "stuff" stuff.

To be successful, you need to take a package along as you move out well before daylight on your first day of elk hunting. That package should include external stuff—the equipment you need to take and field dress an elk and get it and you back to camp without getting lost or frozen—and internal stuff—the physical and mental skills needed to use your equipment.

CHAPTER 11

Safe and Confident Movement in Elk Country

The main impediment to successful location is fear—lack of confidence, to put it more politely. But there's another aspect. Misplaced confidence actually gets people into more trouble. The key to avoiding either extreme is having the right gear and knowing how to use it.

THE IMPORTANCE OF MOVEMENT IN ELK COUNTRY

The elk hunter needs to be able to move freely to successfully perform that first phase of the hunt, location. Elk populations never "fill up" their very extensive summer range, and sorting through all of the parts of that range where elk are not located is a sometimes extended prerequisite to finding where they *are* located. Determined (and enlightened) effort, with diligence and persistence, will turn up an elk.

It sounds easy. But if you've tried it, you know this effort is not to be taken lightly as you read this in the comfort and safety of the familiar surroundings of your home.

TALES OF THE "ROAD-HUGGERS"

If you stay with it long enough, elk hunting will introduce you to all sorts of characters that frequent elk country and represent themselves as elk hunters. I've been at it for quite a while, and seem to still turn up new types. Some of the most amazing are the ones—all nonresidents so far and all guys, as you'd expect—that talk the most, and loudest, about their experience in the great outdoors. The amazing part comes to light when discussions circle around eventually to getting lost, how to keep from getting lost, the pros and cons of GPS units, and the merits of compasses and maps. There's always one element aloft and amused at all of the techie and map geeks. Compasses and maps and all that stuff, they say—don't need 'em . . . never have. I was impressed, wondering how these individuals managed to avoid the embarrassment that's come to most of the master guides I'm acquainted with at some time, guides who've lived their entire lives in sight of the mountains and still have become completely "debooberated" there from time to time. But I eventually found out the secret from one of these guys who don't need maps: Always take care to never ever get out of sight of the road!

AVOIDING GETTING LOST

Reading a map and using a compass are two of those things that are very easy to understand how to do in theory but sometimes difficult to do when they become necessary. I suggest that you get your hands on one of the many books on the subject and practice until you are confident in your skills. You don't need to be in the mountains or the wilderness to hone your skills. It's actually more difficult to keep your bearings in a flatland thicket, swamp, or forest than in an area with more terrain relief, where you can keep up with prominent terrain features. Just get out away from populated areas and roads and wander around for a while using a USGS quadrant map of the area to get accustomed to a map of the scale you'll need to use for hunting and to practice going from one point to another even when you can't move in a straight line. Even if you can't get access to areas without roads, you can hike along safe, public secondary roads and learn a lot.

When moving cross-country through an area with a significant elk population, the hunter will often use the extensive network of elk trails. That's a good idea, since the elk invariably find the easiest, least energy-consuming route, whether up, down, or around the mountain. The hunter will eventually learn the hard way (or can read it here) that the best way to get from one point to another in really steep terrain is usually not the most direct route according to the map. Pay attention to the contours on the map and choose the route that most closely stays on the level rather than going up and down. It takes a lot of energy to regain that lost elevation once it's been given away. I've noticed that these tips are more important to the mature hunter than to the youngsters, but we'll just leave it at that.

Gobal Positioning System (GPS) Units

For a safe, comfortable hunt, it's essential to know where you are and which way you need to go in order to get to your hunting area, your camp, and important points in between. Until recently, this has always translated to a good map and compass. This concept should now be expanded to include Global Positioning System (GPS) units. These useful tools can indicate your location on a map. It's incorrect to think in terms of using either a GPS unit or a map. They complement each other. The GPS indicates your exact position by coordinates. Then you can locate your position on a map carried separately or on a map stored in the unit and displayed on a small screen with an indicator of where you've been and where you're going. Some units can now be programmed with topo maps to make a complete, self-contained unit. The software map is a handy alternative to the cumbersome "hard copy" map. You might think that the map in the GPS eliminates the need for a paper map. But a paper map of appropriate scale allows instant overview of the surrounding area in greater detail than possible on the small GPS screen. You can see at a glance that little bad place, swamp, rock field, or jump-off where you'll spend the rest of an exhausting day at best, followed by a miserable night of nursing an injury at worst. And the map is still indispensable as backup: It works even when you're in a bad area to receive a satellite signal, and it never runs out of batteries. Call me old-fashioned, but I'll always have a map along.

We use a Garmin GPS device that was top of the line when we got it. Product development is intense in this field, so you should check for the latest models in a major outdoor store catalog or online. The hint at the preferred source of the latest version is deliberate. A big outdoor outfit with a reputation to uphold is more likely to check out the reliability of the stuff it sells than the little discount shop down at the mall.

Maps

Maps to be used while hunting need to be contour maps with contours spaced closely enough to allow you to recognize landforms in your immediate vicinity. For you to stay oriented to big terrain features in the surrounding area, your maps also need to cover enough area to allow you to pick out more distant major landforms. The 7.5-minute, or 1:24,000 scale, topographic (topo) maps published by the United States Geological Survey (USGS) work very well for these purposes. These maps, termed quadrant maps, are designated by the name of either a population center on that particular map or a prominent landform in an area of low population, which is the usual case for the maps you'll need for elk hunting. They may be ordered by phone from the USGS at 888-275-8747 (888-ASK USGS) or downloaded (http://store.usgs.gov). A free index of the quadrant maps for any state can be found online, or you can call the USGS to have them send you one. Use the index to find the maps you need. It's not a bad idea to get the surrounding maps as well, even if your hunt will be in the center of a map. Sometime, if you get a tiny bit "confused" as to your location (most experienced elk hunters will never actually admit to being lost), you might want to pick out a prominent landform feature on the adjacent map to get your bearings. At the time you need it, the extra fifteen bucks or so that you spent for that other map will seem like a good investment. Coordinates of the place that you're interested in are handy as a check if you can get them. USGS products and services change all the time; check for the latest maps.

There are other Internet sources that can supply maps in both aerial photo and contour format. You can get the location by population center or other cultural or landform features. You create the scale of the map printed by means of a zoom feature; for example, you can zoom in to create a 1:24,000 scale equivalent to the 7.5-minute quadrant map.

Forest Service (202-205-8333) and USGS 1:100,000 scale Bureau of Land Management (BLM) version maps are also handy since they show land ownership, cultural sites, and natural features, along with a vicinity map for statewide orientation. The exact boundaries of land ownership may be essential in some areas for you to know where you can legally hunt. These maps may be ordered from the USGS or Forest Service by phone or online.

Finally, as with all of the other gear you could possibly need, good old Cabela's and other outdoor retailers sell an array of maps. Check the latest catalog.

Maps of game management areas are available from state Fish and Game Departments along with the rest of the rules and license and tags or other types of permits that you'll need to hunt. Contact information for each state can be found in the state-by-state rundown in Chapter 3.

WHAT TO DO IF YOU DO GET LOST

If you're with an outfitter, there will be some sort of standard procedure to follow in case something happens to prevent you from getting back to camp if you're hunting alone or get separated for some reason. You need to work something of a similar nature if you are with any other group. Otherwise, the standard, or "code," of the West seems to be three quick shots in succession, with the sequence to be repeated at intervals.

This universal standard presupposes that this is done well after dark so that it won't be mistaken for someone shooting at game. If you're not with a group and don't have someone to come and look for you, you're just playing the long shot that someone will hear and be inclined to come.

Being lost without injury is not too uncommon, and hardly qualifies as an emergency in itself. Handling this problem is mostly a matter of not making the situation worse by getting injured as well. Since getting lost is not a dangerous situation in itself, and can be handled by extension of outdoor skills training, we'll consider it first.

Some of the most useless advice I've ever seen in print is not to panic when you're lost. Of course you're going to panic—you're lost! The moment you become "a little confused" in the woods, you realize that these soothing words are always written by a successful professional writer in a cozy office or study. You wonder if this writer has ever gotten any farther than the privy from a wilderness camp without a guide at the elbow. And you're out here and you're cold and hungry and it's starting to snow and the wind's getting up and it's getting dark and what was that growling sound over there behind that tree? I'm handling this a little on the light side for a reason. This is one situation that can be made a lot worse by your own mental approach to it.

If you calm down and if you think about it, being lost in and of itself really doesn't matter at all. All you really care about is getting lost and not being found until after you're dead. So all you really have to do is to keep from dying of hypothermia, an accident, or an encounter with a predator (an *astronomically* remote possibility). Stay where you are; stay warm and dry; and you did tell somebody where you were going, didn't you? If you didn't, maybe you should panic. Sorry, I couldn't resist; I'll get serious.

Being Lost: What It Feels Like

The first thing you need to master is the initial sensation of confusion and disorientation that comes when the internal gyroscope between the ears loses all sense of direction in the wilderness. And don't feel immune as you read this in the comfy surroundings of your home, safe in the company of friends or family. Take it from old Tom, nobody's immune.

There are a lot of many-times-told Tales featuring lost first-time elk hunters; there are a lot more Tales less often told starring experienced hunters and guides becoming temporarily confused as to their location and direction of travel. Tales from the latter category are more entertaining in that they involve that sense of confidence that comes with experience. They are somewhat more instructive in that they usually illustrate some carelessness or oversight that can affect both new elk hunters and those who have been down the trail a few times. Some of the best Tales in my repertoire feature yours truly either alone or in company of Old Herm, master guide of the Bitterroots and extended adjacent areas.

The first Tale of this group is intended to convey the sense of confusion and disorientation of the initial stages of being lost and the preferred initial moves toward getting your bearings back (as opposed to a panicked rush off of the mountain in the direction you're headed).

THE TIME THE FOG LIFTED TO REVEAL THE CREEK IN THE WRONG PLACE AND FLOWING UPHILL

I was hunting in the Boulder Creek drainage one season when it seemed that the normally unusual weather of the Bitterroots was more unusual than usual. I had walked out while it was still dark one clear morning. The air was clear, absolutely transparent. The stars were bright even in the faint light of the sky that starts the transition from night to day long before the sun finally makes it up over the mountains to the east. I had always considered the Boulder Creek drainage as one of those places where an experienced elk hunter just *couldn't* get lost. Yeah; sure. Make that *shouldn't*.

The reason that it is so easy to keep up with yourself and everything else is that this place is completely oriented by its topography toward the one major creek, which is one of the few creeks in Idaho that twist along in one general direction, with all of the tributaries coming in at close to right angles. If you go up one of the tributaries around a few major bends, you had better check your topo map often and keep your compass out to keep up with your direction of travel at all times, but if you hunt the slopes either side of the main drainage, it's easy to keep up with the major drop-off into Boulder Creek. On the side of Boulder Creek that I was hunting, the creek ran along one side of a high ridge; on the other side of the ridge was the Lochsa River. The standard outfitter/guide advice was that if a separated hunter became disoriented, all he or she needed to do was to head downhill, then follow the side of the river or creek downstream to come out back at the river camp. Simple, clear instructions that didn't mention the intervening rock slides and slippery slopes that would be in the way. The result was that lost hunters would often show up in a battered condition along the highway across the river the following afternoon.

As I climbed out of camp along a familiar trail under the stars, getting turned around was one of my least concerns as I gasped for breath—because the most outstanding characteristic of the slopes of the Boulder Creek drainage is that they are steep. Straight up-and-down steep. Lots-of-switchbacks-in-the-trail steep.

Suddenly all of the stars blinked out and the sky went absolutely dark. Two-miles-into-a-cavern-system dark. Not wanting to use a flashlight in the area I intended to hunt, I sat down on the edge of the trail and waited for it to get light before I moved on. It was like sitting under a wet blanket that shut out all light.

Eventually the light from the rising sun weakly penetrated the gloom enough to light up the trail a short distance ahead of me, and I moved on. I came to the point where I planned to get off the trail and moved off through the area I planned to hunt. I've never liked to hunt in fog so thick that you can't see beyond 30 yards or so. Humans depend almost exclusively on their vision to locate game. Most game animals depend on their sense of smell to avoid danger, and that seems to work about as well in the fog as under any other conditions. Elk will circle around downwind to check out suspicious sounds and take off, usually before the hunter is aware that they're even in the area. So on this morning I tried to make the best of less-than-ideal conditions by moving along slowly and quietly, stopping often and long to look and listen for moving elk. Even though I couldn't keep up with the usual landmarks, I kept my bearings by the lay of the land in my immediate surroundings and by the sound of the distant creek in the stillness far below.

Then, just as quickly as the fog had formed, it lifted. I moved up the slope a short distance so that I could see over into Boulder Creek, just to make sure that all was well with my sense of direction. All was not well. The creek through this straight section below was making a sharp turn, in the wrong direction, with the water making a mad rush through the rapids uphill!

Disorientation is a strange sensation, and it's not pleasant. It's as if your body is steady but your brain is dizzy and confused. I fished the compass out from deep in the backpack where it had migrated due to disuse. It was malfunctioning and pointing in the wrong direction and obviously useless. I attempted to face downstream aligned with the creek below, and the wrong arm was directed toward the creek. Nothing worked. I worked my way downslope, and came across the trail going uphill in the wrong direction. My unerring instinctive sense of direction told me to head down the trail. Logic said that my sense of direction might not be as good as the broken compass pointing in the wrong direction. I headed up the trail. It soon turned downhill in the right direction as my internal gyroscope straightened out. As suddenly as things had gone haywire, all was right with the world again.

This next little saga makes a few important points: Don't overstate your qualifications, to either your hunting companions or yourself; if you do get a little confused, it's usually a better idea to stay put rather than taking off when you don't have any sense of the direction you're heading; and you should know the standing procedures for signaling your location.

THE BIG BUCK HUNTER GETS LOST
AND POPS OFF A FEW ROUNDS

On the evening of the day before the season opened, Herm and I rode over past the Stanley Hot Springs on the government trail up past Huckleberry and made a spike camp, to be in place among the elk on Greenside well before daylight on opening morning. We were in company with a new hunting companion, the Big Buck Hunter, on his first elk hunt. He was a little on the windy side, with dozens of stories, each featuring some variation of slipping unseen over a hill and coming on hundreds, or at least a lot, of big mule deer bucks. He even bought along a photo album of the mule deer kills he'd made!

Bull elk were bugling around us all night while we tried to get some sleep, which was a tough proposition considering our excitement and the hard ground under our sleeping bags. It was no problem at all to be awake well before daylight, ready to eat a quick cold snack and get out among them.

The plan was for the Deer Hunting Legend to walk up the creek for a short distance and take a stand. Herm figured that he would have no problem with this, considering his unerring sense of direction and vast amount of outdoor experience that we had been hearing so much about.

Herm and I made a big circle through the general area where the elk were located according to the bugling, and swerved past the place where the Big Buck Hunter was supposed to be located. The plan was to pick him up and continue the hunt. No Master Hunter to be found. We were standing there, wondering where else he might be, when we heard a single shot off in the distance, then another. All of the bugling bulls shut up. Now they were intently focused on looking for trouble rather than letting possible trouble know where they were. We moved on along the general route we had planned, but now we neither heard nor saw any sign of bull elk in the vicinity, just tracks of bull elk leaving the area. Meanwhile, the randomly spaced shots continued from different locations as if from several sources, or a single source on the move at a rapid cross-country pace. Herm figured that the Great Hunter had put one down after a chase punctuated by several not-so-well-placed shots. He finally decided that even though it was still relatively early in the day, since all of the elk had gone silent and were on full alert and taking off out of the area, I might as well ride back to camp with my bedroll and tell the packer to bring over the heavy dressing and quartering gear and enough of the pack string to bring an elk out of a bad, deep hole.

I accomplished my mission. The packer took off with the string, and I decided to hang around camp and the afternoon soup pot for a time. When, after a reasonable time, the triumphant hunter didn't show up with Herm, the packer, and the loaded pack string, I decided to go out on a late-afternoon-and-into-the-evening hunt down the creek below the camp, and put off congratulations to the lucky hunter until I returned after dark.

Eventually, I was back in camp, it was night, and nobody was back from the mountain. After a while, it was really late night and the packer finally came in with an empty pack string. He had talked to Herm, and the Big Buck Hunter was lost. Much later still, Herm returned with the Legend in tow, much deflated from when I last saw him.

For some reason known only to himself (the rest of us thought it might have had to do with dark timber and strange sounds), he had walked away from where he was supposed to stay, and immediately got turned around. When he realized that he was lost, he fired a single shot in the air (not the three shots in rapid succession, as is standard in the West) and then kept moving! He would fire a shot and then move on while Herm tried all day long to locate him, both of them walking in ever widening circles through prime elk hunting area. Herm finally caught him after dark when he stopped walking and started yelling, exhausted and out of ammo.

We didn't hunt that area again for a while, and the Great Hunter was much less outspoken for the rest of the hunt.

Just to make sure that I'm not picking on the first-time elk hunters exclusively, I need to include at this point a couple of little incidents to show that, under certain circumstances, momentary minor confusion can happen not only to experienced hunters, but even to master guides of the Bitterroots.

WHICH WAY'S NORTH, TOM?

Old Herm and I were working over a new area during archery season. It was another of those days that start out with clear, cool bluebird weather, and end with weather fit for a scene out of a horror movie. Of course, neither of us gave a second thought to the fog and snow setting in, being old mountain hands from way back—Herm considerably farther back than yours truly—so we didn't even bother to check the compasses before we headed back to camp while we could still see our hands in front of our respective faces. We knew the area well enough to know that all we had to do was walk due north along the back of the high ridge off to our right that stretched the length of the edge of the drop-off into Squaw Creek. So, with Herm leading the way, we trudged confidently through the fog, making our way over the slight ups and downs of the steep little ridge.

Just as we were crossing a little muddy stretch between the rocks and it was beginning to occur to me that it seemed like it was farther going back along this route than I remembered, Herm broke our cadence and we came to a stop. "That looks like the print of a great big wafflestomper boot like you're wearin' going in the same direction that we are. Which way's north, Tom?" I confidently pointed a finger north. "Got a compass with you?" asked the master guide. I was already fishing it out of my backpack. The needle pointed in exactly the opposite direction from north as indicated by my finger. We looked at each other, then at the ground. There was a slightly less distinct set of boot tracks, indicating a lighter individual, that matched the ones that Herm was standing in. We looked at each other again and then we looked all around through the fog and snow.

"Herm, are we lost?" "Not as long as you have that compass, eh?" We turned around and continued walking north in the opposite direction, me in front this time, holding the compass out in front to make it easier to follow.

Just getting your internal gyroscope reset for north doesn't mean that it always stays fixed after that. Herm and I have made kind of an ongoing joke of it just to remind ourselves that we're not perfect, in the gyroscope department at least. I'm not too sure about Herm in some of the other departments, and I'm sure he'd say the same of me.

WHICH WAY'S NORTH, TOM? THE SEQUEL

As part of a master tactical maneuver to surround and mop up all of the hapless trophy bull elk in a steep little creek basin, Herm and I stood looking over the edge of one of the steepest jump-offs in Idaho: rocks and stunted trees down the side in front of us; thick brush up the other side. It was going to be fun. We took some small comfort in knowing that the rest of the bunch would have just as bad a trail down, then back up again, as we would. Just in different locations spaced around the basin calculated to intercept escaping elk. Just before we dived over the side, I looked at my compass one last time to check what it looked like where we would come out. It looked a little rough. It was a little rough. I'd been up the other face the season before. I also noted that it was due west, more or less, from where we stood. Off we went.

We looked for elk, watched our footing, tripped, slid, and sat down without planning to down the steep sides and little ridges dropping off into the little creek below. We sat down to watch for moving elk and to just look around in general about halfway down. Right on cue, it was starting to get foggy just as our chances for a shot were starting to go up as we neared the bottom.

"Which way's north, Tom?"

I pointed. "Which way's north, Herm?"

He pointed in another direction as I located my compass.

"This compass is confused again." It pointed in a different direction from either of us, and indicated that we weren't crossing the basin as we had in mind. We were heading down the creek toward the worst brushy hole in the entire area. It's funny how those little ridges that make for slightly easier going always *seem* to be dropping off in the direction that you want to go, whether they really are or not.

The next Tale regarding the general subject of lost hunters makes the point that a good honest self-assessment is the first step to staying out of trouble in the lost-and-found department.

I'll state the moral of this little session up front. If you're interested in how you'll be found and retrieved in case you get lost, you should check with the outfitter or with the state authorities where you intend to hunt so that you know what the deal is. The arrangements and protocol for search and rescue vary throughout the various elk hunting states of the West. Colorado, for instance, tacks a small search and rescue surcharge onto the sale of every license sold (or at least it's on all of the licenses of the nonresidents; I can't speak for the natives). By this arrangement, everybody chips in to effectively share the cost of finding the small percentage of hunters who get themselves lost.

Idaho has, or at least had at the time of this next little Tale, a different setup. If you got lost, the county sheriff's department called out the chopper and looked for you. This was a pretty expensive endeavor, and somebody had to pay for the service. At first it was the state or county, but after much tax-payer complaint they changed the rule and decided that the hunter who had to be found would pick up the tab for the finding. That arrangement would seem reasonable, but brought on more complications. It seems that a lot of the findees, once safely found and drinking coffee back in a warm tent, said that they hadn't really been lost at all. They hadn't really needed that expensive search, and since it was usually the outfitter who had called for the search, they said the outfitter could pay the cost of the tab out of those excess profits from the outfit. You don't have to know that many outfitters to guess how well that outcome went over.

Change #2 to the procedure was quickly enacted: At the beginning of every hunt, the outfitter would hold a "come to the altar" meeting with all of the booked hunters, and everybody went on record with their preferences of when they wanted to be searched for if necessary. This set up some of the most entertaining exchanges I've ever heard in an elk camp, or anywhere else for that matter. The one I'll relate here is from one of the most physically capable and confidently self-reliant hunters I've ever had the privilege of accompanying along the elk hunting trail. It's a funny story—but on a more serious level, it makes the point that a little honest self-appraisal can prevent some anxious moments out in the woods.

HOW LONG SHOULD WE WAIT BEFORE WE CALL OUT THE SEARCH HELICOPTER?

All of the hunters had arrived in the base camp on the river the night before we were scheduled to pack in to the mountain camp. Everybody was excited about the prospects of the hunt, the first wilderness pack outfit hunt for most of our little drop camp group and for the hunters signed on for the main outfitter camp. The time of settling up of payments due and all of the other administrative stuff was at hand.

You've probably already guessed the star of this Tale. This was Wes's first time out on an all-out wilderness pack-in elk hunt, and he was excited. This was the same trip in which Wes had in the forefront of his mind the admonishment his mother-in-law had made just as we left regarding a recent article in the news about the two half-devoured elk hunters apparently surprised by a bear while cleaning an elk. (See "Wes and the Bull and the Bear" in Chapter 7.)

In any event, the outfitter dutifully asked each hunter around the group assembled their preference for delay before an expensive helicopter search was to begin, and each answered according to experience, survival training, and bravado.

One said something to the effect that if he couldn't make it back on his own, don't bother; he was dead anyway. Another, more realistically, said to send out the searchers around midnight when they could look for his fire. Another said to call them in the morning when they would be able to find him in the daylight. Another said in the afternoon of the next day. Then came Wes's turn.

His strong, decisive voice rang out: "If it's two hours after dark and I'm not back, get that thing in the air and out here as fast as it'll fly."

Lost Hunter—What to Do

Now we come to the practical response to getting lost. You need a sequence of activities to complete, one after the other, to keep yourself on track or you won't get anything done before dark. If you don't have a sequence of activities, you can use mine: Locate a dry place that will stay dry (or at least not collect water if it rains), start a fire, finish preparing your shelter, change into dry underclothes and socks, eat, drink, and be miserable.

Before it gets too late, stop looking for the way back to camp and start looking for a dry place to hole up where you can make a fire. The best place would be on dry ground, have shelter from precipitation, and be out of direct wind exposure. A thick standing green tree is good protection against the rain and turns a surprising amount of water. In case it leaks, you can stretch out a poncho or thin plastic sheet carried for the purpose for further protection against wind and rain. The ideal setup would be a downed tree trunk with a dry side that you could make your fire against. You can break off or saw off some dry low pine or spruce limbs using the wood blade of a Wyoming saw. You want to have the fire just to the side of the shelter so that heat is retained under the shelter without the chance of catching it on fire.

INJURIES AND OTHER EMERGENCIES
Avoiding and Responding to Injuries

The best way to avoid injury from falling over ledges, rock slides, and steep slopes is to stay away from such places. Of course, sometimes elk hunting requires traveling over less than optimal ground surfaces. In these cases, you should use caution and be ready to prevent or minimize injuries.

Elk trails are very different from maintained human trails. If you're moving fast, keep your arms close to your body in case of a surprise slip, and tumble rather than trying to break your fall. Trying to break your fall will often result in an arm or shoulder injury.

Moving across steep terrain without a trail for sure foot placement is very hazardous. Each step onto grass or gravel, not to mention snow, presents the risk of that foot dropping out from underneath you before you can react. Your immediate reaction when faced with traveling over such terrain should be to get low and create more points of ground contact. A high crawl is more stable than our usual upright gait.

As opposed to a simple case of getting lost, an injury or medical emergency in elk hunting country that immobilizes a person or results in any significant loss of blood must be taken very seriously. You won't have the luxury of the time or, in the worst case, the ability to deliberately prepare your shelter and start a fire. You have to work with the materials in your backpack, which should include a poncho to separate you from the elements; a thermal bag to keep all of the body heat you can generate; and some concentrated, high-energy rations (not to be confused with snacks) to keep your internal heat stoked. This is also a situation when you're better off with a companion.

You should know enough about first aid to stop massive bleeding and prevent shock in yourself or a hunting partner. Learning CPR is a good idea. I don't know the overall statistics, but according to all the tales forming my frame of reference, there are more heart attacks in the mountains than accidental shootings. I'll not attempt any instruction in CPR or first aid in this guidebook, other than to advise that you get some training from a professional. The techniques you learn from a professional will include use of some pieces of equipment or material at hand to stop major loss of blood. Make a point of having anything mentioned in the class in your backpack.

Carrying the Proper Equipment

Here's a sometimes overlooked but important point regarding safety training and its associated stuff. It's always a good idea to check the contents of that daypack one more time. Skills with emergency equipment are of no use if you don't have the stuff you need with you, when you need it, in good shape, and where you can get to it if you're not operating at full capacity mentally as well as physically. I can't make the point too often that any training in outdoor skills that require certain materials will do you no good unless you have the stuff available in workable condition when you need it. It's tough to find an electrical plug for the charger on the GPS unit where you're going. How about bringing a spare battery? Maybe a compass and map? That terrific buy on a cheap toy compass isn't a very good deal if it comes apart in your pocket. The fire starter stuff needs to be dry. Neither will it do you any good if you lose it or leave it in camp. There is some stuff that you should not count on your guide to have, even on a first-class guided hunt through an outfitter. Guides are often in such good physical shape that it's not second nature for them to consider getting out of a rough spot with dark and a storm closing in. They're surprised when they're slowed down by a flatlander hunter who can't see in the dark or hike straight up a sheer cliff like the twenty-year-old guide who's done it all of his young life.

Lightning

Fairly considered, you're probably in less danger out hunting in the wilderness than going about your daily activities back home, particularly in light of critical skills required to avoid danger. The prospect of facing your everyday task of "simply" driving at highway speeds through the congested freeway systems of major metropolitan areas strikes fear in the hearts of outfitters and guides who spend most of their lives in the West. That's even throwing in some of the most fearsome, hair-raising mountain grades that you can imagine. But it really gets down to a matter of what you're accustomed to, and you may run up against some unaccustomed situations on your first elk hunt. The ones you've thought about, like the bears, cougars, and wolves, probably worry you out of proportion to their true potential danger. If you can, sort of zero out your preconceived apprehensions and bear with me while we consider the things that top the list of what can cause trouble for hunters, according to my direct experience, and the experience of people I've hunted with, especially the packers, guides, and outfitters I know.

There are some situations that you might encounter in the mountains that just won't normally occur to those of us who are native flatlanders. Although it's not anything like a common occurrence, being struck by lightning is one of those risks, this one bearing very high negative consequences. The fact is that the possibility of being struck by lightning is significantly higher on mountain slopes and near mountain peaks than at low elevations on flat terrain. Coupled with the fast changes possible in mountain weather, it becomes a factor to be aware of. There are several precautions that you can take to minimize the risks if you get caught in a lightning storm, which is as likely to be associated with snow as with rain during the elk hunting season.

If you're out hunting on open faces or near pinnacles or peaks when the weather turns threatening, you may be in an area of highly mineralized rocks, since they are usually most resistant to weathering. The mineralization also makes them very conductive to electricity and, therefore, the exact location of most of the lightning strikes. Move down toward more gentle slopes before the storm closes in on you. People familiar with the mountains seem to prefer a saddle or the bottom of a drainage if they can get to it. If lightning strikes close to you before you clear the area, you're in trouble; it *does* strike repeatedly in the same location. If you are caught out in this situation, the mountain professionals I'm acquainted with advise that you keep moving out of the area, avoiding lone trees and rocky prominences. If you're on horseback, dismount, hang your hardware on the saddle, and lead the horse.

This Tale makes a couple of points concerning weather in the mountains during elk hunting season and associated consequences for the elk hunters.

RELAXING BRIEFLY ON A MINERAL ROCK FACE
DURING A THUNDERSTORM SNOWSTORM

Wes and I were hunting above the Big Bend of the North Fork during the early part of the general elk season. Up until the time of this Tale we had experienced warm "bluebird" weather, almost too warm for elk hunting. On this particular morning, the appearance of the sky indicated that that might change. We had walked out to a steep little pass overlooking a deep, steep little creek named, very inappropriately, Flat Creek. We stood in the pass looking down, considering how, or maybe if, we should tackle that hole, throwing in the possibility of a storm moving in. The sound of a bull elk's bugle rolled up from below and answered both questions. Elk had been hard to find, and here was one accommodating enough to locate himself. The call seemed to come from just below our own elevation and around the valley. We wouldn't need to go down into the deepest part of the hole and have to retrace our steps straight up in order to get out. Weather or not, we took off around the side of the slope at roughly our own elevation, with the steep ridge above on one side and the creek below on the other.

We moved slightly down and around the drainage, looking for the elk and trying to hear another hint of its exact location so that we could consider a surround move. No luck. We eventually moved well past the point where the bull should have been, carefully looking for fresh tracks along the way. We finally found tracks, and tried to make sense of their clues. It looked as if the elk might have circled around and seen or scented us, then moved down toward the bottom of the steep canyon, even steeper in the part of the drainage where we now stood than at its head where we started. Then we heard another bugle from far below on the opposite side of the canyon.

Considering the steepness of the possible approach to the new position of the bull; the fact that he had probably somehow sensed our presence; the now obvious fact that a heavy storm was moving in; and, finally, the reality that we would probably be well past the point of being walked out by the time we made it out of that hole, we decided to turn back toward camp by climbing straight up the slope we were on, cutting across a well-established trail along the top of the ridge from where we were, and following the trail back to camp, which would be a lot easier than sidehilling cross-country with rain or snow coming down. We started climbing up the very steep slope.

The stops to rest a minute and take a "blow" came fairly often on that climb. In addition to the steepness of the slope, we had to pull through areas of rugged outcrops interspersed throughout the thick brush. We came to yet another almost vertical outcrop face, and sat down on a couple of handy rocks protruding up through the dirt and brush at the bottom of the outcrop face to rest a minute and build up steam before we tackled the almost vertical face itself.

As our labored struggle for air slacked off slightly to the point that we could talk, I noted the very dark storm now closing in from across the canyon, the direction that had been to our backs until we stopped to rest. While I was sitting there taking in our situation, Wes broke the silence with conversation, as he was the only one of the two of us with enough breath to speak, and made some comment as to the fact that there weren't all that many real hazards on a wilderness hunt. This was his first hunt and I think he may have been revisiting the "Wes and the Bull and the Bear" Tale. I replied, in a soft voice without excitement because I couldn't muster enough breath for a more forceful utterance, that there were only two true mortal dangers out there: an untrained horse spooked on a trail through bluffs, and being stuck on an exposed mineral face in a thunderstorm.

I had no more than wheezed out "thunderstorm" with the limited amount of air I could get over the lump in my throat when lightning struck the opposite but not so far slope with an instant roar of thunder. Close! Close—and that rock face where we sat was exposed because it was hard. Hard because it was a mineral outcrop, judging from the color of the rocks that I had just taken a much greater interest in. But it wasn't a good time, and certainly not a good place, for an esoteric discussion of geology. "Don't need a lightnin' rod," I muttered, turning the barrel of my slung rifle downward. Wes took the point and turned the barrel of his rifle down also. Not a good time or place to talk about the physics of lightning either. "We'd better get the hell off of this face before . . ." We left that place a lot faster than we came to it even though it was steeper going on up. Now that I think about it, we didn't even need to rest again all the way to the top. And the snow started to float down through the darkness as a few more booms encouraged us along our way. It was dark and the snow was thick, but we could still figure out the way up. And we stayed to the brush rather than crossing the bare rocks of outcrops.

Another risky situation that flatlanders don't usually notice pertains to the combination of wind and trees in the mountains. Wind gusts channeled by the terrain can seemingly explode through restricted areas on occasion, flattening every tree. Professional outfitters and experienced hunters keep this in mind when selecting campsites, and standing dead trees lined up with the tents are the first to be used as firewood. They will keep a wary eye even while riding through some areas such as thick stands of mature lodgepole pines when the wind suddenly picks up.

Cold

It has always amazed me how folks who show so much fear and respect for cougars, wolves, and bears can be absolutely indifferent to the most effective and consistent killer lurking in the mountains: cold. Hypothermia poses a danger that most hunters seem to be aware of, even if they aren't particularly well informed on how to deal with it. In plain terms, the experts say that the name of the game is keeping your body heat in your body by not allowing it to escape. The first line of defense is to insulate yourself from the surrounding cold air. That's done with what you wear. The main problem that I've observed is that hunters show up with clothes, well insulated if they're dry, that become poor insulators of heat when they are wet through, which often becomes the case. That usually translates to using garments that insulate with wool rather than down. You need to carefully select your clothing to make sure that what you're wearing will keep you warm in wind and rain as well as snow and cold. More on this in Chapter 15.

The best solution for keeping warm if things get serious is to make a fire. You don't want to be reduced to a personal struggle with hypothermia and the clouded judgment that accompanies it. If you're suddenly caught in such a situation by accident, through an unexpected downpour or by falling into a cold creek, bravely resist the impulse to settle down and relax and wait for what usually comes next (death). Move around, using your energy reserves to stay warm, visualize the impulse to rest as a physical danger, and fight back with your mind and body.

Frostbite is less of a mortal danger than hypothermia. Extensive damage from frostbite such as loss of limbs is often associated with extreme extended exposure to cold and a near brush with death due to hypothermia. Exposure to cold and wind much less severe than life-threatening conditions, with minor discomfort that may go unnoticed at the time, won't result in severe damage such as the loss of a limb or appendage, but can still lead to long-term, nagging tingling and aching of ears, fingers, and anything else that is small, has limited circulation, and sticks out from under cover. As with hypothermia, the first defense against frostbite is also proper clothing. Keep all of those little parts covered and warm. As an example, you'll use split deerhide leather shooting gloves to wear under most hunting conditions, but if it gets really cold, you'll want some serious mittens or thick gloves more on the order of what you would use for riding a snowmobile. Keeping the rest of the snowmobile suit in your vehicle is a good idea if you'll be in an area where a snowstorm can strike without warning.

A related condition, commonly called trench foot (from the situations where it becomes a major problem), occurs at temperatures well above freezing when feet are cold and wet for extended periods of time. Trench foot takes longer to do its damage, and is easily avoided if you take care of daily maintenance of boots, socks, and feet—which means thoroughly drying all three every evening. That's easy to do if you're not preoccupied with something more immediate, like fighting a war. The right gear for your feet also helps make the job easier: wool outer socks, polypro liner socks, and waterproof or Gore-Tex boots.

You may not find it very entertaining, but the U.S. Army's *Basic Cold Weather Manual* (FM 31-70, available at www.globalsecurity.org) has the most specific and comprehensive instructions for getting by in cold weather.

A couple of notes are in order regarding snow in the mountains. Snow makes the entire place beautiful; it's great for serious tracking associated with elk hunting and the not-so-serious tracking of reading the morning news of what went on with all the small animals overnight. But for those of us who are destined to be forever the flatlander, just in the mountains for the hunting season, snow opens up all sorts of possibilities for us to put ourselves out of action. You need to wear boots with the best traction possible and watch your step on as well as off the trail. Footing can be treacherous when snow-covered grass on the edge of the trail looks just as solid as snow-covered dirt or rock.

Snow also changes the appearance of trails and the terrain in general to the point that you can lose your way in an area that you easily navigated the day before the snow fell. The best way to avoid the problem is to develop the habit of noticing and being aware of not only your immediate surroundings, but also where you are relative to major landmarks as you move through the hunting area. Then you won't be disoriented when the familiar trail suddenly blends in with the rest of the ground.

Snow problems extend to the road trip out of the hunting area. A set of tire chains can literally be a lifesaver, preventing slides over the sides of mountain roads or avoiding being stranded in a storm.

On the subject of roads, avoid going too far off of the pavement on a mud line road in areas known (check with the locals) for bad mud conditions after rains. There are unbelievable differences in the nature of different soils when they turn to mud, grading from slick to sticky. Even tire chains are of little use when the mud balls up around the wheels.

At the other extreme of elk hunting conditions, on early hunts in the southern part of elk country, you should always carry enough water

Things look a lot different in the snow. Be careful not to get disoriented.
STEVE BURSON

for a day of hunting—at least a couple of liters, or two 32-ounce sports drinks. Dehydration is not to be taken lightly.

You Can Safely, and (Relatively) Comfortably Reside Anywhere in Elk Country If You Can Make a Fire

Making a fire is an essential skill for folks inclined to wander about in the wilderness in cold, wet weather, regardless of their purpose for being there. It's also a skill seldom used by most of us in our everyday lives. Some outdoor types seem to have a knack for fire starting, and can appear to use one wet match against a large wet log and have a roaring bonfire going in no time. The rest of us, unless a West Texas pear burner is available, and it never is, need to be more deliberate in our technique and the materials that we use. At least that's the *usual* situation during elk hunting season—but there are occasions when putting out our fires, avoiding starting fires, and avoiding deadly consequences of fires already burning become the key skills.

There are many different circumstances in which you might need to start a fire: in camp when you would like to have a fire in a camp stove, out on the side of the mountain for a nice-to-have warm-up during an extended pause to rest or regroup, or for a need-to-have source of warmth for yourself and to dry clothes during an unplanned night in the open.

If you don't get into the details of why and how stuff burns, making a fire is simple and straightforward. You somehow get a part of a combustible substance, in this case firewood, above its ignition temperature, and it starts burning. It's easier to get a small area of a splinter or thin wood shaving up to temperature than a little part of a big, cold log, even if the log is absolutely dry (which it won't be). Moisture makes it even harder, as its evaporation cools the combustible material back down. Paper, as long as it isn't damp, is easy to ignite due to its thinness. More paper and you have a good means to keep the sustained temperature of the wood up longer than you can with a single match. If the match goes out, you're back to square one.

In the camp, you should always have the stuff to make a fire on hand. You'll need some foot-long pieces of stove wood from a standing dead tree—pine, cedar, tamarack, or whatever is available and favored locally—split to a handy size, about 2 to 3 inches thick. The fire is started by using a match or lighter directly on the wood or to ignite dry scrap paper to set ablaze the thin edges of split kindling, which in turn sets the thicker sections of kindling on fire, which sets the full-sized stove wood on fire. Outfits that hunt predators through the winter usually have a stash of "dude dust" around camp to help the clients make a fire for themselves as the occasion demands. It's made of magical secret ingredients that smell like sawdust mixed with diesel fuel. Don't improvise with gasoline. It's also not good practice to heat up the small propane bottles on a fire so that they work better. Have I seen it? Think I could make this stuff up?

Out on the side of the mountain, you'll need to be carrying your fire-starting stuff with you, and it needs to be dry. It's a good idea to carry both a lighter and matches with you. The lighter is less sensitive to falling precipitation and wind, and is more convenient for applying a sustained flame to start the fire, but lots of them don't work as well when it's really cold—which is, of course, when you really need them. A candle can be used to apply a sustained flame after it's lit with a match. Both lighter and candle are less sensitive to moisture than a match. You can carry a few matches in a small, capped bottle. You can also keep matches dry by carrying a box of them in a sealed plastic bag with the toilet paper. Some outdoor types carry a traveling fire-starting kit that includes candles, paper, and special kindling from the big mail-order outfits. Those of us who have been cold at one time or another usually carry all of the above.

You'll need to rustle up some firewood to make the more substantial fire along with some smaller pieces to cross from kindling to real fire. The difficult part here can be finding suitable dry firewood. Usually, even in an old forest with limbs all around, the wood on the ground will be wet. You'll need to break off some low, dead limbs for your firewood. The pros will start a fire against a standing dead stump, locating the only dry place on the whole thing to start it burning. We flatlanders are better off lighting some small dead limbs about the diameter of a finger in a little stack so that flames from the pieces on the bottom lick over the pieces on top, heating them up and igniting them. You can then add larger and larger pieces.

A note on axes: Unless you're already an accomplished expert with an axe before you get to the big woods, be advised that close proximity to a sharp axe in camp won't make you any handier with it than you were back in your suburbanite flatlander backyard. I need to give you this admonishment, because, for some reason, outfitters and their employees seem to think that everyone else grew up swinging an axe or sledgehammer into a wedge just like they did. It's probably best if you carry the wood for a little while until you get a chance to observe the correct technique first. And don't stand directly in front of the other beginners, because that's the direction the blade will fly in case it gets away from them.

Eventually you need to start considering how to put the fire safely out. The stack needs to be made with a little thought to "destacking." If you take all the pieces apart, it's easy to extinguish the separated pieces. The pros know when and how that stump will smolder and go out when the fire gets to the wet part. The rest of us can set the whole place on fire, when and if we ever get a fire started.

This explanation of the general idea of fire making should be followed up with some practice, just in case you're like most of us and don't have much natural ability. You need to get out and do a little camping where you can make some campfires, preferably with material you collect at the campsite. Alternately, you can take some (preferably natural) material with you to make a fire. Practice making a fire under different conditions—wet, dry, windy—using different starter material.

FIREARM SAFETY

The number of miscues or accidents with firearms is really very low when compared to other kinds of wrecks and troubles you can get into, but the consequences of an accident with high-powered hunting firearms can be horrendous. Pay serious attention to the manufacturer's instructions. Even if the safety precautions that come with the firearm seem a little overdone to you, you should be as concerned about your own safety as the manufacturer (and its lawyers who reviewed the instructions).

Keep firearms free of dirt, debris, and moisture, which can collect in liquid form inside the mechanisms, then freeze to a solid, potentially defeating the control of operation of the firearm, including the operation of the safety.

Internalize all the information pertaining to firearm safety you can get your hands on. Make it intuitive. Before the shot, arrange any cooperative approach toward elk with other members of the hunting party so that there is no chance of the elk coming between different members without each of them being aware of the presence of the other. During locating and stalking, be very aware of everything surrounding your intended prey, in a wide-ranging sense during locating, then narrowing in focus during the stalk as you distinguish the elk selected from inanimate surroundings and from other elk that may be in the immediate vicinity. By the time you have reached the stalk stage, you have switched from all senses to sight as the primary focus. By the time you have entered the kill stage, you have long isolated the specific elk as your objective with nothing else animate in the immediate vicinity or behind the intended quarry.

HORSES AND SAFETY

Follow the lead of the packer and guides around the riding and pack stock (for more, see "Don't Mess with It" in Chapter 20). Outfitter riding horses are usually very good with inexperienced riders, but they're still horses. Nearly all horses are subject to panic—"gettin' boogered," as it's called out west—if they're surprised with a sudden flatlander stunt that they haven't seen before. Let them know you're around, with soft-spoken words, if you're behind them. Stay clear of their kicking reach to the rear and you'll usually be okay. Lead your horse with the lead rope attached to the halter rather than with the bridle reins. That will give you more clearance and allow the horse more room to pick its way along the trail. Outfitters are careful to reserve the biters, which have danger areas to the front, or horses with other bad traits, for the guides to ride.

Whereas the majority of horses present a danger only if spooked and will otherwise put up with a lot, a significant percentage of mules sometimes show a little of their father's disposition. In case you don't know, their fathers aren't selected for their sweet temperament. Unless they've been part of your childhood, as in, "You kids stay out of the pasture where that old Jack is," you don't appreciate the full meaning of the term "jackass" as applied to beings other than breeders of mules.

For the most part, only other mules, and usually the packer, know the mood of mules at any given instant of time, although even packers can get ambushed on occasion. Be advised that mules are very athletic, and it is physically within their prerogative to nail anyone they choose right between the eyes with a shod hoof anywhere within their danger zone, which is about a 10-foot radius all around. From a flat-footed stance, they can make a little crow-hop straight up to clear the ground, and then arch their backs in midair to kick out for an unbelievable distance. You don't want your first look at a mule trick to be the last thing you ever see. Better leave them alone. They're not part of the regularly scheduled entertainment.

NOW FOR CONCERNS ABOUT THOSE BEARS, COUGARS, AND WOLVES (AND MAYBE SOMETIMES SNAKES—AND SPIDERS, CENTIPEDES, SCORPIONS, VINEGAROONS, AND THOSE NASTY BEETLES AND TICKS . . .)

Cougars and wolves usually seem to find better things to eat in the mountains than a flatlander. The main caution folks familiar with the mountains take is in regard to cougars and small children. The sounds the little kids make either in fun or in distress seem to trigger the cats. Cougars are incredibly stealthy, quick, and strong. They would be a major danger if they were more aggressive. They seem to be timid in the presence of dogs. Usually. Little lapdogs might look more like slow-moving protein than a threat.

Wolves, on the other hand, attack dogs as a natural reaction, and will savagely kill all dogs they perceive as a threat to their territory. They're usually inclined to leave people alone, although I'll admit that being surrounded by a pack of wolves in the gathering darkness would probably give me the creeps (but that possibility won't affect my elk hunting plans).

Bears are in a class by themselves. Don't mess with the Griz. If you come across one that isn't yet aware of your presence, just ease out the way you came in. The old, dangerous bears usually hear poorly and see only slightly better, but have an unbelievable sense of smell. It follows that your route in leaving should be downwind from the bear. Trouble with a grizzly usually derives from its territorial instinct. It may make a bluff attack to run you off. If it patterns a human as a serious intruder, a grizzly can be deadly. However, they don't seem to consider humans as prey. If it perceives that it's taken care of the intruder, a grizzly is through with you, hence the official advice to play dead.

The black bear is seldom aggressive, and I don't normally interrupt my elk hunting agenda if I come across one, but, that said, I never turn my back on one. The trouble with the black bear derives from the fact that it'll eat anything that it can get without too much trouble. When a black bear makes the news, the details usually sell lots of copies. A typical scenario has some variation of the hunter(s) being found after going missing for several days. Clues at the scene of one such incident that had extensive news coverage some time back indicated that two hunters had been field dressing an elk and had been surprised from behind by a black bear. It had somehow managed to dispatch both of them, and then proceeded to eat parts of all of the bodies. (The half always devoured first is the juicy, soft half—just in case your morbid curiosity demands a mental image.) A black bear, if it's so inclined and perceives that it can take you unaware, doesn't want to go to the trouble of killing you only to let you go to waste, so playing dead is not a good strategy with these creatures. A black bear is also less inclined to use the bluff attack as a tactic than a grizzly. It's usually, or at least often, serious. If a black bear perceives that you're aware of its presence, it usually either backs off or sits down and looks to one side to signify that it's not looking for trouble. You can go on about your business. Remain alert in case it has backed off to circle around for another approach in hopes that you won't notice the next time. Like I said before, I never turn my back on one, even though I know that more people are blasted by lighting than eaten by bears.

Now about those snakes. About the only snake that you'll ever be concerned with is the rattlesnake, and usually, it's not even a consideration. Usually. Elk generally prefer areas where snakes either can't, or prefer not to, operate. For elk, the cooler, the better, preferably with plenty of water in the vicinity. Not so for snakes. Dry is okay for them, and warm is essential, since they're not warm-blooded and can't create their own body heat. The only areas where elk and snakes might overlap would be in the lower elevations and warmer regions of the elk hunting states, usually in the Southwest. The best way to check for the possibility of rattlers in your elk hunting location is to pull into a local gas station or roadside diner and strike up a friendly conservation. Then at the appropriate point, ask, "Any snakes around here?" and you'll hear probably more than you'll ever want to know in no time.

If there are snakes in the area that you plan to hunt, just wear boots with high tops and watch where you step. Not to get into a Tale, but also watch where you sit in the dim light of early morning. A warm human body feels nice to a cold snake body. For this reason, I don't sleep on the ground in snake country. The ground in snake country is also home for spiders, centipedes, scorpions, vinegaroons, and those nasty beetles that are said to bite the lips of ground-sleeping cowboys and transmit unimaginable miseries. Most of that last group isn't really dangerous, but just put it in the category of another personal thing.

A special case that's not usually a problem for elk hunters is disease-carrying ticks; they aren't around in the fall. Check for them during any spring or early summer scouting trips.

I'll cover one last point before leaving the general subject of critters that can cause trouble. There's one critter that inflicts severe injury to hunters every year, but you seldom hear about it. It doesn't make spectacular press, and it isn't even commonly found out in the wilderness. It's a little spider, the brown recluse, and it's to be found inside that seldom-disturbed part of the closet or trunk where hunters store their coats and gloves and other cold-weather hunting stuff between seasons. It hides in the clothes until the victim disturbs it by putting on the garment after months of storage. Take care to check and/or treat all garments, and that includes caps and gloves and mittens. I make a habit of crushing, wrinkling, or rolling up anything that's unhandy to turn wrong-side-out (shooting gloves are a notable example), so that if it has a spider in it at all, it's an obliterated one. Yet another personal thing with me.

GETTING OVER DANGEROUS SITUATIONS AFTER THEY HAVE PASSED

The best way to handle accidents, we would all agree, is not to have them. But they do happen—that's why they're called accidents. Just be cautious and enjoy your elk hunt. Don't let fear spoil the fun. And don't let recriminations, if something bad does happen, spoil your life. All things pass. Come back and try it again.

CHAPTER 12

Making the Kill with the Rifle

Among the several choices the elk hunter has to make is the type of equipment he or she is going to take the elk with. This chapter will give you the information you need to be able to pick the best rifle and learn how to use it effectively.

AMMUNITION

I begin the discussion of equipment for actually making the kill with consideration of ammunition. Don't we start with guns? Nope. This book is all about elk hunting. From an elk hunting perspective, we don't care as much about the gun as the cartridge and the bullet it fires. You're interested in bullet delivery on the right spot on the elk. The specifications for that bullet are defined in terms of construction to hold together as energy is transmitted (integral core and expanding point), cross section (.30 caliber and bigger is better), and energy at target impact (2,000 foot-pounds and more is best). I'll just cover the essentials of guns as tools for elk hunting.

At this point I will correct what you've probably read if you've ever read anything about gun selection for elk hunting. What you read was probably something like this: "Elk are big, tough animals. Use enough gun." Actually, that should read, "Elk are big, tough animals. Use enough cartridge."

Now, to get into specifics. High-powered hunting rifle cartridges firing high-velocity, expanding bullets kill quickly, primarily by hydraulic shock. This shock is produced when the kinetic energy of the high-velocity bullet is explosively transferred to tissue, extending to a volume much greater than the wound channel. This is in contrast to high-velocity military cartridges with non-expanding bullets, pistol cartridges and muzzleloaders firing low-velocity bullets, and broadhead-

240

tipped arrows, all of which kill more slowly by producing wound channels. Damage is restricted to organ damage and loss of blood through the wound channel.

The consensus among the guides and experienced elk hunters I know is that the minimum you need for hunting elk is a combination of .30-caliber, 180-grain bullets, striking with 2,000 foot-pounds of kinetic energy at the point of impact. A larger caliber with more kinetic energy is better as long as the greater recoil doesn't keep the shooter from firing accurately. The point of impact should be the chest cavity of the elk, and the bullet needs to be a modern, premium design like a Nosler Partition, which is strong enough to stay together while all of the energy is transferred. This

In Win Mag: A Winchester 70 with 1 to 4X Leupold and a custom Browning BLR with large-aperture peep sight.

combination won't kill an elk instantly, but the wounded animal should go no farther than 40 to 100 yards, and you'll still be able to find it.

These requirements can be translated into the maximum range at which a shot should be taken based on the cartridge:

.30-40	150 yards
.308 Win	250 yards
.30-06, .35 Whelen, 8 mm Rem Mag	300 yards
.300 H&H, .300 Win Mag & Short, .300 Rem SA Umag	400 yards
.38 Win Mag, .375 H&H, .416 Rem Mag, .416 Rigby	400 yards
.300, .340 Weatherby Mag, .300 Rem Ultra Mag	500 yards

Coming up short on caliber per stated criteria, but marginal with premium bullets such as Nosler Partitions:

7 mm Rem Mag	200 yards

Short on energy, but with good bullets, capable at short range (less than 40 yards):

.30-30, .32 Win, .300 Savage, .444 Mar	40 yards

Will anything less kill an elk on a good day? Has anything else killed lots of elk in the past? Sure, but ethics require that we use enough cartridge to kill a big elk even without luck on our side that day.

You'll not find an excuse in this book to use anything less than what's available and adequate, which is always well above state game regulation requirements. It's up to you to stay within range limitations. For most of us, the range limitation above 350 yards becomes a matter of the shooter-rest combination. In practical terms, that translates as a minimum to any rifle that you can shoot well in the .300 Winchester Magnum class. If recoil is not a problem for you, the .338 Winchester Magnum class is preferable. (The Winchesters seem to be the "lightest" kickers in these respective classes, according to my experience. I routinely use both.) If the recoil of the .300 might reduce the number of practice rounds that you'll fire, I would advise that you go with the 30-06 and accept the reduced range. Then, if you see the bull of your dreams through the scope of your .30-06 about 500 yards or more out, don't be tempted to "stretch the barrel," as Gene and Herm would say. Get closer.

Don't decide that recoil is a problem until you've put in some practice as suggested in this chapter. Pull the rifle stock tight into your shoulder and lean slightly into the recoil so that your entire body reacts to resist and absorb the push. If you don't have good muscle tone from conditioning training or a regular job involving hard physical activity, use what I term the thick fluffy recoil pad for practice. You'll never notice the recoil as you take that shot at the big elk. The official name of a good big fluffy is PAST Recoil Protection Super Mag Plus Shield from Battenfeld Technologies of Columbia, Missouri (www.battenfeldtech nologies.com, available from Cabela's).

You'll get over a sore shoulder; you will *not* get over hearing loss if you don't use adequate hearing protection. The earmuff designs that completely cover the ears are better than simple earplugs.

Lots of shooters get the heavy rifles, can't handle the recoil, and figure it's easier to get a muzzle brake to lower the recoil than to get their arm muscles in shape. Muzzle brakes come with a downside: muzzle blast. Folks who retail guns let this info slide, in my opinion. It's not overkill to wear earplugs with muffs over them when muzzle brakes are in use close by! And make sure that everyone present has hearing protection in place before a shot is fired—especially little kids. Ear protection is needed at all times for everybody when shooting .22s to .458s.

I don't reload my ammo. I don't recommend it to you either, as far as hunting is concerned. The reason I don't reload is that now you can get premium bullets, such as Nosler Partitions, in commercial loads. If you like reloading as a hobby, that's great. The rest of us will be at the range, at the gym, or running over the fields getting ready for elk season.

For those who do mix reloading with elk hunting, I'll offer an elk hunting Tale that you can use as a reminder to keep your reloads properly sorted.

Sometimes little mix-ups happen with the elk hunter's stuff. Sometimes little mix-ups happen in communication. Sometimes, regardless of the mix-ups, it all comes together; other times all of the little mix-ups happen at the same time, resulting in a snowball effect.

THE RELOADER AND THE SHORT SHOTS

I came in late one afternoon after beating myself up on the steep, slick, snowy slopes all day. I was just settling in to get a big bowl of stew and shoot the breeze around the hot stove with Old Herm, who was already back in camp, when the Old Reloader came storming into camp, making enough racket to wake up and stampede the entire string over the corral fence.

"Saddle up the meat packers, Herm! I got 'im! Mike's down there on the first ridge over from the high lookout above the kitchen, with a bull with a rack as wide as he can reach!!" He stood panting, shirttail pulled out from the headlong rush back to camp through the brush, with outstretched arms, palms turned forward with fingers in to express the width of the huge bull elk rack. Herm waited as he settled down and got his breath back sufficiently to give a better translation of the location. As the hunter wound down, Herm was spinnin' up in excitement.

Now for a little note on the Old Reloader. In the world of elk hunting, the hunters are divided into sitters and runners. There are other names for both types, but I won't go there right now. The Old Reloader was pretty much a sitter. He was also big into guns and shooting, but most of all, he was into reloading. He knew guns and cartridges and powers and loads and bullets and on and on. He could tell you the exact ballistic table, the rise and drop of the bullet, for any given range, any particular bullet, from any particular cartridge, out to hundreds of yards. He had scope settings for different ranges using his lightly loaded "Squid" loads and a completely different setup for the "Full House" stuff he used for hunting. As I recall, he carried a folding shooting support in his daypack with a rather large spotting scope. He was a *shooter.* So he would probably sit on a stand with the chance of a long shot if he could have run the ridges all day. It always struck me as a little funny that he ran (not literally, you understand) with the Iron Man, who was almost completely innocent of knowledge about things firearmswise. The Iron Man, on the other hand, could give lots of pointers on conditioning techniques. Taken together, you could pick up a lot of useful stuff with these two in camp.

Back to the storyline . . . Herm had by this time heard enough to start getting excited, and not just over the good fortune of the Reloader. Herm needed some pictures of big trophies coming out of this new area for advertising purposes.

"How many points?" he asked.

"Don't know!" Two very quizzical and one semi-quizzical, counting the cook, looks drew a fast explanation. "I stayed where I'd made the shot, while Mike hiked over to the place where the bull was standing when I shot, so that I could spot him and wave him into the place where the bull disappeared to after I shot, so we wouldn't lose him." That made sense. "I shot several shots, and at first the bull acted like he wasn't hit at all. Then he started moving along the ridge and disappeared into the brush. I guess he must have moved down the ridge and dropped, and the brush was too tall for us to see him, because Mike was just down the ridge from where the bull had been standing when he spread his arms to show how big the rack was." In his excitement, he reiterated in detail the main cause of that excitement: "When Mike got to the place where the bull was, he stretched his arms out"—here he demonstrated again—"that the rack was this wide! I headed on back to get you to get out there with the pack string to bring the quarters and mount in before it got dark."

"Sounds like a plan" was all that Herm said as he started gathering up saws and pack tarps and headed for the corral. He was out of camp in no time.

I stayed in camp with the Reloader. I knew the ridges, and that was a long shot to knock a bull over. I was starting to pick up interest in this reloading business. I ate my soup and the Reloader got more and more excited. By the time that I was full of soup, he was very excited to the point that I hoped that I didn't have to waste one of my nitros on him. He was going crazy excited waiting to see what that trophy rack was going to look like up close. It was getting full dark when Mike and Herm showed up. They were not excited, and the pack saddles were empty. They couldn't find the bull.

The Reloader was dropping into the bottomless gloom of dejection where elk hunters go when they face the awful fact of a once-in-a-lifetime shot missed, or, even worse, an elk mortally wounded and never recovered.

"But what about your signal that you'd found the bull and the rack was this wide?" he asked, demonstrating one last time without enthusiasm.

"I signaled," demonstrating arms thrown out in an unanswered question, palms up in puzzlement and helpless despair, "that I can't find a damned bull elk, any blood, nothin' around here anywhere! The tracks played out, and you took off before I got back to you. I went back and looked and looked, but couldn't find bull blood, tracks, nothin'. Finally Herm showed up and I thought he'd gone crazy." The guys said they'd go out the next morning and look some more.

Supper was glum. The Elk Tales that evening were about wounded elk not found, and ended early. Before long, we had all turned in except for the Old Reloader, who was messing around with his stuff.

Suddenly, a long mournful wail of obscenities turned the area surrounding the camp blue and turned everybody out. Sounded like we had an exorcism job on our hands. Should we make the victim drink mule liniment? Eventually an explanation emerged intermittently through the expletives. "I mixed up my [expletives deleted] reloads! I took the [expletives wow! deleted] practice loads out this morning! I was [expletive, goodness! deleted] shooting exactly 33, [expletive, mercy! deleted] feet low at that [expletive, expletive, ow, even in an elk camp, even the mules are blushing they're so embarrassed! deleted] bull!"

Don't hold me to that exact figure for the bullet drop. After all this time, I can't remember it precisely as it was quoted.

But I do remember the "note to self" I made later as I lay half asleep in my sleeping bag in the darkened tent. I recalled an image of an elk hunter hurriedly loading stuff into his pack for the day's hunt, not giving a thought to which one of the two identical boxes the different reloads were stored in he was grabbing. Note to self: Never reload. I saw the Reloader in my mental image in the dark tent . . . "Now which box did I put the Squid loads in? Which box was the full house stuff in?" Another note: Practice with what you hunt with. What was it someone had told me? "You really don't need to practice with the good, expensive hunting rounds . . . just use a cheaper round of the same power and bullet weight and recoil to practice."

You can carry everything else wherever you want to, but carry your ammo, other than what's in the gun, where you can reach it instantly at all times. Don't worry about protecting it from anything except losing it. I use an elastic type belt carrier that holds twenty cartridges. At one time, I carried a few extra loose rounds in my left shirt pocket where I carry other shirt pocket stuff, away from the shooting shoulder. I don't do that anymore. A short, hard ride on a horse with a thing about jingle noises got me over that habit.

SELECTING A MODERN HIGH-POWERED RIFLE

I'm sure I'm in good company in that I've spent countless hours of my youth studying the relative merits of different types of big game rifles. At the end of all that reading, which, in retrospect, could have been more profitably directed to other fields of research, I have reached a conclusion: They're all better than my shooting and probably better than yours, too.

Most experienced elk hunters seem to eventually end up using a bolt action. They're more accurate than most of us will ever be with our shooting (which also goes for most of the rest of the actions); they're more than adequate to handle the elk cartridges discussed earlier; and they can be relied on to get a shot off every time as long as they're thoroughly cleaned every few months, including the bolt. You can always stuff another round in with a bolt action.

If I were just getting started as a high-powered rifle shooter, I wouldn't go all out for a lightweight rifle. You'll notice the greater recoil more during practice than you'll notice the lighter weight while you carry it, even if there's a lot of difference in the weight. Some of us got into one of those very high-level discussions once about lightweight rifles. It finally reached the point of making a trip to some very accurate scales to settle the case. The custom rifle that cost enough to cover the cost of a good used truck with a good dog in the back weighed in with its oversized scope less than 2 pounds lighter than the off-the-shelf standard with a good fixed 4-power. Lose the weight off of your middle instead; you'll be better off.

On a separate, but related topic, I don't get too excited over either the short or long rifle barrels. I figure that the guys at the big factory back east have had a hundred years since smokeless powder came along to work it out, and the standard is probably just fine.

I would get a rifle with iron sights and immediately put the front sight hood/cover in a safe place, like that desk drawer that you'll never look in again. The iron sights are always there in the unlikely event that you need them, and the exposed front sight is very handy when leaning the rifle against a tree or boulder—set it between two rough parts of the tree or rock surface to prevent the rifle from falling and knocking the scope sight off zero. It works best for this purpose with the cover off.

You'd probably conclude that I'm not a big fan of iron sights. Actually, that predisposition is restricted to the iron sights usually as supplied on factory rifles, the open V or notch rear sights. Open rear sights require sharp focus on three points at different distances: the very close rear sight, the somewhat close front sight, and the distant target. You'll probably have to try it under different light conditions to prove to yourself that you can't do it. The term "iron sights" also includes aperture sights, or as commonly termed, "peep" sights, which require focus on two points: the front sight and the target. Focusing on those two at once is possible, as demonstrated by millions of tactical sights on service firearms. Done right, these sights are excellent. "Done right," in practical terms, amounts to sturdy construction, an aperture large enough to allow enough light to pass through under all lighting conditions, and enough thickness around the aperture to provide a distinct reference as the shooter's vision is focused on the front sight and the target. The best available sights that I'm aware of are made by XS Sight Systems, based in Fort Worth, Texas.

I definitely recommend the Winchester Model 70. For some scientifically unexplainable reason, its stock seems to accommodate any way I can hold it and fold up around it to take a rest for the cross-canyon shot using a stump, rock, or log. I also definitely recommend the Remington Model 700. For the same unexplainable reason, its stock seems to jump into position for the bull that suddenly appears out of the timber and doesn't intend to stay very long. Either will work okay for the other shot if the occasion should come up. They're both accurate and reliable, at a reasonable price. I match up the rifle with a sight selection to tailor the combination for a particular purpose. For some time now, the particular purpose usually involves attempts to go after big bulls in the thick stuff where they tend to hang out.

Following the philosophy that practice with a .22 version of any action is an extremely good idea before committing to use that particular action on an elk hunt, we extended an invitation for a couple of .22 Henry lever-actions to move in. It's a good idea to mimic the length of throw of the full-power action with the practice .22, and the Henry is long throw.

SCOPES

There are a lot of good scopes on the market these days, which hasn't always been the case. On those occasions when somebody asks me about my recommendations for a scope for a particular type of rifle or hunting, I carefully consider all of the options and then invariably recommend the Leupold. I sometimes get the impression that maybe they're just checking me out to make sure I'm not mentally slipping. I do notice that I don't buy a new scope very often. I just change the old Leus from one rifle to another. And no, I've never had a dime discounted on the full retail price I've had to pay for them. Remember, I'm not an outdoor writer by profession.

I have and use variable-power scopes, and you'll probably get one for your first elk rifle too. And then, unless you're in the trees and want a lower power setting, you'll always leave it on 4 power just like I do, which brings up what I see as the drawback to the ranging scopes or most of the stuff that requires an elk hunter to do anything other than size up the elk and get ready to make the shot: You'll probably have enough to do just to make the shot; you don't need anything else on your hands. The exception—the case in which the variable power really is useful—is using the high power setting for trophy assessment.

My usual scope for elk hunting is a fixed 4-power Leupold with medium weight Duplex crosswires (crosshairs). I have gone from cheap fixed to high-quality variable to high-quality fixed. I found that the variable scopes were usually at the wrong setting, and you don't want to have anything on your mind but the shot when the occasion arises.

After you go to the expense of acquiring a high-quality scope, don't make the mistake of getting a good scope cover to protect it from the elements. I'll explain the math. A good scope will cost $200 or $300 and last well over twenty years in the hands of an amateur—we're not out there all the time. During that time you sink as much as $4,000 to $8,000 per year in hunting trips. Do you want to risk not getting off the once-in-a-lifetime shot sometime during those twenty years because your scope cover was on? That scope is as likely to get busted by accident as to become unusable due to accumulated damage from wear and the elements. Leave it uncovered so that you're instantly ready for that once-in-a-lifetime shot, without anything to think about at the time other than making the shot.

Pack camps are populated by hunters, cooks, guides, packers, and various other wild critters. There are countless Tales about each one and how they interact. You meet a lot of outstanding people of all types over a few years. One type fits a pattern that almost always leads to early success at elk hunting. These are the hunters that show up with almost no elk hunting experience, some with almost no hunting experience at all, but who obviously excel in unrelated sports and hobbies that emphasize physical conditioning. Some of the old hands are always quick to have a little fun at the new hunter's lack of familiarity with elk hunting and the stuff of elk hunting. Some of the old hands often pack out red-faced and empty-handed at the end of the hunt while they follow the pack string with a big rack collected by the "dude." I've been led to conclude that a longtime fascination with the "stuff" of elk hunting is quickly trumped by physical fitness and enthusiasm. I always try to help out the newcomers, if they ask, just so I can share in their pleasure—and sometimes, if you can keep up well enough to hunt with them, they'll get some elk moving that might come your way.

THE FAST MOVER AND THE RIFLESCOPE COVER

Darkness was gathering on the third day of the season. I had been out entertaining myself with a long, casual tour of the trails of the area. That's normally unusual for me, but, also unusual for me, I had taken a bull on the opening morning of this particular season. It had taken about a day for me to figure out that it was more like a vacation to tour the trails than to hang around camp doing jobs that the cook dreamed up to keep me entertained. So there I was, strolling down the trail at a slow pace even for me, when I was overtaken by the Fast Mover, another hunter in the camp, striding along at a pace that would normally be considered a fast jog for most of us. His full name was Fast-Movin' Doc, to distinguish him from his hunting buddy Slow-Movin' Doc.

The Fast Mover was sort of a fitness enthusiast. You know the type— 20-mile run every other day, off days in the gym for four or five hours, 75-mile hike on both days of the weekend, a diet consisting of fresh baked fish and raw fruit. Always makes an effort to carry at least 40 pounds of stuff in his pack to get a little exercise in during his hunt. He slowed down to my turtle pace and we walked along visiting.

It's always a little amusing how folks that you're hunting with for the first time assume that if you take an elk, you must know what you're doing and ask questions. I figured from the questions that he had just missed getting a shot at a good bull. I asked a few questions and determined that he must have moved into one side of a "bull's nest" before he was aware that he had stumbled into a big bull's hideout. A few more questions confirmed my suspicions that he had been moving along at a fast pace through the woods when the incident occurred. That's a common failing of the very physically fit. They tend to walk through a place faster than they can look it over. That's usually not a problem for those of us who are naturally slow paced.

He eventually got around to his main concern. It seems that the bull had made a clean getaway because he couldn't get the cover off of his scope quick enough. He asked about my technique to remove my scope cover when I was in a hurry. (Herm had been telling about the quick, accurate shot I had made to take the big bull on opening morning. With each telling I had gotten a little faster.) I turned and he immediately noticed that my riflescope didn't have a cover. He said something to the effect that I must have lost my cover too. I told him that a cover had never graced my riflescope. As he asked how I kept from ruining my scope, I noticed that he didn't have his scope covered either. I didn't have to ask the question I knew the answer to. He went on to say that he used a set of covers with an elastic band that stretched between the two lenses to keep the front and back covers in place. In the excitement of trying to get into battery with the elk getting away, the covers, propelled by the stretched connecting elastic straps, had shot forward over the side of a drop-off into a steep creek and were lost forever. My comment to the effect that that was a real good place to leave a set of scope covers tipped him off as to my philosophy, but, like old guys usually do, I had to give the fully embellished viewpoint whether he wanted it or not. Since he's a medical doctor and could cover the cost of a new rifle and scope in the first fifteen minutes of a surgery, the economic perspective shouldn't factor greatly into his calculations, but I brought it up anyway, since that's the way I figure it. If it takes forty years to ruin a set of riflescope lenses (I haven't ruined a scope yet) and you can see through them a lot better with a little water on them than with a cover over them, then missing that one shot at the bull of a lifetime for the cost of a scope versus the cost of all of those elk hunts just doesn't calculate.

He didn't say anything, but he did down a big bull later that same hunt. I'm sure it had more to do with Herm's unsolicited advice to move a little slower through the good places, since he didn't have another scope cover anyway. But I haven't seen a scope cover on his rifle whenever I've seen him since.

Bore Sighting

While hunting, you should be confident at all times that the zero of your scope hasn't changed due to one of those little spills that you tend to take in the woods. And you always carry one of those little laser pointers that fit in the barrel to check the scope, and of course the batteries never run out. Right? Just in case, sometime while you're out on the rifle range and want to take a break, remove the bolt from your (bolt-action) rifle. Using sandbags to support the rifle on the bench, sight through the scope at the target at least a hundred yards out and center the crosshairs on the target, making small adjustments as required—not to the scope but to the rest, while leaving the rifle fully supported by the sandbags. Now, without touching the rifle, peep through the barrel and look at the target. When you have moved your eye around so that you are looking straight down the barrel, with the opening of the muzzle being exactly centered with the opening of the chamber, the target should be exactly centered. This is *bore sighting*. Note that you can't really see through the scope and the barrel at the same time. You move your eye to look through one, then the other without touching the rifle. In the illustration on the opposite page, you might use the large rock to line up the barrel, and really squint to get the small rock resting on the large rock centered in the bore of the barrel. The light entering the end of the barrel will help you center the muzzle of the barrel with the darker chamber end. It's easier than it

sounds because your eye naturally lines up along the center of
the bore. Then you shift your eye
to look through the scope, and
you should see the magnified
image of the small rock in the
crosshairs.

Now remember this little exercise and someday, in a mountain
elk hunting camp, you can use it
to prop the rifle on a stack of hay
or firewood or a downed tree and
check the zero of your rifle after
you have bumped it in some
ingenious way. Just pick out a rock
or a leaf about a hundred yards
out to sight in on. It's far better
than shooting up the countryside
to check your sights and annoying
everyone in camp by running off

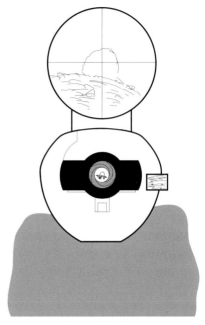

Bore sighting.

all of the elk. Offer to help anyone else in camp who might be possessed
with an urge for some target practice in the middle of your hunting area.
And, if it's too hot for the elk to be moving, and the action's really slow,
you can check your laser gizmo even if the batteries are working.

RIFLE CLEANING KITS

Another piece of gear you need for your modern high-powered repeater
is a cleaning kit to field-clean your rifle at the end of each daily romp.
Mine consists of a three-section rod, a few patches, and a small spray
can of WD-40. The spray does a fair job of displacing moisture in places
you can't reach, although it will eventually create buildup if used in
excess over a long period of time. For the duration of a trip, I prefer the
WD residue to moisture, which will freeze and interfere with operation.

BASIC SHOOTING PRACTICE

This section starts at the beginning, long before plans for the elk hunt
are finalized, even before all of the gear that will be needed is assembled. The comments here are primarily for the beginning rifle-equipped
elk hunter with experience hunting small game or white-tailed deer,
unfamiliar with the heavy rifles, long distances, and quick offhand
shooting encountered in elk hunting. My hope is that I can save you

some time and frustration by passing along some tips on practice that I learned over time the hard way.

The first thing that you need to do after you get your preferred rifle and have a scope mounted and bore-sighted is to buy another rifle. Get an inexpensive .22 rimfire (any action will do since there's really no need to match your bolt-action elk rifle) with an inexpensive scope of the same power as the one you plan to use on your elk rifle. The .22 is a very light gun and good for practice that simulates shooting the big gun, but with ammo that costs next to nothing and with practically no recoil. At the least, practicing with a .22 will save you a lot of time and expense, and at best, it might prevent a case of "big gun heebie-jeebies," the old hunter's technical term for what the pros call flinching.

Shooting Practice Preliminaries

For the first session with your full-sized scoped and bore-sighted elk rifle, I suggest that you go out to the range with a trusted loved one, not one of your hunting buddies. Your spouse is okay if he or she doesn't talk too much (as in spreading around information that will get back to the hunting buddies). The best situation is if your spouse is also your hunting buddy. Your mom or dad or one of the in-laws (if you married well) would be okay too. Take along a couple of boxes of discount-store ammo; no need for the premium stuff you'll use for hunting.

Put up a great big target about 40 or 50 yards out. Both shooter and coach should put on ear protection, and a heavy-duty shooting pad for the shoulder is a good idea as well. Keep your glasses on if you are going to wear them while hunting. Then, standing offhand so that during recoil you can "go with the flow," hold the rifle tight, real tight, into your shoulder and touch off a couple or three rounds, reloading single rounds so that you have time to think about it. Remember the exact sight picture the instant when each shot went off. Your mind will always hold that image. Say out loud where the sight was; that's where the hole should be in the target. The term is "calling the shot." Get somebody to check the target with a spotting scope to see how the calling and shooting match. Without a spotting scope, it's hard to see those little .22-sized holes in the black spot.

Lots of noise with that big rifle. Noticeable recoil. See how you did. You should have a pattern no larger than about the size of a turkey roaster. Don't worry about the location of the center of the pattern for now. If your pattern is in the number-three-washtub range, take a few shots with the .22. Call each shot. Not much noise. No recoil. Better pattern?

Try a few more offhand shots with the elk rifle, but this time have your trusted loved one load the single rounds for you. And ask him or her to leave the chamber empty one time chosen at random without telling you. If you have noticeable recoil when the hammer falls on an empty chamber, you have a little more work to do before attempting more precise shooting. Do it with the .22, holding it tight against your shoulder every time you shoot. Tight enough to turn the knuckles white on the nine fingers you're not using to pull the trigger. With that tenth finger, carefully pop off each round. Pull that thing into your shoulder until you almost shake, and shoot some more.

The low-priced .22 may have a 10-pound trigger pull and that's okay. We experienced amateurs never have our rifles tuned up to have a light trigger pull. We like them hard to pull, just like the factories make them—that way we don't risk having the gun go off before we're good and ready. We want to have to deliberately pull the trigger even if we're shaking from cold, from breathing hard, or just because we see the biggest set of horns through the scope that we've ever imagined.

Concentrate on getting the shot off with the .22 when the target looks good in the scope. If you hold the rifle too long and the crosshairs start moving across the target like windshield wipers, lower the rifle and rest a minute. Don't worry; you're not a marine recruit here. Relax and enjoy the moment. You can't play around like this in lots of countries, you know.

Getting tired of the .22 after about thirty rounds or so? Try the elk gun again. Shoot the same way you did with the .22. You should be okay to go on to the next stage. If, after six to eight shots, you think you're still jumpy, go home and think about it and try again tomorrow. Before you leave the range, let your trusted loved one try it. He or she might suggest something helpful. That's why I suggested a trusted loved one. If this first session doesn't go very well, the last thing you want is to hear about it again in elk hunting camp. Recoil, like lots of other stuff, is mostly in your mind. All you have to do is pull the rifle into your shoulder hard enough that all of your mass is involved in the recoil reaction. I can say that much not as an amateur, but as an engineer; my work has involved design of several machines that operate on principles of recoil reaction. My personal experience with target practice in company of my loved ones indicates that the weight limit for enjoyable offhand shooting of a .300 Win Mag is somewhere well less than 110 pounds. So, if at first you don't succeed . . . practice some more. Do not, I repeat, do not try to practice using loaded-down reload cartridges, then hunt with the full-house stuff. Learn to hold the rifle right, practice that way, and you'll always be ready for the once-in-a-lifetime shot with confidence. And confidence is what counts.

Offhand Practice

I'll now address the most difficult shot you'll ever encounter, one that some hunters are so reluctant to attempt that they pass up opportunities rather than risk taking it. Relax. You've already learned all the technique you need to know in the preliminaries. It just takes more practice with the .22. Practice and more practice. The secret is that you had enough good sense to buy the .22. About eight or ten full-house rounds in the .300 Mag—that's anybody's .300 Mag—and you start losing ground. A good shooting pad for the shoulder will extend that number some, but not a lot. But with the .22, as long as you have the same sight picture as with the elk gun, practice is practice. Pull that hard-breaking factory trigger when the sight picture is right. Again and again. Forget what you've read about squeezing off a round; that term comes from creepy military rifle triggers, the kinds that were tuned with lighter, better-breaking pulls when the military rifles were converted to sporters. That also creates the impression that offhand shooting is a mechanically precise activity, which it is not. Attempting and expecting too much precision initially is counterproductive. All you're after is to be able to hold it in a 6-inch pie plate 40 yards out with a shot you can consistently get off in a second or so after you have the rifle to your shoulder. (Later, I'll teach you how to get the rifle from the sling to your shoulder in a hurry so that you'll have plenty of time to make the shot.) As you practice offhand shooting, focus on the target and the shot going off when the sight picture looks right. Time stands still; motion stops. Instinct is in the making. Don't let the rifle cant (tilt) to either side. The sights will tilt too. Figure it out.

The photos on the next page illustrate the good offhand form of a natural shooter. It's a safe practice to mimic the naturals as you develop your own form. Note how her offhand stance is aligned with the axis of the rifle to react to the recoil of the elk rifle, even though the .22 is acting as a stand-in while she makes lots of practice shots. She'll lean into the heavier rifle more. (The hunter cap looks a little out of place for practice in Texas, but that's what she'll be wearing on the trails of Idaho, unless it's warm there and the tennis visor comes out—which she also wears for practice.) Don't overdo the level of precision needed in this offhand practice. This informal shooting is at a range of 60 yards, at more or less 3-inch black spots; anywhere in the spot is very okay, and you're going for a pattern about the size of a 6-inch pie plate for starters.

A natural offhand shooting stance.

Side view. Bill is in the background with a spotting scope, calling the shots from behind the acoustic blast shield of the open pickup door.

TIPS FOR OFFHAND SHOOTING PRACTICE

Some shooting from the bench at a range of around 200 yards will indicate what, if any, corrections you need to make to center the offhand standing shot pattern on the target. However, I would think twice before I made drastic changes to a good offhand zero on the basis of the initial bench rest practice session.

Go back to some offhand shooting to see if you're keeping the left forearm, stock, barrel, and scope in the same vertical plane. If you hold the rifle at a cant, the sight will be off to one side rather than directly over the barrel. The bullet drop will be straight down, and therefore off to one side of the sight picture of a canted rifle—and all of the trajectory stuff goes out the window.

The left hand lightly restrains the rifle, and the right hand holds the butt of the stock into the shoulder. (You lefties know what I mean for you.) The left hand shouldn't have a tight clinch on the rifle, but most people can't simply rest an elk rifle on a flat palm in the manner of many offhand .22 shooters.

Until now, we haven't changed the crosshair adjustments from the bore-sighted settings done at the store. After a couple dozen shots, you probably have a fair idea of the location of the center of the shot patterns you're producing. Adjust the crosshairs so that your offhand patterns are about in the center of the target.

Long-Range Practice Using a Rest

You've done some offhand shooting by now and have the crosshairs in the vicinity of the center of the target. You're ready to go to the range bench rest to really zero in the rifle. This is the type of shooting where you expect to develop that mechanical precision that you've heard about. Well, up to a point. Art becomes involved when addressing the interaction of three elements: the mechanically precise rifle/scope combination; the unmoving, rigid rest; and the imprecise, flexible shooter attached, more or less, to the rifle. The goal here is to hold the bullet impact inside the 6-inch-diameter pie plate as with offhand shooting; we just move the pie plate out to about 200 to 300 yards rather than 50 yards. The key to attaining that goal is, as you might expect, more practice. The difference is that this time, you get to use a rest to steady the wavering rifle.

Standard practice is to use ballistics tables to understand how the bullet on its way to the target will rise and fall relative to your line of sight. These tables are always to be found on the gun store counter. They're a source of entertainment for the people that hang around there, and the people who run the store use them to sell people more guns than they need because of the new, or different, cartridges that they currently don't have guns for. Ballistics, wind drift, and other details that may not make sense to you now are also available online from manufactures.

Most of the cartridges that are used for elk have a suggested zero at 200 yards; then they should shoot about 2 inches high at 100 yards, and at 300 yards they hit about 8 inches below the point in the crosshairs. My personal practice is to push this out a little for the elk rifle. I like to have the bullet strike dead zero at 250 to 300 yards, depending on the bullet and the rifle. Then I shoot dead-on for about any distance, or as far as I can tell that the elk looks to be a reasonable size in the scope. If the range starts to reach the point that the elk doesn't fill up the space between the posts, I think about it for a second. At all of the intervening ranges, the shot will be about 4 inches high from about 100 to around 200 yards, less for closer and farther. Since the range of most offhand shots is about 50 yards, the bullet entry will be about $1/2$ inch above the point of aim; there'll be some difference between open sights right on the barrel and telescopic sights a couple of inches above the barrel, but both are close enough at 50 yards to become one of the least of your worries.

Many, if not most, people take the first shots with their new elk rifle here, from the bench rest. The reason I suggest starting with a few off-hand shots to become familiar with the rifle becomes obvious with the first few shots from the rest. Recoil may be a little stiff if you're not accustomed to it. If this is where you start, first go through the exercise I suggested in the preceding section. Recoil is more of a problem when shooting from a rest because you can't roll with the punch as in the off-hand shot.

Don't push yourself for too many shots per session with the elk rifle. The novelty wears off quickly, you'll find. Use the .22 to accumulate the practice shots. Be careful to keep the same tight grip you need to use with the elk rifle. You can shoot the light-recoiling rifle with no hold at all from the rest, but that practice has little value, since you need to use the same grip for all of your shooting. Go ahead and practice with the little rimfire .22 at 100-yard ranges. You'll have more shot dispersion than with the heavy centerfires, but the little imperfections in technique will show up at longer ranges and you can make corrections with practice. A few of the little imperfections that lots of us struggle with are things like inconsistent grip or cant of the rifle and scope. Hold either the heavy or light rifle tight to your shoulder with your right hand, with your right elbow resting on the bench. Rest your left hand on two sandbags to give yourself enough clearance off the bench to allow your left forearm to contact the bench surface directly under and in the same vertical plane as the stock, barrel, and scope of the rifle. (Left-handed folks, change hands for all of the above. The bolt handle of your left-handed rifle will be turned around as well.) If recoil is hard on your shoulder in this locked-down and rigid bench shooting, use a recoil pad as thick as required to eliminate the distraction (the PAST works for the real kickers). Out on the mountain, you'll have on a lot more padding due to your coat, and excitement usually makes the recoil imperceptible.

Some Techniques of Shooting and Rifle Handling beyond the Basics

Once you've learned the basic shooting skills under the controlled conditions of the shooting range, you need to make the transition to hunting conditions. Many ranges have or can make provisions to allow you to practice while sitting on the ground or standing while using part of the structure or bench rest for support, particularly during weekdays when the range isn't crowded. The objective is to make all of these supported situations as consistent as possible, and as close to the offhand grip as possible. This sort of practice is easier to arrange if you live in the country or have access to a safe place for some informal shooting. You can practice holding the rifle steady anywhere. It's good to shoot a lot with a .22 to see the results you can produce with a rest compared with the standing, unsupported position. Then you can shoot a few shots with the elk rifle with each type of rest and shooting position to check out the effects of recoil. That recoil pad may come in handy again for some of these positions.

Out in elk country, a rest can be taken by resting the arm and hand supporting the front of the rifle on any solid, generally flat object. The trick of this arrangement is what you do with the rest of your unsteady body. It's usually best if you can lay it over or against the same object; otherwise, it will rock back and forth and make the sight sweep across the target. A variation on this general theme that some long-range shooters use is to sit back against a rest like a tree or rock or your classic pickup truck seat back. The first two backrests result in sharp recoil effects, so I'd recommend using that big old fluffy recoil pad when you first try it in practice. The recoil effect is sort of on the order of what you get in the prone position using a .338, and shouldn't be taken lightly by those of slight build. You can damage your collar bones and rotator cuffs with just a little error in hold! For most people, the main point to address when practicing from a rest position is the effect of the rest support upon the shot placement (to the right or left). The best way to avoid this effect is to keep the support in the vertical plane as nearly as possible.

You can usually find a vertical rest under hunting conditions. Any tree without a lot of low limbs in the way will do, and you can shoot from a standing position. The best rest for most people is to steady the hand holding the front of the stock lightly against the rest, rather than pushing the side of the stock or barrel against the vertical surface. Your unsupported body will tend to rock slowly from side to side, and you can compensate somewhat by slightly moving your wrist to keep the sight on target.

A reasonably steady hold can be made from a sitting position without any rest other than yourself. With some practice, it will become fast and instinctive. This position is particularly adaptable to shooting from a slope—and there's usually a slope wherever you are in elk country. You create the rest beginning with a step back with the right foot (for a right-handed shooter), then square up at a 45-degree angle to the target. Form a base for the rest by sitting on the ground with your legs spread apart and the heel of each foot dug into the ground. The pattern on the ground should be a triangle of equal sides. Then you hold the rifle as if you were going to shoot from a standing position, and lean forward to rest each elbow on your legs in front of each knee. This position is designed for stability, not comfort. It's fast to get into and you don't need to locate a tree or rock for stability. You do need to check to make sure that, from your lower shooting position, you can still see the target that you picked while standing. You'll often see this position illustrated using a sling. Forget the sling for now. Just practice first to develop muscle and coordination without the sling.

You'll need to control your breathing, or you'll produce an up-and-down motion of the sight. Practice until you can instinctively coordinate taking a deep breath and holding it while the trigger finger squeezes the shot off. This technique will also ensure that you go ahead and get the shot off without thinking about it too much. A little oxygen depletion will remind you when you're taking too much time. A fully supported rest should be steady enough for you to notice the sights moving with just the throb of your pulse. Instinct should keep you from squeezing the trigger when the throb is anticipated.

After you've become accustomed to shooting with the consciously maintained tight hold against the shoulder, you may relax a little to see if your patterns improve (in the sense of becoming smaller). Be careful not to let the butt of the stock get too loose, or it will accelerate into your shoulder enough to bring the scope into contact with your forehead, leading to an embarrassing "third eyebrow" mark you'll have to explain to everybody. Steep uphill shots or shots from a near-prone shooting position will have the same unfortunate effect.

Developing Instincts—Practice with the Image of an Elk through the Scope

My target practice routinely uses cave art images as the target rather than conventional rings around a spot. I recommend the technique for everybody. Your instinct for the shot at the elk should be as close as practical to what you've practiced. The target images are scaled so that they can be used at a distance of 30 yards for practice of the 300-yard shot. Elk measure a little more than 30 to 35 inches from the bottom of the belly to the top of the shoulder (the two don't exactly align up and down); to get the image of a real live elk at 300 yards, your paper target at 30 yards should be about 3 inches from belly to shoulder. That distance of 30 yards is about the point where the path of the bullet from the muzzle crosses the line of sight for a reasonably low mounted scope sight or a high peep sight. I recommend that you practice with a .22, so that you can put a few thousand rounds downrange as opposed to the twenty or so rounds you could do with the full-house .300 or .338 Mag before all your nerves are shot and your brain has turned to mush. But note that you could practice with the heavyweight and be reasonably close. You'd probably be better off to use the big shells actually at 300 yards, but targets the full size of the elk are unhandy. Note that my rifles are set up to cross the line of sight again just short of 300 yards, so I account for a hit a little high for the 100-yard shot.

You can tell from the photos that we keep it casual and fun. The first photo is from a gravel pit shooting practice and shows shots for sight adjustment. The cartridge illustrates the scale of image used for practice with a .22 at a range of about 30 yards. In the second photo, my target is stuck up on the support of a real range. The support's never in the right place (range) for a bullet to be at zero like it should.

Experiment with different rests and shooting positions to see the effect on the impact of the bullet. You'll see that the effects can be significant, and somewhat complex when considering long, deliberate shots. Some rests will kick you off target. Check it out in practice.

Elk image on a target board on the side of an earth bank in an exclusive gravel pit shooting club.

A scaled image of an elk at a real range.

Practice Hunting with a High-Powered Rifle

The elk hunter's mindset can't be practiced at the shooting range. The same goes for moving on game using cover and taking shots at moving game. It can, however, be practiced at other times than while actually hunting elk. It can be accomplished by finding some kind of year-round (or at least with more time than the relatively short elk season) hunting activity that approximates elk hunting (sort of). That translates to a type of hunting that involves the same (general) set of activities as elk hunting: location, stalking, and making the kill.

The most obvious hunting activity that springs to mind might be mule deer hunting. It takes place in the same landscape, for the most part, and it includes two of the three phases of elk hunting: stalking and making the kill (location is less complex in the case of mule deer hunting). But mule deer hunting as a learning experience has the drawback for the nonresident that the trip is just as expensive in terms of time and money as elk hunting; the tags are often just as difficult to come by; and the hunting seasons in most states overlap. So the best approach is to look for a hunting activity close to home that simulates elk hunting. Preferably, the three distinct phases should be present; enough elbow room should be involved to allow (or require) you to move over a few miles on foot and handle a rifle on the move, ready for a shot at any time; and enough terrain and vegetation should be involved to help you develop your instincts and intuition of how the quarry will interact with its surroundings under different conditions.

In the part of Texas where I live, coyotes have been an off-and-on problem to the local stockmen, and for some years, I have had an open invitation to keep them thinned out or at least keep them from getting too comfortable in the area during calving time. Rather than calling or waiting along their travel routes, I hunt them on foot, ranging over several farms in what amounts to miles of straight-line distance. Moving along, using fencerows as screening cover, I try to intercept the coyotes, which are also on the move in the early morning. I occasionally attempt to stalk them in their rest areas later in the day. This practice gives me a feel for their movements and location. And routinely carrying a bull-barreled varmint rifle makes handling an elk rifle seem effortless in comparison. I always use a cartridge that comes close to the ballistics of the elk cartridges I use. In the case of varmint rifles, the combination of a 6 mm using a 100-grain bullet is close to a .300 Win Mag using a 180-grain bullet. This sort of year-round hunting is ideal for simulating elk hunting in open terrain. Over time, as I have moved toward elk hunting in thicker cover, I have likewise shifted my year-round hunting toward feral hog hunting. This type of hunting involves a shorter range, and a quicker reaction is required, with shots at moving game being the norm.

Something to consider in your practice hunting is the running speed of your quarry; if you can, relate it in your mind to the speeds of elk at different gaits. According to my best estimates, feral hogs walk at about 5 mph, trot at about 10 mph, and blaze along at a 20-mph gallop. Coyotes walk at about 5 mph, but they seldom walk. Their dogtrot is a good clip, either side of 10 mph. An all-out run is around 45 mph for a couple of miles, then they'll leave the country at 30 mph after a good scare. Wolves aren't as fast as coyotes, according to my best reports, with maybe 35 to 40 mph as their top speed. Their dogtrot is also around 10 to 12 mph.

When I'm involved in year-round hunting, I always carry spare ammo in exactly the same manner that I carry my spare ammo for elk hunting. Likewise, since it is my habit to carry three rounds in my elk rifle—one in the chamber, two in the magazine to ensure smooth operation—that's the way I load all rifles for all types of hunting. That way, I always subconsciously count off three rounds, and then go for the next round from the ammo carrier at my belt with my right hand and drop it into the chamber from the open bolt. It's also a good idea to try out some hunting accessories, such as amber shooting glasses, while practice hunting to become accustomed to them over a period of time and in varying conditions before you take them on your big hunting trip.

Eye-Hand Coordination and How to Attain Steadiness

I've come to recommend more practice shooting than I once considered adequate. And I've come to emphasize the .22 rimfire as the preferred equipment, with a few shots from the heavy hitters now and then just to keep consistent in the restraining pressure against the shoulder to keep recoil under control. Here's why. All of us will shoot the little .22 more during each shooting session, and it's the shooting repetitions that count more than anything. The reason? Only repetition develops coordination between the trigger finger and the eye.

The eye is the boss. The instant the eye has the sight picture for a hit, the finger has to make the rifle fire. Not before. Not after. Not a second after the sights sweep over the target. Not in anticipation, or hope, that the waving sight will cross the target. While the sight is steady on the target. Impossible? Impossible. In an absolute sense, impossible. But there is hope. What you need to understand is the meaning of "steady" in any given situation.

"Steady" for practical shooting is when the movement of the barrel as indicated by the movement of the crosshairs or front sight over the target is limited to the bounds of the area where you want the bullet to strike for a clean kill. If you're close enough at 50 or 60 yards for that pie plate to cover the wandering of the sight with an offhand hold, you're steady enough. If not, you need to get closer or find a rest to steady your movement for an ethical shot; the corollary is that something less than 60, maybe about 30 yards, is your offhand range.

At a range of somewhere between 250 and 300 yards, the point where the bullet in its trajectory falls back through the line of sight, it should impact a target precisely centered. Or above the boresight point by the distance between the center of the scope and the center of the bore, to be exact. The line of sight of the scope has to be in precise vertical alignment to the bore—and a windy day is no good for conducting this science project. I'll cover the effects of the wind shortly. Vertical alignment of the rifle—no cant—and vertical mounting of the scope are critical. The shooter, in an effort not to cant the rifle to one side or the other, will always try to keep the vertical crosswire in a vertical orientation. If that wire is at a cant, the rifle will be fired at a cant. Then the rise and fall of the bullet throughout its trajectory aren't along the vertical crosswire: Gravity always pulls straight down, so the bullet will fall to one side of the intersection of the crosswires of a canted rifle. (My beat-up old .300 Win Mag Model 70 with a slightly tilted scope will still drop one right on the stern of a coyote running dead away at a measured 550 yards—I just have to remember to hold it high and to the left. It's been through a lot and hasn't moved, and I hate to change it. Guess I'm giving away the lengths some of us will go to in order to get those sights just right.)

COWBOY BENCH REST SHOOTING

Accurate determination of sight alignment is usually performed using a bench rest setup. A complication in the case of rifles with noticeable recoil is that they have to be restrained so hard by the setup that the dynamic interaction with the shooter that goes on during the hunt is lost. I've found the cowboy bench rest technique to be the best approach to find out how the sights should be tweaked to account for the imprecise human that's going to be attached during actual hunting. The cowboy bench rest looks a lot like a pickup truck. The (right-handed) shooter takes a position on the driver's side, with the seat adjusted to comfortably support the wiggly-weavely shooter. A fluffy coat or pillow makes a soft buffer between the left rearview mirror and the right hand of the extended forearm holding the rifle sticking out of the window. The shooter relaxes to make sure the position is maintained without strain, then pulls the stock back into the big fluffy recoil pad. (The cowgirls enjoy referring to it as the "sissy" recoil pad in hopes that the 300-pound guys can be induced into not using it when they set off the .300 and .338 Win Mags and any of the big Weatherbys. It never works on us old guys.) When all's well, that bullet drops right through the 6-inch bull of the target.

Pickups are also handy for informal shooting that sort of duplicates the improvised rests you take out where the elk run and there are no bench rests around. Then, when you're out on the western slopes, attempt to duplicate as near as possible the near-optimum support of the practice session. You'll come close using a daypack with a poncho inside, or a rolled-up coat or a hat for a cushion over the downed tree trunk or rock. The bullet will do the same thing out in elk country as it did when you were in the truck. That's assuming everything else is okay and not too excited.

If you intend to make a 300-yard shot that's an ethical stretch, you need to know the range and how the rifle is sighted at that range, and you need to be (softly) welded to a solid rest. Firmly down against a daypack or hat is about right.

"Steady" becomes measured by how much the sight picture moves with your pulse as you hold your breath. Then your eye can tell your finger when to put pressure on the trigger to fire. If you intend to make the same shot after you've just run up the slope and your pulse is pounding so that the sight picture has a continuous jitter, then "steady" means that the jitter of the sight picture has to be contained within the clean-killing pie-plate-sized area of the heart and lungs. Not steady? No shot.

Different scenario. You meet a big bull head-on along the trail at a range of 50 yards. You spin the rifle to your shoulder. Holding for the offhand shot, the sight picture will wave. If you control the waving so that the sight picture stays centered on the chest of the bull, your eye instructs the finger to shoot. If the sight picture is waving back and forth across the chest of the bull and a couple of feet to either side because you're gasping for breath, exhausted from just scaling the side of the bluff, or really, really excited because that thing is just so damned big . . . no shot.

And that's the reason why you need to practice, practice, practice, practice . . . to make your instincts strong enough that your eye knows the sight picture is steady enough and tells the finger to get the shot off at the right instant, regardless of what the rest of you is doing.

When you've reached that point, you're "in the zone." But once you get there, you don't always stay there. Sometimes instincts and conscious thought collide. The answer? I'm afraid it's nothing magical, just more practice to get back in the groove.

Make it part of your life. The fact is that the practice that it takes to internalize the sight picture and finger coordination sort of loses its fascination over a period of time. Try getting your family involved—all that practice seems to go better if you surround yourself with people you enjoy being around. You can make connections at the public shooting range that you're paying all the range fees to, and join a shooting club. Before long, you'll be out there all the time with friends and family, having a great time while you knock off five thousand shots a month. (That's a joke, but five to ten thousand rounds a year is about right.) There are lots of games you can play to make the practice more fun—KD Range Camp Perry, silhouette, and maybe one of the scattergun games that folks really enjoy going off the deep end doing. Sporting clays, which involves thrown clays at all angles, is probably the best training for all-around shooting skills at moving targets, and it can be a good family activity. Kids big enough and mature enough to handle a .410 shotgun love it.

You've now reached the point where you should expect to hit close to your point of aim. You should also begin to approach the absolute focus required for consistency, touching off the round between the bounces caused by your pulse. This focus becomes the mindset you need to make the kill while hunting.

We now move beyond focusing on a target at a known distance. It's time to give some thought to evaluating the unknown distances you will encounter under actual hunting conditions.

ESTIMATING RANGE USING A TELESCOPIC SIGHT

The next tale offers a good laugh at the expense of yours truly, and is a good way to remember one of the main principles of the long-range shot from a rest. Get the range before anything else—that includes even thinking about making the shot in the first place. The range needs to be within ethical limits before anything else happens. I've discussed the technique of determining the range to an elk by using the width of the space between the thick posts of the crosshairs. This method is descended from one Herm taught me to use with an old scope made in the 1950s that he had mounted on an old .300 H&H. The old scope had a series of little oval shapes adjacent to tick marks on the vertical hair. The oval patterns were sized to fit over a deer at different ranges when using a .30-06, but Herm had worked out which oval should fit over an elk on the H&H. At the time, the whole process struck me as being a little far-fetched, but I eventually learned that Old Herm was trying to help out the first-elk-hunt flatlander with the range estimation as much as with the range of the rifle. The "Circle around the Deer/Elk Rangefinder" concept is currently manu-factured by Shepherd Scope and available through Cabela's.

I worked out the crosshair post spacing as a rangefinder technique after the experience of this tale. Up until this sorry episode, I just estimated the range using my sharp young eyes to measure out those imaginary football fields between me and the elk, which, incidentally, was the technique taught in the army before laser rangefinders, which are now also available to the elk hunter. But we didn't need that sort of gadgetry in those days. We just laid out those football fields. Accurate? Yeah. You bet!

THE LONG SHOT OUT OF GOLD CREEK

The rain had poured down day and night for days. So hard that no elk, or anything else for that matter, was going to come out from under that big green tree where it was holed up. There was no point in even going out in that miserable wet stuff. You can walk by within 30 feet of a herd of holed-up elk in weather like that and they'll lie motionless and you'll never see them.

Finally, after what seemed like endless days and nights of downpour, the rain suddenly stopped one afternoon and the sun broke through. Our little party scattered out of the small tent that had made for togetherness in the extreme during the deluge. The rest of the group decided to forget about the bulls for that day, and headed for the hot springs to soak out the cold with hot water on the outside and a bottle of firewater on the inside. I took off to check out the theory that elk pile out into the meadows to graze when the weather makes such a drastic change for the better. It turned out that this was one of those times when the theory was right.

I slipped (in the sneaky sense) over into a little drainage called Gold Creek that cut past the broad face of a prominence called, oddly enough, Gold Hill, which dominated the area along one side of Boulder Creek through the area. This prominence was noted for long open faces with fairly low brush. Just the setup I needed to see if a bull would walk out in the middle of the afternoon to graze after the weather broke after a long rainy spell. And, sure enough, there he was. Standing right out in plain sight as I sneaked up out of the bottom of the creek and pulled up behind some thick brush to look out over the slope.

The bull was standing on the generally flat slope of the side of the moun-tain. The term "generally flat" in Idaho translates to mean that, like almost every square foot of the Bitterroots, it really wasn't flat at all, but was cut by several small drainages. And not being able to see all of the ground across the distance, I was having a difficult time trying to lay out those imaginary 100-yard football fields across that distance. Finally, squinting real hard through my new variable scope turned over to 7 power, I just guessed that it must be about 400 yards—which meant, of course, that I didn't have a clue what the range was. So I just held the crosshairs a little high so that they looked about right and popped off a round. The bull elk, of course, continued to graze along. I wasn't even close enough for the elk to be aware that he was being shot at. Having no better idea of what to do, I fired again with a steady rest so that I was sure to get a round through the chest if I got one anywhere. I fired once higher, once lower, and once in between. The bull finally must have become annoyed by the noise and moved off around the side of the mountain, leaving me to stand there feeling like a dumb flatlander. A self-assessment that matched my performance.

Later, back at camp, my hunting buddies deftly parried my questions as to the reason for their bruised and scraped condition. It was apparent that their horses had gotten drunk during the outing and playfully dumped my companions with the bloodshot eyes off onto the rocks in the vicinity of the hot springs when they tried to mount up for the trip back to camp. They returned fire with some questions as to where was the blood on my hands after all of the shooting up on the hill. Not letting on that I was annoyed when their barbs stung a little, I asked Gene in a nonchalant way just about how far it was across that slope from where I was standing to the bull. He had hunted that slope for years and knew the place like the back of his hand. After getting the precise particulars of my location and what the surroundings of the bull's location looked like, he estimated, "Oh, 'bout 800 yards, maybe 1,000 . . ."

"Guess I must have lost a few of those football fields in the low places."

"Yeah, cranked-up variable scopes tend to shorten those football fields up some."

And that's why, young elk hunter, you use the crosshairs of your scope or a rangefinder to estimate or measure the range instead of trusting those fighter-pilot eyes to lay out those football fields.

Most of the major manufacturers offer telescopic sights with ranging reticles of various designs. Most have marks that fit over some part of a particular game animal at a given range. They're all based on stadia or arc measurement. I'll detail the procedure to give you a practical, quick estimate of the range of elk, or anything else, observed at a distance using most riflescopes. The first element of this technique is to determine an arc measurement on your riflescope. The dealer should be able to give you this type of information, but just in case, I'll tell you for scopes I'm familiar with and teach you how to determine it for yourself using any scope that has some kind of mark or recognizable feature on the crosswires.

If you're using a Leupold telescopic sight with a duplex reticle, either 4- or 6-power fixed magnification, or a 3- to 9-power variable set on 6 power, the space in the center of the crosswires (crosshairs) between the thicker sections, called posts, will cover an arc of 10 minutes-of-angle (MOA), 5 on either side of the center. A single MOA amounts to a spread distance of 1 inch at 100 yards. You hear very accurate rifles referred to as capable of shooting with 1-minute accuracy. That amounts to a spread of 1 inch across a group at 100 yards. So the space between the posts covers 10 inches at 100 yards, 20 inches at 200 yards, and 30 inches at 300 yards.

We'll assume that all bull elk are created equal and are about 30 inches from the top of the back to the bottom of the chest or belly. Then, if you look at an elk through the scope, and it just fills the space between the vertical posts, or the thick part of the vertical crosshairs, that elk is about 300 yards away. If this tip is new information to you, that's about as far as you need to take a shot at a standing elk. (As a point of interest, you can assume that deer are about 20 inches back to belly and would therefore be about 200 yards out if they fill the same space.)

With any other scope, at any power, you can check against something of a known size at a known distance and get it calibrated that way. A 10-inch paper plate on a dark background at a distance of 100 yards works just fine. Using a rest for a steady hold, center the crosshairs in the center of the plate, and note where the edge of the plate strikes the crosshair. Just see what fits around 10 inches at 100 yards on your scope, even if your scope is actually marked in mil-dots! The best reference is relative to the thicker part of the crosshair, or post, on models that have thicker crosshairs on the outside, finer in the middle.

An alternative arc measurement used to determine range for military applications is the milliradian, usually abbreviated to "mil." It's a small (one-thousandth of a radian), dimensionless arc unit,

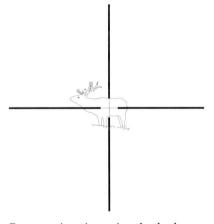

Range estimation using the duplex crosshairs of a telescopic rifle sight. For a Leupold duplex reticle fixed at 4 or 6 power, or a variable at 6 power, this bull is about 300 yards out. For sights set for the bullet to fall back through the line of sight at around 270 yards, it's also a good hold.

which is an alternate way to measure angles or arcs around a circle in terms of π (which is equal to about 3.14, as you may remember from math class); 2π radians equals 360 degrees. Try to not think about it too much. What counts is that the milliradian radial arc distance between the dot centers marked on the crosswires of the scope covers 3.6 inches at 100 yards, and 36 inches at 1,000 yards. You can tell from the funny figures that these inches and yards are a translation. Mil-rads, or mil-dots, as they're termed, are set up for metric units, where 1 milliradian covers 1 meter at 1,000 meters, and 1 centimeter at 100 meters. Don't worry, it makes more sense when translated to the size of an elk in the scope.

In terms of elk size, 1 mil at 1,000 yards (way too far to shoot, but bear with me) covers about 36 inches, slightly larger than a bull elk from back to belly, though you can't tell exactly at 1,000 yards. But at 100 yards, 10 mil-dots make a loose fit over the bull from back to belly. Out where your sight is dead-on at 250 yards range, the same fit would be between 7 and 8 mil-dots. Most shooters who use this system make a table for different game species and memorize it.

Laser Rangefinders

Direct range measurement is possible with laser rangefinders. The way they work is that the rangefinder shines a laser beam off of an animal, or any other object, and precisely measures the time it takes for the light to go to the object and be reflected back; that time correlates to the distance you are from the object. The laser sender/receiver is mounted on binoculars in order to precisely aim the laser beam. The devices, like all electronic gear, are now greatly improved in performance and affordability from the first models. They still have trouble handling targets with poor reflectivity and less-than-ideal lighting and atmospheric conditions. But you can measure the distance from a better reflector close to the intended target rather than the poorly reflecting target itself. Before using one of these devices, check to make sure it's legal where you intend to hunt. A practical rangefinder I've used is the Bushnell Yardage Pro 1200 yard (also available in shorter ranges). Laser rangefinders are now also available integrated into high-end binoculars.

SHOTS AT MOVING ELK

A related topic common to all equipment concerns shots at moving elk. I didn't get into this in the first edition of this book for a number of reasons, most of them having to do with the first edition being addressed primarily to the prospective or first-time elk hunter. But due to popular demand, let's get into it.

For inexperienced hunters, this is pretty simple: Don't take that shot while the elk is running. You take that shot while the elk is standing or walking slowly, and then only if the range is not too far. If the elk is walking, you need to limit the range to 80 yards with the high-powered rifle, 40 yards with the muzzleloader, so that the bullet can get there before that 6-inch spot that you're following in the scope moves from the foreleg back to the liver or gut. The speed of the walk should be slow enough that the lead is still on the front shoulder. If the elk is running or fast trotting, you should not attempt a shot at over 40 yards with a high-powered rifle, 20 yards with a muzzleloader, and with a bow, just forget it. There are a good many of us around who think elk are too important to use for target practice. You don't want to be stuck in a mountain camp after pulling a stunt like that in case one of us happens to be there.

Very experienced hunters, however, can learn the skills and instincts needed to take shots at moving elk in some situations. I've already pointed out that there are a lot of places you can locate that pie plate over an elk that are certainly not ethical shots. There are places you can shoot that will kill the elk, but not before it makes it over several ridges, never to be recovered, at least not by you. But nevertheless, just as that pie plate in the right spot is just as big at 300 yards as it is at 30 yards, the same goes for when it's moving at 20 or 30 mph versus 0 mph. When you get the chance at that shot, you have to make up your mind whether it's ethical in a hurry. I can help you out by giving you some very explicit criteria as to where you should be in skill level at standing shots, and in other areas, before you take running shots at elk.

Shots to take moving elk come in two versions: stationary or swinging barrel. In the first case, you hold a sight picture through a clearing ahead while you follow the elk with both eyes open and fire the instant the shot location on the elk fills the scope. For this stationary barrel shot, the elk should be less than about 50 yards out, moving through the thick cover, and stationary or moving slowly when the shot is made. In the second case, the moving-barrel shot, you swing the sight forward of the shot location and hold the swinging lead as the shot goes off. The fast-moving bullet intersects the shot location on the slower-moving elk. For this to happen, the bullet has to be aimed ahead of the shot location so that it gets to the point you aimed at at the exact same time the shot location on the elk does. Note my focus on the fact that the lead is relative to the shot location. In hunting books and magazines, you'll often see the lead defined as the distance in front of the game animal. This works for ducks and doves, but not for elk. With small game, you're trying to hit the body, usually with a shot pattern; with elk, you're trying to hit a very restricted location on the body. From the heart/lung shot location area forward to the front of the elk is a significant distance. The way the animal holds its neck and the shape of the thick mane will cause confusion when you don't need any (more). Always think of the lead as the distance ahead of the shot location, not ahead of the whole animal, even when practicing with game smaller than elk, such as feral hogs; you'll develop the correct instincts to hit any size game in the right spot. This is the kind of instinct you learn through practice.

Hunters who are really good at moving shots reach a point where they think of the lead as arc distance, or an angle; they make a smooth swing through the arc and shoot when the lead "looks good." I'll go through the exercise of reducing it all to a table, with calculations included, to help get you started. I don't suggest that you put off your first elk until you master everything involved in running shots. It might take a while . . . Keep hunting, and just pass on that moving shot unless it's very close or you can get the elk to stop. On occasion, elk can be stopped by a cow call, whistle, or spontaneous screamed obscenity.

A sort of imprecise nomenclature has developed around leads. An animal running across in front of you broadside, from one side to the other at a 90-degree angle to your line of sight, would be taken using a full lead. That direction of travel of the elk relative to you results in maximum movement across your line of sight and the path of the bullet. The speed of the animal is fully effective in displacing the shot location during the flight of the bullet. In contrast, if an animal is running either straight at you, head-on, or straight away from you, dead away (right on top of your line of sight, in either case), there's no displacement of the shot location relative to the flight of the bullet, regardless of the speed of the animal. No lead is required. All other angles, either toward you or away from you, require something in between no lead and a full lead, in proportion to the angle of the animal's line of movement relative to your line of sight. An angle of around 45 degrees toward or away from your position is referred to as a "quartering angle" and requires about half of a full lead.

Estimating Speed of Elk by Gait

The fundamentals of leads for shots on moving game involve two speeds: the speed of the game, and the speed of the projectile. Complications set in immediately in the case of elk. You can guess at the speed an elk is moving by looking at which gait is used, but that just gets you a range of speeds, as there's a lot of variation within gaits—enough variation that elk moving at about the same speed may be using different gaits. Particularly when threatened, elk are likely to continually change speed and direction while going through or around everything in the way of closing with the rest of the herd and leaving the area. For uninterrupted locomotion, they use three main gaits: walk, trot, and gallop. Each gait has a speed range.

The best speed for taking a shot at elk is when the elk is stationary. Suppress the giggles. Experienced elk hunters instinctively try for the standing shot, and often get one. A quick cow call will often stop a panicked elk in its tracks. And it's been my experience that it seems to take an elk the better part of a second to shift its weight and feet to turn in its tracks and head off in a new direction. (Note that this hesitation doesn't apply when they're in motion and suddenly change direction by rounding a corner to go in another direction.)

The standing broadside shot at a threatened elk attempting to make an escape seems counterintuitive, but experienced hunters get a lot of kills with quick, close shots in "close" elk habitat. Thick timber presents obstacles to bulls with wide racks, and the shooter will get that second that it takes for them to turn in their tracks. Practice, lots of it, embeds the instinct required in eye-hand coordination to touch the shot off at the instant a clear, on-target shot is presented. A single second doesn't last too long. If limbs obscure part of the heart/lung area, the shooter needs to decide if that pie-plate-sized target can be squeezed down to the 4-inch saucer at 30 yards. Don't try it if you're not up to it at that moment.

The normal gait of elk is the walk. Moving along the trail single file as part of the daily undisturbed routine, elk move at 3 to 4 miles per hour, using the slow walk. It's sort of an amble, with heads bobbing around. If they're disturbed and moving out of an area but not pushed, they'll be at a fast walk of around 7 miles per hour with all heads up and looking ahead at the lead cow.

Disturbed elk moving away from the general vicinity of a recognized threat use two actions of about the same speed: the trot and a plunging gallop. Individuals in a herd may be using either. Heavy bulls and some cows use the trot. Necks are stiffened and heads are carried erect. Antlers are tilted back so that main beams are level. Escape will often push the herd off the trail. Heavy individuals push through brush at the trot. Lighter members of the herd, traveling at the same speed, will be running at a plunging gallop, hopping over brush. Which gait an individual chooses seems to be according to weight, which relates to the amount of energy to move at a given speed: Trotting results in a very high energy savings for heavy elk, compared to the gallop, which requires that their entire weight be lifted in the thrust of the gallop. Lighter animals require much less energy to lift their weight, and plunging over thick stuff is easier for them than shoving through, which is no problem for the big boys. You can observe a wide variation of speed with either action as the herd swirls around and through obstructions.

It's not too difficult to discern whether an individual is at the slow trot or plunging gallop (about 20 miles per hour) or the fast trot or plunging gallop (30 miles per hour). The easy slow trot is much less strained than the fast trot, which appears to match the fastest trotters at the horse race track. My technique for a quick, but not scientific, estimate of speed independent of gait is the angle at which antlered bulls carry their heads. The faster the gait, the stiffer the neck to carry the rack, the higher the nose—and the lower the tips of the antlers. If the tips are clearing the rump, the elk are not going so fast, 25 mph or so; if the antlers, when they bounce off of the trees, are plowing up the coarse hair below the rump, the elk is moving fast, maybe 35 to 40 mph.

I don't know if there's a set speed where they break into the gallop. The all-out hard gallop over unobstructed ground translates to a speed of about 45 mph, and is reserved for a few situations: a predator at the animal's heels, the enraged victor of a fight during the rut chasing off the vanquished opponent, or an ill-advised hell-bent determination to pass in front of a Dodge pickup. The fast trot of heavy bulls is at a long stride; their gallop is a short stubby stride that appears very stiff-legged compared to the graceful, long, bounding strides of light cows.

Calculating Leads

Now we get into the analytical aspects of shots at moving elk, starting with establishing some speeds.

You can figure out the appropriate lead using straightforward calculations if the speeds of the moving elk (rough estimates from observation) and bullet (precise manufacturer's measurements) have been determined. The average velocity of the bullet will let you determine how long it will take the bullet to get to the location of the target, assuming you know how far away the target is. Then, knowing the speed that the target is moving and the angle of its movement relative to your perspective will allow you to figure out the location on the target where the bullet will impact. Swing the sights ahead of the running elk until that location is on the pie-plate target area, and keep swinging it at a constant speed, so that you'll be correct at the instant that the bullet leaves the barrel—which you can't pin down exactly because of several variables that include your own response time.

HOW THE CALCULATIONS WORK

First, you have to do some calculations to get everything into the same units of measure, since elk speed is measured in miles per hour, bullet speed in feet per second, and leads in inches.

1 mile/hour = 5,280 ft / 360 s = 1.47 ft/s

At a range of 100 yards (300 feet), a bullet at about 3,000 ft/s takes 300/3,000, or 0.1 second to go the 100 yards.

Let's say the elk is moving at a fast trot, about 27 mph. To convert that to ft/s, multiply by 1.47, yielding a speed of 39.7 ft/s. So, in the time it takes the bullet to go 100 yards (0.1 s), the elk goes 39.7 ft/s times 0.1 s, or about 4 ft. Similar calculations for a slow trot of 20 mph give you about 3 feet traveled in that 0.1 second.

If your sight is marked in arc increments of minute-of-angle (most are not), the marks coincide with 1 inch at 100 yards, so you could actually measure out the lead (in inches at 100 yards) with your sight.

Telescopic rifle sights marked in arc measurements of milliradians (mrad) are becoming more popular, so let's look at how to convert this information for them. Our little exercise converted to the mil-dot scheme would translate as follows:

The lead for the fast-trotting elk of 4 feet at 100 yards is about equivalent to 13.3 mrad; the slow-trot lead of 3 feet at 100 yards is equivalent to about 10 mrad.

The table on the next page uses actual data for a .300 Win Mag with 180-grain Noser Partition bullet to determine the correct leads for shots at elk at different gaits and ranges.

What the Table Tells Us

Close shots are no problem with elk moving at any gait. Walking elk should not present a problem except at extended range; shots at trotting and galloping elk at range should be passed by all except experienced experts. (Note: If this is new information to you, you're not one.) And I suggest that you get accustomed to arc measurement—note that the mil-dot leads are always the same.

TABLE 1: LEADS FOR SHOTS AT MOVING ELK BY RANGE AND GAIT

Range (yd/ft)	10 yd/30 ft			33 yd/100 ft			66 yd/200 ft			100 yd/300 ft			200 yd/600 ft			300 yd/900 ft			400 yd/1,200 ft		
Average bullet velocity (ft/s)	2.950			2.916			2.872			2.830			2.705			2.585			2.480		
Time to Target (s)	0.0102			0.0343			0.0696			0.106			0.2218			0.348			0.4838		
Lead																					
Gait	feet	inches	mrad	feet	inches	mrad	feet	inches	mrad	feet	inches	mrad	feet	inches	mrad	feet	inches	mrad	feet	inches	mrad
Slow walk (3 mph/4.41 fps)	0.045	0.54	1.5	0.151	1.8	1.5	0.307	3.7	1.5	0.489	5.9	1.6	0.979	12	1.6	1.53	18	1.7	2.13	26	1.8
Fast walk (5 mph/7.35 fps)	0.075	1	2.5	0.252	3	2.5	0.512	6.2	2.5	0.816	9.8	2.5	1.63	19.6	2.5	2.56	31	3	3.56	43	3
Slow trot (20 mph/29.4 fps)	0.3	4	10	1.01	12	10	2.046	25	10	3.263	40	10	6.53	78	10	10.23	123	11.5	14.23	171	12
Fast trot (30 mph/44.1 fps)	0.45	5	15	1.513	18	15	3.07	37	15	4.9	59	16	9.79	118	16	15.3	184	17	21.3	256	18
Slow plunging gallop (20 mph/29.4 fps)	0.3	4	10	1.01	12	10	2.046	25	10	3.263	40	10	6.53	78	10	10.23	123	11.5	14.23	171	12
Plunging gallop (30 mph/44.1 fps)	0.45	5	15	1.513	18	15	3.07	37	15	4.9	59	16	9.79	118	16	15.3	184	17	21.3	256	18
Hard gallop in a clear area (45 mph/66.2 fps)	0.675	8	22	2.271	27	23	46.1	55	23	7.35	88	25	14.7	176	25	23	276	26	32	384	26

Techniques

Being able to make successful running shots at big game comes with practice. Lots of practice. Here's how you get the skills you need to make shots at moving elk:

- Practice shooting at stationary targets until the correct sight picture causes your finger to instantly fire the shot.
- Observe elk (in real life and in videos) in order to be able to recognize different gaits and variations in gaits.
- Practice shots on moving game such as predators and feral hogs. Other activities that can help you develop your skills include shotgun sports: skeet, trap, and International Clays. Gun clubs often work up creative contraptions to move deer targets for practicing running shots. These sports call for two techniques of holding leads: constant and pull-through (with the eye controlling when the shot is fired). The constant lead holds the lead ahead of the target with a constant swing of the sight/barrel. The swing-through, where the sight and barrel swing from behind the target and continue along the axis of the target through to a point in front of the target, is preferred by experts. It assures that the sight leads along the axis of movement of the target, in this case elk, for any inclination of the terrain.

Estimating the Effects of the Wind on the Bullet Path

Estimating the effects of the wind on your bullet is less straightforward than estimating range. Old-timers referred to it as "wind doping." I just refer to it as "risky business" when it comes to elk hunting. As opposed to shots at moving elk, there's a variable that you can't completely account for—the wind. So my take on estimating wind effects amounts to a "go–no go." If wind will affect the flight of the bullet to any extent, don't try that long-range shot.

The effects of wind drift from a side wind on any given bullet design fired from any particular cartridge can be determined from precise measurements taken by the manufacturer. Table 2 shows the effects of a 10 mph full crosswind on some typical hunting cartridges.

The drift decreases for winds angled away from full crosswind in a nonlinear pattern: Wind at a 45-degree angle is $3/4$ of full crosswind; wind straight toward or away from you has no effect. The higher its ballistic coefficient, the less a particular bullet will be deflected by the wind. Wind drift increases exponentially with distance traveled; deflection goes up as a multiple of the distance, as opposed to a linear increase with increasing range.

TABLE 2:
WIND DEFLECTION IN INCHES AT DIFFERENT RANGES

Cartridge	100 yd	200 yd	300 yd	400 yd	500 yd
.308 175 Match	1	3	7	14	22
.300 Win Mag	.7	2.8	6.3	11.8	19.2

The manufacturer's published wind drift data is usually for a 10 mph side wind. The drift for wind speeds other than 10 mph may be calculated by multiplying the 10 mph drift by the multiple of the wind speed: 20 mph wind results in two times the drift; 30 mph wind results in three times the drift (good luck, elk won't be likely to be moving unless pushed); 5 mph wind results in half the drift of 10 mph; and so forth.

With the deflection due to wind drift at the range of your target established (or estimated), the shot is taken with the barrel pushed into the wind to compensate for wind drift. You're making the wind deflect the bullet into the shot location on the elk. This can be accomplished by either of two techniques: Range the elk using the crosshairs and move the sight picture into the wind the required amount; or, using a telescopic sight furnished with a windage knob graduated in MOA or mil-dots, move the sight into the wind the number of MOA or mil-dots required at that range and fire holding the crosswires dead-on. It does require some calculation. Note that you have to keep up with how you've left those crosswires set!

So the tricky part becomes estimating the wind speed. The best way is to use a wind velocity meter to measure the wind speed in your vicinity, then use the telescopic sight to note the effects of the wind on movement of grass, trees, and the elk (if it stands at some distance) to see if it's the same there as where you are. That assumes that you have the time and inclination for a little science project as you get spun up looking at the big bull elk. Mountain winds are notoriously variable. Estimates of wind speed without instruments are based on the movement of vegetation: 10 mph wind causes tree branches and limbs to sway, and grass to sway back and forth; 20 mph wind causes trees to sway, large limbs to whip back and forth, and grass to form ripples and waves. At 30 mph, go back to camp; elk won't be moving and a dead tree might blow over on you. Direct measurement of wind velocity can be made using an anemometer. You may hear hunters refer to the instrument as a Kestrel, which is the trade name of the most widely known manufacturer.

The most tricky wind effects result when wind is blowing around the canyon in different directions. Estimation of the effects on drift becomes an art form—or pure luck.

There's one other effect of wind you have to keep in mind: its effect on you. Offhand, unsupported shots in wind on the order of 15 knots are usually more influenced by movement of the shooter due to the wind rather than the effect on bullet path after it leaves the muzzle. The best solution is a rest, and finding a rest adds to difficulties already present. Carrying shooting sticks makes sense in this situation. You can also use a shooting sling if you've worked with it a lot.

SLINGS, SCABBARDS, AND RIFLE HANDLING
Slings
Our first order of business is to get our definitions straight. In the world of competitive rifle shooters, military snipers, and all the other groups who are shooters first and foremost, "slings" always refers to shooting slings. In the world of outdoor sports, "slings" always refers to carrying slings. The two are not the same, in primary function, design, or even appearance, if closely examined. A carry sling is a sling that supports the rifle on the shoulder to avoid the fatigue of carrying it by hand. Carrying slings are not designed to be used to assist in shooting. The tactical carry slings that hang the rifle at a ready position (to shoot from the hip) soon become unpopular with your companions because you'll be pointing the barrel at them now and again while moving along the trail.

Slings for Carrying Rifles
I like a conventional leather sling for carrying the rifle on my shoulder. Take my word for it, you will too after that first day of trying to locate elk in rough terrain. Mine doesn't have an oversized cushioned pad over the shoulder, just a widened section of the strap. A good plain leather sling keeps the rifle on your shoulder when you want it there, and doesn't slow you down when it's time to get it off. A high-quality carry sling just doesn't seem to wear out. I have used the same one for going on forty years, and it appears to be holding up better than I am. Hunting rifles are usually furnished with detachable swivels, which are all interchangeable. So you attach the sling to one set of swivels, then change it from your elk rifle to your varmint rifle to your deer rifle. Which brings us to my main point on carrying slings: Pick one, then get used to it as if it were a part of you. Practice with it attached to the rifle. And, I'd suggest, don't use it as a shooting sling. At least until you've become very good without using a sling.

The sling carry is usually over the shoulder of the shooting side (the right side for the right-handed), lightly held in place by the hand on that side holding on to the small of the stock. Some individuals, square of shoulder and small of neck, can saunter along the trail swinging both arms freely with a slung rifle seemingly keeping itself in place, but most of us need to hold it in place. In unusual circumstances, the rifle may be slung diagonally across the back or chest to leave both hands free. Lift the rifle so that the sling goes over your head to the far shoulder. The sling should not be extended from the usual length you use for the one-shoulder carry, so that it fits tightly diagonally across your chest with the rifle diagonally across the back, pointed either up or down. The rifle may be carried against your chest if you need to go low through brush tangles. Note again that these carry techniques are for the unusual circumstances where you need both hands free to carry something or for climbing. Getting the rifle into battery, or shooting position, from the diagonal carry is hopelessly slow.

Most hunters don't use the current military-type slings that allow the rifle to dangle freely in front of the chest in a horizontal position, for several reasons. Long, heavy hunting rifles (with no pistol grip and a relatively large scope) usually need to be held with both hands with this sling, which interferes with a natural fast walk. Narrow trails tend to result in the rifle being pointed forward toward anyone walking ahead, and the rifle will catch brush if the hunter needs to move through the thick stuff, particularly if using a poncho. Also, the rifle tends to pull the upper torso forward.

When making a stalk where you have plenty of time to move the rifle from sling carry into position to make a shot, it's best to carry the rifle with your shooting hand around the small of the stock and your other hand in a shooting grip around the forward part of the stock. If the rifle is carried cradled in the elbow of the off arm, it's actually rather slow to get into battery.

Many close shots are missed or never made due to a lack of technique and practice in bringing the rifle to battery from the normal sling carry. Too much of the time available for assessing and making the shot is taken up by awkward movements that leave the rifle in a poor shooting position. Some will actually shoot a high-powered rifle from the hip in this situation. Yep, just like in the movies. Very bad idea. There's a tendency to tighten the dominant hand around the small of the rifle stock as part of pulling the trigger, preloading the arm to pull back and up with the recoil.

With the following technique, it takes about a second to bring the rifle to your shoulder into a good position to make a shot. I started using it to bring a bull-barrel varmint rifle from sling carry to my shoulder while varmint hunting cross-country on foot. Handling an elk rifle is effortless in comparison. The technique works well with a leather sling that doesn't stick to the shoulder, but not so well with a more high-friction material such as padded neoprene. All the motion is in a vertical plane, as opposed to removing the rifle from your shoulder with your left hand and swinging it around while trying to locate the right hand on the stock in the process. In addition, with this technique, you won't be pointing the rifle at anyone unless they're directly behind you, which is unlikely. I've seen excited hunters manage to point the rifle at everyone else while taking the sling down and around their arm.

The first photo in the series on the next page illustrates the normal carry, with the fingers of the right hand around the small of the stock to lightly hold the rifle in place, and the weight of the rifle supported by the shoulder (0.0 seconds elapsed time).

To begin the transition, grasp the rifle more firmly with your right hand by the small of the stock, with your thumb against the pistol grip. Lift the rifle to transfer its weight from your shoulder to your right hand. Let the rifle spin in a vertical plane to the rear under its own weight, with the barrel to the rear and the rifle upside down (0.3 second).

Let it continue to rotate to a point where the barrel is pointing almost straight down. The rotation is fast at this point, as you can see from the blurred barrel and flared sling (0.5 second).

As the barrel of the rifle passes vertical, swinging forward, grasp the forestock with the off hand (0.7 second).

Supporting the weight of the rifle with the left hand as it continues to swing forward, roll the right hand around the small of the stock at the pistol grip, hooking the lower part of the pistol grip against the side of the right hand above the thumb to maintain location (1.0 second).

As the barrel continues to rotate forward and up, the rifle is now right side up and both hands are in firing position. Bend the right elbow to pull the butt of the stock into contact with your shoulder. Your attention has been focused on the sighted game up to this point, and if there is a shot to be made, move the safety to fire as the elbow bends (1.2 seconds).

Pull the rifle firmly to your shoulder while leaning into shooting position, looking through the scope, which should have the target centered along the line of sight of the right eye (1.4 seconds).

I perform the entire process without conscious thought, so that I'm totally unaware of the individual actions it takes to change from carry to battery. My hunting companions say that it looks fast and smooth, and have clocked it at a second from initial reaction to battery, give or

0.0 sec   *0.3 sec*

0.5 sec   *0.7 sec*

PHOTO SEQUENCE BY WES MCQUIDDY

take a tenth of a second. I shoot from a half second to a second later, depending on how long it takes to assess the elk and clear the shot.

This technique works for me; you can take it or leave it with my blessing. Some of my friends say that it's a good practice not to try it for the first time with your new custom rifle while standing on a concrete floor. You get the idea why I don't formally recommend it for every-body. And I don't recommend it for anybody unless he or she is willing to practice it.

1.0 sec

1.2 sec

1.4 sec

Alternate carry.   *Alternate carry with poncho.*

An alternate sling carry and sling to battery move that's almost as fast and has better ground clearance begins with the carry illustrated in the photo at top left. This carry is preferred by some, usually those square of shoulder and small of neck referred to earlier, and used by everyone wearing a poncho. The rifle is slightly lifted and rotated to the right (for the right-handed) around the axis of the barrel. This clears the arm with the sling and leaves the rifle in an upright position. The left hand then grasps the stock and begins lifting the rifle to the shoulder as the right hand slides back to the pistol grip.

The right hand can also throw the poncho back at this point. You're now at 1.0 second elapsed time, with less motion than in the previous sequence. For either technique, the dismount of the slung rifle from the shoulder needs to be a smooth reflex so you can keep your attention focused on the quarry.

Shooting Slings

The best shooting sling designs are derived from, or are absolute copies of, centuries-old military designs used to carry a traditionally stocked rifle on long marches and to provide extra support and stability for long-range shots after the sling was reconfigured from carry support to firing support. Preparation amounts to unfastening the sling from the lower end of the stock, forming a loop that fits around the non-shooting arm above the biceps muscle, extending the sling as the rifle is brought to the shoulder, and wrapping the sling around the non-shooting hand as the forearm of the rifle is grasped. This pulls the rifle into the shoulder of the shooting arm and stiffens the arrangement of the rifle and upper body in any of the standard military shooting positions—standing, sitting, kneeling, or prone. Slings and speed don't go together under stress, and only countless hours on the target range using slings and structured shooting positions will result in using either as second nature, even without factoring in effects of terrain on repeatable stance and footing. Somebody along the way over the last century, in an effort to achieve speed with a sling, came up with what's referred to as the hasty sling. It amounts to wrapping the non-shooting arm around a too-long carrying sling. I'm sure somebody thinks that it's a good idea, but I haven't run into that person yet.

I would recommend that you not be tempted to try shooting slings as far as elk hunting is concerned. You can't count on enough time to get strapped up just right. You never know if the shot offered will be at a range of 30 or 300 yards (which is why my scope is always a fixed-power one or a variable one set at about midrange). You may only have a couple of seconds for that once-in-a-lifetime shot. Even if you had time to get ready, your sights would need to be zeroed for whatever hold you would have, with whatever sling support you're using, in whatever shooting position you might take, with or without a rest. I consider it best not to even think about it. Practice more without a sling. With a variety of shock-isolated rests. And don't cant the rifle.

Scabbards and Riding

The opportunity for the close, unexpected shot doesn't always come up while you're moving along on your own feet. You can't shoot from the back of a horse with a high-powered rifle, so you have to get down *and* get the rifle out of the scabbard before you can make your shot. There's a little technique to drawing a rifle from a scabbard as you dismount, but it's still easier than attempting to draw it from the ground while you try to hold an excited horse that's wheeling around or trying to bolt. Hold the reins and go for the saddle horn with the left hand; flip open the fold-over flap that covers and secures the rifle with your right hand. Then rise in the stirrups to begin your dismount as you simultaneously grasp the rifle by the small of the stock (that's the area of the pistol grip). When you stand up in the stirrups, you have the reach to withdraw the rifle as you swing from the saddle, steadied by your left hand against the saddle horn. The reins should still be in your left hand after you dismount; with any luck at all, you will be standing to the side of the horse, which will give you more leverage for control if it's needed. Maybe you'll just let the horse go bucking down the trail with the other horses with some of your companions still enjoying the ride while you chamber a round and take a shot at the big bull elk that just walked out. It happens for the lucky. This technique is illustrated in Chapter 21.

I don't recommend a saddle scabbard with a hood, just a snap flap to retain and mostly cover the rifle except for the butt of the stock. This is the same perspective that holds that it's better to have your scope uncovered all the time so that you won't miss a shot during those twenty or thirty years it takes to mess up the lenses of the scope; if you are blessed with enough hunting time to mess up the butt of your rifle stock because the scabbard does not completely cover it, be thankful. I have a couple of stocks that look pretty bad, and the rifle shoots just as well as it ever did. If you really worry about that sort of thing and are in for a wet ride and don't see much of a chance that you'll see an elk, you can cover the stock with a light plastic bag, which you'll never notice if you want to draw the rifle in a hurry.

Finally, here are some tips to ensure that a live round will always be in the chamber of your rifle when you want one there. I always carry three rounds in the rifle, and at least ten or more in an elastic ammo carrier within easy reach on my belt. Why only three in the rifle? Because the somewhat oversized rounds used in elk hunting can stick or jam in the magazine and fail to spring up to be engaged by the bolt to be chambered for the follow-up shot. My procedure is to load three rounds into the magazine, the usual full capacity, pushing each round at either end to ensure that it slides clear of the ends of the magazine. Then I chamber a round from the magazine when I start hunting, leaving the remaining two under reduced spring pressure from the follower, further reducing the chance of a jam. I know after the third shot that the rifle is empty (a person has to be pretty excited not to be able to count to three), and I know to leave the bolt open while I draw a round from the ammo carrier and drop it directly into the chamber and close the bolt, keeping track of the game throughout the entire procedure. No wasted motion; nothing to remember.

Choosing a Rifle Scabbard

An outfitter normally furnishes a rifle scabbard as part of his or her services. You'll need your own for horseback or off-road vehicle hunting otherwise. I use a full glove type, without a cutout for the rifle bolt. It has an integral flap that fastens with a snap, no hood. Like the sling, I

(Left) Frank gets creative and straps the near-side model on the far side, inverted and handy to get to in case of very bad trouble with a string of mules. This zip-up case is perfect for transporting an extra rifle if a lot of brush is involved. (Right) Frank illustrates a scabbard carry for steep trails with one of his riding mules, Bruce.

Custom gun leather, from left to right and top to bottom: banjo-case-style gun case; scabbard with snap selection design to fit any long gun, from short lever-action to shotgun; and near-side flap-closure scabbard.

want it to hold the rifle for me most of the time, and let me have it back without delay when I decide that I want it back. Whatever scabbard you get, you need to put in some good practice getting off of horses and taking the rifle with you. You can expect the best of scabbards to rub the finish along both sides of the rifle barrel near the end. They're deliberately designed to do that so that the old hunters can recognize the new ones and keep an eye on them.

My almost forty-year-old holster scabbard, restitched after it got into Herm and Leroy's outfit's tack shed and had an outfitting career for several years, had seen its best forty years, and it never secured a long rifle completely. So I found a master saddlemaker who would put up with my ideas to make a suitable bow scabbard, and while he was at it, he made a flap model with multiple snap settings so that any rifle, or shotgun, can be carried.

The scabbard/gun case zips around the top like a bow case to protect a scoped automatic through rough country rides around the swamps during that long part of the year when there's no elk hunting season of any flavor. That's a big automatic with a big magazine. The down south off-season pig hunters will know what I'm talking about. It also protects a rifle for horseback transport into elk camps. I guess it's referred to as a half "banjo case" design in saddlemaker lingo.

High-quality custom leather gear is relatively inexpensive compared to other high-quality shooting stuff. It's available from Ken Grimes, 5940 County Road 165, Kaufman, TX 75142, telephone (972) 932-3917 or (903) 880-2370 (cell). Leave a message that you'd like a scabbard, gun case, gun case/scabbard, or anything else you can imagine. If it can be made out of leather, he can make it. Be advised that leather gear made out of the heavy saddle leather isn't going to immediately take the shape of whatever you put it around. It has to be oiled and the rifle or whatever stuffed in real tight for a time until the leather takes the correct shape. Ken says that it takes less time if you soak it in water with the rifle in it for a few days, the way the old cowboys made their boots fit good and tight, but that can be kind of hard on the rifle. I just oil it and wait and check it every so often.

CHOOSING AND HUNTING WITH A MUZZLELOADER

My best advice to the beginning muzzleloader hunter is to use the most effective and modern gun and components that are legal in the state where you intend to hunt. The modern muzzleloader eliminates a lot of the complexities of operating the original muzzleloaders and their modern reproductions. You eliminate a lot of the complications from the weather, for instance. With traditional muzzleloaders, the old admonishment that you "keep your powder dry" takes on a whole new meaning, and it's hard to do in a heavy rainstorm. Even in practice, you can concentrate on your shooting rather than on the niceties of measuring and tamping the power just right if you use the pre-measured fixed powder. The traditional designs also normally use open sights. A scope usually allows the beginner to more quickly pick up game, either near or far, and helps to pick up intervening limbs in the thick stuff. Until you become an elk hunter with some experience, keep the shooting of the old-fashioned front-end loaders as a separate activity. Either shooting black powder or hunting elk is enough of a challenge when considered one at a time.

The prospective hunter should check with the state Game Department regarding any questions of legality. Many states have restrictions on caliber and other details of muzzleloader charges allowed for elk hunting, and they are subject to change.

Muzzleloaders can now be used with percussion caps of different types as well as modern primers. Balls or bullets can be traditional or of modern design, including sabots for modern bullets. Novice elk hunters should try to eliminate complications and complexity of use of the gun while simultaneously learning to hunt elk under conditions that can become adverse (caps and power can take up moisture in wet weather). Wind complicates the loading of loose powder, so some muzzleloaders use the "ready-roll" pellets rather than loose powder; others stay with the loose powder because the pellets sometimes tend to lose chips that adversely affect the consistency of the load.

There are different types of muzzleloader rifle designs available: the in-line, which appears externally to resemble a modern centerfire, but with a ramrod under the barrel, and the traditional type with exposed hammer and ignition cap, which is hardly distinguishable from rifles 150 years old.

The in-line design refers to the configuration of the plunger-type hammer alignment with the percussion cap, nipple, and charge. As opposed to the traditional design, it's practically weather-proof and can be designed with lock times as fast as a centerfire. The modern in-line muzzleloader lends itself to mounting a telescopic sight, which is a distinct improvement over open sights. Major manufacturers now produce modern muzzleloader designs. Both traditional and modern designs are available from many smaller domestic and foreign manufacturers. Remington makes an excellent muzzleloader that handles and operates like their high-powered repeaters, except for the loading, of course, and

Cabela's lists a wide selection of all types of muzzleloader designs. My friends who hunt elk with muzzleloaders exclusively report that Thompson is an industry leader in in-line as well as traditional designs.

If state regulations allow it, a scope is invaluable to allow you to see intervening brush, to help in dim light, and to estimate range. However, some states require use of open sights when hunting with a muzzleloader. I would caution that the heavier muzzleloader loads are hard on scope mounts due to the shock of the muzzleloader discharge.

I recommend that your practice sessions with your muzzleloader give more emphasis to offhand shooting with close shots in mind rather than long-distance shooting from a rest. Muzzleloaders are never flat shooters and their rainbow trajectories tend to make distance shots an exercise in accurate range estimation, not to be recommended for the inexperienced elk hunter. The ethical range limitations of muzzleloaders dictate that you move in on elk during stalking rather than attempting a long shot. A laser rangefinder helps determine ranges.

You can develop the one-shot mentality through turkey hunting and one-shot small game such as squirrels (the latter with small-bore rifles). Develop mobility for locating and stalking with challenging no-calling, no-bait hunting of coyotes, bears, and feral hogs. Enthusiasts that hunt a lot of game other than elk often use smaller-caliber rifles for small game.

Clubs, reenactments, and shooting meets are a major aspect of muzzleloading as a hobby. The shared experience with like-minded enthusiasts helps the newcomer acquire the considerable body of information needed for successful muzzleloader hunting of elk. I recommend you get lots of experience and insight into the care and feeding of muzzleloaders before taking on elk hunting with a flintlock muzzleloader.

CROSSBOWS

I put crossbows in the same class as rifles and muzzleloaders on the basis of difficulty of mastery. They're usually grouped, incorrectly in my opinion, with archery equipment, since they have a little bow (usually a compound, sometimes a recurve) mounted on the stock to propel the bolt, which looks like a very short arrow. But what defines the crossbow as a system in basic technical terms, which is my frame of reference, is the stock that the shooter pulls to his or her shoulder, the sights (often scopes) used to aim the piece, and the trigger pulled to release the projectile. State regulations may place crossbows in either rifle or archery season, sometimes restricting their use during archery season to hunters unable to draw a conventional bow. The techniques and tactics used with a crossbow closely align with those used with the muzzle-loader due to their similar characteristics: They have limited range and power, fire a single shot, are slow to reload, and don't need to be drawn (a large movement that attracts attention when in close proximity to game). The effective range of the crossbow is less than that of the muzzleloader, and about the same as that of compound bows, and the missile is larger and slower than the muzzleloader bullet, allowing nimble game alerted by the distinct thump of the crossbow to jump away from the bolt.

The elk hunter equipped with a crossbow needs to keep a few cautions in mind:

- An elk can easily be struck with a crossbow bolt at a range exceeding the precision and energy required for a clean kill.
- Extreme care is necessary when handling a set crossbow, as the entire mechanism is under full load at all times and, in many designs, exposed to external hazards that could cause it to fire accidentally.
- Constant inspection is necessary to ensure that the mechanism is not damaged by rough wilderness handling and conditions.
- Have any used crossbow considered for purchase examined by an expert. (Be aware that many experienced archery bow repair experts won't work on a crossbow, or even look at one, due to previous bad experiences.)
- Regulations regarding use of crossbows for hunting vary widely.

Practice Hunting with Crossbow

The one-shot mentality of muzzleloader hunting also applies to crossbows, including the need to reload quickly under pressure. Safe mobility for locating and stalking should become second nature for the crossbow hunter. Feral hogs are the ideal crossbow practice game: You'll have lots of close stalking action, hunting is available all year across the South and Texas, and there are not many regulations to complicate your main purpose, which is to learn how to handle and make the kill with unfamiliar equipment. Go for the heart and lung shot. Hogs are tough quarry, which will help you get the feel of the killing power of your equipment as second nature. You might carry a high-capacity firearm as backup in case the pig you stick is running with twenty or thirty friends and family members.

CHAPTER 13

Making the Kill with the Bow

Making the kill with a bow is much more difficult than with a modern, high-powered rifle or muzzleloader. More on the order of an athletic activity, it requires an extension of physical capabilities in addition to a higher level of the basic elk hunting skills. It's been my experience that learning to use a bow to hunt elk will make you a better elk hunter regardless of what you have in your hand from then on.

The new bowhunter should be aware that different schools of thought exist within the overall ranks of bowhunters as to the most effective, the most pure, and the most pleasurable way to pursue the sport. Each group tends to advocate its own approach and recruit new hunters to its own group.

The first group, maybe the largest, and certainly the least hell-bent, consists of those who are hunters first, and sometimes bowhunters to add to the overall experience—and sometimes to extend the season. Their choice of equipment is based on efficiency: the most effective at taking elk, at the least expense in terms of time, practice, and money. Sights, string releases, and bows, usually compounds, tend to minimize the transition between rifle and bow. Their equipment also tends to accommodate the existing physical attributes, or lack thereof, of the hunter, rather than requiring the hunter to undergo extensive training (specifically upper-body strength development) in order to be able to use the bow.

The second group is populated by bowhunters who hunt with the bow exclusively. Many of this group use the bow not necessarily for the challenge, but because they consider it to be the most effective equipment for their particular style of hunting. Archery seasons overlap with the rut, and hunters who are expert with the bow and the bugle and cow call can count on filling the freezer before the woods get crowded during the general rifle season.

Hunters in this group use a wide range of equipment according to their preference and physical type. The majority use compounds of various types with sights and mechanical releases, but you're also likely to see a lot of finger-release shooting using compounds. Many are stickbow (wooden recurve or longbow) shooters who don't need the let-off of the compound bow. Some use instinctive aim rather than sights, again, not for the challenge, but because it's fast. They don't come to full draw, then aim, and then release the arrow, as is the usual practice with the compound bow; they draw and release the arrow in one smooth, and apparently effortless, motion.

The third group of bowhunters is the smallest in number, but these hunters more than make up for it in their fierce devotion to their sport, which is traditional archery, first and foremost. They use traditional longbows fabricated by professional craftsmen and cedar-shaft arrows, and they shoot instinctively (without sights). A subset within the group consists of the primitive archery enthusiasts who make their own equipment from natural materials, going out into the woods, finding a suitable tree, cutting and shaping it, and possibly adding reinforcement. You don't see them around much. They're always out hunting or shooting at targets.

OLD TOM'S (VERY) CONDENSED HISTORY OF THE BOW

The invention of the bow and arrow was a stroke of pure genius. Pulling back to propel the arrow forward is counterintuitive. The process of storing energy from the deformation of the elastic bow and then releasing it to propel the arrow is many steps removed from the direct process of throwing a spear. Primitive bows were universally self bows, that is, bows made of a single flexible piece of wood. Over time, the composite bow, made of wood reinforced with sinew, was developed and widely used. These reinforced bows allowed more elastic energy to be stored in a short bow, particularly advantageous to the mounted archer. Research has shown just how advanced some of the "primitive" bows of our ancestors were. I've learned appreciation for their ingenuity as I designed and fabricated several high-performance bows, using graphite and fiberglass instead of wood, bone, antler, and sinew.

Modern interest in archery for hunting and field-shooting contests began about the time of the passing of the last Native American bowhunters. Fascination with the novelty of primitive weapons prompted a few individuals in the early twentieth century to become interested in handcrafting bows and arrows made from natural materials. Enthusiasts made their own self bows, following traditional patterns and copying museum specimens and samples fabricated by the few remaining craftsmen, who also instructed them in shooting and hunting techniques.

Books and magazine articles by notable authorities such as Howard Hill described the use of bows in adventures in exotic locations. So it naturally followed that lots of kids set about making their own bows. Most discovered that it required a good bit of craftsmanship and patience, two commodities in short supply for most of us. That bois d'arc ("bodark") growing in the fencerows of our North Central Texas farms was considered to be prime bowmaking material, but most of our results were mediocre at best. As far as shooting was concerned, lots of practice with intense focus on the target was supposed to result in consistent hits. Not so much for most of us, who had just a passing interest in archery and soon moved on to other things. But hardcore devotees continued to develop equipment and apply their product to field competition and sport hunting. Bows made to classical patterns of selected woods by specialized craftsmen are referred to as traditional bows.

The modern bow came about with the advent of modern aerospace materials and processes. It didn't take long for bowmakers to adapt glass fiber into composite bows, and almost immediately afterward they found that the ancient recurve designs produced the most efficient bows. Arrow manufacture proceeded apace, with aerospace-specification aluminum tubing being used for arrow shafts. But the most efficient use of advanced composites turned out to be in compound bows, which use pulleys and wheels to maximize the efficient storage of the energy you put into them by pulling back on the string.

One of my favorites of the vintage compound bows was, still is, the Oneida. It's a compound that looks and shoots like a jazzed-up recurve. And you never draw to a stop. It's the exact opposite of an old, very short, hard-to-shoot Ben Pearson two-wheeler I still have and like to shoot because it points out my sloppy habits.

My serious-use bow for some time has been a Mathews SoloCam top-of-the-line extended draw. Just say Mathews. Bowhunters will know.

HOW BOWS WORK

The number of words spoken and written concerning the best selection of bows and arrows is exceeded only by the words concerning the best selection of guns and ammo for elk hunting. In either case, the detailed discussions in enthusiasts' magazines always seem to go well beyond the point where enlightenment ends and confusion begins. The general consensus is that a bow-and-arrow combination to be used for elk hunting should generate somewhat over 60 foot-pounds of kinetic energy.

Some bows I have known and still shoot. From the left, the first two bows are field archery bows made decades ago by Wing archery, light bows that I used for target practice (same idea as using a light rifle for lots of practice). The second is a takedown with the limbs attached to the magnesium risers. The next three bows are hunters by Wing: a takedown design (same as the field bow), a conventional Wing recurve, and an experimental model made with unidirectional fiberglass/off-axis unidirectional graphite laminates. Next is the Oneida, the compound that looks like an exotic recurve. Next is a tough little Ben Pearson two-wheeler, the lone survivor among the two-wheelers I've used. On the far right is my Mathews.

This photo illustrates arrow carry. For a long time, I used a Cat quiver or some version of a back quiver for elk hunting. I always had trouble from overhanging limbs as I rode a tall horse down the trail. Now I use a quick detach with the short compounds. They about match my arrows in length.

The general consensus also is that most elk hunters don't know how to relate that figure to the draw weight of a bow and the speed of an arrow/broadhead combination of a given weight. For the record and the interested reader, I'll briefly explain Old Tom's Rough-and-Ready Physics of Bows and Arrows.

The design of archery bows remained essentially unchanged from around 30,000 to around 30 years ago, staying close to the basic concept of a string tied to either end of a stick to hold it in the shape of a bow. The modern recurve bow is based on the same principles as ancient ones, using fiberglass laminates instead of animal sinew to power the flex of the bow. Ancient or modern, conventional bows exhibit a progressively greater resistance when drawn, reaching a peak at maximum draw.

Compound bows changed all that. Their various arrangements of cables, cams, and limbs are designed to produce progressive resistance to the draw up to a certain point and then reduce it (called the let-off). The effect is that at maximum draw, much less force is required to hold the string back while the archer takes aim and releases the arrow. There was initial resistance to universal adoption of the compound bow at first. I suspect that it may have partially been due to the appearance of the things, which look like contraptions when compared to the graceful curves of a conventional recurved bow. They look a lot nicer after you shoot them and realize their many advantages. The compound bow, while making the selection of a bow more complicated, allows hunters of all sizes, genders, and physiques to participate in bowhunting.

The way bows and arrows work is straightforward when considered on the level of basic physics. The archer pushes on the bow while drawing back the string with an arrow in place on the string. The total distance of the push and pull to change the shape of the bow is called the draw length. This change of shape of the bow stores elastic energy. Let's say that we have a very simple bow composed of a string tied to both ends of a stick. We draw the bow to a draw length of 30 inches (2.5 feet). The force to pull the string back goes from 0 pounds at the start to 48 pounds at full draw. That's an average of 24 pounds of force over a distance of 2.5 feet, or 60 foot-pounds of stored energy when you multiply it out.

When the string is released, the bow returns to its original shape, transferring the elastic energy of the bent bow into the arrow as kinetic energy (energy in the form of movement). The amount of kinetic energy is equal to the mass of the arrow multiplied by $1/2$ multiplied by its velocity, then multiplied by its velocity again. The same bow always puts the same amount of kinetic energy into the arrow (with slight variations due to more or less efficiency under different circumstances), which means a light arrow, with less mass to move, will fly faster than a heavier one.

The arrow flies to the target, losing some energy due to wobble as it leaves the bow and some more in flight due to the resistance of the air. (The energy lost to air resistance is proportional to the velocity squared, so that the faster the speed, the more energy is lost.) Another physical property associated with motion is momentum, which is equal to the mass of the arrow multiplied by the velocity. When the arrow reaches the target, the remaining kinetic energy and momentum of the arrow in flight are transferred into the work required to penetrate whatever it strikes, elk or tree. If the arrow penetrates through the elk or tree, it exits at a much lower speed, having lost a great deal of kinetic energy in penetrating the object.

Much is made of the relative advantages of kinetic energy and momentum as measurements of the effectiveness of an arrow on its target, but we don't need to get into that debate. Here's what you need to know: If two arrows strike identical tissue with identical broadheads and identical kinetic energy (i.e., shot from the same bow), but different weights so that one is lighter and traveling faster than the other, then the heavier, slower arrow will achieve greater penetration.

Through trial and error, bowhunters have established the arrow/broadhead weight and bow draw weight combinations suitable for elk hunting. Weights much lighter than 450 grains require very high velocities to carry the 60 foot-pounds of kinetic energy needed to pierce elk hide and are difficult to stabilize for consistent flight. There are practical limits to how fast a bow can shoot an arrow, and extremely light, fast-moving arrows lose more energy in flight than heavier, slower arrows. At the other extreme, arrow weights much heavier than 650 grains require bows of very high draw weight and/or long draw distance to generate sufficient velocity for reasonably flat trajectories.

The physics notwithstanding, the most effective shot is the best directed shot: low in the front of the chest and passing through the heart and/or both lungs.

ARCHERY EQUIPMENT

For the beginner, I suggest some experimenting with different types of tackle setups before you buy one. A good archery range with a professional shop and/or a shooting club will usually have some kind of arrangement to allow the beginner to try different archery tackle setups before committing to purchase a specific set of equipment.

Bowhunters who are experienced in deer hunting will probably have their own opinions on archery tackle. The only suggestion I might offer is to review your gear and practice techniques from the standpoint of mobility and range estimation. The convenience and durability of the quiver, along with practicing drawing arrows from the quiver so that it becomes second nature, are more important in elk hunting than deer hunting. Under some circumstances of stalking, you're more likely to have an opportunity for a second shot, or even a third, while elk hunting than while deer hunting. Those opportunities may be lost if you can't get another arrow in place as an automatic reflex.

Selecting a Compound Bow

Several factors go into choosing a bow: your wingspan (the distance from fingertip to fingertip when you extend your arms and hands) so that the let-off matches your draw length, your physical capability, the ease and stability of tuning the bow, and your own personal preference. If you're a new bowhunter, get a truly qualified pro to set you up with a bow you can handle, and determine the weight, length, and stiffness of arrows that will work well in combination with it. Most states specify minimum draw weights for bows used for elk hunting, so check the regulations where you plan to hunt. When it's left to their own judgment, some elk hunters go all out for maximum kinetic energy, using light arrows. Many, maybe most, use a bow with a draw weight sufficient to generate around 70 foot-pounds of kinetic energy and use a heavier arrow/broadhead combination, around 600 grains or more. I use a Mathews SoloCam Switchback LD 32-inch draw.

Selecting a Recurve or Longbow

The first consideration is which type bow to use. Longbows are traditionally made completely of carved wood, and called self bows. The limbs are D-shaped in cross section, with the flat side toward the outside, the tension-loaded side. The tension side may be reinforced with high-strength elastic material such as unidirectional fiberglass (which replaces the animal sinew used in primitive bows). Tactically, a longbow is just that—long. You have to get accustomed to handling it through brush and in tree stands, but it's smooth to shoot. Longbows are usually aimed instinctively, which means they can accommodate odd shooting angles (no sights to get messed up by the cant), but this takes a lot of practice.

Unidirectional glass-powered recurves are short, handy, as powerful as the shoulders and arms of the shooter, and more durable. The beginner stickbow shooter is faced with the decision of whether to use sights or shoot instinctively in the case of recurves. Sights make learning to shoot more straightforward for most, but with sights it takes a little longer to sight, and the bow has to be oriented vertically.

Arrows and Broadheads

Arrows are matched in stiffness to the bow. Arrow shafts all flex in response to the force of the bowstring as it accelerates the arrow into flight; therefore, there are limits to the acceptable flexibility of arrows for a bow of given pull weight and draw length. Manufacturers release tables showing which arrows work with which bows. Most arrows are made from aluminum or graphite tube, available as blanks that are then cut to length to provide a customized fit for the draw of the individual bowhunter. Easton Archery has been a quality supplier for a long time.

> Easton Archery
> 5040 W. Harold Gatty Dr.
> Salt Lake City, UT 84116-2897
> (801) 539-1400
> www.eastonarchery.com

I currently use Beman carbon arrow shafts a little on the heavy side, at 9.5 grains per inch (ICS Hunter 300 model).

The hunting point of the arrow, called the broadhead, screws into an insert permanently attached to the arrow shaft. The bowhunter normally practices with points without cutting blades, called field points, then hunts with the broadheads. Some practice is normally done before hunting with broadheads in place to make sure the sights are set correctly for the broadhead design, since different points can affect arrow flight.

The broadhead designer, for at least the last 30,000 years, has been seeking a design that will efficiently penetrate the hide, pass through muscle and other softer organs, and punch through or divert around bone rather than sticking. The shape has stayed basically the same for most of those years, slowly evolving from stone to iron and then to steel while retaining the familiar arrowhead shape. Recent years have seen a bewildering variety of new designs developed for the modern hunter. A few years back, the general consensus of elk hunters favored the variations of the flat-faceted chisel-pointed shafts with three or four detachable razor-sharp blades. The chisel point was considered to better deflect around bone while the three blades effectively cut through and across the grain of tissue. The choice of most was the Muzzy with a chisel-point three-blade design in the 125-grain weight. More recently, improvements in design and materials have resulted in a comeback of the cutting-edge designs such as the Magnus in 100- or 125-grain weight. If there is any order to hunter preference, the heavy-arrow school of thought seems to favor the chisel-point designs, while the lightweight, high-velocity group goes for the cutting-edge designs. Some states have requirements in regard to broadhead cutting blade shape and size that can be confusing. I suggest that you get a copy of the regulations and go over them with a bowhunting expert or equipment professional.

I currently use G5 Outdoors 125-grain Montec Broadheads.

Arrow Rests

It's important to select an appropriate arrow rest for elk hunting, as bowhunting elk often requires fast and unexpected movement. Some rests hold the arrow in place, while other designs simply allow the arrow to lightly rest on the contact surface of the rest. Some rests really provide no restraint, and are only good for stands. For elk hunting, I recommend that you find a rest that provides the most secure restraint while still allowing you to tune the bow. Most of the rests that will secure an arrow seem to tune easier with mechanical releases than with a finger release (due to the lateral arrow motion associated with a finger release). The following are some possibilities:

- Carolina Archery Products (CAP)
- Whisker Biscuit Drop-Tine QS
- Bodoodle Zapper 300

Rests for instinctive shooting with recurves provide support on two sides, which is normally adequate support for shooting with a tilted bow. Traditional bowshooters normally use the index finger of the grip hand to hold the arrow in place until the string is released.

Some bowhunters like to use handheld or bow-mounted (where legal) laser rangefinders. They're handier when you're hunting from a stand and have time to set them aside for an unhurried shot. They're available in a wide range of quality and prices. Optical rangefinders are less expensive, but usually take more time to operate. Note that bow-mounted electronic sighting and ranging devices are illegal in many states.

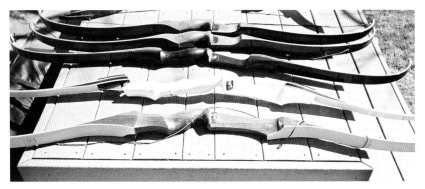

Arrow rests used on recurves. Typical light plastic vanes are mounted above the shelf on field archery target bows, sometimes with light plunger contact. The bow must be held vertically or the arrow will fly off to the side. Hunting bows that have shelf arrow rests may be aimed instinctively and can be canted.

If you have experience in rifle shooting or plan at some time to hunt elk with a rifle, I recommend using a sight that gives a mental image the same as the riflescope. For the same reason, I suggest you use a trigger-type string release device. There are now several variations on my long-time favorite, which is made by Winn Archery Equipment of South Haven, Mississippi.

Bowsights and Other Accessories

Traditional longbows and primitive composite bows are normally instinctively aimed, without the assistance of sights. You look at the spot where you want the arrow to hit as you draw and release, the way a pitcher looks at the catcher's mitt while throwing the baseball. Naturally gifted instinctive bowshooters find this to be easy; the rest of us can achieve instinctive aiming with a high dedication to practice, as long as we stick to short shots.

Modern recurves may be instinctively aimed, but they are often aimed along the arrow as it rests on the arrow shelf within the window of the riser section. The bow is drawn consistently so that a marked point of the string is brought to the same point on the shooter's face to sight through the string. (That point is usually on the lips, and the point on the string is a button, sometimes called a "kisser button.") When aiming along the arrow and looking through the string, you adjust the elevation of the arrow instinctively to account for the range. The arc distance between the point of the arrow and the target may be referred to as the gap.

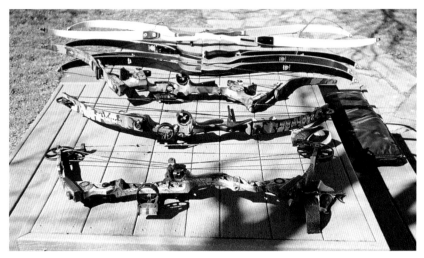

Bowsight options. I currently use three fiber-optic aim points. The adjustable crosswires on the Oneida are left over from my transition to sights from the stickbows in the rear.

Compounds are usually aimed using sophisticated bowsights. However, while you might raise some eyebrows doing this, there's no physical reason why you can't shoot instinctively with a compound bow, and if you're sure you'll never hunt with a rifle, you might be interested in learning to shoot this way. If you invest the time to get good at this type of shooting, you'll have fewer distractions on that morning when the once-in-a-lifetime shot comes along.

My first bowsight was a crosshair adjustable for range. Many bowhunters used aiming pins set for different distances. Fiber-optic point bowsights are now considered the standard. If you have a lot of experience deer hunting with a certain type of sight, that's what you will want to use to hunt elk. For beginning bowhunters who don't yet have a favorite setup, I suggest a single fiber-optic illuminated point in combination with a bowstring-mounted peep sight. The single aiming point tends to be less confusing when the chips are down than the multiple pins for different ranges. Leave the sight set for about 20 yards, practice at this distance, and think twice before taking a longer shot. Consider adding more points as you gain expertise, including lots of practice hunting at 20 yards.

But there's one common denominator for aiming all equipment used in elk hunting, be it traditional bow, recurve, compound bow, muzzleloader, or high-powered rifle: Shoot at a spot on the elk, not the entire elk. The elk hunter must always aim instinctively at the heart/lung area, discussed in Part I.

I recommend the use of a trigger string release for the beginner. A mechanical trigger release is easier to master than a consistently correct finger release, and in my opinion, it's easier to use as second nature when you have a big elk in the crosshairs. A trigger release that attaches behind the wrist increases the draw weight that you can pull, as well as increasing your control of the string release. I use a trigger release so that I have the same type of reflex to get the shot off, whether I'm using a bow or firearm.

CARRYING ARCHERY TACKLE

Think in terms of mobility in general, as well as mobility through brush and other sorts of stuff that tends to grab you and your equipment. This always seems to happen at very inconvenient times during elk hunting. If you plan to hunt using horse transport, you'll want to get a saddle scabbard for your bow and arrows. You'll probably find a back quiver inconvenient for riding on a horse, although it's great for cross-country travel on foot. Most saddle scabbards will accommodate a bow and a bow quiver.

For elk hunting, I recommend either a bow quiver or a back quiver to carry your extra arrows. Experienced archery hunters like to remind retread rifle hunters that arrows are always loaded once the broadhead point has been attached. The quiver needs to restrain the arrows and cover the broadheads while still allowing you easy access to them. Always practice with the quiver that you plan to use while hunting.

The commercially available scabbards for carrying bows and arrows come up short out on the slopes where the brush is thick and things can get rough. Pictured on the next page is master saddlemaker Ken Grimes's expert execution of a scabbard that began with a design idea of mine, which, happily, he didn't pay too much attention to, so it worked out real well. It is made of top-grade saddle skirt leather to protect the equipment from sticks and stones and securely contain it. If you'd like one, see Ken's contact information on page 288. And get in line . . .

In the case of bow scabbards, as opposed to rifle scabbards, you don't need to be concerned with quick access. Get off, get ready, and start a stalk.

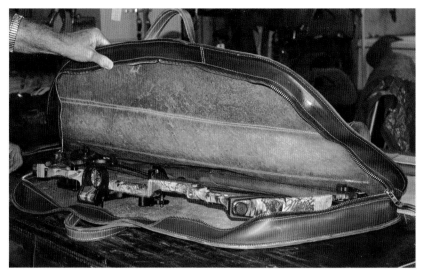

Checking my case for fit and function with my Mathews extended-draw bow during development. Reinforcement stiffens the bottom of my case in its current configuration, and I'm experimenting with different padding and Velcro and leather strap arrangements to secure the bow. It actually seems to work satisfactorily as shown here, with the heavy leather sides of the case clasping the bow.

Frank and Butch take a spin to check mobility before hitting the trail along the Idaho-Montana border in the Bitterroots. He has adjusted the scabbard to tuck in behind his leg to fend off brush and hang free of the mule's back hip to avoid rubbing. It's a little easier to get everything to fit together on the larger horse, but mules are better at keeping ground contact restricted to the shod parts in the steep, slippery, weathered granite places.

GETTING STARTED WITH THE BOW

The overriding consideration in practice with the bow is to plan for a lot of it—a lot more than is required for hunting with a rifle. Each new elk bowhunter will need to do some self-sorting to determine his or her individual starting point of practicing to develop skills to the level it takes to ethically and successfully hunt elk with the bow. Always use the complete arrangement—bow, arrow, sight, trigger release, and quiver—that you plan to use while hunting for practice, with one exception: Always practice with a field point of the same weight as your broadhead hunting point.

Practice using 2-D or 3-D archery targets is invaluable for the bowhunter. It becomes second nature to shoot for a spot on the image of the animal—essential for quick, offhand shots in heavy cover, with either the rifle or bow. Part of the game in 3-D competition is range estimation, and range estimation is probably the most important element for success in bowhunting.

If you want to learn to shoot instinctively, start close to the target, just a few yards away, and progressively move back as you become confident in your aim. As you become more proficient at a range of about 20 yards, introduce obstacles close to one side near or along the path to the target. Such obstacles are the most common causes of misses in practical hunting situations. Practice until they don't distract your aim.

Shooting Tips

The most common shooting error is grasping the handle of the bow while aiming and releasing the arrow. Most writers have suggestions as to how to grip the bow consistently so that inconsistencies don't develop during release of the arrow. Here's mine: Don't grip the bow. Until the arrow has cleared the bow and is on its way to the target. Really. As you begin the draw, release all restraint of the bow by your left hand except for a pivot contact with the web of your hand between the thumb and index finger. The force of the draw will hold the bow in place during the draw, and the force of the reaction of the bow as the string propels the arrow will continue to hold it in place until the arrow clears the string. Your hand will instinctively grasp the handle of the bow when it begins to jump away, as long as you don't give it conscious thought. It's worked for me every time for more decades than I'd care to discuss. I've never had to use a safety string, but I've seen other shooters using a loose string to attach the bow to one hand.

A common failing of the elk hunter who has hunted extensively with a rifle before taking up the bow is that we don't, by second nature, adequately clear our bow shots above the line of sight. This failing explains why I don't have a bow-shot six-point mount on the wall (remember the Tale with the hanging twig in Chapter 9?). Always remember that the arrow will rise well above the line of sight. A few experiments with a paper placed above the line of sight between shooter and target will demonstrate just how much. Another problem is range estimation. The answer for the beginner is to just keep it short, about 20 yards, and set up your tackle to shoot around 3 inches high if you're 10 yards closer, 3 or 4 inches low if you're 6 to 8 yards farther. With experience, you can graduate to multiple fiber dots adjusted for greater range.

Practice Hunting with the Bow

Go beyond target practice with your bow. Practicing what would appear to be completely unrelated kinds of hunting can develop skills that can be transferred to elk hunting. Practicing with deer hunting is a given, but also try expanding your hunting to no-call, no-bait hunting of coyotes, bears, and feral hogs.

Your equipment and techniques need to accommodate the movement required for locating and stalking. Many experienced white-tailed deer hunters have done practically all of their hunting from stands. Over time their entire setup can evolve to become very limited in mobility. Learn to move with your archery equipment if you intend to move while hunting elk—and you probably will. Familiarity in handling the equipment leads to improved safety as well as more successful hunting.

One particular item that is often overlooked, but then turns out to be a pain in elk hunting, is the arrow rest. Practice with an arrow rest that is practical for the hunting situations you expect to find yourself in—one that provides some restraint in case you have to tilt the bow as you shift position. An arrow rest that allows the arrow to lightly rest on the contact surface of the rest works only out of a stand or on the practice range.

Practice Hunting with Calls

If you plan to use an elk bugle or cow call while elk hunting, you will need to do a lot of practicing with them long before you head for the mountains. It's also a good idea to practice hunting with calls before you go after elk using calls. Using mouth calls for year-round predator and spring turkey hunts will allow you to become accustomed to using calls during the excitement of the stalk. It just might help prevent your cow call from sounding like the high-pitched squawk of a terrified chicken as you attempt to settle down a nervous lookout cow while you're moving in on a big bull. Practice with elk bugles and calls is tied closely with the type of call you select. This is another instance where you might want to try different types of equipment before you commit to one. Some types of calls may be more difficult to operate than others for a given individual.

CHAPTER 14

Equipment for Field Dressing and Preserving the Kill

BLADES: KNIVES, SAWS, AND AXES

Knives are essential tools for a successful hunt, no more, no less. Some hunters develop such a high interest in knives that knives and knife collecting become a hobby in itself for them. These individuals collect references on knife designs, steel alloys, heat treatments used in making knife blades, and makers of custom knives. They'll also get into the fine points of knife sharpening, with opinions on optimum techniques and sharpening equipment for each type of blade. But most of this specialized knowledge won't help put an elk on the ground, or get it to the locker any quicker, for that matter. So there won't be any details on designs, alloys, heat treatments, or famous knife makers in this chapter, and the dedicated enthusiast should feel free to skip to the next chapter. I'll assume that the rest of you, like me, just want a knife that will work reliably and safely at a reasonable cost.

There have been significant developments in knives over the last thirty years, and with each development is a generation of hunters who favor the type of knife that was new when they arrived on the hunting scene. Because a lot of the old hunters from each generation are still hanging around hunting camps, moving slower but still losing, loaning, or giving away their favorite type of knife, new knives of each older type are still sold today. The most important point in selecting a knife for elk hunting is easy to remember: Every make of every type of knife made by the well-established manufacturers will serve the purpose of field dressing an elk.

Not so many years ago, everyone, at least everyone who lived out in the country, was familiar with knives to some extent as a working tool, and carried a folding pocketknife as a part of everyday life. Knives were always good selections as Christmas presents, which is how I came by some of my most cherished possessions, including all of my original deer and elk hunting knives. In my family, the term "knife," was translated to mean a Case XX. You said "pocketknife" or "hunting knife," and that took care of all of the technical specifications as to which Case XX you were talking about. In other families it might translate to a Schrade, a Craftsman sold through the Sears catalog, or something from another of the few domestic knifemakers in business at the time.

All of these knives would now be considered to be of "moderate" hardness, somewhere on the low end of the range of what's available today. Most hunters didn't know anything about the alloy, the heat treatment, or the Rockwell hardness of their favorite knife. They just knew how to sharpen it the way their granddads taught them. The hunting knives were always fixed-blades with clip points (a clip point is one formed by the back of the blade sweeping in a concave curve into the cutting edge to form a sharp point). You expected your knife to become dull while field dressing an elk, but a few swipes with a small whetstone would quickly restore a sharp edge. These knives were always carried on the belt in a sheath, where they were subject to being lost in the rough terrain frequented by elk hunters. The prospect of rolling and sliding down a steep slope with an unsheathed, fixed-blade clip-point on the belt has led some of us to carry these knives sheathed and in the daypack. This has the added advantage of removing at least one item carried on the belt or in the pockets, reducing the weight trying to pull your pants down.

This nice, stable, easy-to-remember body of knife knowledge began to change with the advent of stainless steel knives, which were significantly harder. A typical alloy would be 420 or 440 stainless steel alloy treated to a hardness of 58 to 60 on the Rockwell hardness C scale. Stainless steel and ceramic blades are now available with hardness off the Rockwell hardness C scale. Buck, Gerber, and Kershaw knives are a few of the current most popular brands. Case has added some models with stainless steel blades to its line of traditional models. Some manufacturers make the flat statement that their blades won't dull when used for the purpose intended. If they do, they offer to sharpen them for you at the factory. Reliable locking, folding knives were first introduced by Buck, then offered by all manufacturers, along with hard rubber or other synthetic nonslip handles.

As more knife materials became available, a wider variety of designs became common. Blades were made with specialized shapes to handle certain tasks more efficiently (and sell more knives), leading to sets of multiple knives in a single sheath. Many modern blade designs have serrated edges or have a serrated section in combination with a conventional section.

The most popular specialized blade is the skinning blade. Its defining characteristic is the rounded or blunt point formed by tapering the back of the blade toward the intersection with the cutting edge, which itself is often "bellied out" to make the knife blade wider near the point end. Skinning blade designs often include a specialized "gut hook" in the back side of that typical "fat" width of a skinner. This cuts down on the possibility of getting into the intestines while splitting the belly open during the preliminary stages of field dressing, and having to deal with the consequences for the duration of the job.

Smaller blades better adapted to the delicate job of caping make a nice combination with a skinner. The little blades also work well for efficient removal of all the meat from the bones with minimum waste in preparation for a backpack trip.

There are a lot of experienced elk hunters that don't like the modern knives with their space-age blades, synthetic-looking handles, and folding designs. I, however, belong to the group that wants to get the job done and get in before the storm breaks or the meat spoils and will use any edge that I can take. Pun intended.

Elk hunters seem to pay little attention to the other blades really essential to field dressing an elk—saws and/or axes. As discussed in Chapter 10, quartering an elk for packing out to the road requires separating a lot of bone, and is not a job for a knife. Most elk hunters prefer a small light saw that breaks down for a compact carry. A favorite is a "Wyoming" type breakdown, which comes with blades for wood and bone. Also handy is a single-blade "pack saw," available in various takedown designs, with a bone saw on one side of the blade and a wood saw on the opposite side. Outfitters often like to use an axe to make quick work of bone splitting, even though axes are heavy. It's handy enough for them since the axe shows up with the pack string to finish the quartering job as the quarters go on the pack stock. There's usually a really good hand with an axe in the outfit, and the job is finished amazingly fast. A lot of hunters also carry small axes. Gerber makes several small pack axes that weigh only a little more than a pound. However, the average hunter doesn't have the skill with an axe that the best outfit hands are blessed with, which makes for a rougher split and lots more bone chips than when we use a saw. A much neater result can be achieved in a hurry if two hunting partners each have an axe with a flat hammer surface on the back. One can hold the axe blade in place on the bone to be split and steady the carcass, while the other strikes the stationary axe with the flat back of the other axe. All of the axes and saws mentioned are available from mail-order outfits and large outdoor stores. You can get an excellent setup of the double axe arrangement down at the hardware store in the form of a couple of shingle axes at the expense of a little more weight.

Whatever blade combination you choose, you need to carry suitable sharpeners. Different types of knives have different requirements and preferred means for sharpening. Failure to match sharpening equipment to the type of knife can be inefficient or remove excessive amounts of steel, leaving a rough edge. The different types of high-hardness stainless steel and ceramic knife blades will hold an edge longer than the traditional blades, but are much more difficult to sharpen with a conventional stone. Some hunters carry sharpeners with fixed carbide blades to restore dulled edges of high-hardness blades. These devices will literally shave chips from a knife blade of moderate hardness, and usually leave a sharp but rough edge. A conventional whetstone is best for old-type blades, and will do the job just fine. Diamond whetstones will sharpen blades of any hardness using the traditional sweeping strokes of whetstones. Ceramic-coated sharpening steels operate on the same principle. Another good choice is a ceramic hone, which looks like a bar, triangular in cross section, with flat sides and rounded corners. The flat sides work well on conventional blades of any hardness, and the rounded corners are designed to restore serrated edges. Unlike the knives, axes, and saws, sharpening tools weigh next to nothing. You can afford to carry a conventional whetstone for your traditional knife, a ceramic hone or diamond whetstone for your high-hardness stainless steel or ceramic blade, and a small tungsten-bladed, fixed-angle sharpener for a quick, rough fix on the knife, or the axe, or the saw for that matter.

As far as my own choices go in regard to the blades that I take out into the woods, it depends. On a pack-in trip, I'll probably have two setups, just in case. On opening morning, I'm full of confidence, excitement, and too much strong, black coffee, and I'll have a Kodi-Pak knife set (available from Cabela's), which includes a skinner and small caper/boning combination along with a small saw perfect for splitting a pelvis and adequate (barely) for cutting across (not splitting) a backbone. I'll also have a cheap but sharp imported lock-back folder, which I usually find on sale down at the Tractor Supply Store, for the single nasty belly patch job. On opening morning, everything's light and easy to carry. A few days into the hunt, and my knife selection depends on my mood. If it's obvious that we haven't located the elk and it's going to be a long haul to find them, I may be down to the import and a weighs-next-to-nothing, stays-sharp-always Gerber folder, and use the rest of my weight quota for water, snacks, and enough sandwiches to stay out until dark.

CHECKLIST OF FIELD DRESSING GEAR

First, review all you need to have in the pack in the way of blades: A small sharp knife is needed to remove the belly patch (after this one job, it is stored in a plastic ziplock bag to prevent it from contaminating the meat, or even coming in contact with your hands to transfer odor to the meat). You'll want a large skinning knife with a gut hook for the bulk of field dressing. A small saw edge is needed to split the pelvic bone between the hindquarters, and either a saw or axe to split the backbone in order to separate the quarters. A small skinning knife is required to cape the head, and a saw is required if the rack with a skull base is to be separated from the rest of the head.

Here's a checklist of the required blades, along with the other miscellaneous gear you need:

- Small sharp knife for belly patch
- Ziplock bag
- Large skinning knife with gut hook
- Small saw edge
- Saw or axe
- Small skinning knife
- Game bags
- Cord or rope for hanging quarters
- Rubber gloves (elbow length)
- Toilet paper
- Flashlights (multiple small ones to be carried in different pockets or packs, just in case)
- For quartering: portable axe as well as Wyoming saw

CHAPTER 15

Clothes for Elk Hunting

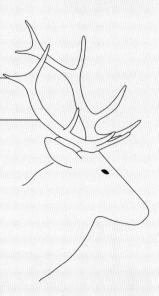

GEAR TO HUNT IN SAFETY AND COMFORT
In this chapter, I'll present some general considerations regarding the elk hunter's ensemble, and then go into detailed discussions and specific recommendations for the most important items. Your personal outfit not only is the key to comfort and prevention of sidelining injury, but also contributes greatly to the feeling of well-being throughout the course of the hunt.

GENERAL CONSIDERATIONS
The gear that you wear and carry should contribute to your hunting success just like the equipment you use to take the elk. All clothes and equipment to be carried should be selected with some thought given to possible effects on locating elk and then making a stalk and kill.

A primary consideration is to pick clothing and equipment that minimize the chance of your being detected by elk. This translates in a practical way to the three Us: remaining *Unseen, Unscented,* and *Unheard.* My advice has always been, if you have to decide between being comfortable and being unnoticed, pick unnoticed. But I'm changing my position on this one with greater "maturity." I now consider how much comfort is traded in for how much stealth—because discomfort can affect your hunting success as well. A low level of discomfort endured over a period of time chips away at your ability to make a challenging shot if the occasion demands one.

Visual stealth becomes progressively more important from the ground up to the head. The upright stance and rhythmic gait characteristic of humans appear to be the primary triggers of the danger instinct for elk, so it's better to confuse the upper part of that shape. Avoid

Match your camo to the local vegetation, and pay attention to sheen. If the surroundings contain vegetation that gives off a sheen on a sunny day, camo with sheen is less obtrusive than a drab commercial camo outfit. This outfit is accessorized with a BLR custom-sanded no-sheen stock, among other slick mods—the textured surface is less noticeable than the highly reflective shiny stock, and also has a surer grip.

apparel that reflects ultraviolet light or gives off an ultraviolet signature, such as felt hats of light colors and any material washed in detergents with brighteners. It's a good idea to check your stuff in ultraviolet light. I'll leave it to your own imagination to figure out the best way to approach this testing. Nondestructive testing areas at aerospace structural fabrication and repair facilities come to mind, as well as clubs and bars with special lighting effects. Or maybe you could just get a black light. Wash everything without bleach or other brighteners, which will also produce an ultraviolet signature. Baking soda works for washing clothes too.

To stay unheard, avoid metallic noises from rattling of loose articles. Separate or fasten together loose metal items. Pants should be of material that does not make noise while moving through brush. My experience has been that elk don't panic at the sound of footsteps or even breaking sticks to the extent that the rhythmic swish of noisy leg coverings through brush sets them off. It might be due to the fact that the noise humans make moving through brush is very distinctive. The rhythmic swish of each leg as it moves forward can be discerned. Four-legged creatures brush their entire bodies through the brush, making a continuous sound. In short brush you can sometimes hear the individual legs move forward, but then the sound repeats faster than a human's stride, with the quick steps of two sets of legs. The intensity of the noise made when wearing conventional raingear is much higher than anything else in the woods.

Keep clean and avoid scented deodorants. Use deodorants that absorb rather than cover up body odors; baking soda–based Arm and Hammer deodorant is good.

Of course, your clothing has another purpose: protecting you from the elements. You need to select clothing for warmth without overheating, and the best method is to dress in layers. A good elk hunting coat stays on securely while open so that you can open it up to cool off while traveling, then fasten it back together quickly and smoothly when you stop. The best material for cold and rainy weather is wool; brushed cotton is great when the weather is warm and dry and will stay that way. But you can't count on the stay-warm part with any certainty in elk country. Cotton should be considered only for early, warm-weather hunts, with wool available when the cold comes. It always does in elk country, often suddenly. Wool is also good thermal insulation even when wet.

After you have assembled your clothing and gear, you need to do a dress rehearsal to see how it fits, what it's going to weigh, and whether everything will work together. Do some target practice, hiking, and practice hunting with all of your gear in place. You need to practice the way you're going to hunt: Wear your coat, hat, and daypack to the range one day. Reload from the ammo carry that you will use hunting. Make it automatic. You may get a few funny looks out on the practice range, but that's far preferable to an unpleasant discovery with an elk in sight or holding up operations on opening morning while you adjust straps and pack and repack stuff. You need confidence to have luck, and preparation is the way to get it. Don't get yourself into a situation where you have to do anything regarding clothes before you can shoot, walk, and so on. Don't let dressing, undressing, redressing get you messed up. You won't have any fun, luck, or success if you go around feeling awkward and undone.

A word on safety as it relates to clothing: Avoid any clothing that might give another hunter's imagination an excuse to mistake you for a

The well-dressed elk hunter wears blaze orange when required. CRAIG ADAMS

game animal. As starters, that translates to no black (bear); no russet of any shade (elk); no gray (deer). Note that even solid olive drab or dark, fine-pattern camo in some fabrics can look black when wet. Avoid wearing fur garments and any fabric that gives the impression of fur. Leave that favorite brown suede riding jacket at home.

Some states require that hunters wear blaze orange headgear and vest on the upper torso during rifle seasons. It's a requirement that tends to compromise the camo effect, but you should be happy to comply, since these are usually the same states with lots of hunters out during short hunting seasons, and you want them to see you for what you are under the circumstances. You should make a special effort to screen yourself from elk by intervening vegetation when at all possible. The theory is that the color-sensitive eyes of the primates in the woods (humans) can see you through the screen, while the color-insensitive but ultraviolet-perceptive animals (everything else, including elk) can't pattern you through the screen. Note that a camo pattern on all clothing other than the vest and cap still makes the human pattern less recognizable, depending on the background.

DETAILS AND SPECIFIC RECOMMENDATIONS
Boots and Socks

Boots are a complicated choice and very important—right up there with the equipment to take the elk. Your coat, hat, rifle, or knife may be a poor choice or not fit you correctly, but they won't hurt you or put you out of action to ruin your trip. Your choice of boots can either keep you in the hunt or put you out of action for the duration of the hunt. Their primary function is to keep you moving and prevent injury from falls, slips, or blisters. Their secondary function is to keep your feet warm and dry, or, failing that, at least warm while wet. Stealth is a low priority for boots; the noise you make while walking will mostly be of no great consequence, except when you're bowhunting under dry conditions.

My approach to boot selection will be to first cover those essentials that you need to have right no matter what kind of boot you get, and then to present the other options and the associated trade-offs, so you can do the rest of the deciding yourself.

The main thing, first and foremost, is to get a good fit, and that means out on the mountain rather than just in the store. I'll elaborate. When you are moving through rough terrain, your feet change size and shape progressively over time. The change seems to be a function of your weight and possibly age, as well as how rough the area is. Regarding the fit, the first step is to get an accurate size under your normal circumstances with help from a true professional. Don't depend on the part-time salesperson at the mall. The best place is a professional-grade work-shoe store; my second choice would be the athletic-shoe store. Check the width accurately as well as the length.

Note that fit means how the boot feels over a good pair of wool socks—on the third day of the hunt. By the third day, your feet will be about a half to a full size larger in width. Switching to thin socks to accommodate your wider feet is not a good approach. Thin socks may not be warm enough and may even wear through with a day on the slopes; you'll quickly develop blisters in unimaginable places. Start with a thick sock arrangement and finish with medium thickness.

To determine the right size, you need to accommodate either a very thick wool sock over a thin undersock, or, if you prefer, two moderately thick wool socks. To do this, take your size with one sock on. With this procedure, you'll have a boot that will fit on the first day with two socks on each foot and on the last day of the hunt with one sock on each foot. The limit to thickness of socks for starting the hunt is if your foot is free to shift around in the oversized boots needed to go on over the extra thickness. If your boots are initially too wide, your feet will tend to slide to one side if you need to sidehill around slopes. You'll often develop stiff knees due to the lack of lateral stability. You never seem to encounter this situation other than when hunting. Even if you hike in the mountains, you normally stay on trails, which will keep your feet on ground that is level from side to side.

Another aspect that pertains to all boots is clearance toward the toe when negotiating a steep downhill slope. Some designs of outdoor boots and shoes will allow the foot to slide forward until your down-slope weight is restrained by the contact of your toe against the end of the boot. A very short time is required to lose your toenails. To guard against this problem, when you try on footwear for hunting, stand on a steep (45-degree) incline for a few minutes. Use the stand in the shoe store. If you feel your toes in contact with the end of the boot, try another pair. Proper footwear for steep slopes will restrain your foot with the lacings across the top of the foot.

Hiking exercise, the more the better, will help you check out the fit and weight of the boot you select. Work up to 10 miles of walking for each session if you're stuck with only flat terrain for your exercise. Suitable practice hunting (meaning lots of walking is included) will partially serve this purpose.

Now for the choices and the trade-offs. The first that comes to mind with boots is stealth versus traction. Some of my bowhunting companions at one time would go to a lot of effort to keep down the noise from their footwear, to the point of wearing tennis shoes with tape around them on the order of football preparations. I never would trade traction for quiet. Put it in perspective: How much noise are you going to make when you slip and mess up your knee? Your choice of pants is more important than your choice of boots in the area of stealth.

An associated dilemma—that leads to another choice and another trade-off—is that the boots with the best traction on steep slopes usually run on the heavy side. In the case of footwear, heavy is bad, even worse than extra weight around your middle or in your pack. You only have to lift the weight you carry from the hips up one time to get it up the slope; the feet have to be lifted up and set down several times over the same distance. The other side of the coin is that if you compromise on traction too much, you can slip and twist your knee or take a tumble and be completely out of action. The only guidance I can offer is based on the principle that "the bigger they are, the harder they fall." I'm in the big category, and consider myself somewhat clumsy even in my native flatlands. My choice of boots tends to favor traction over light weight. If I'll be hunting cross-country, I always go with Vibram soles on a rather substantial boot. For the normal mix of weather conditions to be expected on an early hunt, my favorite boot for traction is a Red Wing Model 699 logger/lineman/motorcycle work boot (around $300 through a Red Wing retail dealer last time I checked). This boot also has a slightly elevated heel. It's the non-steel-toe version of their logger boot

Model 2218. I also use Herman Survivors with Vibram soles for a change-out. If I'll be walking and riding without much cross-country, I use Wolverine Dura-Shocks 8-inch Kiltie Lacer. You'll note that neither of these boot models is insulated like most dedicated hunting boots are. I've had problems with the insulation not staying in place on some boots I've tried in the past. I just count on the wool socks for the insulation. Wool insulates even when wet, and my feet stay wet a lot the way I operate. Waterproofing is always recommended for boots. Many guides and packers in elk country prefer Obenauf's Heavy Duty LP.

A good women's boot with high-traction soles is the Danner Model 42234 Pronghorn Camo-Hide GTX. Danner is considered the standard for hunting boots by many elk hunters. A thin under-sock is often worn with medium or medium-heavy ladies' wool socks. This combination will handle most cross-country and steep trails encountered in elk hunting.

Under conditions where I plan to cover a lot of ground and high traction won't be required, I prefer either a lighter army combat boot as currently issued with the canvas side panels and the Panama sole, or Wolverine work boots with ridged shop soles. They can be resoled with Vibram soles for all-out traction at the

When location requires a lot of ridge running, JoAnne goes for comfort and mobility in the pants and boots department. She's also found a novel approach to combining traction and light weight when she needs to cover lots of miles over sometimes treacherous footing—motorcycle boots with traction soles. Compared with the stiffer, high-traction waffle-stompers, flexible soles have some advantage when working side ridges. The particular biker boots she uses (Harley Tessa lace-up with zipper) are waterproof too!

expense of more weight. Wool socks again provide the insulation. Both of these boots pass the test of preventing contact between the toes and the end of the boot. I might note that the old-style Munson paratrooper combat boot I used in the service will not pass the toe test. Neither will most of the expensive European-style mountain-hiking boots.

For a late hunt that almost certainly will include deep snow, or in an area of high precipitation, I would go with Sorel or GoreTex boots with wool outer socks and polypro liner socks.

Bowhunters have various theories concerning the best footwear for sneaking through the woods, ranging from track shoes for silence to high-traction, lightweight "Bob" tread soles for fast movement across rough terrain. Most of the big suppliers now carry specialized boots for bowhunting.

When horseback riding while wearing high-traction boots, most experienced mountain trail riders take special precautions to prevent their boots from getting stuck in the stirrups in case of a real bad horse wreck or buck-off. Chances of this happening are minimized if you ride with only the front of the boot in the stirrup.

The boots discussed up to this point are good for situations where walking, or climbing, as is usually the case, is the norm. Some hunts may involve a lot of horseback riding as part of their normal operations or due to special circumstances. If, during planning discussions with the outfitter, you find that a lot of saddle time is likely, you may want to pack a pair of suitable riding boots. Conventional heeled western riding boots, referred to as cowboy boots in areas of the country where cowboys don't naturally occur, are the best choice for spending days in the saddle. Note that the fancy versions made for cowboys (and cowgirls) that dance a lot more than they ride horses will be useless on the ground in the mountains. The soles are too slick and the heels too wide for traction on steep slopes.

Professional outfitters, packers, and guides commonly use special packers' boots. These boots, often custom-made, lace up to fit tight around the ankle like loggers' or linemens' boots but have serious riding heels that work pretty well on steep slopes for the people that wear them all of the time. Custom-made White's boots are traditional in the Northwest. Motorcycle boots work surprisingly well for both walking and horseback riding (on reflection, I guess it shouldn't be that much of a surprise considering what they were designed for). Riding in the mountains involves a certain amount of walking both up- and downhill to make it easier on the horses.

I prefer conventional pull-on western riding boots with the original leather soles and riding heels. This type of boot will work well if the prospective hunter expects to be using outfitter horses, which are not usually given to diving over the side of a trail. When I was part of an association that owned our own pack outfit, I used a series of saddle horses of questionable disposition whose personality quirks provided plenty of entertainment to break the monotony—and my neck too, if given the chance. Somewhere in the back of the closet with my hunting gear is an old pair of boots with reworked riding heels that could be guaranteed to kick out of the stirrup whatever stunt a horse pulled. However, you won't need to carry it that far with good outfitter horses (the operative term here being "good").

My personal favorite socks are Fox River Boot and Field extra-heavy-weight worsted wool ribbed-leg Model 7267 Outdoorsox. Available from the following address:

Fox River Mills, Inc.
P.O. Box 298
Osage, IA 50461

With all the walking you'll be doing, your feet are probably going to need all the help they can get. Pay attention when your feet and toes are trying to tell you something. Those dogs don't bark for nothing. Before the blister blisters, apply a piece of moleskin cut to size. The adhesive side sticks to your foot, and the sliding is now between slick moleskin material (it's actually made of cotton flannel; no moles are used in the process) and your sock. Let it wear off or soak it before removing it, because it sticks to your skin better than your skin sticks to you.

Pants

Pants serve two important purposes: to keep your legs warm while wet or dry and suppress generation of noise while walking through low brush. The rhythmic swish of two legs moving through brush is an unmistakable human sound. Low visibility is desirable but not an overriding concern since surrounding brush usually masks the lower body.

Look for pants made of wool. In the cold and wet, it's the only way to go. Wool is warm whether wet or dry, and it doesn't make a lot of noise as you move through brush. Durability of some wool garments can be a problem on the snags that are always there in elk country.

What else should you consider? Pockets allow you to conveniently carry small pieces of equipment. Tight-fitting pants with no stretch increase fatigue when you have to be moving all day in the location phase of the hunt. Wear them loose or stretchy. Remember to stay away from gray, dark blue approaching black, and russet colors to eliminate

This ensemble is designed for cool speed when elk need to be located. The waterproof boots are nice too.

(Below) A study in camo in a camp along the Dolores River in southwest Colorado. Note how the soft-washed and line-dried brushed cotton reflects light about as much as the surrounding vegetation. The pattern and texture of shirt and pants are often deliberately mismatched.

any chance of being mistaken for a deer, bear, or elk by somebody with a tag and a nervous trigger finger.

The army has given a lot of thought to the problem of keeping warm and dry under field conditions. The old-style cold-weather wool field pants (not dress uniform pants, which are lighter and less durable) are hard to beat. However, they are hard to find, and you may have to go with a modern commercial alternative—or you can try a foreign design found at an army surplus store.

When cold weather isn't a problem and extreme stealth is required (read early-season bowhunting), brushed cotton commercial camo is a good choice. And, as noted in Chapter 6, when the location phase requires a lot of ridge running, go for comfort and mobility in the pants and boots department.

Coats and Shirts

You want your coat and shirt to be warm, but the ability to open both garments to vent off heat is just as important. It's very important to wear camo patterns appropriate to the surroundings. For stealth purposes, don't wear anything on your upper body that was manufactured or cleaned with ultraviolet-reflecting whiteners. Convenient pockets that can be used to secure small items of equipment for easy access are very important.

The military field jacket works just fine for the three most important functions of a jacket: camouflage, adjustable warmth, and convenient carrying capacity. If it's too warm for the field jacket, a woodland camo-pattern BDU jacket provides camo with little weight. You can use a jacket liner in the cold morning and stuff it in the backpack in the afternoon. Available from quartermasters or a local military surplus store. The real article can be identified by the MIL-SPEC designation on the tag:

Coat, Field, Woodland Camouflage
Outershell 50% Cotton 50% Nylon
Lining 100% Cotton

In case of cold weather, a button-in liner is nice to have along (look for the label saying, "Liner, Cold Weather Coat").

In case of snow cover, I use a West German surplus BDU snow camo jacket that I wear over the woodland camo coat. This particular camo isn't all white, but has dark splotches and seems to blend well with snow and brush.

Save your down coat for the ski slopes—its insulation doesn't keep you warm if it gets wet, which will probably happen on an elk hunt. Stay with synthetic insulation. The liners for military field jackets will work just fine.

You should have a high-quality wool shirt for really cold weather. Cotton flannel is good under a light coat for typical early fall conditions when general seasons open. Early hunts may be warm enough to make

A good ensemble for the well-dressed elk hunter as the weather begins to turn colder in the northern region. The hunter in this case has the hat pushed back to help keep cool during a hard climb up a long slope. Note how the coat is open but still showing camo washed with no whiteners. Camo gloves complete the effect.

a camo T-shirt about right throughout the day, maybe starting in the morning with a camo or BDU shirt over it.

I recommend that you don't wear the heavy thermal underwear suitable for waiting in a cold, late-season deer stand for elk hunting. I'll leave it to you to create your own visualization, but if you get over-heated while hunting the steep slopes, this is one part of the ensemble that's unhandy to change out of when heat-induced leg cramps hit. You might need one set of long-handles for around camp in case you get cold at night.

Gloves

It's important that your gloves keep your hands warm so that your ability to manipulate the equipment to take the elk is not impaired by cold. At the same time, your gloves can't be so thick that they restrict the sense of touch, for the same reason. Small hands are more easily chilled and need thicker gloves.

Deerskin leather shooting gloves are the all-around best for shooting. When it's not very cold, I recommend the old-design officers' military dress gloves, if you can find them. I'll usually take a good pair of pigskin leather work gloves along on a hunt to use for serious wood splitting. Wool gloves are better for warmth in the case of folks with small hands. If there's a possibility of weather cold enough for frostbite (and I'd plan conservatively), you probably want to take along some serious mittens, lined leather or thick wool.

Hats

The primary function of the hat or cap is to protect the head from the elements and vent off heat without restricting visibility or hearing. It needs to turn water to keep rain from entering your garments through the neckhole. Try to get one that's water repellent, so that the snow stays on top of the hat rather than on top of your head.

Your headgear also offers an often-overlooked opportunity to camouflage your top part so you look less like a human. It's best to cover all gray or artificially colored hair. Remember to avoid hats made using processes that make them reflect ultraviolet light.

I usually take a bibbed cap with fold-down ear covers on the hunt to wear around camp and under the poncho or field jacket hood on days when it's too nasty to go out but I go out anyway. Most of the time, you'll be active enough to be interested in keeping your head cool rather than keeping it warm, so vents in the crown of the hat are a good feature. Bowhunters often use some form of pullover that rolls up to make a cap, or can be pulled down for a face cover. A balaclava can be rolled up and worn as a beanie; pulled down to cover the top and back of the head, the neck, and, if desired, part of the face; or pulled down all the way to serve as a neck gaiter.

Raingear

Raingear is always a trade-off between keeping you warm and dry and getting you too hot. And if it's very good on both counts, it's probably too heavy to stuff into your backpack and you're more likely to leave it in camp that day that the big storm moves in. Raingear is also really loud. Check how much noise your gear makes when it's cold, not in the nice, warm sporting goods store—yes, stuff it in the freezer. Raingear usually makes a noise characteristic of humans.

In the raingear trade-offs, pick not getting too hot and not making noise. I recommend a military-type poncho, a type of raingear that I have used for thirty years. It's available as army surplus or facsimile. The best surface texture is flat matte, and the best camo pattern is large-pattern woodland, as illustrated on army field jackets. The drawback to this type of poncho is that you get your lower pants legs wet, which

The military poncho is a good, easily stowable raingear option. The GI version is the best for noise suppression.

leads to rain running down your legs and into your boots, even if they are waterproof. On the good side, you can carry your rifle under the poncho to avoid its being soaked (it's not the effect of water in liquid form that we're concerned about; it's water frozen to ice down inside the internal workings that becomes a real problem). The photo illustrates the poncho with hood worn down, which is a lot cooler if you're pulling up slopes. The theory is that the brimmed hat keeps the snow from going down the back of your neck, more or less, and your all-around vision is unimpaired.

WARDROBE: WHAT TO WEAR AND HOW MANY OUTFITS?

Start by researching the weather that you'll most likely encounter in the area (keeping in mind that elevation can make a big difference—the valley town nearby will not have the same weather!) during the time of the year that you'll be there. These conditions will determine the ensemble that you'll need in multiple copies. Figure out how many copies by taking into account the number of days you plan to hunt and how often you'll need to change due to getting too soaked to dry out or to sweating out a set of clothes because of heat and exertion. A washer and dryer won't be available—unless you count the waterhole and clothesline. And you may be too worn out to be interested in either. Table 3 (page 328) has some general suggestions.

Bill blends in with the vegetation sans fancy (and expensive) camo. Note how the color and texture of his clothes just make him "fade away."

At the same time that you research the most likely conditions you'll encounter, find out the most severe extremes in weather that you might suddenly encounter. You need to consider not only the severity of the possible weather conditions, but also how much warning you'll get, how far you'll be away from food and shelter, the likelihood of other members of the hunting party being able to rescue you if you get into trouble, and how well you could expect to make a fire and temporary shelter with the gear you have with you. Apply common sense to these deliberations as if your life depended on it—it very well could. Then take along one copy of whatever outfit or critical item you would need to get by in the extreme conditions.

Finally, consider the effects of your mode of transport from home to camp and then on up the trail to locate an elk. Some arrangements put constraints on the weight and total amount of stuff you can bring and how it can be packaged for transport.

CLEANING AND STORING GARMENTS

After the trip, wash your hunting garments in baking soda a couple of times and dry them in the sun. The wool stuff should be taken to the cleaners, then hung out in the wind to let the cleaning odor air out. Then store it all in tight-weave duffels with cedar chips spread over every layer of garments, in coat pockets, and every other hidden place.

TABLE 3: CLOTHES TO BRING FOR DIFFERENT HUNTING ARRANGEMENTS

Item	Outfitter Pack Camp	Personal Camp on Road	Backpack	Comments
Headgear	Hunting cap and cold-weather hat	Hunting cap and cold-weather hat	Hunting cap and cold-weather hat	
Wool socks	Assortment/change of socks for every day	Assortment/change of socks for every day	1 pair/socks for every day	
Underwear mix for cool and thermal for cold	Change every day	Change every day	Change every 2 days	
Long sleeved camo T-shirt	Change every day	Change every day	1 for hunt in warm weather	
Cotton camo shirt	Change every 3 days	Change every 3 days	1 for hunt	Warm weather only
Cotton camo pants	2 for trip	2 for trip		Warm weather only
Medium-weight wool shirt	2 for trip	2 for trip	1 for trip	Cool to cold transition
Medium-weight wool pants	2 for trip	2 for trip	1 for trip	Cool to cold transition
Heavy wool pants	1 for trip	1 for trip		Cold and wet
Wool sweater	1 for trip	1 for trip		Usually worn under coat
Coats	1 heavy wool coat for very cold weather; field jacket for mild weather, add liner for colder weather		Personal judgment/experience	For riding in cold weather
Raingear	Poncho/rain suit/slicker	Poncho/rain suit	Poncho	Poncho and rain suit for riding and walking; slicker for riding only

You'll also need the following items regardless of your hunting arrangement: boots, gloves, belt (wide for ammo carry), suspenders (per personal preference).

Next season, or next hunt if you can get in some "off-season" hunting (anything except elk hunting for some of us), take it out, shake it out, shaking the cedar back into the duffel, check it out for those recluse spiders—which shouldn't be able to get into a tightly zipped bag—and you're ready to go. Go ahead and wear it with some of the cedar chips still on or in it. They smell better and more natural than we do.

CHAPTER 16

Personal Gear

A GOOD NIGHT'S REST: MORE LAYERING

For most elk hunters, a good night's rest is usually the most critical aspect of well-being that determines their ability to maintain sustained anticipation of success and a high level of performance throughout the hunt. The bedroll determines your comfort level for a significant part of your time elk hunting and your performance level for the rest of the time, so it is a big deal. Your personal sleeping gear needs to be compatible with your hunting arrangements, and adaptable to both unseasonably hot or cold weather. For bedding, as for clothing, the word is *layers*.

This is where personal outfit and gear sort of overlaps with hunting arrangements. If you plan to pack your gear yourself, you'll probably want a down sleeping bag, since that's the best selection for a light bag that can be stuffed down to a small size. If you have transport available, a large bag using synthetic material for insulation is preferable, since it will stay warm when wet. In this case the term "bedroll" is applicable— it translates to an augmented sleeping bag. When the weather can be variable—and the temperature inside a woodstove–heated tent is extremely variable—your sleeping bag can cook you, and then when you unzip to cool off, you'll go to sleep and sometime later wake up frozen. The best solution is to roll up a sheet and light blanket with your bag. Then you can unzip the bag and use it for cover with the sheet under you to separate you from the cot, tarp, or ground underneath. If you get too warm, you can sleep on the bag and cover up with the sheet and blanket. When it gets really cold, you zip up the bag and actually use it the way it's designed to be used. If you normally sleep with a pillow, take a pillow. If you don't normally use a pillow, take one anyway.

It helps keep your neck warm, and, on a camp cot, you may sleep on your side and back more than you normally would back home. Snooze on your tummy, and your back is curved in the wrong direction if that's the way the cot wants to sag. Outfitter deals normally include a camp cot or bunk that you supply the bedding for; lodge accommodation may vary from bunkhouse standard to luxury hotel.

WHEN THE OUTFIT BECOMES PERSONAL GEAR: SPIKE CAMPS, BACKPACK CAMPS, ROVING OUTFITTER HUNTS, AND OTHER MISGUIDED ARRANGEMENTS

A spike camp is a small, bare-essentials camp that can take different forms depending on its purpose and whether it's a satellite off of a main hunting camp or a stand-alone camp. When connected with an outfitter hunting camp, it's often used to avoid the time-consuming trip through the predawn darkness from the main camp to get hunters into the vicinity of elk very early in the day. With a spike camp, you can make the trip in the evening or late afternoon of the preceding day. It's often used on opening morning of the general season to expand the area that can be hunted by individual hunters with guides before elk start heading for deep cover due to hunting pressure. Transport to the spike camp is usually by means of outfitter stock and can include a pack animal or two. In this case, the hunter(s) and guide(s) may use a smaller version of the usual pack-camp wall tent. Sleeping arrangements are usually old-time cowboy-style with bedrolls on the ground, so a backpacker's ground pad can come in handy to soften the rock or stump you usually find against one of your soft places when it's time for bed. (Some hold to the theory that the name "spike" camp derives from the uncomfortable terrain feature that you'll always sleep on in any type of spike camp.) Since the whole purpose of this camping arrangement is to "git in amongst 'em" with as little disturbance as possible, it's often a "cold" camp. That translates to no fire and no cooking. The little hunting party is often dropped off, with the packer taking the animals back to the main camp, ostensibly to avoid the commotion from unhappy horses and mules tied up short all night. By morning everybody has realized that the packers are simply smart enough to avoid sleeping on the rocks if they don't have to—or starting the day with no coffee. The excitement of hearing elk bugling in the night is supposed to overcome all miseries. It usually works for the younger hunters.

Another takeoff on the outfitter pack-camp-based spike camp that appeals to the young and misguided hunter, or the more experienced hunter who should know better, is for the hell-bent die-hard hunter to tie the bedroll to the back of the saddle and go out alone to combine an evening hunt with an early morning hunt in some far-off corner of the outfitter's territory. This is normally one of those activities where you're supposed to check with the outfitter first before taking off. The usual procedure is to take a couple of pack tarps. One goes on the ground, the other over the bedroll—and over your head if it rains or if you hear a large predator in the immediate vicinity. It has been my experience that both will leak during the hundred-year storm that usually blows in during one of these little outings. A person usually doesn't plan ahead for this type of excursion, or he or she would think better of it, but if you did, you might take a small backpacker tent along in your pack. You might check with the outfitter when you book to see if this is a possibility . . . though on second thought, it might be better not to.

Roving outfitter camps are an arrangement I do engage in. There are parts of some large outfitter areas that are very difficult to pack in and out of to sustain drop camps, but a single hunter with a guide that knows the area can use the outfitter's riding and pack stock to rove over such areas, carrying sufficient provisions to support a multiple-day hunt. Small tents can be packed along or dropped off along with some simple camping gear.

There's another group of spike campers, the bunch that uses the spike camp for the main camp—the backpackers. For those new to the camping game, note that a backpack is a large pack mounted on a pack-board, designed to carry a light camp as described below. It's not the bag you carried to high school. That's a daypack, to be discussed shortly—a small pack worn while hunting that holds only the essentials for a day of hunting and an emergency night out.

For the dedicated backpacker, the entire camp is personal gear. Most of the elk hunters in this elite club have very definite ideas about their camps, so these camps can take very different forms when you see them set up. Some use the small, easily packed hiker tents that have appeared on the market with the rise in that activity; various setups with a sleeping bag in an itty-bitty tent are also available. Others don't use a tent as such. They prefer a small tarp stretched to form a single-sided lean-to, completely open on one side. Some will use two lean-tos, one to cover, more or less, the sleeping bag, and another for the provisions and cooking area. These setups work out to be reasonably dry if located in a thick stand of timber that will catch snow and turn most of the rain, or at least keep the rain that does get through coming straight down. The exact location of the sleeping bag is chosen by experience to avoid places where water will collect when it rains. Backpacker spike camp gear should include a pack frame with a detachable pack, so that the pack frame can be used to move the camp, then convert to pack out elk quarters or boned meat if the hunter gets lucky and the work gets serious. A lightweight down sleeping bag rounds out the camp. Utensils and provisions should be chosen to keep weight to a minimum.

A spike camp variation sometimes used by the extremely rough-and-ready amounts to staying out all night. The hunter just picks out a good place and stops when it gets dark. The only provisions for camping are an oversized daypack with some extra food and a light tarp to roll up in or stretch over your "bedroom." In the simplest form, the hunter sleeps with clothes on, with boots replaced by an extra pair of warm socks. You can go an extra step and carry a light sleeping bag and a couple of utensils to heat backpack meals. Then it starts to become a real camp at the expense of carrying more weight while hunting. This can work out okay when the weather cooperates, usually during early-season hunts. It's also nicer in areas where safe drinking water can be easily found so that it doesn't need to be carried. I've heard this arrangement termed a "bivouac" camp when it turns out well. When it doesn't turn out so well, I've heard it called much worse.

REALITY CHECK ON THE PERSONAL CAMP THING

It is essential to research the area you intend to hunt to determine exactly what you need to hunt in safety and comfort. Firsthand telephone conversations with Forest Service officials might be a good place to start. Depending on the area, your questions might begin with the availability of safe drinking water—should the load include all the water that will be needed, or can locally available water be treated or filtered with a small portable unit? At the other extreme, will the expected temperatures dictate a need for extremely warm clothes and portable stoves? Is there a likelihood of being snowed in? If you're new to the backpacking game, you can find a lot of information as well as equipment at a specialized store catering to hikers. Then there's always good ol' Cabela's.

THE DAYPACK AND POCKETS—PUTTING THE GEAR ALL TOGETHER AND MAKING IT MOBILE

Your next task is to make a list of the gear you need to take with you when you leave camp:

> Rifle and spare ammo (yes, people walk out of camp without one or the other)
>
> Hunting license and tag (they need to be with you where they won't be lost or left)

Water—carry and resupply as required

Maps/compass(es)/GPS and altimeter

Bugle and/or cow call

Wristwatch—expendable (not the keepsake) with illuminated dial

Binoculars

Signal whistle (empty .300 or .338 cartridge shell)

Fire starting kit with both lighter and matches

Matches, paper, and tinder shavings—all carried in a separate waterproof bag

First-aid kit

Emergency thermal bag

Poncho or other raingear

Dry woolen socks and underwear in ziplock bag to keep them dry

Emergency rations—not for snacks

Camera (not necessarily only for the trophy, but also for that unforgettable view that you'll forget otherwise)

Flashlight(s)—several small ones rather than one big unhandy one that you'll lose

Flashlight batteries

Game bags with cord or rope for hanging quarters

One-time-use knife for belly patch, with ziplock bag to drop it into

Rubber gloves, elbow length

Toilet paper

Knives for skinning overall and for trophy mount

Tools for quartering—portable axe or Wyoming saw

Regular prescriptions

All of the other good ideas you have for stuff you might like to have along (I try to narrow it down to snacks and lunch.)

All of the hunting gear that you get together should fit together in a convenient package to carry with you every step of the way while elk hunting. The essential stuff is shown in the photo on the opposite page, ready to go into backpack and pockets. Spare ammo is carried on the belt on the left-hand side so it can be easily reached by the right hand (reverse for lefties). Your coat pockets are the best place to put stuff that you need to get to easily without removing the daypack or backpack. That would include GPS or map and compass, water, small binoculars, camera (small, disposable, and waterproof seems to work out best), an empty cartridge shell to use as a signal whistle, small butane lighter to check wind direction, and snacks. You need to leave the right-hand shirt pocket and upper coat pockets empty so that there won't be anything in

Making the most of backpack and pockets when packing gear for hunting.

the way of getting the rifle to your shoulder (for the right-handed shooter). Leave the left side clear for operating a bow. You don't want anything solid in the side pocket of the military field jacket to bump against the stock of a slung rifle.

Most of the loose, light stuff that you don't need to get your hands on quickly will go into the backpack. Carry everything in separate plastic bags with extra air removed. This will include your wallet with the license and tags, an extra compass, deer bags (one for each elk quarter and one for the liver and heart), the elbow-length disposable gloves and a one-time-use knife to deal with the belly patch along with a resealable plastic bag to drop the nasty stuff into, cord for hanging quarters, all of the emergency stuff to make a fire, first-aid kit, thermal bag, and toilet paper (for trail marking, emergency bandage compress, and fire starting, as well as its original purpose) or a roll of paper towels.

The single item that takes up the most room is the raingear. In the photo above, it's already out of the way in the backpack. An alternate carry for the poncho is looped over the belt. It's easier to get at quickly from the belt without having to take the daypack off this way, but it's also more likely to snag on brush and has to be secured so that you won't lose it. (It also tends to drag your pants down if you're like some of us and bigger in the middle than you are at either end.)

Both an axe and saw are shown in the photo. You usually carry only one of the two. For quartering an elk carcass, the axe is faster, but it is heavier to carry. If you are hunting from a spike camp, you'll want a full-size camp axe around. A full-size axe is too heavy to carry while hunting. The axe shown in the photo is actually a heavy roofers' shingle hatchet, the lightest, most effective solution I've ever found. It can be carried while hunting, although it's a little on the heavy side. Note that if you're sure that you will be hunting with another person all of the time (a good idea for a number of reasons), you can split up most of the gear to take care of a downed elk between you. In the case of a pack outfit, you'll have guides along who will carry some of the stuff needed for field dressing any elk taken. If you're hunting alone out of a spike camp, you probably won't range out a great distance from camp, so it might be easier to go back for the heavy stuff rather than carry it all of the time.

Some hunters prefer to carry a lot of gear on the belt, with the fanny pack becoming the primary pack. This is the only way to go for the bowhunter using a back quiver. Military web belts are a practical way to comfortably put a lot of stuff on the belt, and can hold water canteens, knives, axes, and ammo. You can get the rest of the army web gear set to transfer weight from the waist to the shoulders. Most hunters use the backpack as the primary load carrier and limit the belt load to ammo.

The coat is shown as part of the gear for carrying stuff. I recommend a military-style coat for the camo pattern and all of the handy pockets. All of the pockets snap closed to keep stuff from falling out if you flip over a couple of times on a steep slope. You can carry your glasses, maps, and compass in the upper pockets on the left side for the right-handed shooter. Water bottle, lunch, camera, lighter for reading wind direction, signal whistle, flashlights, and other small stuff can go in the lower pockets. Everything that needs to stay dry needs to be in a waterproof bag in case you or your horse thinks you could do with a cold swim in a mountain stream with all of your clothes on. Note that if you put too much stuff in the right-hand lower pocket, it may bump on the rifle stock if you use a right-shoulder carry, as will a large knife on the belt. You'll find that there's a limit to the amount of gear that you can practically, and comfortably, carry on a belt, particularly the belt that also holds your pants up. Remember that the stuff in your pants pockets depends on the belt to stay above your ankles, as do your pants. At some point you begin to appreciate the invention of suspenders to transfer the load from waist to shoulders. Military gear is probably the best-designed and highest-quality equipment of this type that you can get.

Gear packed for riding—for hunting and for transport by pack string.

Oversized saddlebags are handy for keeping essential stuff close to you.

When packing gear for packhorse or mule transportation, you need to have your stuff in multiple small duffels so that the packer can balance the loads on the pack stock. Hard gun or bow cases don't pack well and you don't want them back on the pack string anyway. The outfitter may provide rifle or bow scabbards, but it's best to have your own. Most hunters wear their backpacks while riding in to the mountain camp as well as during the hunt. Backpacks can also be looped over the saddle horn by the straps with the lead rope wrapped over the

Gear packed for ground and air transport.

straps. Packers and hunters with their own horses usually carry gear in saddlebags.

I've already told you about the rifle and bow scabbards Ken Grimes made for me. In addition to them, Ken has made another longstanding wish list item of mine a reality. The oversized saddlebags shown in the bottom photo on the previous page are my interpretation of the cash cases of the Old West cattle drives, with embellishments. The cases can be detached from the center section that goes over the horse and be snapped together to form a single piece of luggage or oversized briefcase. This way, the gear that you want to keep up with won't be loosely packed in with an assortment of stuff somewhere on a mule back in the string. It's also ideal for carrying gear and changes of socks and extra coats and gear for a roving outfitter camp expedition of a few days.

For airline travel, you'll need a good hard carrying case for firearms or bow and arrows. Soft duffle bags seem to work best for clothes. They're also preferred if you will finish the trip by horse, packing in after the flight. Roll or fold clothes to cushion other gear like flashlights, knives, and ammo so that they won't be damaged or poke a hole through the side of the bag.

Tight-weave fabric duffels can be used for transporting everything on the elk hunting trip. They're also the best place to leave your hunting outfit during the hunt at all times other than when you're actually out hunting in it. They prevent your clothes from soaking up all of the considerable camp odors floating around—bacon and other good stuff cooking, smoke from the fire and those with the habit(s), and all of the other distinctly human smells that add to our own unique stinks. Keep the "around camp" sweats in a separate plastic bag, and the hunting garments and undergarments worn next to your skin in another.

You don't absolutely need hard cases for firearms when packing gear for transport in a car or truck, but they ease the ride on scopes if you worry about that sort of thing.

Hard cases aren't needed for a road trip that will require cases and scabbards for riding and pack stock transport during the course of the hunt. Gun and bow cases/scabbards and oversized saddlebags are handy for stowing expensive equipment in the hotel room during overnight stops. Clothes and sleeping bags in duffle bags can stay in the locked vehicle. Reserve space under the topper in the back of the truck for the box of frozen elk meat in dry ice on the trip home. Keeping it in the back prevents the carbon monoxide from building up in the cab with the people. Just in case.

CHAPTER 17

Old Tom's Quick 'n' Easy Camp Provisioning and Rough 'n' Ready Camp Cooking

Y ou will get hungry on the hunt. The easiest way to handle this requirement is to book with a good outfitter who provides food as part of the deal. Hunters making their own arrangements need to know enough to at least get by, and, with a little planning and effort, can make mealtime a pleasant part of the experience.

Planning for provisioning should take into account the number of hunters to be fed and for how long; the requirements for food preservation; and how food will be cooked. The preferences and amount of food purchased depend on the tastes of the individual members of the hunting party. It seems to work out best if one member of the bunch gets a single list together considering the preferences of all of the individual members of the party. The amount of food purchased should realistically match consumption. There's usually a tendency to take too much. Planning realistically also includes consideration of the fact that members of the party will be tired after a day of hunting, and will want a meal that's fast and filling.

The preferences collected from the members of the hunting party should include the manner of cooking, so that the preferred means of cooking will actually be packed and available in camp. The type of camp plays a big part in determining the cooking equipment that will be available. Highly portable pack-in backcountry camps may depend

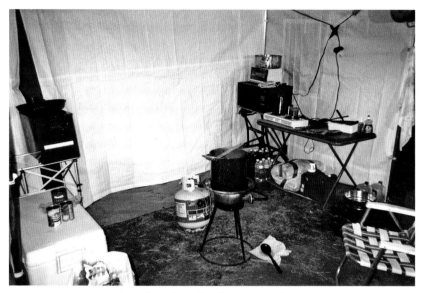

Rough-and-ready elk camp cooking.

on campfires for cooking. This type of cooking also requires a certain amount of skill and experience with skillets, wire grills and spits, and Dutch ovens. Horse transport may allow butane burners. Road-based camps allow use of any type of cooking equipment that can be hauled, but you still need to remember to load it. Some guys just won't leave home without their gas grills. They can also be made to double as effective, if not particularly efficient, ovens. An electrical generator in a road-based camp can be used to power a microwave oven and portable cooktops. Check the power requirements of everything added together against the output of the generator if you plan to use them at the same time. Camp stoves fueled by propane are usually more practical. For fast cooking of large batches of stuff, it's hard to beat a large burner hooked up to a big bottle of fuel. The only thing better than that setup is two of them. Then you can get the coffee and the skillet going at the same time in the morning, and be way up the ridge full of breakfast before the light breaks in the east.

Preservation of food depends on the temperature at the camp location during the hunt. Not the average temperature of the region. Not the temperature when your buddy camped there last year. Not the temperature up on the mountain where you're hunting. Plan for the temperature being a lot warmer, colder, or both when you plan the arrangements for food storage. That understood, for general hunts in the northern regions of elk hunting country and late hunts in the southern regions, the temperature will be below freezing at night and cool to mild during the day. Under these conditions, keeping the food fresh becomes a straightforward routine. Food such as meat that will spoil at normal temperatures should be frozen and packed together in insulated containers. Keep the containers closed as long as the food stays frozen. Take out and thaw food immediately before it is to be cooked. It's far safer not to attempt to keep fish or poultry for any length of time after it's thawed. During the duration of the hunt, most of the frozen food should be used before it thaws. Some hunters open the insulated container and leave it outside in the cold at night, then close it and put it in a cool place during the day, but this can lead to the meat thawing before it's time to use it. Check for signs of spoilage when you use it. The food like milk, eggs, and lettuce that should be kept cool but not frozen should be stored in an insulated container that's left open during the chill of early evening and then closed to prevent freezing during the night and warming during the day. A third set of containers for food such as apples, potatoes, crackers, pancake mix, and canned goods need only be small critter–proof.

If the temperatures are above freezing during the night and mild to warm during the day, different approaches may be used, depending on the hunting arrangements. If the hunt involves packing into backcountry or any other arrangement where portability is important, use either dried or canned food and use all food immediately after opening. The carcass of any elk taken will need to be packed out to the road and taken to a locker immediately or it will be ruined. Note that immediately doesn't equal the next morning or whenever the locker plant opens. The carcass won't chill sufficiently during a warm night. If the arrangements include a road-based camp, one of two approaches to food preservation may be used. One approach is to store the frozen food in one set of insulated containers until it thaws, then keep what's left cool using ice hauled in from the nearest town. Food to be kept cool can be placed in another set of insulated containers cooled with ice for transport. The ice will need to be replenished as it thaws. Again, you need to immediately transport the carcass of any elk taken to the locker in town for processing and freezing. Another approach for a road-based camp, often preferred when warm weather is the norm, is to bring an electric generator and a freezer along with the rest of the camp outfit. Running the generator for a few hours each day will keep the contents of the freezer frozen and freeze containers of water or freezer blocks to preserve the cooled food in insulated containers. The ice or freezer blocks will be exchanged between the freezer and ice chests daily. This arrangement also provides a means to freeze butchered elk carcasses in camp.

Storage of food should always provide protection from the little critters that are always part of the scene in an elk hunting camp. The little critters can be an aggravation. However, bears can be a major problem if they're in the area. I've seen enough results of bear raids on outfitter camps to prove to my satisfaction that there's no such thing as a bearproof container, at least not in a practical sense. I've also seen all sorts of arrangements for food protection that can't be counted on to keep bears out of the chuck: scaffolds, tents (and they never leave through the same big rip they used to let themselves in), cabins, vehicles of any type (they'll usually do more damage than if they got all of the food), or buried outfitter caches. Bears seem to consider any human-produced arrangement directly connected to the grub as just an extension of the container, and go to work on it. To quote some backpacker type of long ago, "There's just no practical way to deter a large, determined animal." The only practical solution that seems to work consistently is to suspend all food containers, including all recently used cooking utensils, in a cargo net 8 to 10 feet off of the ground and 5 feet away from anything that will support the weight of a bear. You can suspend it from an overhanging limb or from a rope or cable stretched between two trees. Of course, the bear can be expected to climb the trees and the limbs and probably work on the tie-offs. Good luck.

Hunting from your own outfit along the road, from an outfitter drop camp, or even with a pack outfit in those situations where the cook gets skunked out, runs off, or never shows up, you could be faced with a prospect more dreadful than an encounter with the meanest bear in the woods: a camp with no cook. Under these extreme circumstances, I offer Old Tom's rough-and-ready camp cooking for the non-cook. The best thing that can be said about this cooking style is that it will get you going in conditions of cold weather, lots of exercise, and no alternative to satisfy your ravenous hunger other than cooking for yourself and your grateful hunting companions. And it doesn't take much time, so the cook doesn't miss a minute of hunting. For frying stuff, all you need is a 12-inch skillet, cast iron for cooking on a fire, Teflon-coated pressed steel for cooking on a butane burner. For stew, a medium-sized (about $2\frac{1}{2}$ gallons) stew pot is required. For baking using a butane (propane) oven, baking or roasting pans such as those used around the house will work; for baking using a fire and coals, you'll need a cast-iron Dutch oven. You'll also need a few big spoons, some mixing bowls, a big fork, a spatula for eggs and pancakes, and a big spoon or ladle to stir stew.

The recipes that follow are for three or four people; for eight people, make up twice the amount stated. If you want your elk camp cooking to be at a higher level than mine, look up Storm Creek Outfitters and sign up for Lorrie's Dutch oven camp cooking class. Make it part of a scouting trip. Folks say that I don't know very much about good camp cooking, but I know it when I taste it.

Starting with breakfast, first we need some coffee to be able to do anything else. Some folks seem mildly surprised that coffee can be made without electricity. You can make it correctly if you have the right kind of coffeepot—one that sits on a burner or stove with insides that hold ground coffee so that heated water perks up through a central stem to the top of the pot and flows back down through the coffee. You need to pay attention to the steam and listen for it to start perking. Then take it off the stove after it's perked a few minutes, before it gets too strong. Pour a sample in a white cup to see if it's strong enough. Some camp cooks take pride in throwing the factory-supplied insides of the coffee perker away so that you have to make the coffee by boiling ground coffee in the pot, then pouring in cold water, which theoretically makes the grounds settle out so that you don't need to strain them through your teeth. Very uncivilized.

Now to cook eggs and bacon, sausage, or ham. Simply fry the meat in a skillet until it looks done. It's normal for it to be partly overcooked, partly undercooked. That's okay, because all we need to do is cook out enough grease to cook the eggs. Take the meat out and break the eggs into the hot grease. Set the skillet off of the stove or burner to keep the grease from getting hot enough to splatter on you. Salt and pepper the eggs while they cook. You can easily tell by their appearance when they're done. If you want to bother, you can carefully turn them over to custom order of the eaters—or just fill up the skillet with eggs and scramble them all together. It's your call, since you're the cook. You can warm bread in the slightly greasy skillet to toast it. A big blob of jelly and you're set. Eat it fast before it gets cold.

You may want to make pancakes on alternate days. Don't mess with making them from scratch; just get a just-add-water mix and follow the directions on the box. You've got to get out hunting.

French toast is a good use for sandwich white bread after it's been around for several days. Make an egg batter of half a dozen eggs, a little less than a cup of milk, a dab of vanilla, and a dash of cinnamon. Soak and coat the bread in the batter for a minute and cook it like a pancake on a lightly greased skillet or griddle. You can get all of this stuff going at the same time, so that breakfast shouldn't take more than thirty minutes or so. A small camp stove with multiple burners is the best way to cook breakfast.

Pack outfits and most private hunting parties have cold-cut sandwiches, fruit, and other easily carried goodies to take along for lunch while hunting. Whole smoked turkey breast makes a great sandwich. But a real delicacy is elk venison heart sandwiches. Soak the freshly taken heart in cold water, making it easy to cut apart to remove the stiffened blood. After it's thoroughly cleaned, boil it in a stew pot until it's soft to a sharp fork, which should take about an hour on a big burner. Then slice it across into pieces about $1/4$ inch thick. Served as a sandwich on the side of a mountain with a little fancy mustard between two pieces of bread . . . mmmm!

For the evening meal, you can cook any slab of meat bought in a store—steak, ham, pork chop, or lamb chop—by frying it in a skillet. All of these cuts will contain enough fat to cook in their own grease; just keep the fire down so that you don't get things too smoky. Too much smoke is smoke you can't easily see through—and it happens just before you have a fire. Temperature is easy to control when using a gas burner; simply turn the burner down. Cooking over a campfire is a little more tricky. You usually set the skillet on a ring of rocks or on a steel grill resting on rocks. Move the skillet around relative to the hot spots of the flame or bed of coals to control the temperature. With either source of heat, turn the meat over after it browns on one side to cook the other side. Repeat the turning until it's cooked through. For meat without its own grease—that's wild-game meat slices (cut them thin across the grain), liver, heart, fish, or any kind of fowl after it's cut into small pieces—you need to start with some grease or vegetable oil in the skillet. I like to pepper meat as it starts cooking with enough ground black pepper to lightly cover the entire surface. I salt meat much more sparingly. Most fried meat goes better if you add thin slices of onion after the meat has cooked some. Same goes for big, mild green peppers if you have some. Meat needs to fry slowly to keep from burning. The small camp stoves are about right.

You treat vegetables like meat that doesn't have its own grease. The staple for hunting camps is potatoes and onions. Peel and slice a couple of pounds or more of potatoes and onions about $1/4$ inch thick. You can pour vegetable oil over them while they're still cold to give the slices a good coating and end up with about $1/4$ inch of oil in the bottom of the skillet. If you use grease, you'll want to warm it up first, but don't get it too hot or it may splatter and blister your skin. Potatoes will be dark brown when they're done. You can sample them a slice at a time (cooled) to see when they start to soften as they cook. Shake salt on the potatoes as they cook, shaking it onto your hand as you go so that you won't put too much on. You can't see salt on potatoes in a dark tent. Two palms' worth of salt shaken over thin will be about right. The eaters can put on more to their taste, but it's the very devil to get the stuff out once it's cooked into the food. It takes a good flame to cook up a 12-inch skillet of heaped-up potatoes.

As an alternative to fried potatoes, you can bake or mash them. To bake, cover the surface of the potatoes with grease or butter, wrap them in aluminum foil, and bake them in a gas-fired oven at 400 degrees or in the coals of a campfire for a couple of hours or until they're soft to squeeze. For mashed potatoes, peel and cut the potatoes into small pieces and boil until soft. Mash all of the lumps out, and pour in a little milk while stirring until you get the correct consistency; add salt and pepper to taste. As another alternative, dice peeled potatoes as if you were going to fry them, but boil them instead. Salt and pepper them, then blend in a can of condensed mushroom or onion soup, partly mashing the potatoes in the process, but leaving them in the diced shape for the most part.

To cook a stew, start by browning about 3 pounds of meat cut into 1-inch cubes in the stew pot or a separate skillet. You'll need to add a little oil or grease for meat that doesn't have much fat in it. Cover the entire surface of the meat with black pepper when you start. Add five medium-sized sliced onions, selected to be a little on the hot side, as the meat starts to turn brown. That flavors the meat more than just adding the onions to the rest of the stew later with the rest of the vegetables. Add enough water to fill the stew pot about one-third full. Get the fire hot enough to bring the water to a boil and stir enough to keep everything from sticking to the bottom of the pot. Add enough salt to cover the palm of one hand to the heating water. Add about 5 pounds of potatoes that have been peeled and cut into 1-inch or so cubes. From this point on, the potatoes are what you use to tell if the stew is cooked. They'll be soft when it's ready. Add inch-long pieces of celery and carrots to cook along with the potatoes. A package of celery that contains a dozen stalks and a package of about a dozen large carrots seems to work out about right. At about this point, cover the surface of the water with black pepper (through the holes of the shaker) a couple of times. You'll want a fair-sized fire under the stew to keep it cooking along, and you'll need to stir it often enough to keep things from sticking to the bottom of the pot. Little camping stoves that use the little bottles of gas are often undersized for this job. The bigger burners that are 6 inches across and that can throw a blue flame about 4 inches high will do the job in about an hour or so. As the stew finishes cooking, you may want to add a can of English peas, corn, and/or stewed tomatoes. At this point you'll find out if you added too much water to start with; if you have to lose some liquid, drain the extra off of the canned stuff and try to save the good broth that has the salt and pepper cooked in. It takes longer to make a stew than the fried stuff, and, in order to make sure that cooking doesn't interfere with quality elk hunting time, I usually make it the afternoon before the season starts, on very hot or very rainy afternoons when there's zero chance of seeing an elk, or in the evening after we've already had dinner. Stew is usually better the next day anyway, and will keep for days as long as the weather is reasonably cool.

Baking using a Dutch oven and a campfire takes a little technique. Some accomplished camp cooks use a Dutch oven almost exclusively for all of the cooking that they do. The normal approach is to build a fire and let it burn down to a good coal bed. Food to be baked or roasted is placed inside the lightly greased interior surface of the oven, which is then set down in the bed of glowing coals. Glowing coals are then spread thick over the lid (which is made with a deep rim to hold coals). The bed of coals is banked a little with ashes and the food is allowed to cook. A lot of the technique involved pertains to getting the heat to the correct temperature and then maintaining that temperature over the required cooking time. Both of these variables depend to a great extent on the wood available in the local area, techniques of banking the coals, and a lot of other secret, mysterious stuff known only to master camp cooks who won't explain it to the rest of us or everybody would be a master camp cook. Roasting meat requires holding the temperature longer, but baking biscuits, bread, or desserts is actually more difficult because they overcook or burn easier. A gas oven with a temperature setting is simple in comparison, disdainfully simple to an expert camp cook. Those of us who are self-proclaimed noncooks easily swallow our pride along with our not-so-badly burned biscuits in a hurry and get on out hunting.

We noncooks also don't spend the time to work up the starter for sourdough bread and pancakes as do the "real" cooks among us. The biscuits in the smash-open cardboard cans and pancake and cake mix from a box work just fine. Plus, the directions are right on the containers.

Pot roasts of beef, pork, or lamb with vegetables make really good camp chuck. Brown 5 to 8 pounds of roast in the Dutch oven, or in an oven roaster if you're using a gas oven. Salt the surface lightly and give it a good covering of ground black pepper. Cook it hot, a little over 400 degrees, for about thirty minutes, then take the meat out long enough to add about 2 or 3 pounds of cut-up potatoes, onions, and carrots. Cook the meat and veggies together at a lower temperature now, a little over 300 degrees, until it's done, which will take from two to three hours. Check the meat for softness with a sharp fork or knife to see when it's done.

To make meatloaf, mix four or five eggs with about a dozen sort of stale slices of sandwich bread, and blend the mixture by hand into about 5 pounds of ground beef. Work in a good covering of ground black pepper and a couple of chopped medium-sized hot onions. Bake for about an hour at a little under 400 degrees.

For dessert, pudding mix is handy and doesn't take up burner time. Lots of camps like cobblers and baked pies that sort of simulate what they remember their grandmother making. You can find instructions on canned pie fillings, and make pie dough from your granny's old recipe or use canned biscuit dough for a passable dessert.

Here's a really good, really fast dessert. I call it "Wes's Take on Herm's Version of Chris's Cobbler," although strictly speaking it's not a down-home southern-type cobbler, but a variation called a "country cobbler." Dump a cup of flour, a little less than a cup of white sugar, a blob of brown sugar, a dab of baking powder, and a dash of cinnamon into a mixing bowl and mix while adding milk until it stirs smooth. Melt anywhere from just a good covering up to as much as $1/4$ pound of butter in a baking pan or Dutch oven. Dump the mix into the melted butter, then spoon in a pie-sized can of your fruit of choice—apple, peach, cherry, pineapple, or whatever. Bake it at a little under 400 degrees for about thirty minutes, or until it's cooked past the gooey stage all the way through, with a light amber brown color on the surface.

Note that the heavy-duty cooking is being done with gas. A microwave is handy for light, quick warming, but that's about all.

CHAPTER 18

Physical and Mental Conditioning

Conditioning is critical to the ability to execute the techniques required by the particular strategy, equipment, and hunting arrangement you have chosen. This one of those areas where you have to reconcile desires with capability. Some people are not going to be able to leap high mountains in a single bound, no matter how hard they train; it's better to pick a different strategy rather than take on something you can't safely handle.

PHYSICAL CONDITIONING

Being in the best state of physical conditioning that you can attain will pay off in elk hunting success in the long run. You will be able to get into the tough places where the big bulls have their hideouts; you will be able to maneuver freely and in a hurry and keep downwind if the big bull comes to the bugle; you will be able to crawl up from the road along the river and hunt the river slopes that nobody else can get to on your own rather than having to book an expensive outfitter hunt so you can use their horses to get back into the high slopes.

I should clarify the meaning of "conditioning." Everyone has some physical limitations; even the competitive Iron Man athletes I have hunted with have their limits.

It's all just a matter of working around your limitations. But some kind of scheme can be worked out for just about anybody to go elk hunting. The point is, if you have some kind of physical challenge, it can be handled. You may want to review the section on hunting arrangements at this point to better understand what I mean. What all of us are trying to do is to hold to a minimum what we have to accommodate as far as limitations are concerned. I, for one, am slow going

Just like a stair-stepper or a 280-story stairwell, but with a better view. With diligent aerobic exercise back home and a couple of days to acclimate to the higher elevation, these gentle slopes are no sweat.

uphill. I just don't have the heart and lung capacity to go fast, and I never did. I can't change that, but I try to stay in condition so that I can keep going at my own pace. I tell my hunting companions that I just take my time and enjoy the view, and give thanks that I can do as much as I can—slowly.

You're going to need to put in some effort to get in shape to go elk hunting. You'll also need some time—probably a year, if you're not already in good shape. Resolve that you *will* put in the required effort and time, then set some realistic goals with the help of a medical professional. A personal trainer initially might be worth the cost in order to save you time and prevent injury. Take it easy at first.

Everybody is different and your doctor should advise you regarding what should be realistic in your case, but here are some guidelines. The twenty- to forty-something age group can handle about all the training they want to. Five miles or more every day would probably be about right. The only exception would be when you're just starting the program; you need to work up to your goal to avoid injuring yourself. If you're in the fifty- to sixty-something age group, you should be able to build up to jog about 5 miles or so on typical flatland suburban surfaces. Note that would be on a three-day-per-week schedule to give us old-timers some time for damage recovery. If you run with the dog every day, you might cut the duration down some, if that's okay with the dog. The seventy-something group can stay in condition to be out there along with the rest of the kids. Just be careful and avoid injury, as it takes a little longer for this group to recover. That translates to avoiding high-impact activities: Fast walking is better than the shocks of a slow jog; full-body workout devices and rowing machines build muscle and flexibility. Exercise equipment that's slightly used is often a very good deal. Just locate someone who gave up exercise and has a set gathering dust. Resellers are a good source and will have checked out what they sell for any mechanical problems. For all age groups, individuals vary. Be realistic and know your limitations. Then push them. Your attitude counts for a lot.

Some of my elk hunting friends belong to the physically impressive group of those who want to be able to leap tall mountains in a single bound. Those who work in office buildings run up and down the stairwells for one hundred stories (twice up fifty floors or ten times up ten floors or you can work out the math while you run). The down part helps the knees; the up part is for everything else. Then this bunch goes to the gym on the off days to work on body strength. If you can run up and down one hundred stories during your lunch break, then go back to work in the office the rest of the afternoon, you can handle the most challenging elk hunting situations. This would also be on a schedule of two to three times a week; cut the number of flights in half if you try it every day.

You really don't need to take it that far in order to hunt elk. Just keep your weight down to a reasonable level, make the 5-mile jog a few times a week, and you can get up the hill. Try to get in some cross-country work wearing your hunting boots along with the track and street exercise.

You don't need to have mountains to get ready for the mountains. Stair-stepper machines and treadmills allow you to work with steep inclines. Both exercise and develop your climbing muscles. Running up and down a high-rise building stairway is probably even better if you have access to one. It's hard to get your downhill muscles developed otherwise. Develop your aerobic capacity by running outside or on a treadmill, then use progressive resistance machines to develop upper-body strength and full-body workout machines for your overall body workout. The machines seem to have less chance of injury than free weights for those of us more interested in elk hunting than bodybuilding.

Special training can help you deal with very steep slopes that occur in Idaho or other locations on the Cascade side of the Rockies. Slopes in these regions can also be covered with loose dirt and other weathered material from the underlying granite. You'll quickly learn to follow elk trails when moving around slopes as well as up and down slopes, but the trails won't always go where you are heading. Your boots need to be fitted at the ankle to provide support, but your ankles and knees should also be strengthened by exercise. Part of your aerobic exercise program might include slow cross-country jogging over rough ground and ground covered by short vegetation. (This had better not include growing crops or you'll get in trouble with the farmer, but with permission, you might use plowed ground.) Sandy beaches or sandy desert country provide a soft surface for resistance, if you can get to them. You can't go as fast cross-country as on paved surfaces. About 3 or 4 miles in an hour should be okay. Again, take care to avoid injury.

Regarding that sobering idea of risk of injury, there's an association that every individual has to address in his or her own way: The little bumps, bruises, and scrapes that can progress in severity toward major falls, slides, rolls, joint dislocations, bone fractures, and so on take longer to shake off as we travel along life's trail. Those of us who want to be out there on opening morning of elk season eventually figure out that it's just a helluvalot easier to avoid the wreck than to recover from it. So we look at all aspects of exercise and outdoor activities from the perspective of risk as well as the payoff. Rather than run cross-country at full speed in the deepening twilight, we walk and augment the program with some reps on the machines; we take the main trail back to camp instead of the shortcut straight down over the rock slides. Make sure your performance expectations are in line with your age.

Hiking is good exercise and easy on the joints for the "mature" elk hunter. In preparing for it, try to simulate what you'll encounter in the mountains. I've mentioned the technique of running up and down stairwells for the upper-level physically fit group. Everybody else can walk (climb) the stairwells at his or her own speed. Other mountain simulations available to the flatlander are earthen embankments, gravel pits, earthen dams, landscape breaks at rivers, roadway and residential developments where the dirt has been shoveled around, and sand dunes along beaches or in deserts.

Bicycle riding will strengthen legs for climbing and save the knees for those of us a little heavy on our feet. A personal trainer might help with special conditioning to strengthen knees and ankles. Strengthening the legs in general in all directions seems to provide additional support.

It's a good idea to do your practice hiking over terrain and trails in the same boots you'll wear for hunting. Your feet and legs need to be toughened to the conditions of the hunt to the greatest extent possible, and you need to learn the little details of foot care required to keep your feet working at top efficiency. Try to do some practice hiking off of improved trails and under rainy, muddy conditions and over some rocks if you can find some, and see how you and your footwear do under different conditions. Most of my buddies, guides included, and I have gone hunting with footwear that seemed great on the flatlands but didn't have either the traction or the durability for elk hunting.

Using a bow and arrow requires extra upper-body strength. Conventional workouts for strength development don't do enough for the across-the-shoulder area, where strength is required to draw a bow of sufficient draw weight for elk hunting. Despite arguments to the contrary, the size and stamina difference between elk and deer means that elk hunting requires more arrow power and penetration. Female bowhunters have to put in extra effort to meet this challenge, but they can do it with modern compound bows.

MENTAL CONDITIONING

The admonishment that a person needs to have the proper mental attitude to be successful in elk hunting is often received like the advice that you shouldn't panic when you realize that you're lost. It's kind of like advice to be confident when faced with taking an important exam tomorrow, or when you're a teenage driver walking out the door to go take the all-important driving test. The confidence is already there when you've received good classroom instruction and then studied so you know the material covered on the exam. It's already there when you've been taught all the driving techniques you need and put in plenty of practice well before the test day. In both cases, you have confidence not because of some admonishment; you have confidence because you know what you're doing. Likewise, if you read through all of these instructions and practice the skills described until you have mastered them to the level described in each section, you'll have confidence regardless of what anybody says. You know that you have what you need to be successful.

If you know what you're doing, you'll be able to enjoy the hunt with respect for the wilderness but without fear of it. As my old guide friend might say, you'll be ready to get lucky. I finally came to understand that "Lucky" could pass for the name of any old bull elk that's been around for a while. But remember, "Ole Lucky" will probably give you the slip a few times before he's on your wall, if that's important to you. The best big-league baseball players are put out two-thirds of the time; the best hockey players may take forty shots before they score the winning goal. They're still the best. They know they're the best, whether the fans do or not. And you're ready to get lucky, or Lucky, even if it's next year or next decade. And your opinion is the only one that counts.

The most important thing about all of this is that it isn't just limited to the elk hunting. You develop this confidence before you go to the mountains, and then you take it away when you leave. Then you bring it back to the flatlands proofed out and verified, regardless of whether you connected with the elk or not. You'll know that you can climb any slope, no matter how steep. It always has to level out eventually.

COMBINING MENTAL AND PHYSICAL CONDITIONING: PRACTICE THE WAY YOU'LL HUNT, THEN HUNT THE WAY YOU'VE PRACTICED

As we draw the discussion of practice and equipment to a close, it's worthwhile to repeat that practice with your equipment should include *all* the gear you will have on your person while hunting. You may need to make a shot in a hurry as you make the transition from locating to stalking to making the kill, and more than just the rifle or bow is involved in this transition. You need to practice the way you're going to hunt, and this includes the wearing of coats, hats, and daypacks and the arrangement you choose for ammo or arrow carry.

It's very important to reload from the ammo carry that you will use hunting. Make it automatic. The same goes for spare arrows. Ditto for muzzleloader reloads. You can maintain absolute focus on only one thing at a time and that needs to be making the shot. Practice so that you can shoot an elk even if you've lost your breath and your mind.

DEVELOPING SITUATIONAL AWARENESS AND PREDICTIVE INTUITION

Elk hunting requires mental keenness; you must be aware of the situation at all times and constantly be planning your next move, the best reaction to any conceivable development. Anticipation goes beyond awareness during the hunt to include maintenance of self and gear. Anticipate all possible developments by role playing them on fast-forward in your mind, and you'll develop a sort of intuition, and be able to come up with a solution without a long process of problem solving at the most inconvenient time.

As I discussed in the chapter on making the kill, practice hunting—any hunting other than elk hunting that involves the same kinds of skills—is a good way to learn how to handle your equipment in action. It also allows you to develop physical and mental skills as well as that elusive situational awareness that's essential to elk hunting. Best yet, you can do it all year, as opposed to that week or so that's usually available for nonresidents to hunt elk.

Coyote hunting is available throughout most of the country and can involve movement and stalking, and challenging shots. The approach to make coyote hunting good preparation for elk hunting is to do it according to the rules of fair chase. No calling to bring the coyotes to your ambush; get out and walk them down. You'll need permission to hunt over a considerable distance in those parts of the country where private ownership prevails. You'll learn to use fencerows as screens against the coyotes' excellent long-range vision, and work into the wind to thwart their keen sense of smell. Moving and pausing at the edge of cover will become second nature. You can expect shots to pop up anywhere from 20 feet to 500 yards. I've made and missed both.

The new game in town is wild hog hunting, usually feral populations, but Russian imports in some areas and mixed in others. The same rules of fair chase apply if you want to make this good practice hunting for elk; hunt on foot so that it's a reasonable analogue of elk hunting with the three phases of locate, stalk, and make the kill. The three phases of the hunt pertain, but the scale of the action tends to be shorter range than with coyotes since there's usually closer cover in pig country and their vision is limited. The added flavor is that the piggies in some areas run in little extended family groups of thirty to forty animals of all sizes, and things can get exciting if they decide to run at the stalker rather than away. The preferred equipment in areas where they're many and aggressive is high-capacity magazines in semiautomatic rifles, and side arms with big clips for the bowhunters. Except, of course, in the case of very fast runners and/or good tree climbers. I, for one, am neither.

Any hunting that includes the three phases of elk hunting makes you a better elk hunter. Even better than the physical familiarity of handling equipment and yourself in exciting hunting situations is the situational awareness such hunting gives you. With this awareness, things don't seem to move so fast about you during the critical phases of completing the stalk and making the kill. With experience, you can master the intuitive level of situational predictive awareness and initiate actions yourself rather than reacting to the situation as it develops.

ATTRIBUTES OF THE SUCCESSFUL ELK HUNTER

I've become acquainted with a lot of elk hunters along the way. I pay attention to the successful ones. They're the ones you can learn from. So my notes on almost forty seasons as of this writing include a list of the notable attributes of these successful hunters. I include them in this section because developing them is part of mental preparation for elk hunting. In addition to a love of elk hunting and elk country—which goes a long way toward a positive experience—the successful elk hunters I've know have displayed the following qualities:

- Determination
- Confidence
- Optimism
- Enthusiasm
- Flexibility
- Focus
- A slightly self-deprecating sense of humor

PART III

Arranging Your Hunt

Part III includes everything a person needs to make an intelligent choice from among the different hunting arrangements available to get the most enjoyable hunting experience. In the Introduction, I mentioned in passing that there's a lot more to elk hunting than taking an elk. It's in this part of the book that we get into these intangibles. Your choices become more complicated when you start to introduce these intangibles, the factors you can't assign a number to: Are you interested in a trophy bull, or is your main goal elk venison? Would you prefer to hunt from an outfitter-provided wilderness pack camp? How important is it to you that there be very few other hunters in the area you hunt? Would you prefer to pack your camp in, and your elk out, on a packboard? Are you physically capable of transporting your gear and camp to a remote hunting area yourself, or would you be better off booking a pack camp hunt with an outfitter? Would you prefer to camp by the side of the road and use logging roads to access a likely hunting area by ATV? I'll not wander too far off into the esoteric, but you'll need to be conscious of these intangibles so that they can be factored into the plan for your elk hunt along with the facts and figures.

CHAPTER 19

Outfitters and Related Arrangements

This chapter will give you an idea of what the deal is with outfitters. It's intended for the person who's thinking about trying what many feel is the ultimate hunting experience, a guided elk hunt out of a wilderness pack camp. Like a lot of nonresident elk hunters, I have more experience with this type of hunt than with any other type of arrangement. I've seen outfitter pack camps from the perspective of the first-time hunter on a guided hunt, and later, after some years of hard-earned inexperience, from an insider's viewpoint as part owner of a good hunter-owned outfit with an outfitter and expert packer as one of the partners.

A good outfitter pack camp is worth the cost for the typical elk hunter with time constraints. The operative term here is "good." There are some that are not so good. It's lucky for us flatlanders that there are many, many times more of the good type than the others. Otherwise, we couldn't enjoy wilderness elk hunting to the extent that we can. It's also in the best interests of the outfitters to keep it that way. Otherwise, hunters would eventually work out other arrangements. The outfitters keep things in line themselves through organizations called outfitter associations, which exist in all states that have elk hunting available.

Although this section is intended to give the reader some insight into the intangibles of the pack camp hunt, it won't be all morning mists and evening campfires. My purpose here is to introduce you to all aspects of the outfitter pack camp. I'll deal in realities, the way pack camps will look to you, not misty memories of just the good part. I'll hand out some tips on how to get along in an elk camp, which usually has the secondary effects of improving your luck as well as your enjoyment, safety, and general well-being. I'll also give a few indicators that can help you tell whether you're in a not-so-good outfitter camp or just having bad luck in a good camp, and I'll give you some tips on how to make the best of a less-than-perfect situation.

DIFFERENT KINDS OF OUTFITTER ARRANGEMENTS
The outfitter pack camp defines elk hunting in the minds of most people who have given the subject much consideration. The picture of a pack string pulling up the trail brings to mind images of an earlier time in the history of this country, a time of the Old West. I suspect that the intangible aspects of the opportunity to be immersed in this image for a time is a part of the appeal of elk hunting to some people, perhaps just as much as the challenge of the pursuit of the elk. There is something real behind that image that draws some of us back to the mountains again and again. You don't always take an elk, but you can have a great hunt even if you pack out with your tag still in your pocket.

Most novice elk hunters will book an outfitter hunt termed as "deluxe," or a "deluxe guided hunt." Note that the term "deluxe" has a whole different connotation than what you'll see in five-star hotel listings. In the context of elk hunting, "deluxe" means a hunt with the full complement of guides, either one guide for each hunter or one guide for every two hunters; a camp cook; a packer; and sometimes a campjack, who handles all of the rest of the camp chores. The outfitter supplies everything except personal gear, including a place to stay, usually a tent with a wood-burning stove and cot or some type of bed off of the ground where you use your personal bedroll; all food and preparation of food; camp chores; all stock required—horses to ride and packhorses or mules to transport gear and provisions and pack out game taken. The accommodations on a deluxe hunt may be either fancy or plain (camp cots or real beds with mattresses). The deal should specify the ratio of guides to hunters, as well as the number of days of the hunt, whether those days include packing in or out, and what circumstances might cut off the hunt early. Most outfitters give you the original number of days you signed up for regardless of whether your tags are filled or whatever, but some consider your hunt over if you shoot and cripple, but don't collect. Others contend it's over if you're presented a shot and miss, or pass on a shot if it's not the trophy you're after. I'm not aware of any convention among outfitters on this point, and most outfitters will go to all lengths to satisfy their clients. I just suggest that everybody knows all aspects of the deal up front.

The guides are expected to primarily help locate elk and coach stalking. They'll also field dress and cape and salt the trophy hide for the trip to the taxidermist (this is usually considered an extra service and merits an extra tip for whoever does the job, although the outfitter will usually defer if he helps).

You'll see some differences in camps in designated wilderness area camps where internal combustion engines are not allowed at all and in national forest or Bureau of Land Management (BLM) land camps, which allow power units but may limit use of motorized vehicles. Horses work fine for transport, but for whoever has the responsibility to keep the camp going, you do miss that chainsaw in wilderness camps. And the hand that swings the axe and pulls the crosscut saw can't be doing other camp chores at the same time. There's very little multitasking in the woods—unless the cook is also the mama of the littlest campjack. So the outfitter's expenses in a wilderness area tend to be a little higher, to go along with a higher "blue sky" cost sunk to get the outfitter concession for the area. But these "drawbacks" of designated wilderness areas are associated with a distinct advantage as far as elk hunters are concerned. No roads! Restricted access! Fewer hunters! All this means a lower disturbance level of the elk. And the herd bulls have better chances of surviving additional years to produce more impressive racks—and to gain more experience that makes them more difficult to hunt, which is another good thing for a lot of us.

Outfitters often offer another arrangement with less service at a lower price than the "deluxe" camp. A "drop" camp (sometimes called a "spot" camp) arrangement involves the outfitter packing the hunters and camp into the area, then simply dropping off the camp for the hunters to use while they hunt on their own. The usual deal is for the outfitter to provide transport for hunters, their gear, and provisions. The provisions may or may not be provided by the outfitter as part of the deal. Provisions may be preset in the camp or packed in with the hunters—the local bears usually determine which. The outfitter may provide the tent and camp stoves, or the hunters may furnish the whole outfit. It's important to remember that if the outfitter doesn't provide everything you'll need, or think you'll need, for the duration of the hunt, 24/7, in any weather, you'll need to take it along in your personal gear. Provisions and comfort contribute to the well-being that keeps you enjoying hard hunting during your time in the mountains. Normally, the outfitter checks back regularly to see if the hunters need anything, and will pack out game if they've had success. Some outfitters offer to provide a campjack to keep camp, and maybe cook or help cook. As with any type of service, the more services provided, the greater the cost. Outfitters who offer drop camps are normally set up to offer a particular package, and it usually works out best to go with the usual arrangement rather than trying to arrange a custom deal. The outfitter may assume that you know the Forest Service rules for wilderness camping; it goes without saying that all of these details need to be understood by all parties before they meet at the trailhead. Drop camp arrangements appeal to experienced hunters who have enough elk hunting and outdoor skills that they don't need the services of guides, and are willing to do camp chores, or may even enjoy them.

Occasionally, you can arrange a deal where you pack your own stuff into an outfitter's area—on a packboard, trail bike, your personal packhorse, or whatever you want to use—and then when you get luck the outfitter will pack out the meat and possibly trophy. Caution: You had better get the deal worked out well ahead of time or the service may come at a high price, if it comes at all—and then it will come at the schedule and convenience of the packer.

UNDERSTANDING OUTFITTERS

To understand the outfitter, you need to put yourself in his old, worn-out, run-down, horse manure–covered boots for a quarter mile or so. To begin with, the wild and free outdoor cowboy life of the outfitter is neither as wild nor as free as it might appear. He, or sometimes she, is a small-business owner with at least five or six bosses. The first boss is usually the banker or some other moneylender. The second is the USDA Forest Service. The third is the state Fish and Game Department. The fourth is the state outfitters association. The fifth is the outfit. The sixth is the client—that's us. Any one of these bosses except the last can put the outfitter out of business immediately; the last takes a little longer. If you want to hang on to the illusion that there is one line of work still around where you're your own boss with the freedom to do what you please out under the western skies just like in the movies, you may want to skip the next few paragraphs.

An outfitter stays in trouble in the money department a lot of the time. In order to get into the outfit business, the outfitter first "buys" an area from another outfitter. Despite the terminology, the "owner" of an outfit area obtains far less than full property rights. It's still public land controlled by the government. The outfitter only has the right to charge clients to pack them and their stuff in and out of the area along with any game taken. They can also charge anyone else hunting in the area that may ask for help in getting game out. (Incidentally, this can be a little expensive for hunters unless you've made previous arrangements, since the outfitter, the only one with the right to do that work, really

Some of that guide and packer payroll time is devoted to tasks other than guiding and packing—like haircuts on the biting and kicking ends of the mules.

Baby getting a new pair of shoes—one of the year-round outfitter expenses not obvious to clients.

isn't under any obligation to help.) On top of that expense, which is about the cost of a farm or ranch, the outfitter needs to buy pack and saddle stock, tack and equipment, and vehicles; pay year-round for the upkeep of same; and meet a payroll for the guides, cook, and anybody else needed to operate the outfit. The only thing that the outfitter can count on year after year is that the stock will need to be fed every day, and the equipment will need to be replaced or repaired every few years.

And those wilderness trails that the old, fire-killed trees happen to fall across don't clear themselves through natural processes. Sometimes the outfitter contracts with the Forest Service and gets compensated for big trail-clearing jobs along the main, government-maintained trails, but the occasional tree over the trail after a big wind is handled by the outfit hands. Fires and beetle kill can bring more trees down than can be handled by the routine arrangements. The resulting problems fall in the lap of the outfitter.

What the outfitter can't count on is a full quota of booked hunters to show up, money in hand, when it comes time to pack up the trail.

The next boss after the money source is the Forest Service, which has just about complete authority as to whether or not the outfitter is in line with all of the federal regulations that go with his permits for all camp locations. Then comes the state Fish and Game Department, which has authority over the game in the area. It controls the number of permits or tags issued, and, indirectly, the composition of the elk herds in the area. Sometimes federal agencies work for, with, or against the state agencies when federal statutes and regulations are involved, like those regarding endangered species such as wolves. Then things can get really complicated.

The state outfitters association is not a government agency; it's made up of the outfitters. It primarily keeps the outfitters themselves up to professional standards. Within the outfitters associations, the large, long-established outfitters tend to look out for themselves when numbers of tags are limited or other troubles show up. These associations are political in that they have some influence in the decisions made by state agencies—mostly, in my opinion, because of us flatlanders who bring a lot of money into the state. We pay the high-priced license and tag fees that go directly to the state, and everybody else shares in the rest of the money that we spend on the hunt.

Outfitters that stay in business realize at some fundamental level that they're in the entertainment business just like sports teams, sitcoms, game shows, or symphony orchestras. There is a difference in that the quarterback practicing passes or the cello player practicing a scale has a pretty good idea of what you expect for the price of your ticket. The outfitter and the hunter don't necessarily have an accurate idea of what they expect from each other in the entertainment to be provided. The outfitter gets ready every fall to provide a hunt similar to those that have satisfied most of his clients in the past. The exact nature of the hunt that he can provide depends to a certain extent on the characteristics of his area, the weather this fall and spring, the capabilities of the hunters, and a hundred other factors over which the outfitter has absolutely no control. As you ask questions and gather information in preparation for booking a hunt with a particular outfitter, you need to do the best you can to get lined up with one that is set up to provide the type of entertainment that appeals to you. And both you and the outfitter need to understand what your measure of success is: flat-out whether you take an elk or not, the quality of the wilderness experience, the level of physical exertion you have to put forth to be successful, good food, good company, good guides, or all or none of the above. You'll need to figure out what your own intangible preferences are so that you and the outfitter can make a deal acceptable to both.

EVALUATING OUTFITTERS

I've known a lot of outfitters, packers, guides, cooks, and hunters over the years; I have close friends among each type. I've never known of a single one of any type that went in hoping to have a camp that was less than the best. However, there *are* some outfitters that are not so good, whether through carelessness or financial troubles or lack of the necessary skills. We'll go over some key signs that can tell you what kind of operation you're looking at: a good one, a bad one, or an offbeat one. Offbeat here is a good thing, often very good. It's just goodness—efficiency and effectiveness—in a form that you're not expecting. Some hunters will pronounce these operations bad on appearance and their hunting experience suffers because of it.

Characteristics of a Good Outfit

Top outfits are always a full-time, year-round operation, the only business interest of the owners, who are also the everyday, hands-on managers. They love what they do and are capable and willing to do any job required to keep the outfit going strong, from talking it up at sports shows to tracking down and field dressing the worst gut-shot-up mess of a kill for the most loud-mouthed obnoxious hunter imaginable. They'll be well financed—the best case is family financed, including extended family—and free of debt owed to conventional lending institutions. Outfit personnel (hands, never staff) are all first-rate and keep their personal problems under their hats. Equipment is well maintained.

Good outfitters can be sorted into grades of good by looking at the riding and pack stock. In all good outfits, there'll be enough stock for the job of shuttling supplies, hunters, and gear to camps without having to

A blue roany measuring sixteen hands, with a rider and her truck for size comparison.

use any animal with a lingering injury. In addition, the better outfits will have riding and pack stock that are well trained, but not too old. The very best outfits can be spotted by the size of the stock. Mounts will be mostly big geldings. All of the outfitters in a region go to the same stock auction sales, and the ones that care the most and can afford the best outbid the others. At hunting shows or anywhere else, all you need to do is point the discussion toward the stock, and the good outfitters get to talking about the stock. Check outfitters' flyers for pictures that include people and horses and vehicles if possible. Stocky horses that seat you close to the top of a truck and are longer from back to belly than your legs are a nice size; either side of sixteen hands high is good.

The Offbeat: Good Pack Camps May Not Look like What You Expect

The outfits, outfitter, guides, and packers might not look like they just stepped off the set of a high-budget western movie production. (Interestingly enough, sometimes they have, bringing in a little cash during the off-season. Packers as outlaws. Bays as cavalry horses. Paints as Indian ponies.)

Some outfits are operated as a whole-family operation. The experienced guide is the father of the packer and grandfather of the campjack. The mother is the camp cook, and she does her job while keeping an eye on the campjack. And you might find other double duties: mixed strings of pack stock with horses used to pack in provisions, then carry hunters; guides that have to cut loose from their regular jobs during hunting season.

AN "OFF-COLOR" OFFBEAT OUTFITTER

The standard color for pack outfit tents is white. Strange complications arise when a tent of another color is used, which usually happens when the outfitter comes across a terrific buy on tents of another color. Green, for instance.

This first came to my attention when Herm and Leroy set up in a new area with a brand new cook tent, one that happened to be green. The first night in camp was fine, as was breakfast early the next morning in the predawn hours. Then, for some unexplainable reason, all of the frozen meat that had been packed in for the hunt suddenly spoiled, even the meat deep inside the cooler that remained frozen. Herm showed me the mournful situation as I pulled back in to camp about midafternoon after a long scouting hike. He couldn't explain the wastage, even with all his years of experience in elk camps. The whole situation looked to be making him physically ill. There was even a green cast to his complexion, at least the parts of his face not covered by his lightly green-tinted beard.

"Let's take a look at it outside," I suggested, "so we can get a better look at it in the sunlight."

We walked out into the open. Herm took a long look at the now fresh-looking slab of meat, another look up at the clear, blue mountain sky, turned on his heel without a word, walked back into the green cook tent, and banged the skillet down on the stove.

The Bad

Now we'll discuss some characteristics to look for as an indication that you're in a not-so-good outfitter camp—and some questions to ask before booking to prevent finding yourself in one.

But first: Don't rush to judge an outfitter based on what kind of success, or lack thereof, you are having. It is called "elk hunting," rather than the European term "elk shooting," for a reason. You're going to do a lot more hunting than shooting under the best of circumstances. Success in itself doesn't work as the criterion to determine a good or a bad outfitter. Weather, luck, and the conditioning and aptitude of the hunters have a lot to do with success. If there are elk in the area, as the outfitter indicated, and the outfitter is doing a good job working within your physical ability to help you get a shot, then he's doing his part.

You can't judge on appearances either. Keep in mind that even the very best pack outfit doesn't have fancy new stuff and luxurious accommodations to match the alternative vacation you could have taken instead of going elk hunting. And the outfitter and staff will not be like the people associated with that other recreation either. Outfitters, packers, guides, and camp cooks are, to use the sawmill term, usually more "rough cut." Maybe "rough cut with the bark still on" might be more descriptive. Most of us who hunt in the mountains wouldn't have it any other way; "slick and smooth" won't cut it in some of the situations the mountains may hand you.

But there are some signs that the outfitter is not one of the good ones. Here are some clues:

Is the outfitter strapped for money? Does the outfitter require a lot of money up front? Has he oversold the hunt for the area and the amount of stock available? He may have put too much money into ads to attract hunters or have debts from past troubles that he is using hunt money to pay off, leaving no money to properly finance the hunt.

Does the outfit have sorry-looking equipment? Old is okay; poorly maintained is not.

What is the condition of the stock? They aren't going to look like show animals, but they should be in good health with no injuries. If they have or quickly develop sore places on their backs from riding or pack saddles, it's an indication that the packer doesn't know what he's doing or doesn't care—either is the mark of a not-so-good outfitter. Is adequate feed for stock pre-positioned in the mountain camps, grain as well as hay? The Forest Service doesn't allow the outfitter to graze stock.

Are all of the camps, both trailhead and hunting, in place when the hunters arrive? Is the outfitter still setting up after hunters are in camp? This may indicate that the outfit job is secondary to other business interests rather than a true full-time profession. Other businesses are okay as long as they tie in with the outfitting and allow time for the outfit during hunting season.

Are the people that work for the outfitter reasonably happy and helpful? I should probably amend this to exclude the cook. Good cooking can more than make up for a bad disposition as long as the cook is not too outright dangerous when armed with kitchen utensils. Note that the folks that the outfitter can find to work at a seasonal, low-paying, demanding job under primitive conditions aren't necessarily going to be members of the church choir.

How about the chuck? It shouldn't necessarily be fancy, but it should be substantial and there should be plenty of it. You shouldn't see precooked stuff. Note whether the cook is allowed to hunt as part of the deal to come along and cook. That can lead to real trouble!

Are guides allowed to hunt on the trip? That can also lead to trouble if a guide shoots a big bull out from in front of the hunters he's supposed to be assisting.

When does the outfitter have you out in the morning—not just on your way but actually out there and ready to hunt? Breaking light to around 10 a.m. (depending on the weather) is the best time to hunt. That means being out on the mountain where the elk are at breaking light.

Are there elk in the outfitter's area? (You don't have to take anybody's word for it if you've covered the techniques of locating elk in this book!)

What to Do If You Realize That You're Out There with a Not-so-Good Outfitter

First, suppress any criminal impulses.

Second, the Better Business Bureau, the outfitters association, your lawyer, and your big ugly cousin Louie aren't out here for you right now.

Third, you need to do something rather than keeping your frustration inside; that's bad for your health. I would suggest that since you're out there, having committed your time and money for the trip, you might as well make the most of it.

Make sure that you have your licenses and elk tags if the outfitter was supposed to get them. You should always double-check that he has them if you sent money for them.

Get with the other hunters booked for the hunt and get organized. What's the situation? In a worst-case scenario, you have provisions and equipment but they're not set up, and no cook or guides because they walked out or stayed skunked up. Get the camp organized. Set up the tent and stoves, get some firewood, elect or select people to cook, chop wood, and do all the other camp chores. You'll soon develop a feeling of being campmates and hunting buddies through the team activity. Then organize the hunt together. Find out who can cover some ground and who needs to be placed somewhere on a lookout.

Get out and try to find some elk. You should be in a pretty area with some timber- or brush-covered mountains. You did take my advice and get some topo maps of the area as soon as you started talking to the outfitter, didn't you? Swing into locating. If elk are scarce because the outfitter has overbooked his area, head for the edges of his area, starting with the most rugged part of it with the thickest cover. That's right, the nastiest part—that's where you'll find the elk if they're anywhere.

Good luck. If you do get lucky, you'll probably forgive the outfitter, book in again, and be friends for life. If you're not lucky but have a good hunt without much help, you'll have the pleasure of knowing that you can hunt based on what you know yourself, and you'll probably forgive the outfitter anyway. If it still doesn't go so well, after you get back to town, there's always the outfitters association, your lawyer, your ugly cousin Louie . . .

You need to be aware that there are some operators who represent themselves as legitimate outfitters when they're really not. They will book out-of-state hunters for a pack trip into an area actually owned by another legitimate outfitter. Outfitters don't have the sole rights to hunting in what is termed "their" area, only the rights to a monopoly as far as packing for money. Anyone else is free to hunt in the area: locals, state residents, out-of-state hunters, or a private outfit of local and non-local hunting buddies. This sort of loose arrangement makes it possible for a shady operator to represent himself as an outfitter to uninformed hunters. The "outlaw" outfitter quotes them what looks to be a very good price for a pack-in hunt, and they sign up. The legitimate outfitters can usually keep up with what's going on in their area and are fully capable of taking care of themselves as far as enforcing the property rights they do have. You, as a hunter, don't want to get caught in the middle of what can result.

There are several tip-offs that you're dealing with one of these shady operators. Legitimate outfitters can usually arrange to pick up your license and tags, at least for general seasons; you usually have to work the draws in person. If the outfitter you are talking to says you have to arrange for your own tags, that's a tip-off that something might be fishy. Also, as you probably know, if a deal appears too good to be true, there's probably something wrong with it. This kind of arrangement might appear in the form of a "special" deal for the next season being offered by a guide, cook, or somebody working for an outfit that you're hunting with. It might be from somebody in a local joint down the road from the trailhead camp. It might be in the mail if somebody gets access to the outfitter's mailing list. You can always determine the actual outfitter for an area by checking with the outfitters association for the state. If you knowingly get into one of these arrangements for whatever reason, you're on your own, and you'll get no sympathy from me.

CHAPTER 20

Pack Camps: A Step Back in Time

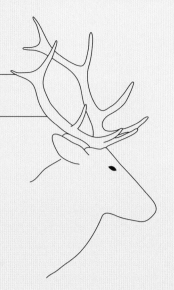

We're looking at the pack camp experience in a stand-alone chapter between outfitter and private arrangements since you may find this kind of camp in both types of arrangements.

Whether you have driven all the way in your own vehicle, or taken a flight to the nearest airport where you transferred to a rental car or were picked up by the outfitter, your final approach to the trailhead will be by road. The country always seems to become progressively more rugged and beautiful as you close in on the end of the road. In the big mountain ranges of the Northern Rockies between Idaho and Montana, the trailhead is often on a river, since the roads often follow the main drainages. That makes for a beautiful drive for the final stretch as you wind through the tall trees alongside the absolutely clear streams, both still remarkable to this old Texas boy even though I've seen them almost every fall for years now. Many of the larger trailheads are sites of old government work camps dating back to the Depression, and they'll sometimes be marked as such on maps.

Outfitter base camps, often called "river camps" since that's where the road is, always strike me as temporarily permanent, or maybe permanently temporary. They're almost always on national forest land, so they're required to be vacated when the outfitter isn't actually using the area—which is often only during the dead of winter while the snow is deep. And some areas are used all winter. Normally, everything except the hitch rail and dirt loading ramp for the stock and the government standard outhouse is on wheels or can be folded up and loaded onto something with wheels for the trip out before the snow gets too deep. But despite the fact that everything looks as if it's ready to roll out at a moment's notice, it's always parked in the exact same spot, year after

These photos taken on the same spot, facing in different directions, illustrate the meeting of wheels and hooves at the trailhead, with vehicles and stock strings coming and going between the base camp and the rest of the country.

year, for the better part of the year. So in the middle of the forest sits this nondescript permanent-looking facility that fits into the landscape as if it belongs there, which it does, with well-worn paths connecting everything—but you know that the whole mess can and will roll out in an intense couple of days' work, usually just in front of the first really deep snow.

This semi-permanent setup at the base camp is the outfitter's link between the hunting camps and the rest of the world. It usually includes a couple of wall tents with temporary-looking bunking for arriving and departing hunters. There will be some sort of a cook tent for the preparation of meals at transition times (while one group of hunters is coming out and another group going in). The cooking setup at the base camp is usually part of the temporary storage for groceries and related provisions going in to the hunting camps. This is usually an old used truck or trailer van where stuff can be stored safe from the year-round critter residents. Other facilities on wheels to support people may include a couple of campers that are used as overnight lodging for the outfitters and other packers coming and going for more provisions or to bring out meat to go to the processor or locker.

Some base camps are used throughout the year. Predator hunts, primarily cougar and wolf, follow the deer and elk seasons in the fall and winter. Snowmobile access allows for midwinter outings for hardy clients in addition to the predator hunts. Spring bear hunts are next, then it's time for spring and summer fishing and camping trips. Forest Service permits for these camps allow tents braced against the snow to remain in place on permanent floors. They can be set up for first-class accommodations.

A good part of what you'll see around the base camp is for support of the pack string and riding stock and storage of tack. A truck van or trailer is preferred to keep saddles and harness equipment out of the weather and away from the crawlers and gnawers of the animal kingdom. Grain and hay are usually stored separately from tack to remove temptations for the little fellows to eat free and entertain themselves by ruining expensive saddles at the same time. Stock will usually be confined to a corral until they are brought out and tied to a hitching rail to be fed, saddled, and loaded with packs or riders for the trip in to hunting camps.

In some locations adjacent to major government trailheads, several outfitters may share a large area in common for their base camps. There will usually also be some other local or nonresident private outfits coming or going to add to the show. The most interesting situation is when everybody has to take turns using the same unloading ramp for the bobtail stock trucks, particularly when everybody is showing up at the start of the general season. You'll see some trucks unloading, some unloaded and trying to get out past others waiting to unload, and all of the horses screaming at each other, with a few kicking the slats of the vehicle they've had enough of after the long haul into the mountains. There may be a rodeo going on as one of the outfits moves out to its base camp. The start of the season around the base camp area may leave you wondering about the mountain solitude you had in mind when you signed up for the trip. Don't worry, it comes later. Just stay out of the way as that string of llamas comes through. Really, I've seen it.

Breakfast in a busy base camp supporting drop camps and guided hunts.
STEVE BURSON

The usual arrangement is for the hunters to get to the base camp the afternoon before they ride in to the hunting camp or to a drop camp. That evening, you complete all of the financial transactions for the hunt and get your license and tags if the outfitter picked them up for you. The repeat hunters in the group have reunions with the packer and guides, and sometimes with their "pets" from the pack strings.

Finally, everybody tries to find a sleeping roll in the luggage before turning in for the night. Keep in mind that anything you unpack now has to be rounded up and stuffed back into the duffle for the trip up the trail early the next morning. I have it on good authority that, over the next several nights on the mountain, you'll miss that flashlight that you stashed to be handy during the night on the river, and then forgot to take up the trail.

The next morning everybody is up early drinking strong camp coffee and getting some breakfast. The coffee and breakfast in some outfits may be a little chancy. Some small outfits may not keep the base camp fully staffed all of the time. In this kind of setup, your breakfast depends on if you're lucky enough to have a cook around that hasn't packed in to the mountain camp already. If not, you have to settle for packer cooking or, more mercifully in some cases, maybe those crackers you brought with you. Everybody's all excited about going up the hill and it doesn't make any difference at this point. You're wishing you hadn't drunk so much of that packer coffee while you alternately get your stuff together and wait your turn at keeping the seat of that single government outhouse warm. Meanwhile, the stock is brought out to the rail and fed some grain and combed a little if they're lucky enough to work for a good outfit and some thought is given to making up the packs.

The pack cover sheets (correctly termed manta—as with most cowboy and packer gear, the origin of the name is Spanish—usually mispronounced by English speakers so that it sounds like "manny" or "matty" sheet) are spread out on the ground for the hunters to put their gear on to be made into packs. From this point on for the next several hours, the packer is the boss. He or she wraps up the gear into packs and picks two packs of perfectly matched weights for each pack animal. It's a point of pride for the packer never to use scales for this process, although there's usually a set around somewhere to settle bets and arguments between packers and guides. By the way, the quickest way to get in the doghouse with the packer is to be sure to put your 120 pounds of stuff in a single bag so that the packer can't balance it, rather than into two 60s or four 30s. That's really too much stuff anyway. The packer may threaten to drag some of it up the trail rather than pack it on the mule. Everything gets worked out within a couple of hours or so. Finally, one of the experts, a guide or the outfitter or the packer, adjusts the stirrup length and cinches up the riding saddles for the hunters. Even if you know a little about saddle adjustments and riding, you might hold back on doing all of this yourself the first time you go up the trail. The steep slopes make adjustments a different proposition, and you can get a bad rub on the horse's hide if the saddle or blanket slides out of position.

ON THE TRAIL

Next, the packer maneuvers the long string of loaded pack animals around to get them straightened out. What may strike the newcomer as aimless wandering for a few big sweeps and circles actually has a purpose—to get the string strung out so that it is actually moving with the lead ropes at the correct tension before going through the trailhead mess. When the whole bunch is raring to go, it's best if the first-time dude hunter doesn't even bring up that flashlight he just remembered he left in the cook tent, much less even consider stopping the procession and dismounting to go get it. As soon as everything is in place and all the packs are riding right, the packer leads the way up the trail, with the mounted riders falling in behind.

In big river country, the ride in often starts by crossing the river just behind the river camp. The most interesting crossings are over suspension bridges. Hair-raising interest levels for the flatlanders if the horses

Loading up.

Crossing an old swinging suspension bridge near a big river country trailhead.

or mules get in step and start swaying the bridge several feet from side to side. Matched mules often get in step on the trail, but the packer usually gets them out of sync when crossing the old cable bridges.

On the mountain trails, the right-of-way belongs to the loaded pack string going uphill. Meeting other strings coming in the opposite direction can get tricky if the view from the winding trail doesn't allow the packers of the strings coming toward each other to see the other in time

A pause for adjustments as drop-camp hunters follow their packed gear into camp. STEVE BURSON

for the downhill string to pull off of the trail at a wide place or a turnoff. There's no reverse in a pack string; in packer talk, "It's hard to push on a lead rope." So the packer may pause from time to time on a gentle slope where the trail will be wider and listen for any indication that a pack string in the distance is coming down the trail. This is also a good place for a regular stop to check and adjust packs that have become loose or that tend to roll to one side or the other because they aren't balanced.

Some riders will get off and walk, leading their horses through part of the long climb into the hunting camp. It gives the horses a break from carrying the heavy loads uphill, and gives the riders a chance to stretch their legs, which are usually unaccustomed to such long rides. Unless you do a lot of horseback riding on a regular basis, you're going to notice stiff and sore places where you didn't realize you had places. Take comfort in the knowledge that the ride in is not as bad as the ride out, since the ride in is usually uphill most of the way. The downhill is harder on the horses as well. You can help by leaning your weight forward when going uphill on steep grades, and back (as if you were sitting at home in a recliner) when going down. The goal is to keep your weight centered over the horse's contact with the ground.

OUTFITTER HUNTING CAMPS

As the procession of pack string and riders approaches the mountain or hunting camp, the horses' ears perk up at the prospect of getting rid of their loads and taking a break. They'll whinny to any horses in the hunting camp, or sometimes for no particular reason at all (as far as we humans can tell). The hunting camp, often termed the mountain camp, will probably strike you as a temporary man-made thing in the middle of a natural surrounding. The prettiest ones have a look of belonging there. Like the base camp, they have paths that tend to give an appearance of permanence even though everything can be loaded and carried off on a horse or mule. A typical camp consists of several wall tents—one or two for hunters, a cook tent, and a tent for the packer and guides—a corral to hold the pack and riding stock, a hitching rail with a stretched tarp or two in the vicinity to keep feed and hay dry, and a tarp over a rail or supported log that saddles are thrown over.

The tents are usually set up using thin, straight trees, preferably standing dead lodgepole pines if available, cut in the immediate vicinity for the ridge and wall poles and supports. Nails along the wall poles serve to hang gear off of the ground, and a string will be stretched for a clothesline to dry the socks and pants legs that usually get wet pulling through the brush.

Though the tents all look the same from a distance, you'll usually find them in a wide range of conditions if you look closely. An outfitter trick is to cover the whole thing with a separate plastic sheet fastened in place at the corners if a tent has suffered enough deterioration to leak. The experienced hunters know how to check out the hunters' tents for potential leaks and places where water might run under the sides. They'll also check the ridge pole to see if the outfitter had to cut a green tree if a dead, seasoned (not rotten) pole couldn't be found, or maybe if the campjack who set the tent up didn't know any better. The green poles will bend under the weight of a heavy, silent accumulation of snow that often comes during the night, lowering the ceiling of the bedroom considerably. Sometimes low enough to add a blanket of snow over the unsuspecting sleepers and provide additional camp entertainment. (It's usually more entertaining to the sleepers in the other tents.) It's a point to remember in case you ever make your own camp.

The hunters' tent will be your bedroom for the next several days. You'll find an odd assortment of sleeping furnishings that range from rough-and-ready board bunks with foam pads to store-bought camp cots, usually with a couple of misplaced pieces. The hunters' tent is usually fairly large and has a camp stove. There may be a campjack to keep wood split for the fire, or the hunters may handle that job.

The hunters' tent in a mountain outfitter pack camp.

And there's always some form of the universal—ranging from the official Forest Service standard enclosed and roofed version to the open-air outfitter variety with seasonal snow on the seat (which may still have the bark on it).

Drop camp bedrooms are smaller, with a small shepherd's stove to warm them up. The hunters handle this job in the drop camp (along with all the other jobs).

Packers grabbing lunch on their way out.

LIVING AND GETTING ALONG IN AN OUTFITTER PACK CAMP

Cooking and eating in a traditional outfitter hunting camp generally follow the traditions of cattle outfits of the Old West, or, at least, the cook's interpretations of the traditions of the Old West. The only thing you can count on is the breakfast schedule of a good pack camp. It will be early. Usually early and noisy. The breakfast atmosphere consists of lights dancing in the corral and tack tent, a chorale of horse neighs and mule yodels, and exquisitely authentic western profanity. It's a scene straight out of a nineteenth-century cattle drive, with the possible exception of those hat-mounted LED lights favored by modern cowboys and packers.

The cook tent is the domain of the cook; it is not to be confused with a lounge or your family room back home. Deference is usually given to the cook by everybody except the outfitter, who is the only one with authority to fire the cook and pack him or her out of camp. The obvious consequence of this action is that then the camp will have no cook. Notoriously bad cooks, drunk cooks, and run-ins between cooks and camps of hunters, or cooks and the guides and outfitter are the stuff of legends to be relived and enjoyed in tales around campfires in later years (but are less enjoyable while they're being endured).

You'll see a lot of variation in the cooking arrangements of camps. Outfitter camps often have some sort of ingenious scheme to make the

Cook's idea of scheduled entertainment for a hunter with a used elk tag.

Hunter's idea of scheduled entertainment for a hunter with a used elk tag.

water run by gravity into the cook tent, through a hose in the stream somewhere up the hill, and maybe some provision to heat water.

Visiting with the cook is done at the invitation of the cook, and depends upon the schedule of the cook. The only assistance to the cook that is welcome is menial help—no culinary advice, no management consulting. One thing that the old-school western cook is very good at, besides cooking, is keeping a hunter that has used his elk tag busy.

The food in outfitter camps is usually good, and made better by the cool of the mountains and the amount of exercise you'll be getting. Breakfast usually consists of bacon and eggs, pancakes, and maybe French toast if the bread is getting stale. You'll take a sandwich for lunch and some snacks when you go out to hunt. Soup is usually waiting when you come in that afternoon or early evening, along with leftovers to tide you over until dinner. Special treats include heart sandwiches and liver and onions from fresh kills whenever one of the hunters gets lucky. Just go with it and try some even if you don't usually order that sort of dish as the daily special down at the diner.

Every elk hunting camp soon takes on its own unique characteristics. It's a matter of the people, staff and hunters, and the conditions of the hunt. A good camp has a sort of primitive fellowship with everyone included. People aren't always the same in a camp as they are in their everyday activities back home or at work. There's always a lot of good evening conversation in a good camp. That's where you can get your classroom training for elk hunting, in the format of elk camp tales if there are good guides or experienced hunters in the group. Some lucky camps may include standup comedians or master storytellers among the outfitter's crew or the hunters. One hunter I know can recite most of Robert Service's classic poems of the Canadian Northwest gold rush.

A lot of the packers, guides, cooks, and local hunters in the Northern Rockies like to play cribbage. In a big camp with a set social structure, hunters usually need to have an invitation to get in on this game; it's easier for hunters to get started in smaller camps because the locals are always looking for another player. It's good to get into these sessions if you're any sort of a card player. You can pick up lots of information on how to improve your elk hunting "luck" in addition to how to play a mean game of cribbage. I'm not a card player, so the most interesting aspect of these games to me has always been the various designs of homemade handcrafted elk-horn scorekeepers.

There will usually be a lot of variation in the intensity of the elk hunters in a camp, ranging from the casual and lazy to the absolutely hell-bent. Some are obviously willing to pay the price of a guided outfitter elk hunt just to get away from it all for a while. (It makes you wonder what "it all" must be like.) There are some card players; there are some high-stakes poker players. Those of us who are neither would be advised to pass on the latter. Like swinging an axe or shooting a rifle offhand, if you're not an accomplished poker player and/or whiskey drinker back on the flatlands, you won't suddenly get better at either just because you booked an outfitter elk hunt. This advice, of course, is only given in the context that it may adversely impact your elk hunting; otherwise, it's none of my business.

Whether your elk hunting is of the ambitious or lazy persuasion, there will eventually be some mornings when it's just pouring down rain or there's a blinding snowstorm and there's a much better chance that you'll get a broken bone or a sore throat than an elk. You'd really be better off to stay in camp and save it for another day. Being in the ambitious group, it took me years to realize this fact, but it's true. You'll encounter hot afternoons with the same low chance of success, but you can at least stay out and loaf under a tree in that case. But for those days that you'll be stuck in camp, you might take along something in your duffel substantial to read. I say something substantial, because information that has been difficult for you to fully understand will often suddenly become clear if read without the usual distractions of your usual background flatlander noise. So, if physics is your interest, take the space-time diagram stuff along. The view of the stars from the top of the world on a clear night helps you see that sort of thing. Same for religion, philosophy, economics, whatever. You'll get more out of it than reading the Cabela's fall catalog from last year that's being used a page at a time to start the fire in the stove of the hunters' tent.

A lot of Tales involve interactions among the humans in elk camps, and a lot more involve interactions between the humans and the wild critters. In pack camp country, where the hand of man touches only seasonally, and lightly at that, the wild critters, great and small, tend to have a somewhat more noticeable influence on the elk camp. Toward the great end of the scale are the bears, and toward the small end of the scale are the mice—which, even though individually insignificant when compared with the bears, are likely to occur in numbers that more than make up for their small size on the annoyance scale.

DENNY AND THE BIG BLACK BEAR IN CAMP

This Tale occurred while I was hunting with the Association, and illustrates a typical incident that happens on occasion while hunting out of a small, quiet camp. This particular camp was located along the trail between two small creeks that came together about 100 yards below the camp. The layout of the camp was somewhat restricted to a few flat places along the slightly elevated ground along the trail, so that it extended for a full 60 yards or so from the cooking and dining area past the tents down to where our saddle horses, the only stock left in camp at the time, were tied.

It was one of those special laid-back evenings in camp that come along under certain circumstances. The circumstances in this particular case were that a hunter had made a kill during the morning hunt. Most of the rest of the day had been taken up with the field dressing chores, saddling and bringing the string out to the location of the kill, loading up the quarters and trophy, and getting Gene started down the trail to the river to get the meat to the processor right away due to the warm weather.

Denny and I found ourselves back in camp a little earlier than usual, since we were going a little easy on the hard elk hunting until transport out got caught up. It was time for some leisurely camp cooking and soaking up the wilderness experience. That's the time to make up an extra large camp stew, taking plenty of time to cook lots of seasoning thoroughly through the whole thing. By the time the late fall afternoon sun was starting to filter through the timber of the slope to the west of our campsite, we had pretty well stunk up the little corner of the wilderness around our camp with a well-blended assortment of meat, onions, and assorted vegetables and seasonings put together more or less by accident by us non-cooks to make one of the best stews I've ever had the pleasure to eat way too much of during the drawn-out cooking process that precedes the official eating of the evening meal. A cool little evening breeze came up to give slight movement to the evergreen boughs and underbrush on the other side of the steep-banked little creek that ran alongside our camp and the trail. The graceful swaying of the bright yellow leaves of the brush in the wind naturally drew our attention as we sat on the ground, leaning back against a couple of the most comfortable trees that an overly stuffed elk hunter ever leaned back against to drink an after-dinner cup of camp coffee. Presently, Denny allowed, matter-of-factly, that the wind coming up these draws seemed to make the brush wave in funny patterns. After a meditative pause, I answered that it must be a result of peculiar patterns of turbulence due to the complicated slopes of the terrain combined with the timber and underbrush. After a much longer pause, while he presumably digested the logic of my suggested explanation, and eventually, correctly, concluded that it was complete gibberish, he casually allowed, "That still wouldn't make some of the brush move while the rest of it was still." A little annoyed at his lack of respect for my non-explanation, I followed his gaze and paid a little more attention to the area he referred to, but I didn't notice anything unusual, or even interesting. He strolled over about 20 feet toward the creek bank for a better look, coffee cup in hand. I really took a hard look at the area of brush up the slope where he had been looking, so I was looking away from Denny as I heard his next utterance.

"Tom . . . it's . . . a *bear!*" he finally got out, in a very low, deliberate, maybe even shaky, voice. In the several years that we had ridden, camped, and hunted together, I had heard, on various occasions, Denny use what I took to be the full range of his tones of expression, and I had never heard that one. He stood a little off to one side of my now concentrated stare up the slope, where I still couldn't see a thing. I glanced over in his direction to check again his line of sight, and would have jumped out of my skin if I hadn't been frozen for the moment in space and time. About 12 to 15 feet in front of where Denny stood like a statue, still holding the coffee cup, the head and shoulders of the biggest bear I had ever seen slowly rose over the edge of the bank of the little creek. Big. Number-three washtub big. Absolutely unafraid to the point of disregarding humans big. Full-screen view on a big-screen television big. Zeroed in on the stew pot big. Big-screen horror movie "We're trapped like rats!" big. That bear was . . . big.

After some considerable passage of time, I fell out of my suspended state, and made a dive for the .338 leaning against a tree. The bear lost its absolute focus on the stew pot and went down below the edge of the bank like the setting sun as I swung the rifle around. A great big furry setting sun.

After a period of time—to this day I couldn't say whether it lasted seconds, minutes, hours, or eons—the bear reappeared down the creek near the location where the horses left in camp were tied. They went absolutely crazy with fear. The bear cleared the creek bank and started across the trail in the general direction of the horses. I popped off a not-too-steady shot as it cleared the trail. It stumbled and made sort of a half roll as it changed directions and headed down the trail and over the embankment where the two creeks on either side of the camp came together. My blood was pumping hotter as I made the change in mindset from prey to predator. I took off in hot pursuit over the embankment, rifle held in a running high port. Clearing the crest, I could see the entire panorama of the streams. Brush covered the entire area but there were a few openings so that a human could move more or less freely about. I began looking for any sign of blood or torn-up ground made by an animal running fast. No blood. No bear. If the bear was still running in a straight line, I was getting way behind in the pursuit. If it had been hit, I might find it fairly close if it sullied up and hid in a pile of the thicker brush. I made larger circles through the brush.

Denny showed up at the top of the drop-off into the creeks. "Tom, do you really think it's a good idea to be down in that brushy hole with a wounded bear that size if you did hit it?" I hadn't thought about that aspect of the situation very much. In my mind, I was still the predator.

It became darker as I looked. Denny stayed back up on the bank out of the brush. "Tom, I really think you're taking an awful chance down there like that," he said in a more insistent tone. I looked around. It was getting pretty dark. I reluctantly climbed back up the bank and went back to the spot along the trail to the point where the bear was when I took the shot. Couldn't see anything other than scrapes on the ground.

The next morning, while I was out looking for elk, Denny and Gene looked along the brush near the streams for hundreds of yards. No sign of blood, tracks, or bear. We finally concluded that it must have been a clean miss and the bear had just stumbled as it ducked the not-too-accurate shot.

THE GREAT PACK RAT PLAGUE

Herm and Leroy had a new pack outfit in a new area. They hadn't been able to get things all worked out on the sale until well after the time of the year when clients usually book hunts, so the first hunt (the archery season) was a little thin on hunters—as in, no hunters. They were still setting up the camp when the first archery season began and I was there, the first and only name signed into their book. Leroy was packing, his girlfriend Chris was cooking, and Herm was practicing guiding archery hunters, with me standing in for a "real" archery hunter who really knew what was going on. Since I was the only hunter booked, I was set up in the hunters' tent, king and only resident of my own solitary domain, or so I thought.

The hunters' tent and the cook tent in this particular camp had an unusual setup. This particular outfitter permit deal included a couple of tent floors that had been in place for as long as anybody could remember. The floors were made of rough-cut planks nailed to a foundation, with dirt filled in around the logs forming the foundation to keep the breeze up through the planks under control. The tents were set up on the floors for use during hunting season, then taken down again, leaving the floor until the next season. This kind of floor is a lot better than a dirt floor when the weather turns bad, which it always does, particularly toward the end of the season. The floor had originally been made to fit a tent slightly shorter than the standard outfitter tent, so that now the tent extended out over the original porch made of small round logs, giving the place a little extra character. It was warm and extra roomy for one hunter, which is good for me because my stuff tends to expand to completely fill up all available space anywhere I stay for a couple of days. This was a fantastic arrangement for me. I had plenty of extra tables and benches, so, before long, I had stuff all over and I could keep up with everything, since everything was always in view. That's an approach to organization that some otherwise completely logical and organized folks never grasp, but we'll stay out of my personal relationships here. Suffice it to say that in that camp in that place at that time, all was well. Just like in the opening scenes of a horror movie. And then the strange stuff started to happen.

Before long, I started to develop a tendency to misplace things. I should say, worse than my usual tendency to misplace things. Then I started noticing that weird stuff was showing up in places where there hadn't been stuff before—bones of birds and small animals, peculiarly shaped sticks, old nails. I finally became convinced that weird foreign objects were appearing in the same locations that my personal objects, like practice field points that I had taken off of my arrows, had been. I was confident enough of my sanity that I mentioned it to Herm. Herm had great fun kidding me about my flatlander introduction to doing business with a pack rat. I was not amused. I had to start stowing my stuff away all zipped up and secured and orderly. And I was on vacation. My much better half would have injured herself in merriment to have seen my gear all arranged as if I were ready for freshman cadet inspection back at Texas A&M.

The situation deteriorated. The rat became bolder at night. There were now strange noises. The most annoying was a fast scratching that came from different locations around the floor, but eventually seemed to center directly under my cot, all around my now-secured stuff. Unseen creatures were trying to get into the bags. They seemed particularly hell-bent on getting into a large cardboard shipping tube that I had used to carry my arrows in on the airplane. The rat, or rats, I couldn't tell in my sleepy condition, were waking me up several times a night. In the dark, I would sling something at them and they would run back under the floor of the tent.

Finally, I'd had enough. I planned an ambush. I opened the end of the shipping tube so that the rat could enter in the middle of the night, waking me up. Then I would roll out of bed and send the rat off into the sunset. Unbelievably, the deal went down exactly according to plan, up to a point. I woke up as the rat crawled into the tube, making plenty of scratching noises in the process. I rolled out of bed, grabbed the end of the tube with the rat inside, and tipped it up in one sleepy, awkward motion. I gave the tube a swing to slide the rat down to the closed end. Herm, in reviewing my strategy, hadn't briefed me on the size of the thing. I had one awful moment as I imagined that I might have a smallish porcupine trapped, more or less. But now I was committed. I continued my roll to my feet, grabbed a broom I had left in a handy location, and slammed the handle end down the tube again and again in a gleeful rage, pounding the lights out of whatever was trapped inside. Finally exhausted, I dropped the tube and broom on the floor. After the couple of minutes it took for me to recover from all that exertion at that elevation, I tipped up the open end of the tube, and, using a flashlight, peeked in the end of the tube to make sure that the unfortunate creature inside would never scratch again. Or so I thought.

Not only was that thing big, it was also tough. The next morning when I picked up the tube to take it down to the cook tent for Chris to cook for breakfast (the code of the West is that you eat what you kill), it was empty! I went into a mild little early morning—best I could muster before coffee—raging fit all over again at the prospects of that thing returning to torment me again that night. And that was my state of mind when I went down to the cook tent for breakfast and described the whole incident to the assembled camp.

It was years later, after I had hunted with the outfit so often that, for all intents and purposes, I was like one of the family—as Leroy put it, "like an obnoxious member of the family that shows up for elk hunting season every fall"—that I learned that Chris the cook, who had in the meantime become Leroy's wife, Herm's daughter-in-law, and the Chairman of the Board of the Outfit, coined a famous quote about the incident. It seems that the combination of the inflection and tone of my "down home" accent, and my general mannerisms, rough as they are, but not so rough maybe in comparison to the packers and lumberjacks around the area, had led her to give me the nickname of "Mister Rogers." And so she described the pack rat incident as something to the effect of "Mister Rogers goes ballistic." Visualize a 250-pound, 6-foot, 4-inch Mister Rogers in the Bates Motel shower scene. Giggling in the cook tent late at night would follow each retelling.

After that incident, I wasn't bothered anymore by pack rat trouble in the hunter tent. But things immediately started to disappear out of the cook tent.

As I recall, Leroy and Chris pulled out for a few days to get ready for the next batch of hunters, so that Herm and I were left on our own. Herm was now acting as packer, cook, and guide (a one-person staff), and I was acting as the hunting party (a one-person hunting party) as we both got familiar with the area and learned the hard way some of the finer points of bowhunting for elk.

We had long since learned to keep everything fastened down or zipped up tight in a bag with no hole large enough for a rat to get through and too heavy for a rat to carry off. Somebody lost a toothbrush (we imagined the rat brushing its little incisors every morning). We were tired of doing business with the pack rats; we were tired of their droppings all over the place, particularly in the cook tent; and we were really fed up with sharing the grub with them, whether they brushed after every meal or not.

It all came to a head one afternoon when Herm and I were back in camp a little early, rethinking our bowhunting tactics and strategy and resting our feet before we went out to get the mule back into the corral after his usual afternoon "jump the corral fence and take yourself for a walk" exercise routine.

Then the noise started. *Thump, scratch, scratch, scratch.* Even Herm, functionally deaf to any sound above about 100 hertz from too much target practice without hearing protection in his younger days, could hear it, although he couldn't locate it. "Where's that comin' from?" He knew exactly what it was. I nodded toward the specially constructed, rat-proof, bear-proof, mule-packable pantry carefully fastened shut over in the corner of the tent. Herm eased over and popped the pantry door open. He and what looked like a 20-pound pack rat exchanged hard stares. "Why you . . ." Herm went for his side arm hanging by the door of the tent.

Herm was back at the pantry in an instant, fire in his eyes. Nothing there. The hammer of the single-action revolver was back and he was trying to stick his finger against the ear turned toward the pantry. I had both ears covered since I wasn't holding a gun in one hand. It didn't take a Sherlock Holmes to figure out what was about to happen next. Herm bent over like something slightly subhuman and peered into the darkened pantry box. His eyes lit up and the revolver came up into battery.

"Herm, I really don't think that's a good—" BOOM! "—idea . . ." My brain was running about two beats behind events, but it was starting to dawn on me that this operation wasn't as well thought out as it should be as far as collateral damage was concerned. The .357 slug, most of a can of cherry pie filling mixed with most of the stuff from inside the pack rat, and part of the back of the pantry box exploded through a hole in the side of the new tent. ". . . because you don't know where that damned mule is . . ."

Herm's eyes flew open wide and his chin came up to meet the end of his nose and his head popped around in that particular Herm mannerism that always reminds me of a hoot owl. He went diving out the front door of the tent, leaving me standing in the same tracks where I had been riveted throughout the entire gruesome proceedings. Herm was around the side of the tent before I could say, "Want me to bring the shovel?" "Naw, that mule ain't out here dead or alive!" he called back in a relieved tone.

All pack camps become their own little society for a few days, and no two are ever exactly the same. There are, however, enough aspects in common that the new hunter needs to be aware of a few general guidelines that will help you get along in an elk camp safely and on good terms with everybody.

First, let's talk about manners:

- Be polite and reserved and respectful to everybody—not just because everyone's armed, but because everybody is going to have to put up with each other for a few days, and in close quarters in case of really bad weather. You may be the paying customer, but in this situation, it's in your best interest to admit that the customer is not always right. Your success, welfare, and safety may at any time depend on anyone you see in camp, both outfit employees and the other hunters.

- You can expect to be well fed and well exercised—beginning early in the morning. Try to stay on the group schedule. Don't sleep all afternoon, and then stay up late at night making noise when everyone else is trying to sleep.
- Your enjoyment of the day's hunt and your chances of success will be improved if you get some rest and sleep before the early-morning call to breakfast. If you're inclined to talk, play cards, or stay awake for any other reason, you should be considerate and not keep others from sleeping. Having paid their money, which in many cases is hard earned and long saved, they deserve to enjoy their hunt without interference from you.
- A related topic is snoring. If you know that you're in the league of world-class noise makers, it would be a good move to work out separate tents or other arrangements with the outfitter when you book the hunt.
- Be orderly with your stuff—don't take up too much room in a group tent.
- Most camps in the low to moderate price range don't have a campjack, so it's usually understood that the hunters will keep their own wood split and their own fire going. If this is the deal, do your part.
- Try to fit in and not be a burden—it's good for your success.

Pitching in and doing your part to help out with hunter camp chores will go a long way toward getting along in a pack camp.

- Tobacco users should be aware that elk country is smokeless territory. Elk hunting season corresponds to the time of greatest wildfire danger in the western forests, and the Forest Service often sets smoking bans in late summer or early fall. Elk hunting techniques usually call for minimum human-associated scents for best chances at success, and outfitters usually require that guides don't smoke. (Unscientific statistics indicate that about 90 percent of outfitters dip, so it's not like they have anything against the use of tobacco per se. It's all about the unnatural odor on the breeze.)

The second set of tips focuses on safety. Some of these topics I covered earlier in the chapters on training, but it's always good to review. You can remember this group as the "Don't Mess with It" list:

- Don't mess with the mountains. Operate within your own realistic limitations. Physical conditioning needs to be done before you get there. I'm always amused when hunters arrive and say they came to get in shape. Of course, these are the ones that can't get out too far, and they hang around camp and annoy the cook. Exercise before your hunt to strengthen important muscles. Be particularly cautious on snow and ice. Stay right side up as much as possible. Watch the wind in the trees and be cautious in conditions of high wind, when huge trees can fall, crushing everything in their path on the way down. Be wary of thunderstorms as well. Lightning can strike you anywhere: on horses, on open faces, under big trees. Mineral outcrops combine all the worst lightning risk elements. Traces of countless strikes can often be observed over areas of outcrops the size of a cook tent.
- Don't mess with the horses or mules (particularly the mules), packs or packing.
- Don't mess with the cook (under any circumstances).
- Don't mess with the guides. (The exception is a lazy guide or one that thinks that he is really one of the hunters; you don't have to put up with that kind of antics. The outfitter is the one responsible for any "straightening out" needed.)
- Don't mess with loaded guns in camp.
- Don't mess with sharp objects such as knives or axes for entertainment such as throwing contests.
- Don't mess with alcohol in combination with any of the above.
- Don't mess with the zero of your rifle, including for target shooting while in camp in your general hunting area. Bore sight your bolt action the old-fashioned way.

And here's a bit of protocol: Tipping, or lack of it, is one aspect of the outfitter experience that can be a little sensitive and awkward to all concerned. The same diversity among packers, cooks, guides, and hunters that makes a pack camp the interesting experience that it is can also lead to misunderstandings and folks rubbed the wrong way. The hunters may include doctors, lawyers, and New York financiers accustomed to dropping big tips on the doormen of their high-rise apartments. Those doormen may have a higher income than some of the blue-collar hunters in camp who have saved for years to cover the cost of a hunt that doesn't amount to as much as one month of club dues for the more well-heeled hunters. And the hunters usually aren't as complicated as the outfit employees, who are often Old West types with different combinations of incomes, pride, ego, material desires, and all sorts of endearing character flaws. Your friendly author doesn't claim to have all the correct answers on this subject, even after years of hunting out of pack camps of various sorts. Whatever I advise will probably come back to haunt me in a pack camp someday, but here goes . . .

Things go better if the hunters get together and try to be consistent. For a particular hunt, it's best to defer to the hunters with the most experience in camps in the area. If you can't get any idea, you might have a representative of the hunters talk to the outfitter to establish the average for the guides. (The outfitter usually doesn't get tipped.) Some articles I've read have suggested 10 to 15 percent of the cost of the hunt for hardworking, capable guides. If it occurs to you, you might mention the tip situation to the outfitter when you book the hunt, particularly if a group goes together. That way, everyone knows what to expect and can plan on it.

The hunters who hunted with a particular guide handle that guide's tip. The tip should be based on the guide's effort and skill rather than the hunters' success. Some hunters add the extra favor of a gift in addition to the cash tip. Knives sometimes change hands if the guide doesn't already have a nice favorite knife in evidence (but usually the guides will just prefer more cash). More often, the gift is some new outdoors gizmo that the guide might not have access to, like this year's high-tech gadget that the hunter will want the new version of next year. Even a rifle as a gift isn't unknown in camps with high-roller hunter clients, but it's unusual. If you were successful and the guide was helpful with caping the trophy, that's worth a bonus. If another guide did the caping task then you should tip that guide as well. If the packer took extra effort to pack the meat out for you to get it to the freezer due to warm weather, that's worth an extra tip.

HUNTING FROM A PACK CAMP

Now that I've reviewed the sights and some of the activities that you might see on an outfitter hunt, let's take a look at your main purpose out there in all of that scenery. That would be the elk hunting. The hunting and how it's conducted depend on the capabilities and temperaments of the hunters as well as of the outfitters, guides, and so on; the weather and the quantity and quality of the elk in the area also affect the hunt. The technical aspects of how to do everything were described in Part I; now we'll see how doing all that stuff with an outfitter guide might look.

You usually head out early in the morning for a hard hunt until the afternoon. Different small groups or single hunters might work different parts of the area and be back into camp early if the hunting area is close by, or the entire group may be out together all day and not be back in until after dark if it works an area some distance away. Hunters in an outfitter camp will often ride horses to an area to be hunted before daylight. They'll then be dropped off for a long run on foot and picked up at another location. It's good to see those horses late in the afternoon, particularly on days when a storm is coming in.

Note that some hunter orange may come out of packs for a ride through areas where you may not know where other camps might be hunting. Hoofbeats might get somebody excited.

Some comments are in order regarding interaction with guides. I've made the point that when it comes to packing your gear on the pack animals, the packer is the boss. When it comes to the cooking and eating schedule, the cook is the boss. But when it comes to the hunting and the interaction with the guides, you finally get to be the boss. Having said that, I should be quick to caution that it's in your best interest to exercise your power to be the boss very carefully. You've paid a considerable amount of money for the services of the guide, and you can make that investment worthless if you keep the guide from doing his or her job. If you know the techniques covered in Part I, you should be ahead of the game, but you'll learn more when you practice those techniques with coaching from a competent guide.

Guides come in all sorts of makes and models. If you had just so much luck in life, and wanted to spend it wisely, you might consider using some of it on your first elk hunting guide. When they are good, they're very, very good; but, when they are bad . . . Some of the best guides are older guys that just like to be out there in the mountains and would be there in the fall even if it weren't their job. My old outfitter and guide friends Herm and Gene were of this type. Bill, another of my guide friends, manages to make a living out in the woods for most of the year. He knows all things of the woods and hunting from an adult lifetime of experience, but also reads extensively and actively works on

Hunters getting picked up for the ride back to camp. STEVE BURSON

specialized skills such as calling. Another of my friends, Mike, would have to be the model young elk hunting guide (haven't seen him in a few years, so I guess he's more "mature" as of this writing); retired military, he taught at the cold weather survival school, could leap tall mountains at a single bound, but would slow down to just the right speed for the client.

These guides, also friends, are not the usual; there seem to be more young men in the profession than anything else. So you often have a young guy willing to take seasonal work for low pay. Guides often have some extra ego, and get into contests among themselves as to who's the toughest, who can move cross-country the best, who can get the biggest elk for their hunter, or who is more consistently successful. You need to be careful and avoid being sucked into one of these agendas so that you try to do more than you can physically handle. On the other hand, these types are going to work hard to get you on an elk, so if you can keep up, that physical training you've been doing will likely pay off with better-than-average success.

Make sure you and the guide are on the same sheet of music. Your preferences as to your objectives, such as trophy hunting, that you worked out with the outfitter when you booked won't necessarily have been communicated to your guide, who is the one who will help you make it happen out there in the woods. This is particularly important if you booked with a third party such as through a booking agent. Make

sure that the guide knows exactly what your hunting preferences are—
trophy hunt only; any legal elk; trophy first, then switch to any elk if no
luck; and so on. Then make sure that you're consistent. In arrangements
where two or more hunters are with a single guide, you should agree
before the occasion arises on who takes the first shot. If nothing is set,
the "code of the West" says, vaguely, that whoever sees the elk first
shoots first. Sometimes, everybody sees it at the same time, or the guide
sees it and says something, and then everybody else cuts loose at the
same time, which can lead to problems if all of the shooters feel that
they connected and the elk turns out to be the trophy of a lifetime. It
happens. Regarding the tempo of the hunt and your speed of travel,
don't kid yourself or hurt yourself by attempting to exceed your capabilities. On the other hand, if you are of the young and vigorous type,
and the old guide is moving too slowly for you, it might be that the
guide is telling you to slow down and do a better job of looking as you
go. Give it a fair try. If you do so, and you still feel that you and a particular guide just aren't going to work, you'll be better off to work out a
change with the outfitter rather than trying to handle it yourself.

The guides that are truly awful usually have some agenda other
than being a hunting guide. Some are into some kind of cowboy thing,
but don't want to bother with looking after a bunch of cows. They're
just out to get some cowboy credentials without a regular job at it, and
can't wait to get back to town to impress and entertain the cowgirls.
Some really want to do some elk hunting for themselves, and want to
locate a big one they can have a go at between hunts or whatever their
deal with the packer allows. I've been on hunts where a guide has taken
an elk from in front of the hunters. Other times their interests are less
intrusive, like dropping the hunter off so that the guide can do a little
trapping on the side. These guide antics are a good outfitter's worst
nightmare. Even legitimate outfitters can get into a corner when somebody backs out on guiding for them on a particular hunt and they have
to hire a guide they don't know.

You can draw some really bad guides, bad cooks, bad packers, and
bad outfitters, but it's been my experience that you're more likely to
draw a really bad financial advisor, stockbroker, or car dealer. Usually
the problem is us. The flatlander hunter who is pretty good in his or her
own specialty thinks that that expertise naturally extends to elk hunting. Also, the typical outfitter hunting guide isn't the type to "bare
souls" and "open up the inner self" to clients, or anybody else, for that
matter. If any sort of problem develops between the two of you, most
guides aren't inclined to "talk out the issues" with you. Same goes for

A merry packer with a pack camp string pulling into the base camp.

the packer, the cook, and the outfitter. They'll just put up with you for a little while until they get to pack you off of the mountain, and you very well may still be wondering why you didn't have as much luck as your hunting companions. And next year you may be wondering why the outfitter didn't have an opening to book you a hunt but managed to work your buddies in. (Or sometimes the buddies get left out as well, which leads to real trouble when the entire story eventually comes to light.) You're not going to have any luck changing the guide, packer, outfitter, cook, or anybody else in the camp. You're better off trying to fit into the program the way it is.

Having said all that, there are some rotten apples in every barrel, and that extends to the elk hunting business just like any other. And there is a limit to what you have to put up with before you are fully within your rights to start looking for indications that you might have booked in with the dreaded bad—'scuse me, with respect to my outfitter friends, that's a "not so good"—outfitter.

CHAPTER 21

Horseback Riding and Related Advice

A lot of the best elk hunting arrangements—best in terms of the quality of the experience and your chances of success—involve outfitters, guided hunts, or wilderness hunting, and that translates to horses. For most nonresidents, horses aren't part of the normal routine. If you didn't grow up on a farm or a ranch, or haven't otherwise had the pleasure of learning about horses early in life, it would be good to fit a little horseback riding into your schedule before you show up at a trailhead, just for familiarization and confidence building. You can find a riding stable of some sort about anywhere in this country.

Regarding the transition from flatland riding to mountain riding, it all gets down to one simple principle: Try to keep your weight centered over the horse's ground contact. You do this by leaning forward when going up a steep slope and leaning back when going down. Some wise old trail horses will help you to remember this technique. I recall a horse named Butch that would always turn crossways on the trail when the packer in front would stop the string to let them get their breath while going up steep grades. That left the weight of the rider nicely centered so that Butch could rest with all four feet evenly loaded. And the flatlander on top usually sat nice and still while turning white as a sheet because the steep places were usually the narrow places along the sides of the bluffs, and Old Butch would have either his front or his rear end hanging over the drop-off.

Riding along an improved trail is usually an easy outing. If you get off the trail, you'll probably have your hands full until you get the hang of it. The packer and guides will usually offer some advice. Take it. You may need to lean this way and that to clear trees and limbs. The horse will be paying attention to where it's about to step rather than your clearance and comfort, and that's what you want it to do. Pay attention and make sure the stock of your rifle goes around the same side of the tree as you and the horse and the rest of the rifle. My scabbard is adjusted to carry the rifle in a more vertical orientation than the norm. This way, there's less chance that the rifle stock will go around the opposite side of the tree from me and the horse.

Mountain riding either on or off the trail in absolute darkness can be a little unnerving the first time you experience it. Just remember that the horse can see in this situation and you can't, which means that the horse is in charge, whether you like that arrangement or not. Also, be advised that you're usually asking for trouble if you turn on a light or attempt to control the path of the horse. Just relax, enjoy the trip, and don't make the horse nervous by smelling like you're afraid. And if the two of you happen to be alone and there's a disagreement as to which one of you is lost, I'm betting that the horse is right. Loosen the reins and you'll probably be either back in camp or back at the river before long. The horse gets to decide which one.

Saddle makers seem to have different ideas of how to make the perfect stirrup strap adjustment. Some of them depend on a mysterious arrangement of sliding buckles to hold the entire assembly together. Stirrup adjustment is not a trivial nicety; you need to have them at the right length so that you can just stand up in them and clear the back of the saddle and all of the rest of the stuff tied to it to mount and dismount. You also don't want your knees bent like a jockey. You won't be able to walk, at least like a human, after a long ride. If you don't know all about stirrup adjustments, it's far smarter to admit that you don't and get some help from someone who does (usually not your flatlander spouse or buddy) before you get on the trail. The packer will have enough trouble keeping the pack string together and can't tie the whole business to trees and ease back through everybody to adjust your stirrups for you or collect the various separate parts of the assembly that you put together the wrong way.

You'll notice more equipment on the front end of your outfitter-supplied mount than you're accustomed to on the flats. The usual practice is to leave a halter in place all the time on pack camp stock. A snap-on lead rope is attached for handling other than riding. A bridle is placed over the halter for control while riding, then removed if the horse is to be tied or led for a significant period. During riding, the end of the lead rope is dallied (looped several times) around the saddle horn. Get someone to teach you the right way to tie your horse using the lead rope. Horses can pull back hard enough to make some knots permanent attachments. They can also use their teeth to pull the loose end of the rope to easily untie some types of knots. It's a good practice to never leave anything of value, beginning with your rifle, on the saddle or even close to a horse that's tied or otherwise not under your immediate control.

PACKING EQUIPMENT ON HORSEBACK

As far as you, the hunter, are concerned, the best way to carry an elk rifle is on the "off" or right side—the side you don't mount from. (You mount from the left side of the horse. That's termed the "near" side. Cowboys, you'll notice, are allowed to make exceptions when they feel like it.)

I can count eight different ways to attach a rifle scabbard. You'll often see packers carry a short, flat-sided lever action on the near side, away from the lead rope to the string. A packer will also normally carry a side arm on the left side, by turning the belt of a "Buscadero" holster rig attached to the belt, or the holster of a "Loop" holster rig, called a "Mexican," or "Texas" rig by old-timers, or by using a shoulder holster. It's all to clear the decks for the lead rope, which can otherwise get around stuff in unbelievable ways. The little lever-action won't get in the way of the packer. Packers could probably mount over a small cannon under the near stirrup and not notice. Their saddles usually fit better than their clothes, anyway. You'll find in Chapter 12 a description of a near-side, custom-made, flapped holster scabbard handy for the hunter/packer of a private outfit.

In old photographs you'll see cowboys carrying lever-actions on either side with stocks either forward or back. I would take that to mean that you can carry a short lever-action any way you want to, and then propose a theory as to why your way is the best way. Photos of Mexican irregulars around the turn of the (twentieth) century illustrate scabbards carrying the bolt-actions of the time along the off side, with the almost fully covered stocks to the rear. The technique was to bound off over the saddle cantle and on over the rear of the horse and grab the rifle from the scabbard just before a light touchdown. Those of us who are flatlanders are better off with our modern scoped bolt-actions on the off side, which makes it easier to get to, in the scabbard with chamber empty, stock forward, scope down, and barrel extending back under the stirrup straps.

A rifle scabbard always comes with straps. When not attached to the saddle, the straps should stay with the scabbard; otherwise, they always get separated and you're looking for a strap or a piece of hay string to tie it to the saddle, which is not only unsatisfactory and unreliable, it's also not cool. When you use the straps to hang the scabbard from the saddle, the straps always go around the scabbard to support the rifle. The tabs or slots serve to keep the straps in the right place, not to support all of the weight like a bucket handle. More information on rifle and bow scabbards, along with illustrations of some options, was presented in the chapters covering equipment.

For planning purposes, you should be aware that wrecks on the trail are always a possibility. If you do much riding off the trail, that possibility may upgrade to a probability in rough country. You need to be able to prevent things from going from bad to worse. Use the saddle horn or cantle for a handhold to assist with balance or to stay on top as long as the horse is upright. (There are no style points here.) You can tell by the feel of the horse if it's going to roll over, run off of the trail in a panic, or buck until you come off. Get your feet out of the stirrups if you're coming off and make every attempt to get completely loose from the horse. Don't get dragged by anything. If your boot is caught in the stirrup, flop over onto your belly so that the toe of your boot points down, so that it'll come loose. In case of a real multiple-roll wreck down a steep slope, try to disengage from the horse. The tendency is for the two of you to roll and slide together. If you realize that you can't get clear of the horse, try to use the saddle horn to control your position so that if the horse rolls over you, the saddle horn doesn't get smashed into your head or ribcage. Don't give a thought about any of your equipment at this point. Just concentrate on getting yourself out the other side of the wreck and roll. Stay clear of the horse's feet as you come to rest.

It's okay under leisurely circumstances to dismount, tie the horse, stretch, rub the sore places, and then walk around and remove the rifle from the scabbard. Circumstances that are not leisurely require more technique. The most common cause of excitement on the trail is for one of the riders or one of the animals to pull what's termed by packers and outfitters "a [descriptive adjective] stunt." The nature and severity of the descriptive adjective depends on the nature and severity of the consequences of the stunt. If really bad consequences result, it will thereafter be referred to as "that hyphenated-descriptive adjective" stunt. You can usually tell by the reaction of the animals and size of their eyes if it's going to be a situation that you can more or less calmly sit through astride your trusty steed, or if you need to consider other options. A little jumping around in a circle in a wide, flat place is just part of the experience. On the other hand, the prospect of a pack string in a crazed panic running by on the inside of a narrow trail through the

Matt demonstrates a technique for taking a rifle along when dismounting.
STEVE BURSON

bluffs and rolling you and the trusty steed over the side is altogether different. If you decide that it's a good idea to watch events unfold without being fastened to the horse, it's best to dismount on the near side as usual, because that's what the horse expects. If it's really bad and you're going to have to jump for your life, you can jump in any direction, but be sure if you slide off the rear that you roll back so that your head clears the kicking zone with plenty of room to avoid those shod hooves that may otherwise come straight back and up into your face.

The other common causes of excitement along the trail come under the general heading of "critters along the trail." The level of excitement depends a lot on the critter. Hornets under horses' tails are very bad. Bears and moose are not so bad. They're easier to avoid, unless they meet the string head-on in a narrow spot through the bluffs.

Finding elk along the trail happens on rare occasions. This is one of those "good news, bad news" situations. The good part is that elk usually don't recognize the image of a human on a horse for what it is. If they've been shot at along the trail by the things with two heads and four feet, they probably won't be seen at a range of less than 800 yards as you ride along. If they haven't had any bad experiences with horses and riders and if you can manage to remain calm as you come into range of the elk, draw the rifle and dismount in a smooth movement, and clear the horses, you may be able to collect an elk right along the trail. That's a big "if." The bad news comes from the fact that the sight of unexpected elk while you're on the trail tends to raise the general level of excitement of both the people and the horses. Add to that the possibility of shooting and you have all the ingredients of a stampede, or at least a pretty good rodeo. There are rules to live by in this situation. Nearly all horses don't like to hear a rifle go off next to their ears, and since they're in a position to do something about it, rule number one is that you don't shoot while mounted. Even if you have a written warranty from the outfitter that you can shoot from the horse like the old cowboy movie stars Gene and Roy, just remember that horses can't read. In the fine print of that warranty you'll find that it is good for one shot only under the best of circumstances. Rule number two is that you can't shoot from the ground either, if your rifle is still in the scabbard on the horse that you've just been thrown off of. Rule number three is that if it's a really good show, you probably won't be holding that horse for long either. You'll note also if the occasion arises that while you're on the ground without your rifle, not only will you not get a shot, but it may be a while before you see the horse, rifle, or some of your companions. If you have the rifle with you, and can avoid being run over, you'll probably have a better hunt that day. The best practice is to take the rifle with you as you dismount. Chapter 12 provided a detailed description of the technique; figure out some way to practice it before the occasion arises. And the vertical orientation of the rifle helps too.

There are several Tales in my repertoire illustrating the fun to be had with horses and mules. Horses and mules are a part of elk hunting pack camps in the high country of the West. They are an essential part of the wilderness experience or a necessary evil—always one or the other, and sometimes both at the same time, depending on the circumstances and the disposition of the human riding or packing the particular critter at the time. If you hunt for enough seasons, the details of a lot of your mounts tend to fade into the soft, pleasant mist of old memories. A few continue to stand out in the mind in vivid, lurid-toned Technicolor. If there's any moral to these stories, I guess it's that I'll put up with a lot from the critters that can get me back into the woods for a chance to find an elk, but I still won't sleep on the ground where the snakes, spiders, centipedes, scorpions, and vinegaroons lurk.

My best Tales that make the point of what not *to do in the trail riding department involve my experience with the Association, a private hunter-owned outfit, and all of the misadventures that can follow from strange horses and a general arrangement that allows the flatlander types to run loose in the High Bitterroots without supervision. A few involve experiences with outfitter hunts. We'll begin with one of those. It comes under the general heading of "Frolics along the Trail—And Sometimes off It."*

THE GREAT BUTANE-TANK PACK-STRING WRECK

This event occurred at the end of my second elk hunt. It was the last hunt of the season and it had been cold. Relentless, frozen-lead-ropes-in-the-morning cold. Our group of hunters was packing out with all of our personal gear. In addition to our stuff, Herm (who was running and packing for that particular camp in addition to guiding) was also packing all of the assorted camp stuff, particularly light but bulky stuff, that he could "top pack" over our gear or load on extra mules to cut down on the number of trips he would shortly need to pack the camp out. Some of those light, bulky items included four "empty" 5-gallon compressed butane gas tanks used to supply fuel for cooking on camp stoves. There were two tanks on each of two mules in the middle of the string.

The trip out was going smoothly as the procession got about halfway down the mountain, through an area called the Bluffs. We had just cleared the "Steep Place," where the trail narrowed in some places to a notch chipped into the rock face about halfway between the creek below and the top of the ridge, 800 feet up and 1,200 feet down. (A standard joke in Idaho is that a steep place is defined as a trail section where a rider can see the stream at the bottom inside of the toe of a boot in a saddle stirrup.) The pack string mules were walking along with their characteristic downhill gait when things are going well—long, carefree steps downhill, swinging their butts back and forth with the packs swaying, leather creaking, stumbling over rocks in the trail now and then.

And nobody was giving much thought to the fact that it was warming up nicely as we approached the bottom of the trail. Warming up the trail, warming up the riders, warming up the stock, and warming up the butane tanks jiggling along, tied to the packsaddles of the mules.

We need a little technical dissertation at this point on the workings of pressurized butane tanks for readers not familiar with how the things work. Butane is a gas at atmospheric pressure and normal temperatures. It's stored in pressurized tanks so that it stays in liquid form and therefore doesn't take up so much room for storage. Regulators control the gas pressure to step it down for release into the atmosphere as a gas at normal temperatures so that it can be ignited for use. As a safety precaution, the regulators are set to pop off and release excessive pressure by allowing small amounts of gas to vent into the air if, for any reason, the pressure inside the tank becomes dangerously high. Then there's no chance that the tank will explode with disastrous consequences. The pressure inside the tank will increase when it's warmed, as, for example, when a tank disconnected as empty in the cold on top of the mountain is packed downhill to the lower elevations of the river camp. When the safety valves on the regulators pop off, they give off a very distinctive sound—and it's loud.

The very loud *peachesssssssss* broke the tranquility of the late morning. The ears of every mule in the string instantly stuck straight up and extended about 6 inches longer. Those of the saddle horses weren't much shorter. The eyes of the mule actually packing the tank stood out on stalks with the realization that the fool packer had loaded him with a sack of frozen rattlesnakes for this trip and they were about to thaw out. All of the mules instantly changed their gait to the danger mode they reserve for dark, stormy nights and other occasions such as this one: short little catlike steps, not a creak from the leather. Every experienced rider in the group took up the slack in the reins and got lighter on the saddle seat. Lots of low, soothing "Whoas" along the line strung out along the trail. Herm was reassuring the horses and mules. Several of us knew what the next number of this show would be.

It wasn't long in coming. After a couple of minutes that seemed like hours, another tank popped off with what seemed an even louder *peachessssssss!* The ears on every animal, packed or ridden, stuck up even farther, if that were possible. All of the people were on the alert by this time as well. Knowing full well the probable direction of the stampede to come, I started to dismount, because it was obvious from my position at the end of the line that animals couldn't pass on that part of the narrow trail and would likely in their panic bowl horses they ran into off the trail if they hit from an inside position. We had fortunately moved past the bare rock section of the bluffs and had some trees and brush on the slope below. As expected, right on cue, all of the tanks popped off at the same time.

The rodeo was on. The tank packing mules went absolutely nuts and jerked the rest of the string over the side of the trail, some bucking, some rolling down the bluff. Some lead ropes broke loose, like they're supposed to, at the hay string (bailer twine) used at the actual attachment of the lead rope to the saddle of the next mule. Others stayed attached as the following animals went with the flow. Herm dived off of the lead horse and plunged down the bluff to rescue mules that were starting to catch on trees and brush on the side of the slope, some right side up, others on their backs on top of the inverted packsaddles.

A capsized mule in this type of predicament will usually wait patiently for some help with all four legs curled up, like a dog sleeping on its back in the sun. A packhorse under the same circumstances will often flail away with all four feet and continue to struggle until it has broken something on itself or a would-be rescuer. Packers tell of horses getting a kink in their intestines that can be fatal. The immediate remedy for a trapped pack animal is to unfasten or cut loose the saddle so that it can right itself, sometimes with a little human help if it's stuck against a stump or tree or rock. The attached strings of animals still tied together are cut loose so that they are free to get themselves back up to the trail if they can.

Some of the riding horses had seen enough, and attempted to turn around and bolt back up the trail. I stepped from the stirrup on the near side, which happened to be the downhill side, and got in front of my horse to keep it pointed down the trail. I caught the lead rope of the first horse coming by just at the halter as horse and rider shot by and just managed to pull its head around and stop it without all of us going over the side. All of us—me, both horses, and the lady on the runaway who only signed up to come along with her husband, the Professor—had eyes about the size of goose eggs. Some of the other hunters along the line had by now dismounted and were either holding horses or climbing down the slope to retrieve or rescue mules. Amazingly, there were no broken bones in the entire bunch of pack mules.

As the mules either made their own way up or were led back to the trail, they were loaded up again. Repacked mules were started down the trail, led by hunters in singles or pairs. The whole process of repacking, repairing, and reloading took hours.

That hunt that ended with the great butane tank pack string wreck formed a club for those who enjoyed the experience. For those who didn't . . . well, none of us ever heard from the Professor or his wife again. But I was to continue hunting for years with Zak, Howie, and a constantly changing membership of the New Jersey Roughriders.

I occasionally draw comments due to my habit of riding geared up, cinched down, and dressed out. I wasn't that way until a certain ride one lazy morning on the Jingle Mare . . .

THE GREAT LOOSE CARTRIDGES IN SHIRT POCKET JINGLE MARE BUCKOFF

The Association had been out for a morning hunt. It was one of those easy-going days toward the end of a hunt, when the group has already sent a bull or two out to the locker, and we all had about had our fill of it for another year. One of those days when hunters aren't up to the same level of excitement as on the first part of the hunt. One of those days when we were relaxed and enjoying just being out in the mountains in beautiful fall weather. One of those days when the flatlander mind gets lazy and hunters can get into real bad trouble.

Real bad trouble on this day came in the form of a big mare. This nice mare had come to the local auction sale barn where the outfitter found her from downstate somewhere. That usually serves to put a horse buyer on notice of trouble. It doesn't take a genius to ask the question, "Wonder why somebody didn't buy this good-looking horse back there where they knew her when she came up for sale?" But the boys reassured me that they had been riding her around the place and she had turned out to be a horse fit for "the little kids and the grandmas" at the summer family get-togethers.

That morning, we had decided—being lazy, remember—to just throw the saddles on the horses and ride rather than walk the half mile or so down the trail and around the lake below our camp. We would leave the horses on the shore of the lake and climb up the far mountains from the lake for the morning's hunt. Taking the casual outlook even further, we thought that we'd just skip making the horses deal with the bridles, and steer with the lead ropes for that short distance along the trail, where the horses would follow each other along single file out of habit anyway.

We finished the hunt for the morning and were glad to have the ponies waiting for the little pull back up the trail to camp. They were really glad to see us too. We saw from tracks and what's politely referred to as "other unmistakable sign" that they had been visited by a couple of moose that we saw were still around in the distance along the lake, and even a bear, while they were helplessly tied up short. Their eyes were still kind of big, not out-on-stalks-big, but on full alert.

They settled down in a little bit as we talked to them in soothing tones that we really wouldn't leave them tied up to be stomped by moose and eaten by bears while we were out on the mountain goofing off. We cinched up the saddles about half tight, maybe actually about a quarter tight, and started up the trail for camp, partly steering with the lead ropes, mostly going along with what the horses wanted to do. Big mistake.

My horse decided to pause for a few nibbles along the side of the trail, which was okay with me. Then she realized that we were being left behind with all of the bears and moose and decided that maybe we should catch up, and she started jigging up the trail behind the rest of the string of horses, which was still okay with me.

I digress for a moment for a little background so that you understand why what happens next happens before I tell you about it. It had always been my habit, up until the time of this Tale, to carry a loose round, sometimes two, in my shirt pocket in addition to the spare ammo carried where you *should* carry spare ammo, which is on an elastic carrier worn on the belt. It might have been (actually it certainly was) a holdover from my youth, when I always hunted with a single-shot .22 rifle or a single-shot 12-gauge shotgun because single-shots were what we had. Extra shells, the normal term for cartridges at that place and time, were carried in shirt pockets, except, of course, when the shooter was wearing bib overalls. That was the fastest reload arrangement. That was the arrangement that everybody who actually lived in the country used, as opposed to the sportsman types who came from town out to the country and carried repeaters. Anyway, that's what I was doing with loose cartridges in my shirt pocket that morning. I may have even unloaded the rifle for the ride and dropped those rounds into the shirt pocket as well.

As we jigged up the trail, the loose cartridges started a merry little jingle in time with the jig of the mare—*jingle, jingle, jingle*—that is burned deep into my memory as my first inkling of trouble that morning. The timing of the jingles started to spread apart as the jigs got farther apart because we were going higher with every jump—*jingle . . . jingle . . . jingle . . .* In no time at all (but it seemed like a long time what with time standing still) we were into a full-bore, all-out, wild-eyed, I'm-gonna-buck-you-off-and-stomp-your-daylights-out, arched-back, high-leapin', stiff-legged-landin' rodeo. And it just went on forever, what with time standing still like it was.

A couple of geological epochs passed before my companions took notice of the unusual activity back down the trail. Actually, their horses caught on first and thought that they might get excited and join in the fun as well. Horses are like that. It was about that time that Gene started my time like they do in the official rodeos. According to him, I stayed on well past the eight seconds it takes to qualify and had accumulated a helluvalot of style points too, but that didn't make any difference with the mare, or me either. You can tell by the feel when a horse has decided to buck you off, and a horse can tell whether it can or not. It was no contest actually, with no reins and a very loose saddle. Most people don't realize that you can actually stay on longer with a loose saddle than a tight one, since the jughead underneath can't get as much pop on you. (Most people have more sense than to get into that type of situation in the first place.) But that doesn't make any difference, because what you can't do is to stay pointed up. A couple of side steps well done will get you leaning a little bit over to one side with no way to straighten back up again. Then the up and down is much more effective.

About this point was when the mare decided that it was a good time to change from bucking to a good all-out bolt through the brush to get around the rest of the string and start a dead run up the trail, where she could knock me off and hide my dead body somewhere. At the same time, I decided that I wasn't going to do any better trying to ride upside down than I was doing right side up, and I might as well start looking for a good place to land. About that time, a 5-foot-tall broken-off tree stump came into view beside the trail up ahead. It was about lined up with my head, mounted as I was straight out to the side of the mare by that time. That stump was coming up fast, and she was making a straight line to go just to one side of it, with me going through it if I could. The ground directly in front of the stump started looking better and better as a place to lightly touch down, and I started trying to kick out of the stirrups. I bounced, slid, and rolled for about 15 feet and came to a stop just in front of the stump.

Since time was no longer standing still, it took a little while for me to get around to moving everything, and a little longer to get over my surprise that everything was still attached, moved in the right places, and in the right directions. It took still longer to locate my rifle in the brush back down the trail. The mare felt a lot better about everything after she got me off, and Gene caught her without too much trouble. I decided to finish the short trip back to camp on foot. To hell with that cowboy thing of always getting back on a horse that's thrown you off to show it who's boss. We'd pretty much decided that question. Particularly with no reins and a loose saddle.

Everybody lived through the night. I was none the worse for wear except that my hide was two-toned with a purple paint job on the hip that I landed on and about a dime's worth of hide removed from one elbow where I bounced and slid along the trail. We packed up camp for the trip out the next morning as planned. I walked out and hunted through some good spots and had a great time. I had about walked out the soreness from the buck-off by the time I got to the bottom.

Meanwhile, back in camp, the guys were loading up for the trip out. They were still mystified as to what had set the mare off the day before. As far as mountain trail riding is concerned, a horse that has quirks that can bring on a bucking fit like that when you don't know the quirks is like sitting on a barrel of black powder or short-fused dynamite and playing with matches. They thought that as long as they were leading her out, they would trying packing her with a light load to see if she might work out as a packhorse, until they figured out what went through her head. They made up a pack with some odds and ends that included our tin cans and other garbage that we always packed out like good environmentalist cowboys. They tied the mare up short and loaded her up with the light pack.

She stood there just as nice as could be until a can in the garbage made a little rattle. Then she gave a little jump, which of course made all of the cans rattle. Then she went berserk. Still tied up short, she jumped around and around and kicked and snorted and bawled and fell and turned over and kicked upside down. The guys couldn't believe their eyes at the fit she had as it just went on and on. She managed to somehow spin around, still tied up short, and buck and kick some more. Nearing exhaustion, she settled down just enough for them to slip in close enough for the dangerous task of cutting loose what was left of the shredded pack and give her enough slack on the rope to fall to the ground. There she lay until she recovered. There was a little speculation as to what might have happened to Old Tom if he'd have got tangled up in that spun-over saddle and got "drug and stomped." I'm glad I didn't hear it.

Sometime during the discussions and speculations while all the stock settled down, the Association, less Tom, in the best Sherlock Packer tradition, concluded that there must be a connection between the jingle of the loose cartridges that Tom had in his pocket and the rattle of the cans in the pack. Some horses have quirks like that. They thought about checking out the theory then and there, but thought better of that idea, since they were on the wrong side of the bluffs, and there was no point in asking for trouble by getting the entire string even more "alert." They did do the test later, back home in the horse lot. I never heard any more about the results of that experiment or about the Jingle Mare. But, I wouldn't be surprised if a few weeks after that, in a sale barn far, far away . . .

There's a little epilogue to this Tale that I'll relay as a point of caution to any young hunters who manage to somehow get themselves scraped along a trail that the bears and moose have used for a path and all of those other things that they proverbially do in the woods.

About a week after that, while I was goofing off at a black powder shoot, it was pointed out to me that my elbow looked sort of funny. Like a pink grapefruit. I hadn't noticed, since I never pay much attention to the back of either of my elbows, but a pink, oversized elbow when you're shooting offhand in a short-sleeved shirt sort of stands out like the proverbial dog balls, even to a bunch of black powder shooters who don't usually don't pay much attention to things like other people's physical infirmities. When the doc checked it out the next Monday, I found out I had a nasty infection that put my arm in a sling for a few weeks. It had gone from the dime-sized skin surface scrape down into the bone and tendons of the entire elbow assembly. A little antiseptic at the time would probably have prevented all of that, including the little ache I have in that elbow in cold weather as a souvenir of that ride on the Jingle Mare.

Episodes like this next little saga are probably less frequent in outfitter pack camps these days what with the insurance companies and their lawyers look-ing out for us. In retrospect, maybe that's not all bad. Anyway, this Tale comes under the category of "scouting on horseback; or, off-the-trail action." Speaking from experience, don't try this unless you're a trained professional, and I don't know where you'd get the training other than the "University of Real Hard Knocks and Scrapes," which is the graduate studies branch of the more well-known "College of Hard Knocks."

CAPTAIN AND TOM TAKE A SLIDE

I had joined the cavalry with a bad knee on my first elk hunt after a few tumbles through rock slides and a change of camp. Herm, John, and I rode out of Pass Creek camp on a hunting-scouting trip up the Seven Lakes Trail past the Stanley Hot Springs. I was riding Captain, one of the best mountain trail horses I ever had the pleasure of riding. Captain was one of those horses that are all heart. If you wanted to go there, he would take you there without any questions, whether going there was a good idea or not.

When you're actually hunting from horseback rather than riding along an established trail, you're in for a more adventurous, rougher ride. The terrain usually offers a few complications; in this case, the very steep slopes were covered with a thick layer of litter, including the remains of old, burned-out cedars from the widespread fires in the early part of the twentieth century. As these downed cedars deteriorated, long natural planks formed under the loose litter of second-growth timber, along with boggy seeps in creases of the slopes. We had ventured well off of the trail looking for elk sign when the fun started.

The first incident of the trip was a good warmup for the thrills that were to follow. Captain and I were slightly separated from Herm and John, and we were going down a steep slope when Captain's back feet suddenly shot forward out from under him. He made a nice recovery and proceeded to slide down a 20-foot-long plank on his behind and his extended upright front legs. I was left standing in the stirrups, which were sliding along the plank in close formation with my mount's three-point ground contact. Some strange combination of physical forces stayed in balance to keep us upright in that unlikely posture throughout the entire 20 or 30 feet of the trip. I'm sure that it would have looked like a fast slide to an uninvolved spectator, but with time standing still due to our velocity, it seemed like a long flight to yours truly. I finished at the bottom still standing astride Captain, with him still sitting on his behind. It looked like a good time to step off while I still could, which I did. The horse stood up, none the worse for the trip; the only physical indication that it had happened at all was the size of our eyes.

Both horse and rider settled down after a bit, and we continued my introduction to scouting on horseback, with me trying to stay in the saddle through the thick, low limbs and Captain trying to keep his shod parts as the only contact with the ground through the occasional little bad place with steep, treacherous footing.

Before long, we rejoined our little group and began sidehilling along the upper reaches of a creek, single file, with Captain and me bringing up the rear. You'd think that I would ride into less trouble if I was in line behind the experienced mountain guides, but it was not to be. We approached a very steep, soft, seepy spot. The horses and riders ahead made it through and Captain and I followed right along without giving it too much thought. It turned out to be one of those places that become more unstable with the passage of each churning set of hooves. Some horses might feel the ground yielding to their weight and refuse to go on. Not Captain. On he went. The rider can sense that the horse is losing its footing some time after the horse, and, in an instant, I could tell that there was trouble on the way. By that time, it was already too late to rethink the plan or attempt to get off, because I would have just thrown the horse off balance. I was already leaning, to keep my weight centered over the ground contact of the horse, when I felt his front feet start to go out from under him. I hit the side of the hill at the same time as the front of the horse, and down the hill we slid. And slid. And slid, rolling over and over and spinning around, with the horse trying desperately to find footing and the rider trying to keep the saddle horn out of his ribs and head. The rolling over and over in a situation like this is not quite as bad as it sounds, since the weight of the horse is pointed straight down, and on a slope as steep as the one we were on, only 200 or 300 pounds of the horse mashes the dismounted rider against the ground. That's not so bad as long as it's not concentrated at a single point on the horse, like that saddle horn, or on the ground, like a rock. The spongy, soft ground of the seep was relatively forgiving.

We went rolling and spinning down the slope, kept together by gravity and the shape of the slope, despite my best efforts to create some separation. Luckily, I stayed clear of the thrashing hooves. Time stands still in this kind of situation, and your attention is well focused. You tend to remember every joyous moment of it. I remember vividly closing my eyes tightly as the horse rolled over me, and opening them again as I went over the top of him. On one roll and spin, I was looking right into the horse's wide, terror-stricken eyes. On another, I was looking right up the other end.

Eventually, after traveling about 30 feet, during one of my turns on top, I saw a small tree to one side of our line of flight, and managed to grab it with one hand as we slid by. The horse went on rolling and sliding for about another 20 feet until the ground leveled out slightly. Herm came running past me as I lay hanging on to the tree, trying to get oriented. He was making giant strides on the steep slope as he kicked off into space with each leap. He bounded right past me on down the slope to where Captain was struggling to his feet. He worked Captain over at some length. Finally, after he had rubbed over every leg of the trembling horse and made sure that he was okay, Herm looked back up at me and calmly asked, "You okay, Tom?"

Sometimes the talk around the evening fire gets around to mules. Here's enough information for you to at least follow the dialogue . . .

MULE TRIVIA—PLOW MULES, PACK MULES, AND SUNDAY MULES

The uninformed (that would be most people who live where there are paved roads in this twenty-first century) are under the impression that "mules is mules," all produced by mating a jack—which is the short form of jackass, the correct and accurate term denoting a male donkey—with a mare, or female horse. The nonbreeding hybrid offspring is about as strong as a donkey, which has astounding strength for its size, and close to the size of a horse. But, like anything else in this or any other century, if you learn a bit about them, you find out that things are a lot more complicated. There are several types of mules, bred for different specialized tasks, and the different types aren't interchangeable between those tasks. Due to the multitude of different combinations of jack and mare used to breed mules, extremes in mule configurations run from very large, slow plow mules to small, agile, fast-stepping pack mules.

A less well-known trait of mules is their longevity. A twenty-year-old horse is considered old; a twenty-year-old mule is still in its prime and can be expected to lead a productive life until well past the age of forty. In an earlier time, mules and men grew to maturity together and grew old using the same plow.

I've noted that good pack mules used for elk hunting seldom come up for sale, but when they do, it's usually because they've outlasted their owner's hunting days and the younger generation isn't interested in hunting. More often, the owner wouldn't think of parting with his or her mules, but is willing to let them go hunting with well-qualified hunter-packer friends just to get in a little packing work as sort of a refresher course each fall. I've been on hunts with these old mules on loan from even older elk hunters, gray and long in the tooth, but ready and willing to take on the steepest mountain trails once more.

Harness mules can be either plow mules or wagon mules. Harness mules of either type won't normally put up with anything heavy on their backs. Plow mules are bred for pulling—and they're good at it. Pack mules, on the other hand, are bred for strength in the back, for carrying heavy loads, and for agility along with endurance. When a pack mule feels resistance on a line from the back, instead of pulling harder like a harness mule would, it will slow down or stop to let the mule behind catch up or get past the bad place.

Mules have several advantages over horses as pack animals. Although horses, since they are larger than mules, can carry heavier loads than mules, they don't have the endurance of a mule. More importantly, horses are much more likely to startle and bolt and stampede than mules, which can lead to disaster in a pack string along a narrow trail in rough country. Mules are generally considered more intelligent than horses, and won't throw themselves over a bluff in a panic to their death as will a horse. On the downside, some mules, unlike horses, will hold a grudge and take revenge later on in response to a real or perceived slight or transgression on the part of their human handlers. Some small pack outfits both pack and ride their horses as a matter of economy, since it is relatively easy to train a horse to both pack and ride, depending on the requirements of the hunt. A mule that can be ridden by an inexperi-

A big top-class mule with a full-time job as Sunday mule.

enced rider, however, is a treasured rarity. A few really lucky folks, like my friend Frank, have strings of fine riding mules.

Pack mules seem to come in a wide variety of sizes and colors resulting from widely different ideas as to the optimum pack mule configuration. Pack strings are usually uniformly matched so that the string has about the same natural step and gait, but I've seen strings ranging from large, slow-paced, heavily packed Mississippi-type mules to smaller, athletic, fast-stepping, little mules hardly larger than donkeys that can scamper through brush and downed timber as if they were on an improved Forest Service trail.

Mules have reputations of being faithful workers, giving their all day after day, year after year, until they are retired or meet an untimely end on the job. If you'll permit a personal example, one of my granddad's old plow mules was pulling his load in the harness one day, and unexpectedly, without any complaint or sign of distress, he either overheated or had a stroke or heart attack and lay down and died in the traces right there in the field. My shocked and heartbroken granddad grieved long after tractors allowed the mules on the place to retire, and carried that memory of faithful service until the end of his days. That tale is still good for a few misty eyes among the old-timers at family reunions, yours truly included.

A Sunday mule is very special. Most mules are dynamite with long ears, but a Sunday mule will have a sweet and gentle disposition and can be trained to ride. The sweet disposition is essential so that the mule doesn't wake up on any given morning in a bad mood and take advantage of the situation and do you in when you attempt to ride it. Any mule is athletic enough to throw a rider off and give him or her a working over on the way down or after he or she hits the ground. The name derives from the fact that it's a mule that can work for you all week and then can be ridden to church on Sunday, traditionally the day of rest for mules and people alike.

CHAPTER 22

Deluxe Hunting Arrangements: Deluxe Camps, Lodges, Tribal Hunts, and Foreign Hunts

For the hunter who can afford to pay a little more, some other paid elk hunting options open up. The arrangements in this chapter cost more than the usual outfitter deal or any of the personal or private arrangements, and the client should expect a high-quality experience. Keep in mind, though, that we all have different measures of quality—success, a trophy, luxury digs, and so on.

EXTRA DELUXE OUTFITTER WILDERNESS CAMPS

A variation on the standard outfitter camp is the super deluxe combination base camp and hunting camp. This sort of setup is located somewhere that allows year-round access, using snowmobiles in the middle of winter, under special permits that allow semi-permanent tents with floors. These camps work well for folks (like JoAnne) who enjoy the wilderness but really don't care to sleep with a rock poking into their ribs all night. After about the third night, a good night's sleep on a real bed might sound like a good idea. And your "luck" might be better with bright eyes and those "mature" joints not so stiff.

PRIVATE LAND

Hunting of free-ranging elk on privately owned land occurs under several different circumstances of land ownership. Some large ranches contain enough land for hunting free-ranging elk of a resident population.

A few accents for the décor.

The most interresting furnishings in this camp, such as the bar, have been handmade by the guys, using chunks of seasoned trees that didn't split well to make stove-sized pieces of firewood. STEVE BURSON

Some places border federal park or other special-use land where elk occur and are free to cross into the private land, where they are hunted. A lot of privately owned land in the West blocks public land behind it from easy access from public roads, effectively limiting public access. This also tends to limit public use for activities such as hunting. This is not an unusual arrangement for cattle ranches that front on roads or running water.

The way you go about hunting from private land is primarily a function of the terrain. Very rough terrain where considerable distances are involved may require a pack-in hunt similar to an outfitter pack camp hunt. The physical arrangement of the hunting camp is the same as discussed in Chapter 20. Hunting under these conditions requires the same skills, techniques, and conditioning as previously described. Easier terrain allows the use of wheeled vehicles and usually works out to involve a commute from lodge to hunting area.

LODGES

A more common arrangement on private land is to hunt out of a permanent hunting lodge. You can find all sorts of variations on this basic setup advertised. We just discussed cases where privately owned land backs up to public land or even national parks that are closed to hunting but hold large populations of elk in summer. These elk then migrate through the private land at the onset of winter, which adds greatly to the numbers of elk beyond the resident population. Success in this situation depends on the weather and other factors controlling the timing of the migration. The number of elk taken is controlled by the length and timing of the season and the number of tags and permits issued.

Depending again on the terrain, hunters may go out on foot, on horseback, or in four-wheel-drive vehicles to the general area where the elk range. In the case of easy terrain and minimal hunting pressure, elk may be located and closely approached by vehicle to begin the stalk. Since the nature of the terrain determines how physically demanding the hunt will be and how close the hunting area may be approached by vehicle, these hunts can be the least physically demanding of any elk hunting. However, they may be less satisfying to some hunters than the wilderness hunt in rugged backcountry. The other side of the easier access, however, is that those hunters with permanent physical challenges can have the opportunity to hunt elk. Their satisfaction in overcoming their own challenges as well as the challenge of the hunt evens it all out, and my hat's off to them.

Easier terrain usually means more roads and possibly more people, which are usually associated with fewer elk in the area overall. The lower elk population in turn means that a limited number of tags are available in these areas. The prospective hunter may have to apply for a permit for several years before drawing a tag for the area of choice. Tight control of the number of elk taken serves to produce highest-quality trophy bulls.

The package for a hunt in this kind of area often includes luxurious hunting lodge accommodations that, combined with a good chance at an impressive trophy bull, make for quite a hunting experience for those who can afford it.

TRIBAL LAND HUNTS

You can also make arrangements to hunt elk on tribal lands in Arizona and New Mexico. The costs and trophy possibilities are significantly different from one area to another, so you should be able to find a hunt to match your circumstances and objectives. Details are available online. If the chance to take a trophy bull is your primary consideration, these pricey hunts are actually a bargain. They eliminate the cost in time and cash of years of hunting for the "Big One" in less productive areas. Sometimes your success in taking a trophy in these areas depends more on what you're looking for. Tribal representatives have explained to me how hunters with the means to cover the cost of these hunts may hunt for several weeks and never see a trophy to match the ones they already have on the wall. They'll choose to save the "young, small" 300- to 350-point bulls for another year! These clients aren't too concerned about getting enough meat to make it through the winter.

ASIAN HUNTING

A new opportunity for elk hunting that has recently emerged with changing political situations throughout the world is hunting in Asia.

Most elk hunters are under the impression that "elk are elk" wherever they might be found throughout Asia. That's about half right—the east half.

Europe and the west half of Asia are home to red deer. Natural populations of Western European red deer are indigenous throughout the Caucasus Mountains of south and southwest Asia and Asia Minor and are commonly referred to as *maral,* Persian for red deer. Wapiti species, also widely referred to as *maral* just to keep things confusing, range to the east and north from the area of their origin, the Himalayan foothills of Central Asia.

When looking for an elk hunt in Asia, you should be aware that not all of the elk are the same as the ones we have in North America. Diminutive five-point wapiti species adapted to temperate forests on mountain slopes exist for the most part in small numbers, but there are a few populations large enough to be huntable, including the Manchurian wapiti and the Alashan wapiti (the same species in different habitat and geographic distribution). The larger six-point Siberian wapiti are identical to the North American form, with some small differences attributed to different quality of habitat. There are two subspecies of Siberian wapiti: the Tianshan or Tian Shan wapiti from the Tian Shan mountain range of Siberia, and the Altai wapiti from the Altai mountain range of Siberia (smaller with less impressive antlers than Tian Shan wapiti). To avoid unpleasant surprises, make sure you are booking your hunt in an area that has the kind of elk you want.

You should also be aware that some introduced wapiti and red deer populations outside of Asia, notably in New Zealand, are often released or transplanted farmed deer rather than indigenous free-roaming populations of wild animals. Ask plenty of questions when booking and make sure you are getting the kind of hunt you want.

If you want to plan an overseas hunt, you need to be aware that in some of the areas where elk hunting is available, the availability of medical care or communications with the outside world may be quite limited. In addition, we Americans tend to be somewhat unaware of local political problems, social unrest, or pervasive corruption or criminal activity in specific areas, which could lead to our unwittingly walking into a bad situation. You need to realize just how much you're depending on your booking agent or whoever has made the arrangements for you. My conversations with references while I was in the process of considering booking a foreign hunt (specifically, in Mongolia) indicated that it's difficult to

Manchurian wapiti, a typical five-point variety.

translate your preferences for trophy hunting, for instance, that you worked out with the booking agent to the Mongolians actually running the camp and guiding you on the hunt.

ELK HUNTING ARRANGEMENTS THAT AREN'T

There is another kind of arrangement advertised as elk hunting that you may come across anywhere money talks—which includes the whole world. It involves privately owned land stocked with elk that are not free ranging. An elk-proof fence encloses the entire place to prevent the elk from escaping. In this case, the elk are also privately owned stock, and for a price, can be killed without any requirement for a license or tag or season or the skills, conditioning, and techniques discussed in this book. This kind of setup, commonly referred to as a "high-fence deal," is outlawed in some elk hunting states.

The key question to ask if you're offered a fishy-sounding deal that makes a guarantee of elk hunting results is, "Is this hunt fair chase?" A fair-chase arrangement usually involves a wilderness outfitter area that contains two or three honest 300+ bulls along with some smaller bulls and a bunch of cow herds and is going to be on the order of 2,000 square miles. So if the deal offered is going to happen on a 500-acre ranch, there's another red flag.

This book doesn't consider such arrangements. This book, as I have said, is about elk *hunting.*

CHAPTER 23

Hunting
on Your Own

In a carefully chosen area, elk hunters with the right qualifications, if they plan carefully from vehicle selection through provisioning and cooking, can have some successful, very economical, and extremely rewarding hunting without hired professional assistance. You'll note a pattern in the arrangements in this chapter: Expenditures and personal capability are inversely proportional.

The key to success in making your own arrangements is to approach everything logically and realistically. If your party doesn't include experienced packers and passable cowboy types, then buying stock and equipment won't automatically create a pack camp operation, and doesn't make sense anyway unless you're hunting a large area without roads of any type.

If you can't stay on 'em, fix 'em, or drag 'em back up to the washed-out logging road you fell over the side of, and don't know for sure whether the things are allowed in the area you're going to hunt, you might as well leave the four-wheelers at home. And if all the members of the party can't carry the camp up, and elk quarters down, attempting to backpack hunt the pockets of steep river bluffs just isn't going to work.

I'll begin with arrangements that rely on boots as your primary transport and grade toward arrangements that use wheels for transport. Then I'll review different arrangements referred to as "private outfits" in western terms that use riding and pack stock for transport and, in general appearance, resemble "outfitter outfits." These tough but economical arrangements are definitely not for everybody, but they can be and are applied with great success, usually by the young and lucky, and meet the requirements that some of us bring up every so often: "What this country really needs is a good, $1,000 elk hunt for non-residents."

Your hunting arrangements for the *minimal* road-based camp should include the following elements:

- A primary vehicle to make the trip in and to haul and/or tow everything
- Shelter (may be the primary vehicle, or may be towed or hauled and set up)
- A source of warmth
- Food and means of food preparation
- Sleeping arrangements
- Transportation between camp and the hunting area

In economic terms, the best arrangement is the one that requires the least investment dedicated solely to your personal elk hunting arrangement. That translates to using things you already own, or gear that has multiple uses.

Minimal setup for a road-based camp—simply shut the doors and move out.

If you spend some time around camping areas during elk hunting season, you'll quickly realize that there's a road-based camping arrangement made for every taste and budget.

If we leave the hiking with a large daypack and tarp and sleeping out all night without a camp to the real die-hards, the most basic approach that provides the essential elements of an off-road hunting arrangement is the backpack spike camp. This kind of arrangement requires the use of your own vehicle or a rental vehicle, backpacks, backpack tents (individual bivy tents or a single lightweight tent for the whole group), a handsaw or axe and fire-making material, dehydrated backpacking food and the utensils needed to eat it, and sleeping bags and ground pads. You carry the camp to the hunting area by foot and backpack the elk out to the road. Be advised that this type of hunt involves staying out in the weather, and it can be a little rough for most tastes if the weather doesn't cooperate. Another caution: Be careful not overestimate what you can do physically in the pack-in, pack-out department if you choose this option.

If some sort of minimal trail (two-wheel) or road (four-wheel) network exists in the area so that you can get some motorized wheels in to the arrangement, all sorts of possibilities open up. Without the requirement to carry everything in and out, your range is extended considerably. Just a note of caution from an old elk hunter who's seen the best-laid plans go haywire at one time or another: Don't get yourself so far back in on wheels that you can't get yourself out on foot if things don't go as planned. Maybe through the snow on a bad leg from going over the side on your wheels. Always consider the worst-case scenario. Then add a safety factor.

Moving up to the general-use road-based camp, we find arrangements that are the minimum for most folks. The required equipment becomes the use of a large personal vehicle; a full-sized tent to accommodate all the hunters in the party; propane gas tanks with cooking stoves, space heaters, and lanterns; a chainsaw and wood stove; camp cooking gear and groceries in critter-proof containers; cots and bedding. You use four-wheelers, horses, or your own two feet to get out to the hunting area and to bring game back.

Hunting from a road-based camp has an often overlooked advantage over pack camp trips: You can jump in a vehicle and head down the road several miles to check out a completely different area without having to pick up camp and make a major move. Sometimes, it seems, just a change of scenery can improve your luck. A large party may want to split up to scout different areas before or at the start of the season, then combine forces to use drive and stand tactics. Sometimes you may just want to split up to hunt different areas for no better reason than that some of you prefer the looks of one area over another. My experience indicates that you usually have better luck hunting an area that looks good to you rather than one where you really don't think that there are any elk. Maybe you look harder in the better-looking area.

In this arrangement, the vehicle you have determines the kind of road required to transport the camp to the vicinity of the hunting area. Vehicles you can use range from go-anywhere four-wheel-drive trucks and SUVs, suitable for primitive or deteriorated logging roads, to vans and pickups pulling horse trailers, both of which have relatively poor ground clearance and therefore require improved roads. The hunters may prefer four-wheelers for elk hunting with a motor sports emphasis or horses for the cowboy experience—or far-ranging individual hunting on foot, packing out meat by packboard for the physically fit and dedicated elk hunter. The camper, or hunting-cabin-on-wheels, approach brings all the comforts of home in compact form to the mountains. Campers can range in size and price range from expensive motor coaches pulling trailers to light truck-mounted or towed campers. Typical camper trailers are small and accommodate parties of four or five hunters, with all their cooking and sleeping requirements, and, in the case of larger rigs, full bathroom arrangements as well. Groups of hunters often travel in separate vehicles, some pulling the campers, others pulling trailers hauling off-road vehicles or horses. The campers are confined for the most part to improved roads due to their size and limited ground clearance. They'll be left in the camping area along the road.

Tents along the road can involve a commute on the road network to different hunting areas, or a walk out from the tent to hunt the immediate area.

Road-based camp arrangements run a large range. Some road-based parties will have several spacious camper trailers for the people and comparable trailers to haul several head of riding and pack stock. They may approach the level of a hunter-owned pack outfit, absent only specialized packer skills, although they operate from the road with more comfortable living arrangements rather than from a pack camp up in the mountains.

Horse trailers and campers are significant investments for one-time-a-year use if you're interested in using them only for elk hunting. Year-round maintenance of horses is also expensive and takes a lot of time unless you happen to live out where the rooster crows in the

The amateur cowboy option on the move, with hunters, camp, and horses in one load.

A motor sports hunting camp option: The camper transports four-wheelers, then becomes sleeping quarters.

morning and the coyotes howl at night. You can rent campers and motor homes, but that cost has to be rolled into the one-time cost of the hunt. If elk hunting is your main interest rather than year-round camping and trail riding, a lower-cost approach is to use tents, which are inexpensive compared to campers and motor homes, and small trailers and electrical generators, which can be rented at a reasonable cost. The most useful feature of generators when hunting the early season of the

A road-based camp using several one-person tents.

A more rustic tent camp.

southern part of elk hunting country is that you're then independent of the cold storage facilities in some distant town. Some road-based camps bring freezers with them on their trailers—the nights will likely be too warm to keep meat from spoiling otherwise. Most of the fixed cost of this kind of outfit is in the vehicles, which have everyday utility for the rest of the year. One vehicle in the group needs to have four-wheel drive and a set of tire chains to handle the roads between the camping area and the hunting area under all foreseeable weather conditions.

I'll make a note of caution here regarding towed campers or trailers for the flatlander considering an elk hunt (or any other mountain road trip in the fall). Big trouble can result from the combination of campers or trailers without brakes and steep mountain secondary roads with a little snow or ice thrown into the mix. The old term "hog on ice" comes to mind, with apologies to the hogs. Without its own brakes, the towed load tends to push the towing vehicle around, even on dry pavement, and any loss of traction pushes the combination out of control and can take it over the side. Even four-wheel drive and chains on the towing vehicle may not be enough to avoid trouble with a heavy camper or trailer.

The best efforts to see that a hunting party is outfitted and fed can't guarantee that the hunt will be a success. Some thought should be given to the party size and compatibility. Most of the parties you see camped by roads during elk hunting season have hunted together for many seasons past. Many of them are made up of relatives, with a few close family friends joining in. They all know each other and what to expect from each other. They've decided years ago who can, and will, run the ridges and who prefers to sit on the lookouts and watch for elk that the "bird dogs" kick out. Many have evolved from runner to sitter through the years within the same party. Fathers and sons or daughters hunt together for years, and the relationship subtly changes as to who is looking out for whom. You encounter these groups while hunting: the older guy, the middle-aged man or woman, with the third generation playing the part of the bird dog. The size of the party has likewise evolved to something that everyone is comfortable with, and they keep it that way. It's hard for an outsider to break in. I've also noted that outfitter pack camps evolve toward a certain number of hunters and guides that matches what the camp can comfortably accommodate. Experienced outfitters quickly sort out the runners and sitters so that everyone is comfortable and has fun. Outfitters that stay in business are good at that sort of thing.

You won't have all of this background work behind you when you set out to put together an elk hunting party for the first time. You may not realize that people on an elk hunting trip often aren't the same as back in the neighborhood, office, or plant. Some will pitch in with the chores and expenses without reservation, coordinate with the group while hunting, and help watch out for each other. Some won't. Some turn out to be loners; others, and this is a quote, "prefer to enjoy their solitude with somebody." Everyone in the group should be aware of these aspects of the hunt before they sign on, and the group should talk about—but not belabor—such things as how expenses and camp work will be handled, how game taken will be divided or not (maybe divide the meat and field dressing effort, with the shooter keeping the trophy), and who takes the first shot if two or three are hunting together. Some people are light sleepers; some snore as loud as a chainsaw. Notice all of those separate campers in the photos? Will you prefer multiple small tents for sleeping and a separate cooking tent rather than one big tent? Some conversation and planning before the trip can make it go a lot smoother.

I can't help with your details, but I can make one suggestion for your consideration regarding the size of the party. Usually, more seems to work better than less, up to a point. If the hunters are family or friends of many years, so that they know what to expect from each other under different circumstances, a hunting party can be made up of three or four people. For people not so familiar with each other, I like a minimum of six to eight in the bunch. I'm not sure why, but maybe a bigger group can absorb the heat of the little frictions without combustion.

Some very nice high-dollar pack outfits with campers and horses may be seen in regions where good roads pass through mountain areas with improved trail networks. The southern region in particular has hunting areas where motorized vehicles are prohibited but that can be reached by good roads. If your group owns two heavy pickups, one to tow horse trailers and another to tow a nice camper, this can be a very

Frank and the mules share the deluxe trailer—camper in front, mules in back. Frank usually does the driving but he says some of his real smart mules can take a turn . . .

The private hunter-owned outfit that I threw in with for several years: the Association of Rough Ridin', Bull Huntin', Straight Shootin' Elk Hunters of the Idaho Bitterroots, or the Association for short. The Association worked mostly because of the guy riding just ahead of the photographer—the packer. He's the reason the packs are on the topsides of the mules at this point on the trip. I learned about shooting elk instead of trees from the rider wearing the baseball cap. As careful as he is accurate, he never chambers a shell until it's time to make the shot, so I guess you'd say he's fast too.

The Association string going in.

Cooking arrangements in hunter-owned camps are more austere than in out-fitter camps, and often outside. Fun only in good weather. GENE KUYKENDALL

practical option. I've observed several family outfits each with a horse trailer and camper set at trailheads. Several states have draw units with limited road access that can be effectively hunted using riding stock and pack strings.

My friend Frank, a riding mule enthusiast, has a first-class outfit for long-range road travel with sleeping accommodations for people in front and stock in back of a deluxe trailer that travels as a single unit. His playpen includes all of elk country.

Then there are the hunter-owned outfits (sometimes called local outfits) that share an area with professional outfitters and are more or less the equivalent of a professional outfit. When they are good, they are very, very good, as they say. When done right, these outfits are a lot of fun, and usually successful in taking elk, although that's only part of the total experience. Usually, the same group of hunters could success-fully hunt elk with any arrangement.

The other side of hunter-owned pack outfit camps is that when they are bad, put together by a group that doesn't know what it is doing, they can be very, very bad. If the group doesn't include at least one member who can pack a horse or mule, which is a mystic and difficult-to-learn art, they are a bad deal for all concerned. That includes themselves and anyone else who happens to be on the trail as they rodeo along.

Dedicated mountain camp private outfits usually skip the road-based campers and horse trailers. Their stock travels in the two-ton bobtail trucks commonly used by old-time outfitters. The lower metal sections of the sideboards are uniquely dimpled to the outside from impatient mules kicking the sides with corked-shod feet, and there'll usually be a few notches on the wooden upper section from bites. The passengers perk up and get in a better mood when the rig gets under way with the canvas cover off in good weather. The sound of the open road with the wind through their ears sort of thing.

Hunter-owned outfits and hunter-owned drop camps usually have a single tent, the same style as used in an outfitter drop camp. A single-tent camp will usually use the tent for sleeping with the ground as the mattress, and the cook tent may be replaced with the great outdoors.

CHAPTER 24

Intangibles

You can do your best to increase your chances of taking an elk, but in reality, the only thing that you can be absolutely sure of is that you'll go on a hunt. You can't control whether you're successful, but you can control what your hunt is like—how you live and what you experience during the hunt—and the totality of what you take away from it. Your pleasure should be determined by this experience of the hunt and those other intangible things you take home, not the results of the hunt (results narrowly defined as an elk carcass on the ground, that is). The satisfaction and pleasure associated with these intangibles of the hunt work together with physical well-being and mental preparation to allow you to put forth the sustained high level of effort essential to becoming a consistently successful elk hunter (again, in terms of that narrow definition of success). And so it's worth spending some time thinking about these intangibles.

My objective in this chapter is to discuss a few intangibles that are important to many hunters so that you can decide for yourself what's most important to you personally. I'll also give you the hard information to pick the arrangement that will provide the intangibles you're looking for. The next chapter will get into a methodology for taking intangibles into account when you're selecting a hunting arrangement.

Elk hunting means different things to different people. To some it's all about bagging that big trophy bull. For others, it's enough just to be out in the mountains. The camp experience can be as important as the actual hunting—and this might mean deluxe accommodations with real

For some folks, just getting to spend time in a place that looks like this is one of the most important parts of the elk hunting experience.

beds to you, or it might mean hunting out of a little pack camp tent very like what your great-great-granddad the frontiersman used to use. The equipment you choose is another intangible—rifles can take elk just like bows and arrows, but for some people the bows in their hands are an essential part of the hunt without which it just wouldn't be the same. Knowing that you're doing it well—the satisfaction that goes with using your hard-learned skills, techniques, strategies, and wisdom to take an elk—is another intangible aspect of the hunt.

The intangibles are about yourself and what you bring back from the hunt. For many of us, part of that intangible pleasure of the hunt is what we learn about ourselves and what we're capable of. It's diving down into some obscure place called Larson Creek and back out (that's straight up back out) the other side. Riding through the bluffs along Boulder Creek without fear on a pitch-black night when you can't see the horse's ears and can hear only the creek far below. Or on a clear day when you can see the creek way, way down below. The absolute confidence of knowing that you can handle a high-powered rifle with skill, regardless of your size or gender. It's being back home and talking to someone about wildlife sounds when they've only seen a wolf on television and you've camped with them howling all around when the echoing of one long moan hasn't stopped before another begins.

THE INTANGIBLES OF PLACE

The first-time elk hunter soon learns that elk hunting is about much more than taking an elk. It's about fall in the Rockies, views that are felt more than seen, colors with aroma, little lakes tucked under the bluffs that bring to mind gems in granite. It's about sunrises so cold that they snap when they hit the sky, mornings that begin mild and clear and end with a foot of snow by noon, ridges that sing in the wind like angels, threads of fog through moonlit pines on the slopes. It's the elation of coming up the other side of a nasty little creek and realizing that you haven't broken your neck or even a leg, and it's an elk bugle that echoes down from a point. It's nights by smoky fires and the telling of inaccurately remembered tales of hunts gone by.

TROPHY HUNTING

We'll begin with one of the more tangible intangibles: trophy hunting. In Part I, I presented the techniques and tactics involved in closing with the herd bull, and in Part II, we looked at the skills and gear you need to take him. Now we're talking about the mental decision to be a trophy hunter. Trophy hunters are self-designated. There's no indoctrination, certification, recommendations, or waiting to see if you've been accepted into the club. It's straightforward. You just decide not to shoot at the particular elk in front of you, so you can wait for that trophy.

In the beginning, I guess I started out as a trophy hunter. You don't know if you're a trophy hunter or not until you've passed up a shot at an elk because it's not a trophy. Some elk hunters, the "lucky" ones, take a trophy bull early and easy. Too bad. Think of all the fun they missed—all of the fun I enjoyed while accumulating the skills, conditioning, and inexperience during those long intervening years between that first hunt and that first real trophy. But, in any event, this is the way it got started.

THE DUDE FROM TEXAS MAKES A CHOICE

Opening day, breaking light on the Boulder Creek drainage above the Lochsa several miles upstream of Three Rivers Point, where the flow of the Lochsa combines with the Selway to form the Clearwater. The old Idaho elk guide and the hunter from Texas lay flat and looked across a large boulder perched on the side of a steep brushy slope. It was just legal shooting light.

The trophy is the first and foremost goal of some elk hunters. CHRIS KUYKENDALL

The guide knew what he was doing; the hunter most definitely did not. He was what was, and is, called a "dude" among the locals. The worst kind, a "flatlander dude," unfamiliar with either elk hunting or the mountains. He had slowed them down by stopping three times on the way out of camp to throw off coats suitable for waiting for white-tailed deer on a Texas deer stand, far too warm and heavy to climb these slopes (slopes where his boots slipped repeatedly). His rifle was a .308 Win lever-action with a four-power scope and a carrying sling borrowed from the outfitter. But he did manage to see with the guide the sudden movement in the tall brush as two elk spooked, probably by hunters from another camp coming up from below, and suddenly plunged into a small open area.

"Elk—shoot, shoot!" the guide half whispered.

The hunter's pulse pounded as he checked off the elk one by one through the scope. "Cow, cow; no horns on any of 'em" went through his mind. Cows were legal.

The guide repeated louder in a hoarser tone, "Shoot, shoot, they're gettin' away!"

"Didn't come this far to shoot a 'slick head.'"

The old guide's jaw hardened. Perhaps a little misunderstanding? A little misunderstanding with a seasoned elk guide. "Okay, let's go look for a big bull for you."

What followed was three days of getting out before first light, climbing up and down the steepest, longest slopes the Texan had ever imagined. He was young. The guide was old. On those slopes, their legs were like young rubber and old iron, respectively. Late in the morning (less late each successive day), the plan was always the same: The guide would go around one way, the hunter another; the bull elk would run over to the hunter, maybe; but, anyway, he should find an easy elk trail back to camp after a short run. But it always seemed to work out that instead he found a hole that a feeder creek had cut through the eons it had plunged into aptly named Boulder Creek, or he found that a rockslide blocked his way back to camp. The flatlander had a PhD in engineering; the guide hadn't made it through, if to, high school. But it took the college-educated flatlander three or four days to realize that Idaho elk hunting might not necessarily always be like this; he might be what's called in the trade "gettin' dumped off."

That realization came to him as he struggled down yet another rockslide and then waded through the rather deep, cold, and swift Boulder Creek at the bottom to get across to the government trail that led back to camp. Just at that time, as scripted in the old TV westerns, the outfitter came riding up the trail with the mule string, bringing in supplies. Trying his best not to show too much annoyance over his realization that he had been "had," he expressed gently to the packer, "Gene, I think I'm going to need a little more personal guiding than I'm getting, or I'm not only not going to get a big bull elk, but I might even get hurt out here." The packer, in his customary understated manner, allowed that, "if you can make it back up this trail to camp, we'll move you over to Herm's camp to see if it improves your luck." And he did. The guide wasn't in camp when the flatlander got there. Never saw him again. (Years later he learned that Gene's words to the guide were generally to the effect that he had better get out of camp before that Texan limping up the trail got there, or there might be real trouble. So much for attempts at subtlety.) At any event, the Texan "joined the cavalry" at this point and hunted from horseback for the rest of the trip; he did a good bit of scouting with the outfitter over a newly acquired area, survived a couple of mishaps riding off the trails (one of them a grand slide and roll that would be talked about for years), enjoyed the company of a guide who later went on to run a guide school, and experienced the rest of the beautiful package that goes with the Bitterroots in early fall. And sometime during the last days of that hunt, he heard a big bull's bugle echo across the canyon. He packed out with his tag still in his pocket.

Just before he left to go back to Texas, Herm shook his hand and said, "Well, Tex, you're a persistent cuss, just not real lucky like that other Texan, the one from Houston. Come back next year and I'll make you the same deal. I'll help you find that big one, and cape out the trophy for you." With that, he wrote out a refund check. The deal was that if you didn't get a legitimate shot at a five-point or better, you got a refund. If you decided (your choice) to take a cow or lesser bull instead, no refund. Herm and Gene hated to write refund checks, and they didn't write many. Hunters usually shot at the "slick heads" (cows) or the "raghorns" (immature bulls). The guy from Houston that Herm had mentioned wasn't faced with that decision. At breaking light of opening morning of the early hunt, a seven-point bull had walked out about 75 yards in front of him and stopped to present a standing suicide broadside shot, which he easily made. Within a couple of hours, he was ready to go back to Houston, through with elk hunting. His goal was to collect a good specimen of every game animal. He didn't need to hunt elk anymore. He was lucky—I guess.

Occasionally, when a hunter is holding out for a trophy bull, the shapes and proportions of immature antlers can result in curious consequences and teach a lesson in looking hard before that shot is taken. Mountain conditions of low visibility due to fog and heavy snow as well as thick brush and heavy timber can make you see what you want to see.

ANTLERS IN THE TREES

I was hunting through light timber with interspersed slashes of thick, high brush. On the edges of the timber, individual trees stood apart. Trees standing like this typically have dead lower limbs that have been shaded by limbs higher up the tree. It was the first time that we had hunted the area, and that usually means that you don't take the easiest route cross-country. So it was that a hunting buddy and I were sidehilling a slope that fell off into a creek below Long Lake way up above the Lochsa in the Idaho Bitterroots. Although you might say that we were, on average, moving on the level, and it would look to be so on a contour map with a good spacing between the contours, we were alternately crossing rises where the more durable underlying rock formed prominences, and then pulling through heavy brush and stands of timber where the more easily eroded rocks formed depressed crossings.

It was one of those dark Idaho days when the heavy snow comes and goes and melts on the brush, and the elk hunters who just have to get out anyway get soaked by wet from above, wet from below, and wet from the brush in the middle. But it was a great day to be out trying to locate elk that were lying under a heavy green tree somewhere and wouldn't move until you almost stepped on them.

We were pushing through yet another of the countless low draws filled with soaking wet heavy brush when the next snow shower came across. The sky went dark and the big wet flakes of snow came down like a thick curtain of white chicken feathers. As I topped the next rise, plowing on through the snow and brush, I suddenly caught a glimpse of a cow elk in the brush ahead, then another, then another. My excitement level picked up considerably. I looked around for a bull with the bunch, checking the outer fringes of the main gathering of cows. There he was, standing under a large tree on the next rise at about my level, his entire body easily visible across the depression, the upper part of his antlers obscured by the low dead limbs of the tree.

I could tell through the snow and dim light that he was an antlered bull as he turned his head slightly to reveal brow tines and rack that went up into the lower limbs of the tree. Expecting any shots that day to be at close range, I was carrying a .30-40 lever-action Winchester 95 rifle manufactured at the turn of the last century with the original open sights on the theory that a sight picture through a telescopic sight would amount to mostly flying snow and water collected on the lens. That was a good theory for that day, but that open sight didn't help to evaluate the trophy very much either. But I could see the bulk of the body clearly and I took the shot. The bull went down immediately.

I plunged through the brush that separated me from the spot where the bull went down to make sure he stayed down. He was breathing his last as I approached. I put a shot into the ear from a .22-caliber I often carried to safely and humanely put lights out when required.

Then I took a good look at the antlers and realized that this wasn't the old trophy bull that I was expecting from all of those antlers tangled in the tree limbs. This young one would be for the skillet, not the taxidermist. My eyes hadn't failed me. The brow tines really were heavy, but they made up most of the mass of the entire rack. It was sort of an ambitious four-point rack that tapered to thin fast above those impressive brow tines. The impressive part of that massive upper rack was still up in the dead limbs—in fact, it *was* the dead limbs!

That raghorn rack became an antler mount that serves a couple of purposes. Most of the young elk hunters and would-be elk hunters who come by remark on it, to the effect of, "What's this hat rack doing up here with the trophies?" That's a perfect lead-in to a little line of philosophical thought that they need to be exposed to, as well as to a practical caution. The first thought pertains to the question, "Why do we hunt?" I think it has to be related in some way to getting back out to the place we came from, our home before concrete and steel became popular, before farms, workshops, and computer-filled offices became our place. Not that dissimilar from the various breeds of hunting dogs, for thousands of generations, the humans that wouldn't, or couldn't, hunt were systematically weeded out of the gene pool. As humans, our basic urge to hunt is based first and foremost upon some primeval compulsion to kill for subsistence, not for prestige or ego—for the skillet, not the taxidermist. One could probably make a case that the trophy came once we got a little breathing room above the minimum survival level, and that's where some of our troubles as humans began.

The more practical lesson is that the elk hunter needs to be damned sure of what he or she is shooting at. You cannot let your excitement overcome you so much that you aren't sure of your target. In my case, it resulted in me shooting an animal that just barely fit the letter of the law of the definition of an antlered elk in some states.

That little raghorn rack leads me to a final couple of thoughts on the concept of the "trophy." As I said earlier in this book, ivories can make small, wearable trophies if incorporated into jewelry; you can also consider elk-skin clothing a trophy, and it's the telling of the tale that the decoration brings to mind that truly makes that big rack a trophy. But sometimes, the best tales result from a miss, or never getting a shot at all! And, if you "waste" a number of years stumbling and sliding around the big slopes on the general pretext of looking for big bull elk, a certain level of enlightenment eventually dawns on your befuddled

"Tom, I just love to hunt elk." And he gets one every so often, too.

consciousness: The most treasured trophies you've accumulated aren't even tangible things! The tale that you take away from the experience is the real deal. And, unlike the trophy mount, which will certainly eventually be surpassed by that young hot-shot, that tale can always improve with a little burnishing (something many old elk hunters get really good at).

OTHER RECREATIONAL OPPORTUNITIES IN ELK COUNTRY

Another very tangible intangible is the availability of outdoor sporting opportunities other than elk hunting that you can participate in on your wilderness elk hunting trip. The first step toward these opportunities is to check the seasons for game other than elk. The first choice for many elk hunters is mule or white-tailed deer, which usually have the most available tags in most areas. These species are not always available in the same area where you'll be hunting elk, of course. Mule deer usually hold to open, rocky or brush-covered areas. Mule deer may be found active in the middle of the day, and I've filled my mule deer tag at high noon during very warm weather, when trying to find elk at any time other than very early or very late was very long odds. Whitetail hunting

I know folks who would make the trip just to see the salmon end their run in the pools of the high country.

may be best early or late in the day, when you'll be concentrating on finding an elk, but if you get lucky and fill your elk tag, you may be glad to have the whitetails in the area, too. Moose, sheep, and goat tags are usually very limited for nonresidents. Some major predators, including bears, cougars, and, recently, wolves, are often available for hunting to reduce their impact on deer and elk populations. Encounters with bears can occur anywhere at any time; the only downside to a shot at a bear is that all elk in the area might make a big move due to the disturbance. Running across either a cougar or a wolf will be longer odds, but you'll often hear wolves on a wilderness hunt. Grouse of various species are to be found throughout elk country. Some hunters carry a .22 handgun to fill the specialty platter at supper—although it's best to warn the cook and get a favorable reaction before bringing in more work to fit into his or her already full schedule.

A favorite non-hunting activity for me has long been trout fishing. For years while I was designing and producing graphite fishing rods for Skyline Fort Worth, I made checking out experimental fly rods on mountain streams and lakes part of my agenda for my elk hunting trips. We would also set aside time to catch one of the ocean salmon runs when everything came together at the right time.

THE TRADITION OF HUNTING

And now we begin to move toward the more intangible intangibles, beginning with joining the age-old tradition of hunting.

We have a rich heritage of hunting traditions, and an important part of hunting for many is to participate in some version of one of these traditions. Our hunting traditions date back to the dawn of humanity, drawing on an overworked phrase, but the essential ingredients of the most popular current arrangements are considerably more recent developments.

The first European settlers of the New World arrived with an internalized background of late medieval European society. That society was based on agriculture, with a very narrow base of land ownership and therefore of wealth and power. Hunting practices reflected this arrangement, with hunts often being a sort of ritual that served to remind the lower classes of their position in life. They would drive all wild animals they could round up toward concentrated groups of the wealthy, who enjoyed the excitement of the wholesale slaughter of every living thing that came their way. The sporting nature of the entire event resulted in the wild animals being termed "game" animals. The drivers might get a small portion of the kill according to the "generosity" of their masters.

The accommodations of a hunt are an important "tangible intangible"—but for some hunters it's the deluxe lodgings that are important, while others prefer to follow in the footsteps of our far-back ancestors and rough it.

When European settlers came to the New World, things were different. Now survival dictated that they learn how to farm newly cleared fields, fish the waters, and hunt the woods, often initially under the tutelage of Native Americans. Direct participation in hunting and fishing, a privilege of the upper classes in Europe, became an absolute necessity along the frontier of the New World of North America. Pursuit of wildlife wasn't a game—it was essential to existence.

As the settled area expanded farther west and the more coastal areas grew prosperous and developed other industries, hunting and fishing evolved into recreational activities. In this environment originated the American version of a literature of outdoor sports. The frontier underwent a transformation as it broke out of the eastern hardwood forests and encountered the great central plains of North America. The plains became conduits of travel rather than destinations, and adventurers and fortune seekers flocked across them, sending back fanciful written accounts for the consumption of those leading a less exciting existence in the settled East. The reality of frontier life began to mingle with the myth of the frontier as the dwellers of the settled East consumed these imaginative reports. Trappers and frontier scouts and Indian fighters captured the imagination of those leading humdrum if productive lives far behind the excitement of the frontier.

As the frontier developed, weathly individuals in the industrial East began traveling to the wilderness along improved lines of transportation. Sport hunting arose among well-off Americans and visiting Europeans. These hunts were grand affairs with fancy accommodations, retainers, and expert guides chosen from among notable frontiersmen. Impressing accompanying reporters and the slaughter of obscene numbers of game animals seemed to have been the primary, if not the stated, objectives of these extravagant excursions into the wilderness. Even as big game resources were being rapidly depleted, however, an awakening conservation movement, often spearheaded by enlightened sportsmen who would come to be known as "nonresidents," was making efforts to preserve big game populations for future generations.

As the era of the frontier drew to a close, less ostentatious private fishing and hunting trips by a much broader base of well-off businessmen and professionals replaced the well-publicized excursions of the rich and famous. The American version of the industrial revolution resulted in a middle class with the economic resources to utilize the emerging network of railroads for pleasure travel. Fishing and hunting opportunities could now be enjoyed by well-off middle-class professionals. Journeys into the wilds of North America that fifty or fewer years earlier had required months of rough cross-country travel by horseback or wagon could be made in the comfort of railway sleeper and lounge cars in a few days.

With the evolution of the American public road system and reliable, affordable private vehicles to traverse it in the mid-twentieth century, those of modest means finally were able to participate in nonresident

Camp camaraderie and camp tales around the fire are important intangibles.

hunting opportunities. And in the last quarter of that century, afford-able air travel meant that even flatlanders with full-time jobs and not a lot of time off could fit in a cross-continental hunting trip.

Sorting the Facts and Traditions from the Myths

It's an undisputable fact that there existed at one time a few frontiers-men along the western fringes of the American frontier. As the frontier broke through the eastern mountain ranges, the original backwoodsmen making long hunts were succeeded by new adventurers: trappers, min-ers, market hunters, cowboys, and fortune seekers who crossed the plains to the Rocky Mountains and the Pacific coast. A lot of the stories about these new frontiersmen were embellished for the entertainment of readers back east. But it's not all myth: In order to survive, these adven-turers became good, very good, at living off the wilderness, at getting through with no one to depend upon but themselves and their party.

Today, the myth of the wild and free frontiersman lives on, and even the most sedentary participants of outdoor hunting and fishing sports can experience a sense of freedom in natural surroundings, even if their pas-sage is bought by the day from landowners. The myth that a person, just by being an American, can competently hunt large game, fish, boat, ride horses, and safely wander in wild places is unfounded and dangerous. But the myth, or the self-image, of the competent outdoors enthusiast can be fulfilled with a little guidance and a lot of discipline and hard work.

Livin' on the edge. BILL WISENBURG

THE INTANGIBLE OF TIMELESSNESS

To me, the timelessness of the places I hunt is another great intangible of elk hunting. I pass by the location of a Tale that happened last season, three seasons, thirty seasons ago—and the scenery often seems unchanged. Other times, it's hardly recognizable, my memory distorted with the excitement of the moment.

A pause under an eight hundred-year-old tree, by chance located on a spot that the fires have missed and that was hard enough to reach that loggers didn't bother to convert it to dead sticks for humans' temporary shelters. I think of the animals that have walked past, and the human elk hunters—recently for recreation, before that for survival. I think of all the life that has gone by this tree, and its predecessors before it—perhaps on an intermittent basis as the ice sheets advanced and retreated. Only ten tree lifetimes ago, elk came through a newly formed passage through the ice mountains to this land of mountains and vast lakes. Twenty trees ago, most of the land was covered by ice and the elk lived on the other side of the ice in Beringia among an exotic menagerie of now mostly gone beasts. A whole forest of old trees would come and go in the time it took for the western mountains to be pushed up by unimaginable forces from below. It helps you grasp just how much more there is to this whole hunting thing than taking an elk. And you give thanks to the creator for the capacity to comprehend, to be in that place at that time, to have the capacity to be in the pursuit of elk, and to possibly see an elk, and to possibly take an elk . . . in descending order of precedence.

We hunt elk, we live our lives, in an eyeblink of time.

And then sometimes it's just for the moment.

When I'm out on the mountain, coming back from a long run when it's too hot for the elk to be out, sometimes we'll just step off of the trail and live on the edge on purpose for a moment. Back in Texas you sure don't look down and see a river a few thousand feet below. It's even more fun when Tom the horse decides that it's a good place to practice some of his dance moves. It's common knowledge in the South and West: "It ain't a sport if it can't kill ya."

There's more to elk hunting than any single aspect of elk hunting—or all of the aspects added together. And you'll turn up more aspects every hunt.

CHAPTER 25

Designing Your Elk Hunt

This chapter is about designing an elk hunt to match your personal preferences. Assuming you've read, or at least looked over, the preceding information, you're aware that an elk hunt can take many different forms. The quality of the experience, cost, and probability of successfully taking an elk can vary over quite a range of possibilities. Likewise, your personal resources in terms of skills and conditioning, time available, and affordable cost will vary over a significant range for each individual. Selecting the hunting arrangement from the many possibilities that will best match up to a dozen desirable characteristics can make your head spin. And I, or anybody else, can't give you the formula for a successful hunt. That's because the measure of success is personal for each of us. I've been on hunts that I thought were great with other hunters who thought the same hunt was a disappointment, sometimes even though they took an elk or passed up a shot on an elk. About the only thing you can be sure of is that the biggest ad in the back pages of that outdoor magazine, or the best-looking website, or the first skinny cowboy packer outfitter you happen upon at an outdoor show is gonna cut long odds of filling all your heart's desires at a reasonable cost. Unless you pick lucky, of course. More on that later.

One approach that might be preferred by independent thinkers who might also prefer to make their own arrangements is to bend the pages back at Chapter 3 and just start looking for a place to hunt (as in scouting from afar per Chapter 5). Your techniques of searching don't need to be particularly elegant. You can search online for "elk hunting" plus the name of any national forest, major landform, tribal reservation, town, or city picked from a map or from the descriptions in Chapter 3, and you'll turn up everything of interest to elk hunting in that particular area. If you're thinking in terms of making your own arrangements, you can order maps from the USGS and use them to get details of topography and to start developing a feel for the nature of hunting in the area. Contact the state Fish and Game Department for information on success rates and details about licenses, tags, and landowner permits for private land. Check with the forest service regarding camping permits if your selected area is in a national forest. Alternately, your search will also turn up outfitters and lodges, and you can contact them for the details of the deal, success rates, and the nature of their hunts. Enough searches of enough places and enough contacts will eventually turn up arrangements that you like. Good luck.

But you may find your search was too successful—turning up a lot of different possibilities that all look good. Especially if you're a first-time elk hunter, you might not know right off whether a tribal land hunt or a lodge hunt or a backwoods outfitter hunt best fits your definition of success. How do you pick?

For a deliberate approach that fits at least my logic, we'll start with the things that can be measured. We can easily put numbers on the costs of different hunting options. Those numbers will be reasonably accurate, since they are advertised and usually paid up front.

Another key piece of information—your chance of success in taking an elk with a given hunting arrangement—is harder to pin down. We can look at figures for success rates associated with particular outfitters, but this is where the data available starts to get a little shaky. There usually isn't a general source of success data available for specific hunting arrangements independent of the people who stand to profit from the deal. The good outfits will provide legitimate references for you to contact, and you can use them to get a reasonably good idea.

We can also look at success rates according to where you hunt. States make overall average hunting data available, and it's compiled by publications of interest to hunters, and can be broken down according to equipment used. Statewide data is too general to be very useful in arranging a specific hunt, but can be a good guide for special seasons in specific areas using particular hunting equipment.

Finally, you need to objectively evaluate your own level of hunting and outdoor skills and conditioning; these aspects will have an important effect on your success rate. Of course, you are entirely within your rights to dream of downing a world-class trophy with a bow and arrow on your first hunting trip. You're also free to plan on bringing it out yourself on a packboard, and you can go after your dream without the benefit or expense of an outfitter and expert guide. I do regret having to remind you at this point, however, that, if you do not have extensive experience bowhunting or the physical conditioning and outdoor skills required—remember, my friend, you are, after all, just dreaming.

It should come as no surprise that the most important bit of information that you would like to see—the precise, two-decimal-level-of-accuracy success ratio for the area and hunting arrangement you are considering, taking into account, of course, your skill level and the weather conditions on the day of your hunt—is never going to be available in convenient, tabular form. What I can do is provide you with tables of general information and firsthand examples that will help you figure out for yourself where a potential hunting arrangement you're evaluating fits into the broad scheme of things.

The information in these tables includes both summary information on generic groups and details on specific arrangements that I've tried out myself, had friends who tried, or found reliable reports on. The generic outfits are sorted by cost ranges so you can put the contacts you come across into the appropriate group. The information on these deals comes from outfitters, master guides, booking agents, and tribal representatives; my outfitter friends who are active in outfitters associations stay current on outfitter prices and competing arrangements in their own and surrounding states. These tables are up-to-date as of the printing of this book, but costs and success rates in a given area will change over time. When you go to plan your hunt, use online research and contact with representative arrangements to keep your tables current.

Success rates are dependent on several factors. Regulatory control of the timing, which relates to the rut and weather conditions of the various hunts, is probably the biggest factor in evening out the success percentages for archery, high-powered centerfire repeater rifle, and muzzleloader; the skill and conditioning of the enthusiasts using the different types of equipment help as well. Success rates are also high for the fortunate hunters who obtain permits for restricted hunts. A comparison of archery success rates throughout the states indicates the effect of permit control within each state; it would appear that the states with proportionally more special permits also have greater success rates, even though total elk taken will be lower than in other states with greater elk populations.

The data in the table may verify things you expected as well as revealing more counterintuitive things. One overall lesson you can get from it is this: Relative to other big game, elk are hard to come by. Trophy elk are *very* hard to come by. You can improve your chances by the hunting arrangements that you choose. You can spend more money to book with an expensive outfit with some type of access restriction where you're more likely to get a shot at a trophy; alternately, depending on the rules of the game in a particular state, you can get lucky or be patient and accumulate points to draw a permit for a hunt in a permit-controlled area for an improved chance at a trophy. In some areas, a combination of high access fees and draw luck for hunting on private land results in a very good chance at a high-quality trophy.

In areas of more general public access, your success can depend on lots of factors. Some of them are completely out of your control: weather, the rut or lack of it, and so on. Others, like the number of elk in the area, are indirectly under your control since you can choose one area over another; the outfitter and guides you hunt with fall into that same category. A factor that you have a great deal of control over is your own skill and conditioning.

A notable shortcoming of all this data is that it doesn't measure the overall satisfaction that does or does not come from the hunt. That gets back into the intangibles.

Table 4 presents summary data on moderately priced outfitter arrangements. Each listing is a composite—with the exception of the last, which is a noteworthy outfitter in that it makes a point to accommodate physically challenged hunters at a very economical price. The summary profiles combine my firsthand information with the insights of my outfitter contacts. Use them as standards of comparison with potential outfitter arrangements you have located through advertisements, outdoor sports shows, and Internet websites.

Table 5 lists some more expensive arrangements. The costs for specific tribal arrangements are what I've been quoted; my contacts were aware that I wasn't prepared to sign up for a hunt at the end of the conversation. If you are prepared to sign, you might do a little better. The top trophy tribal hunts are famous and stay booked with repeat customers. You've got a better chance for a deal with private land hunts. You'll probably need to work with an agent for Asian hunts.

Table 6 is intended to illustrate different variations of private arrangements. Your actual costs will depend on how much commitment is made to setting up an outfit and to what extent trucks, trailers, stock, and gear are available from related family enterprises. Success rates are a function of hunter capability.

EVALUATING HUNTING ARRANGEMENTS USING FACTORS OF MERIT

This section presents an approach to guide you in selecting the area and hunting arrangement that are right for you.

Arrangement and Equipment	Area/State	Cost ($)	% Kill	% Trophy/Pts	Hunter Capability Required	Quality of Hunting Experience
Top-Quality Deluxe Wilderness Camp (High-Powered Rifle)	Rocky Mountains in ID, western MT and WY, and northern CO	6–8+K	50 when guided 1:1	10/300+	Adequate shooting skills; good to moderate physical conditioning	Excellent
Top-Quality Deluxe Wilderness Camp (Bow)	Rocky Mountains in ID, western MT and WY, and northern CO	6–8+K			Adequate shooting skills; excellent physical conditioning	Excellent
Family Operation, Moderately Priced Wilderness Camp (High-Powered Rifle)	Rocky Mountains in ID, western MT and WY, and northern CO	4–6K	20 to 30 when guided 2:1	2/300+	Adequate shooting skills; good to moderate physical conditioning	Excellent
Family Operation, Moderately Priced Wilderness Camp (Bow)	Rocky Mountains in ID, western MT and WY, and northern CO	4–6K			Adequate shooting skills; excellent physical conditioning	Excellent
Guided Pack Camp Hunt (High-Powered Rifle)	Canada	8–10K	50 when guided 1:1		Adequate shooting skills and physical conditioning	Excellent
Outfitter Drop Camp (High-Powered Rifle)	Rocky Mountains in ID, western MT and WY, and northern CO	3–5K	10 to 50	5/300+	Success highly dependent on hunter skill and conditioning level	Excellent
Hunting from Vehicle or on Foot, Based in Hotel in Town	Eastern MT	3–4K	10		Adequate shooting skills and physical conditioning	Moderate–low
Silver Spur Outfitters, New Castle, CO	West-central CO	3–5K lodge and pack camps			Stand hunts accommodate wheelchair-bound hunters (6-pt trophy)	Excellent

TABLE 5: COSTS AND SUCCESS RATES FOR TRIBAL LAND HUNTS, HUNTING FROM LODGES ON PRIVATE LAND, AND ASIAN HUNTS

Arrangement and Equipment	Area/State	Cost ($)	% Kill	% Trophy/Pts	Hunter Capability Required	Quality of Hunting Experience	Comments
Tribal Reservation (High-Powered Rifle)	San Carlos Apache Reservation/AZ	30-K	Hunter prerogative	40/340+ 20/400+	Immaterial	Excellent	
Tribal Reservation (High-Powered Rifle)	White Mountain Apache Reservation/AZ	18K	Hunter prerogative	95/300+ 40/340+ 20/400+			
Tribal Reservation (High-Powered Rifle)	Jicarilla Apache Reservation/NM	5.5K	Hunter prerogative	95			
Tribal Reservation (High-Powered Rifle)	Mescalero Apache Indian Reservation/NM		Hunter prerogative	95			
Private Land Adjacent to Mescalero Tribal Land (Rifle)	NM	12–15K		95/300+ 40/340+	Adequate shooting skills and physical conditioning		
Private Land Adjacent Mescalero Tribal Land (Archery)	NM	12–15K		95/300+ 40/340+	Adequate shooting skills and physical conditioning		
Private Land with Deluxe Lodge in Area of Low Elk Population—Draw or Landowner Tags	Eastern CO, WY, MT	12–15K					
Public Land, Trophy Unit	AZ, UT, MT	3–5K		40/340+ 20/400+	Adequate shooting skills and physical conditioning		Extremely long odds that can be improved by working a complicated preference point system
Top-Quality Deluxe Wilderness Camp (High-Powered Rifle)	Rocky Mountains in ID, western MT and WY, and northern CO	8–10K	50 when guided 1:1	10/320+	Adequate shooting skills; good to moderate physical conditioning	Excellent wilderness experience with special tent accommodations	
Economical Lodge/Camp on Private Land in Areas of High Elk Population	Southwestern and central CO	3–5K	5	2/270			
Asian Hunt, Tian Shan Mountain Ranges	Siberia, Mongolia, and adjoining regions	10–14K	90				Elk in Tien Shan (sometimes referred to as *maral*) are same species as North American elk
Altai Mountain Ranges	Mongolia and adjoining regions	10–14K	90				Elk in Altai (also refered to as *maral*) are five-point species similar to precursors of North American elk
Lodge	Brjansk and North Ossetia, Russia	10–14K	90				Red deer

TABLE 6: COSTS AND SUCCESS RATES FOR PRIVATE ARRANGEMENTS

Arrangement and Equipment	Area/State	Cost ($)	% Kill	% Trophy/Pts	Hunter Capability Required	Quality of Hunting Experience	Comments
Mountain Pack Camp (High-Powered Rifle)	Rocky Mountains in ID, western MT and WY, and northern CO; areas closed to motorized vehicles in UT, AZ, and NM	20–50+K (investment) — Usual outfit involves owning or investing in an old truck, a tent camp, and stock (which require land and upkeep)	Depends on hunter capability	Depends on hunter capability	Adequate shooting, woodsmanship, stock handling, and packing skills; good to excellent physical conditioning	Unsurpassed in national forest and designated wilderness areas closed to motorized vehicles	Check regulations and permit requirements for access and camping. Wilderness areas require certified weed-free hay for stock
Road-Based Camp with Riding and Pack Stock	Areas with reasonable road access and trails in the Rocky Mountains in ID, western MT and WY, central and southern CO, and UT, AZ, and NM	50–150K (investment) — Usual outfit involves trucks with stock trailers for long hauls	Depends on hunter capability	Depends on hunter capability	Adequate shooting, woodsmanship, stock handling, and packing skills; good to moderate physical conditioning		Check regulations and permit requirements for access and camping. Wilderness areas require certified weed-free hay for stock
Road-Based Motor Coach/Camper, with or without Trailed 4-Wheelers	Areas with reasonable road access and backpack trails or 4-wheeler trails	10–100K (investment) — Depends on selection	Depends on hunter capability	Depends on hunter capability	Adequate shooting, woodsmanship, and 4-wheeler riding skills or excellent physical conditioning for backpacking		Check regulations and permit requirements for access and camping
Road-Based Tent Camp, with or without Trailed 4-Wheelers	Areas with reasonable road access and backpack trails or 4-wheeler trails	2K — Assumes vehicles available	Depends on hunter capability	Depends on hunter capability	Adequate shooting, woodsmanship, and 4-wheeler riding skills or excellent physical conditioning for backpacking		Check regulations and permit requirements for access and camping
Backpack Mountain Camp (High-Powered Rifle or Bow)	Rocky Mountains in ID, western MT and WY, and northern CO; areas closed to motorized vehicles in UT, AZ, and NM	1K–	Depends on hunter capability	Depends on hunter capability	Adequate shooting, woodsmanship, and planning skills; excellent physical conditioning	Unsurpassed in national forest and designated wilderness areas closed to motorized vehicles	
Backpack from Road (High-Powered Rifle or Bow)	Rocky Mountains in ID, western MT and WY, and northern CO; areas closed to motorized vehicles in UT, AZ, and NM	1K–	Depends on hunter capability	Depends on hunter capability	Adequate shooting, woodsmanship, and planning skills; excellent physical conditioning	Unsurpassed in national forest and designated wilderness areas closed to motorized vehicles	

The most efficient methodology to develop selection criteria for elk hunting arrangements is to establish a set of factors of merit that include both data and the intangibles of elk hunting. Then you can score each of the arrangements you're interested in in terms of each of these factors. How all potential clients on average value all intrinsic factors of merit for a particular arrangement tends to set the price for that arrangement. To win the game, you want to select arrangements that have intrinsic factors of merit that match the factors of merit that you consider valuable.

The following will be our factors of merit, which we'll rate on a scale of 0 to 10 (10 is best):

- Probability of taking an elk: 100% = 10; 0% = 0
- Affordability
  Adapt this to your budget; I use $10,000+ = 0, under $1,000 = 9, $2,000 = 8, $4,000 = 6, and so on. You'll want to update this scale over time to adjust for inflation.
- Probability of taking a trophy (excepting deals where you pass on the 330s)
- Quality of the wilderness experience
- Comfort and convenience
- Camp camaraderie
- Accommodation of limited physical capability
- Level of physical challenge
- Accommodation of limited level of hunting skills
- Accommodation of limited level of outdoor skills
- Hunting skills development
- Outdoor skills development
- Hunting time per dollar
- Solitude and control of schedule
- Hunting area
  Take into account both the area available for hunting and the number of other hunters likely to be encountered while hunting. An area of 100,000 acres without any other camps or an area of 500,000 acres would get a 10. Outfitter areas of up to 2,000 square miles with five or fewer camps go off the scale. Some of us like that.
- Probability of satisfaction with quality of hunt
  Your confidence that the hunt will be as advertised.
- Avoidance of permanent investment
  Ability to use the outfit without committing to investing in and maintaining long-term purchases. No investment commitment other than paying for present hunt = 10.

If we assess the value of different hunting arrangements, assigning a set of intrinsic values to the factors of merit—that is, values that don't reflect personal preference or bias—then all of the hunting arrangements that are widely used should have about the same numerical grade. That, in fact, is the technique used to check whether or not you've assigned appropriate values to the factors of merit. We can run evaluations on several of the existing arrangements widely used by paying clients as a check. Since they are all commercially viable, they should calculate to have about the same total value. Comparable evaluations of non-commercial arrangements should yield lower totals, meaning that they exist due to other factors, such as for purposes of game management or personal preferences.

We'll rate a few different hunting arrangements for these factors of merit as examples:

- Tribal land trophy hunt (This kind of hunt costs more than $30,000, so we'll give it an affordability of –5, but the trophy potential is 15. Kinda off the scale.)
- Lodge or expensive pack camp in an area with restricted access
- Lodge or expensive pack camp in an area with restricted access and with hunting permit by drawing
- Moderate to expensive outfitter pack camp on public land with access restriction due to remote location
- Moderately priced outfitter pack camp on public land with unrestricted access
- Outfitter drop camp
- Hunting trip in Asia
- Hunter-owned pack outfit
- Road-based outfit using ATVs to access hunting area by logging roads
- Road-based or spike camp using packboards

First we'll list the factors of merit values for commercial arrangements (Table 7), and then we'll take a look at arrangements that aren't required to be commercially viable to exist (Table 8). These examples will serve as a model to help you evaluate the potential specific deals that you turn up. The factors of merit can act as a reminder of questions you can bring up as you discuss deals for different arrangements.

TABLE 7: FACTORS OF MERIT FOR COMMERCIAL ELK HUNTING ARRANGEMENTS

Factor of Merit	Tribal Lands ($30,000+)	Lodge or Pack Camp with Restricted Access ($8–12,000)	Lodge or Pack Camp with Permit Drawing And Restricted Access ($8–12,000)	Outfitter on Public Land with Restricted Access due to Remote Location (Guided) ($5–8,000)	Outfitter on Public Land with Public Access (Guided) ($3–6,000)	Outfitter Drop Camp (Unguided) ($1–4,500)	Trip to Asia ($10–14,000)
Probability of Taking an Elk	10	7	8	6	4	2	10
Affordability	-5	0	0	3	6	8	0
Probability of Taking a Trophy	15	6	8	4	2	2	9
Quality of Wilderness Experience	6	8	8	10	8	9	10
Comfort and Convenience	10	10	10	6	4	2	8
Camp Camaraderie	6	8	6	8	6	8	5
Accommodation of Limited Physical Capability	8	8	10	3	3	2	5
Level of Physical Challenge	2	2	3	7	7	8	5
Accommodation of Limited Level of Hunting Skills	7	6	6	6	6	4	9
Accommodation of Limited Level of Outdoor skills	8	8	8	6	6	2	10
Hunting Skills Development	8	9	6	9	6	2	5
Outdoor Skills Development	0	0	0	2	6	10	0
Hunting Time per Dollar	0	0	0	0	6	8	0
Solitude and Control of Schedule	0	0	0	6	5	9	0
Hunting Area	10	10	8	7	5	4	10
Probability of Satisfaction with Quality of Hunt	10	10	10	10	8	5	9
Avoidance of Permanent Investment	10	10	10	10	10	10	10
Total	105	102	101	103	98	95	105

TABLE 8: FACTORS OF MERIT FOR NON-COMMERCIAL ELK HUNTING ARRANGEMENTS

Factor of Merit	Hunter-Owned Pack Outfit	Road-Based Camp Using ATVs	Road-Based or Spike Camp with Packboard Transport (Requires Very High Hunter Capability)
Probability of Taking an Elk	6	2	6
Affordability	3	9	10
Probability of Taking a Trophy	6	1	4
Quality of Wilderness Experience	10	3	8
Comfort and Convenience	2	6	0
Camp Camaraderie	10	3	6
Accommodation of Limited Physical Capability	4	6	0
Level of Physical Challenge	10	4	10
Accommodation of Limited Level of Hunting Skills	1	3	0
Accommodation of Limited Level of Outdoor Skills	1	7	0
Hunting Skills Development	9	2	10
Outdoor Skills Development	9	2	9
Hunting Time per Dollar	6	9	10
Solitude and Control of Schedule	9	5	10
Hunting Area	7	3	3
Probability of Satisfaction with Quality of Hunt	10	3	2
Avoidance of Permanent Investment	0	0	10
Total	103	68	98

PREFERENCE-BASED SELECTION

At this point, you could just pick the hunt that most appeals to you at a price you can afford. This approach works well when your preferences are few and don't conflict with other factors. A prime example is the prospective hunter who just wants to get a record book–class trophy, and has the cash in hand to fulfill that wish. The best choice for this individual will be a hunt on tribal lands. For the hunter who needs to accommodate an extreme physical limitation, the highest value will be a lodge hunt. In either case, the next step is to move on to the next chapter for how to get started booking a hunt.

But if you're willing to take a little longer, you can use the other half of this methodology, which takes full advantage of its capability. It's the best approach when you have several preferences that may in some cases conflict. You start by creating a preference profile for yourself that corresponds with the list of factors of merit that we used to evaluate the different hunting arrangements; assign each factor that is important to you a number. If you want to be precise, you can rate each preference on a scale of 1 to 10 (10 being most important), or you can keep it simple and just give each of your preferences a value of 10.

Say, for example, that you're an experienced hunter with a high degree of physical fitness, and you want an inexpensive, really wild wilderness hunt that will allow you to develop your outdoor skills and hunting skills. You don't care much about whether you take an elk or not; you are in it for the experience. You don't have a lot of extra cash, so the affordability of the deal will be an important factor. Your preference profile might look like this:

Probability of taking an elk	1
Affordability	10
Probability of taking a trophy	1
Quality of the wilderness experience	10
Comfort and convenience	1
Camp camaraderie	5
Accommodation of limited physical capability	0
Level of physical challenge	5
Accommodation of limited level of hunting skills	0
Accommodation of limited level of outdoor skills	0
Hunting skills development	8
Outdoor skills development	8
Hunting time per dollar	10
Solitude and control of schedule	8

Hunting area	1
Probability of satisfaction with quality of hunt	1
Avoidance of permanent investment	1

The next step is to weight the intrinsic values of the hunting arrangements you're considering to take into account your preferences. You do this by combining them line by line, multiplying each factor of merit by the preference rating you gave it. You add all these numbers together to get a total score for the hunt. Continuing our example of the wilderness experience hunter, the calculations for the tribal lands hunt look like this:

Probability of taking an elk	10 x 1 = 10
Affordability	–5 x 10 = –50
Probability of taking a trophy	15 x 1 = 15
Quality of wilderness experience	6 x 10 = 60
Comfort and convenience	10 x 1 = 10
Camp camaraderie	6 x 5 = 30
Accommodation of limited physical capability	8 x 0 = 0
Level of physical challenge	2 x 5 = 10
Accommodation of limited level of hunting skills	7 x 0 = 0
Accommodation of limited level of outdoor skills	8 x 0 = 0
Hunting skills development	8 x 8 = 64
Outdoor skills development	0 x 8 = 0
Hunting time per dollar	0 x 10 = 0
Solitude and control of schedule	0 x 8 = 0
Hunting area	10 x 1 = 10
Probability of satisfaction with quality of hunt	10 x 1 = 10
Avoidance of permanent investment	10 x 1 = 10
Total	**179**

You can do these same calculations with multiple hunting options to determine the hunt that best fits your preferences. You can also compare important factors individually to evaluate trade-offs. Table 9 illustrates a full comparison of commercial hunting arrangements for the wilderness experience hunter in our example. The hunt from an outfitter drop camp gets the highest score by far, indicating that it matches up most closely with the hunter's preferences. The two outfitter hunts on public land also get a lot of points, and might be good second choices for the hunter to consider.

TABLE 9: COMBINING PREFERENCES WITH INTRINSIC VALUES OF ELK HUNTING ARRANGEMENTS

Factor of Merit	Tribal Lands ($30,000+)	Lodge or Pack Camp with Restricted Access ($8–12,000)	Lodge or Pack Camp with Permit Drawing And Restricted Access ($8–12,000)	Outfitter on Public Land with Restricted Access due to Remote Location (Guided) ($5–8,000)	Outfitter on Public Land with Public Access (Guided) ($3–6,000)	Outfitter Drop Camp (Unguided) ($1–4,500)	Trip to Asia ($10–14,000)
Probability of Taking an Elk	10 x 1	7 x 1	8 x 1	6 x 1	4 x 1	2 x 1	10 x 1
Affordability	−5 x 10	0 x 10	0 x 10	3 x 10	6 x 10	8 x 10	0 x 10
Probability of Taking a Trophy	15 x 1	6 x 1	8 x 1	4 x 1	2 x 1	2 x 1	9 x 1
Quality of Wilderness Experience	6 x 10	8 x 10	8 x 10	10 x 10	8 x 10	9 x 10	10 x 10
Comfort and Convenience	10 x 1	10 x 1	10 x 1	6 x 1	4 x 1	2 x 1	8 x 1
Camp Camaraderie	6 x 5	8 x 5	6 x 5	8 x 5	6 x 5	8 x 5	5 x 5
Accommodation of Limited Physical Capability	8 x 0	8 x 0	10 x 0	3 x 0	3 x 0	2 x 0	5 x 0
Level of Physical Challenge	2 x 5	2 x 5	3 x 5	7 x 5	7 x 5	8 x 5	5 x 5
Accommodation of Limited Level of Hunting Skills	7 x 0	6 x 0	6 x 0	6 x 0	6 x 0	4 x 0	9 x 0
Accommodation of Limited Level of Outdoor skills	8 x 0	8 x 0	8 x 0	6 x 0	6 x 0	2 x 0	10 x 0
Hunting Skills Development	8 x 8	9 x 8	6 x 8	9 x 8	6 x 8	2 x 8	5 x 8
Outdoor Skills Development	0 x 8	0 x 8	0 x 8	2 x 8	6 x 8	10 x 8	0 x 8
Hunting Time per Dollar	0 x 10	0 x 10	0 x 10	0 x 10	6 x 10	8 x 10	0 x 10
Solitude and Control of Schedule	0 x 8	0 x 8	0 x 8	6 x 8	5 x 8	9 x 8	0 x 8
Hunting Area	10 x 1	10 x 1	8 x 1	7 x 1	5 x 1	4 x 1	10 x 1
Probability of Satisfaction with Quality of Hunt	10 x 1	10 x 1	10 x 1	10 x 1	8 x 1	5 x 1	9 x 1
Avoidance of Permanent Investment	10 x 1	10 x 1	10 x 1	10 x 1	10 x 1	10 x 1	10 x 1
Total	179	255	227	384	434	523	246

Note that in working through the selection process, you have to consider what is actually important to you. This helps you formulate specific questions to ask outfitters when investigating arrangements, and might be useful if you want to try working out a customized arrangement for yourself or a small party with common objectives.

This approach can also be used in the case of a hunter with a single, nonnegotiable priority—such as a single-minded trophy hunter for whom money is no object, or a hunter who has to work around some physical limitation. You can play around with the approach, assigning a larger priority to the single factor that's important to you (a disabled hunter might assign 100 to "accommodation of limited physical capability") or assigning a negative value to the factors that work against you (such as "level of physical challenge"). Either of these approaches will weight the results more heavily in favor of your single objective.

SELECTION BASED ON THE "PICK LUCKY" APPROACH

There is one selection process that can't be helped by this methodology: the "pick lucky" approach. This theory is similar to the proven "blind hog" theory, as in "Even a blind hog (if it roots around in the dirt long enough) finds an acorn once in a while," but it is much more efficient. It's a good concept to guide the elk hunter. It also works well in selection of a spouse, or career, or anything else important to you. I have to highly recommend this approach since it worked so well for me many years ago when I was arranging my first elk hunt.

CHAPTER 26

Making Arrangements for the Elk Hunt

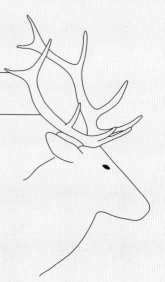

THE BARE ESSENTIALS

All elk hunting arrangements have the same basic set of requirements:

- A license and tag, whatever other type of permit the state Game Department requires
- Legal access to the land you wish to hunt
- A means to get into the area selected with your gear and camp there, or a means to get back and forth to the hunting area from the place you are staying outside the area
- A way to get any elk taken out to the meat processor
- Transport from home to the hunt and back

These requirements can be met in one of two ways: either by booking with an outfitter or lodge, or by making all of the arrangements yourself.

GENERAL CONSIDERATIONS

Arrangements for elk hunts have an annual cycle. Experienced elk hunters start making arrangements for next year's hunt at the end of this year's hunt, if not before. Desirable areas with limited tags and permits may require that you start your arrangements years in advance. The same goes for top outfitters in good areas. Some areas in some states require that you apply for tags or permits that are issued on a lottery basis. Sometimes preferential treatment is given to those who have applied before.

Arranging an elk hunt requires making some connections. You need to get in touch with a good outfitter or lodge; or, if you use your own outfit to pack in or hunt from the road, you'll need to make connections with state authorities for permits, license, and tags, as well as making any other arrangements with public or private organizations or parties to get access to the location where you'll be hunting. If you're making the arrangements yourself, you need to make sure you're working with fresh information, because local hunting conditions change over time. Game Departments continually change their policies and regulations to control the numbers and type of elk in the state.

A longstanding approach to making elk hunting connections that still works is through personal acquaintances who have hunted elk successfully in particular areas and are willing to share information about hunting arrangements in "their" area or even invite you to join their hunting party. They might have a standing arrangement to book with a particular outfitter year after year, or they might operate as a private pack outfit or road-based arrangement. If you don't have any personal connections with hunters in the area you are interested in, you can check out outfitter advertisements or make connections with outfitters at outdoor sports shows, or you can start by getting information from state Fish and Game Departments to set up your own arrangements.

A lot of the looking and arranging and making connections that until a few years ago took a lot of personal contact or specialized knowledge can now be easily handled through the Internet, which is fast becoming the preferred way to make connections for elk hunting, just as with everything else pertaining to life in the twenty-first century. Those of us who spent a lot of time in the last century might as well get used to it. A lot of readers will be hooked up to the 'net through their own computers; everybody else can get online via local libraries, accommodating friends or businesses, schools or colleges, or young acquaintances from the age of about nine through thirty. And anybody with a computer connection just loves to show you how to use it to do searches and that sort of thing. You can also find some Internet addresses of key organizations in Chapter 3, along with the last-century-type address and the good old telephone number. Also check out the information on getting maps in Chapter 5; regardless of the hunting arrangements you choose, you'll want to get your own set of topo maps of the area you'll be hunting.

BOOKING WITH AN OUTFITTER OR LODGE THROUGH AN AGENT

A booking agent can work with your selection criteria and handle all the arrangements for you. Booking agents are sometimes oriented toward somewhat more expensive arrangements, but, by the same token, they are more likely to be hooked up with the better-quality outfits and lodges. Good booking agents have checked out their deals to eliminate the real ringers, because they don't want to have disgruntled clients. Working with a booking agent doesn't cost you money out of your own pocket, at least not directly. The agent is paid by the outfitter or lodge, but agents usually represent the high-dollar outfits that roll agents' fees into the cost of the hunt. On the other hand, the cost of that hunt will be the same whether you book directly or through the agent. If you're interested in an Asian hunt, a lot of the foreign arrangements seem to be hooked up exclusively by agents, which seems fair enough since they've worked up the whole deal using connections that most of us couldn't get together even if we wanted to. You can locate booking agents through advertisements in outdoor and elk hunting publications, or by means of the Internet.

BOOKING DIRECTLY WITH AN OUTFITTER OR LODGE

A lot of the real good old outfitters stay booked up with a waiting list year after year without ever advertising, relying strictly on word of mouth between hunters to bring in new clients as the old ones decide to sit by the fire and talk about how fast they could get over the mountains in times past rather than trying to keep up with the young guides.

If you don't have some sort of inside connection to get booked in with a good, well-established outfitter, you'll have to try out an outfitter that's advertising or attending sports shows in an effort to book hunters. You can either get in touch with an outfitter operating in an area of interest to you, or pick an outfitter that you like the looks of and then find out about the area from the outfitter. At this point, you should be trying to determine the reason that this outfitter is out beating the bushes for clients: Is the outfitter a bright, young, ambitious and hardworking individual trying to get a long-term family business off the ground? Or does the outfitter come across to you as a shrewd businessperson investing a lot in advertising to book a lot of hunters because there aren't enough satisfied return hunters to keep the business going? Or is it some combination of the two? What you're trying to do is get in on the start of a good outfit on a good deal and become one of the contented regulars. The chapter on outfits and outfitters should help you formulate questions and talking points to help you evaluate the outfitters you're considering.

Regional outdoor sports shows are set up early in the year to provide a forum for prospective hunters to make personal contact with guides, outfitters, and lodges. Some of these shows are huge, such as the one in February of each year in Harrisburg, Pennsylvania, where hundreds of outfitters, along with everyone else with something to sell or promote in the general categories of outdoor sports, show up to make contact with thousands of prospective hunters from all over the Northeast. Similar but smaller shows take place across the country, usually in late winter and early spring. Some seem to be restricted to expensive outfits catering to well-heeled potential clients, but most are addressed to the less affluent rest of us as well. You'll find the time and location of these advertised in the sports section of the local newspaper, or you can find out about them online. These shows are a good deal for everybody. The hunters and outfitters can size each other up, ask questions, and develop their own personal opinion of whether they are a good match. This is the basis of the "pick lucky" approach that I recommend as an alternative to evaluating and weighing the factors of merit. You can still use those factors of merit from the previous chapter to guide your own line of questions to determine whether you and a particular outfit match up. I don't recommend that you attempt to thoroughly acquaint the packers and outfitters with the philosophical aspects of your most important intangibles of elk hunting. They'll have other people to talk to.

Outfitters advertise in publications that cover outdoor sports, shooting sports, or, more narrowly, elk hunting. If you're responding to one of these ads, you can ask your line of questions over the phone. It'll just cost some telephone time and you can't look them in the eye as you listen to the answers.

You can also make connections with outfitters using the Internet. A fast way to find a lot of outfitters is to search for the name of a state plus "elk hunting outfitter"or "hunting outfitter." State-run outfitter boards are also a good place to start looking for a good outfitter, as are the outfitters associations of each state. Outfitters association websites usually have a search tool that allows you to look for outfitters in a particular area of the state and for a particular activity. Each association seems to have a unique approach. It seems that the big, well-established, expensive operations carry more weight in the associations than the start-ups and the upstarts. The other side of that coin is that there's usually some reason for ongoing success, and going with a well-established outfitter might carry less risk, maybe with some premium.

There's one thing that's sure with outfitters: If you're thinking of booking with an outfit that the outfitters association for that particular state never heard of, you'd better jump back! That's the one sure sign of an outlaw outfit. Cut your losses and slip out the back, by the window if that's your only way out.

Most first-time hunters find themselves in unfamiliar territory when they get into the details of specifying an elk hunting trip. I've covered the various types of outfitter hunting arrangements and what they look like, but remember that the actual deal you get is the deal specified in writing by the outfitter. All of the details should be worked out and written down before you show up at the trailhead.

The hunting arrangements discussed to this point all have one general characteristic in common: Once you have made your choice and made the payment to reserve your spot, your duties are done as far as arranging the hunt are concerned. The outfitter or lodge will help you obtain the necessary permit, license, and tag to hunt. You can also be sure that the elk season will be open in the area and all the other details will be in place. All you need to do is arrange to get yourself to the designated place at the designated time. This peace of mind comes at a price. The folks conducting the arrangements add a little to their price to cover the time and trouble of making the arrangements. You'll appreciate what a bargain this is if you decide to handle everything for yourself, which is what we now turn to.

MAKING YOUR OWN ARRANGEMENTS

We have a noble purpose in assuming all of this trouble; this is the only route to that elusive goal, achieving what the world has long needed: the good nonresident elk hunt for under a grand—or as close to it as we can get.

We'll weasel from the start. That $1,000 will be out-of-pocket money. We'll assume that the big investments for whatever type of outfit we use have already been made. You have a truck already; you have an ATV to play with all year round; you and the spouse and kids just love to have horses and mules around the house even if you never considered going hunting with them. (That last one is more of a long shot, but it's possible.)

Step one: Get the license, tags, and any other permits required in the state you wish to hunt (see Chapter 3). You may start by picking a particular state, or you may get information from all of them and then go with what's available. Be sure that you check all of the regulations of the state(s) that you're interested in; some may have extra requirements, such as a hunter education course completion certificate. Note that the cost of the license and/or tags is a big part of the cost of an economy hunt. Some states have different prices for different types of elk, and for the sake of economy, you may want to go for the lower-priced cow permit rather than pay extra for the chance at the trophy bull. This choice may also improve your chances of success in the draw.

Step two: You'll need to find out about the road network and the terrain of any area that you are considering for the hunt. There are several ways to do this. Maps are available for each of the national forests, and indicate road networks and camping areas, which can all be keyed to coordinates. You can then use those coordinates to order USGS contour maps, which will have terrain features at a large enough scale to be useful for hunting.

Step three: Verify that the area you have chosen to hunt is in the state Game Department game management area that your license and tag are good for. The maps in the brochures are not accurate enough or at a large enough scale to make this check. You need to get a map that plainly shows the geographic features in the detailed description of the game management area (always included in the very fine print of Fish and Game brochures or guides). This is never a problem when you book with an outfitter, because the boundaries usually stay the same year after year. If the outfitter is confused, there's something wrong. Better check out the outfitter.

Step four: Check with the Forest Service to see if you need camping permits or need to pay any additional fees to use the public land where you intend to stay. Make sure of the ownership of the land where you are camping and hunting. You might plan to arrive in the area a day or two before you actually start hunting to get oriented and acclimated to the elevation and terrain and rest up after the trip. You might note from the maps that there are a lot of places to stay outside of the boundaries of the public land. If you plan to stay in commercial lodging of some kind, make reservations well ahead of time if you're hunting at the beginning of the season, or if the season is short.

Step five: Get out there. Get a discount airline ticket and rent a vehicle or drive your own vehicle as long as the condition of the roads will not be a problem with that particular type of vehicle (e.g., using the old Caddie on washed-out logging roads). Note that if you plan to use bonus miles for airline travel or plan to get a steep discount, you will need to commit well ahead of time. This is usually not a problem, since you'll be getting hunting permits early in the year anyway and seasons are established at the first of the year. Be careful that you don't spend all of the money you saved on the ticket on the rental vehicle. The super discount compact car may not be adequate to carry your gear or get over the primitive roads into the place that you plan to hunt. A truck or SUV rented for a week or more may cost a lot. You don't always need that kind of vehicle, though. Lots of paved roads pass right by hunting areas that are remote as far as other hunters are concerned due to rugged terrain straight up from the road. Just set up camp and hunt from the camping area near the road.

Not too bad! Note that flying, renting a vehicle, and staying in town runs the cost up. You can use these figures as a starting point to develop your own estimate of costs.

HOW ARE WE DOING ON THE $1,000 LIMIT?

License and tags	$350 to $550
Transportation (gas to drive or discount airline ticket)	$250 to $350
Rental vehicle (required with airline travel)	$500
Provisions and meals (camping or some meals in town)	$200 to $300
Cheap place to stay in town for seven nights (no camping)	$400
Misc. (maps, other incidentals)	$100 to $300
TOTAL	**$1,000 to $2,400**

There are, of course, several cautions in order when you make your own arrangements so that the trip doesn't cost you more than you plan in dollars or otherwise.

First, don't attempt to exceed the true state of your physical conditioning to hunt (up) from the road or from a spike camp, planning to pack out an elk if you're lucky. All safety precautions covered earlier go double here. And you're taking a much greater risk if you are completely by yourself.

There are separate considerations if you plan to use your personal off-road transportation, either pack stock or motorized. It may be that some areas just won't work for your own private outfit, depending on its composition. Check the road by map and by firsthand inquiries with someone knowledgeable at the local Forest Service office, if possible. Motor homes can be a very big problem off of the main roads, and any kind of trailer can be trouble.

You should also be aware of possible unanticipated consequences when using flatlander riding and packing stock in the mountains. Ownership of horses and the means to transport them does not a "local outfit" make. Horses that are unaccustomed to the smells and sounds of the mountains are always nervous and easily panicked. In trails through rough country, there's usually no good place to run it out, and it's very likely that they'll go over the side with packs or the rider trying to kick loose. The aftermath will be memorable, but it won't be memories of a nice, inexpensive elk hunt. I always recommend, if asked, and sometimes when I'm not, that the cowboy types book with an outfitter for their first mountain elk hunt just like any other flatlander, and enjoy using his stock. Considering the risk, you'll probably save money, and have a helluvalot more fun. Then if you want to play the mountain elk hunt game on your own, buy some mountain stock. Hope you're a good horse trader. Be aware that the good stuff that comes up for sale through general public access channels is usually "mature," usually because it's outlived its original owner and the kids weren't interested in hunting.

Transporting horses and mules has complications as well. All flat-lander horse trailers have fairly low ground clearance, particularly the bumper-hitch designs. They might not have the clearance needed for old logging roads. Short flatbeds (bobtails) work better for ground clearance, but then you'll need a dirt ramp to unload the stock. Ramps are usually found around designated trailheads, but not universally. The flatbeds are also hard on the stock for a trip of any distance. The animals aren't physically separated as in specialized horse trailers. This gives them the opportunity to bite and kick and stumble, despite your best efforts to tie them up short.

Other possible complications include restrictions on bringing hay into many areas. Any hay needs to be certified to be free of seeds of certain noxious weeds that are fast becoming a problem in some areas.

THE "TRIP" PART OF THE ELK HUNTING TRIP

Plan your trip so that you don't kick off the hunting activities in a state of exhaustion that first morning. The big bull may pass your location as you snooze, or trot off while your slow reactions waste those priceless two seconds that are allowed the elk hunter every forty or so seasons.

HOW *NOT* TO MAKE THE TRIP

Once upon a time, this other misguided elk huntin' nut and a much younger (not young, just younger) version of me left our suburban homes (elevation about 400 feet above sea level) on a Friday afternoon after our jobs and drove from Texas to Colorado (elevation about 11,000 feet above sea level), only stopping for fuel and arriving late in the afternoon the next day. We immediately crawled under our carefully planned, 83-pound backpack loads and started up the trail. We had planned to hike up another couple thousand feet and camp for the night. Sounded like a reasonable plan back at the office.

It wasn't. At least, not after the first quarter of a mile, when the trail turned straight up. Gasping along in front, I had sunk well below the point of utter collapse into a quivering blob in the dirt along the trail. I was able to manage a wobble up to that bush, then to that next bush, and on, and on, sustained only by terror of the absolute humiliation I'd face for the rest of my career if I crapped out on the hike. Suddenly—Hallelujah! Blessed sound! "[Gasp] [weakly] Tom . . . I don't think I'm gonna make it . . . "

Suppressing my next gasp and momentarily holding my breath, I said hoarsely, "You need a break?" We camped just off the trail right there, sleeping on the ground. Cached the stuff and hunted up the hill the next morning.

CONCLUSION

Now about the luck thing. It's very important, so I deliberately saved it for last, just to help you remember. If it doesn't make sense to you this first time you see it, review the book again with this last word in mind. If it still doesn't make sense, hunt elk some, and then read it again. I call it Elk Hunting Fact of Life #1. I learned it through my own elk hunting and through observing the experiences of others. I've since extended this wisdom to life in general. It's become the only advice I ever give anymore:

If you are given the choice between being good and being lucky, pick lucky every time.

There is a corollary: Once you are successful, in elk hunting or life in general, after you get the big bull or fill the cow permit, after you have been lucky in love, once you land the big job, have a high performing investment portfolio, and enjoy good health and all the other blessings of life that you can imagine, and you are feeling good about yourself because you've done so well, just remember and remind yourself, "I did pick lucky."

Good luck. Looks like a storm's comin' in with a lot more snow. Time to get out of here.

See you down the trail . . .

ACKNOWLEDGMENTS

My thanks go to those who taught me about elk hunting . . .
The elk hunters: Herm, Gene, Mike, Denny, Dan, Bill, James, and Steve.
And all those old bull elk.

INDEX